Making Thatcher's Britain

D0874354

Margaret Thatcher was one of the most controversial figures of modern times. Her governments inspired hatred and veneration in equal measure, and her legacy remains fiercely contested. Yet assessments of the Thatcher era are often divorced from any larger historical perspective. This book draws together leading historians to locate Thatcher and Thatcherism within the political, social, cultural and economic history of modern Britain. It explores the social and economic crises of the 1970s; Britain's relationships with Europe, the Commonwealth and the United States; and the different experiences of Thatcherism in Scotland, Wales and Northern Ireland. The book assesses the impact of the Thatcher era on class and gender, and situates Thatcherism within the Cold War, the end of empire and the rise of an Anglo-American 'New Right'. Drawing on the latest available sources, it opens a wide-ranging debate about the Thatcher era and its place in modern British history.

BEN JACKSON is a University Lecturer in Modern History at Oxford University and a Fellow of University College. He is the author of *Equality and the British Left* (2007).

ROBERT SAUNDERS is a Lecturer in History and Politics at Oxford University. He is the author of *Democracy and the Vote in British Politics* (2011).

Making Thatcher's Britain

Edited by

Ben Jackson and Robert Saunders

CAMBRIDGE
UNIVERSITY PRESS

University Printing House, Cambridge CB2 8BS, United Kingdom

Cambridge University Press is part of the University of Cambridge.

It furthers the University's mission by disseminating knowledge in the pursuit of
education, learning and research at the highest international levels of excellence.

www.cambridge.org
Information on this title: www.cambridge.org/9781107683372

© Cambridge University Press 2012

First published 2012
Reprinted 2012

A catalogue record for this publication is available from the British Library

Library of Congress Cataloguing in Publication data
Making Thatcher's Britain / [edited by] Ben Jackson, Robert Saunders.
    p.   cm.
Includes bibliographical references and index.
ISBN 978-1-107-01238-7 (hardback) – ISBN 978-1-107-68337-2
(paperback)
1. Great Britain–Politics and government–1979–1997.
2. Great Britain–Social conditions–1945–   3. Thatcher,
Margaret–Influence.   I. Jackson, Ben, 1975– editor of compilation.
II. Saunders, Robert, 1978– editor of compilation.
DA589.7.M365   2012
941.085´8–dc23   2012016905

ISBN 978-1-107-01238-7 Hardback
ISBN 978-1-107-68337-2 Paperback

In memory of E. H. H. Green (1958–2006)

Contents

Contributors

LAURA BEERS is Assistant Professor of History at American University.

RICHARD FINLAY is Professor of Scottish History at Strathclyde University.

ANDREW GAMBLE is Professor of Politics at Cambridge University.

MATTHEW GRIMLEY is University Lecturer in Modern History at Oxford University and a Fellow of Merton College.

STEPHEN HOWE is Senior Research Fellow in History at Bristol University.

DAVID HOWELL is Professor of Politics at the University of York.

BEN JACKSON is University Lecturer in Modern History at Oxford University and a Fellow of University College.

JON LAWRENCE is Reader in Modern British History at Cambridge University and a Fellow of Emmanuel College.

MARC MULHOLLAND is University Lecturer in Modern History at Oxford University and a Fellow of St Catherine's College.

ROBERT SAUNDERS is a Lecturer in History and Politics at Oxford University.

CAMILLA SCHOFIELD is Lecturer in Imperial History at the University of East Anglia.

PETER SLOMAN is a DPhil student in the Faculty of History at Oxford University.

FLORENCE SUTCLIFFE-BRAITHWAITE is a PhD student in the Faculty of History at Cambridge University.

JIM TOMLINSON is Bonar Professor of Modern History at the University of Dundee.

RICHARD VINEN is Professor of History at King's College London.

Acknowledgements

The chapters in this collection were presented in draft form at a workshop in St John's College, Oxford, in September 2010; and our thanks go first to all those who participated in the lively debates at this event. We are especially grateful to those who acted as respondents: Hester Barron, Anne Deighton, Brian Harrison, Iain McLean and Glen O'Hara. We would also like to thank Chris Collins, Gregg McClymont, Ross McKibbin and William Whyte, who either spoke at the workshop or commented on the papers presented. Their ideas and their time were greatly appreciated. We are particularly indebted to Brian Harrison for generously allowing us to draw on the timeline in his book, *Finding a Role? The United Kingdom, 1970–1990* (Oxford University Press, 2010), for Appendix 1.

We are grateful, for financial support, to the Oxford University History Faculty, St John's College, Oxford, and the John Fell OUP Research Fund; and to Aileen Mooney and Martin Conway for their guidance in securing this funding. The John Fell grant enabled us, among other things, to employ Peter Sloman as a research assistant. Peter proved an outstanding asset throughout this project: it has been a great pleasure to work with him and we are indebted to him for the enormous amount he has contributed to this book.

The research for this volume could not have been undertaken without the assistance of innumerable librarians and archivists, and we are truly thankful for their help. We are also grateful for permission to quote from the following papers and archives: the Margaret Thatcher Foundation website and the Margaret Thatcher papers at the Churchill Archives Centre, courtesy of Lady Thatcher; the papers of the National Viewers' and Listeners' Association in the Albert Sloman Library, Essex University; the Alfred Sherman papers at Royal Holloway; the Donald Coggan papers at Lambeth Palace; the papers of Enoch Powell at the Churchill Archives Centre, with the kind permission of the Trustees of the Literary Estate of the late J. Enoch Powell; the Conservative Party

Archive in the Bodleian Library, Oxford; the Labour Party Archive at the People's History Museum, Manchester; the papers of Lord Hailsham at the Churchill Archives Centre; the papers of the Institute of Economic Affairs and Milton Friedman, both held at the Hoover Institution, Stanford University. We are especially grateful to Andrew Riley at the Churchill Archives Centre and to Chris Collins at the Thatcher Foundation for the assistance they gave to so many of our contributors. We are also indebted to Cambridge University Press, and in particular to Michael Watson and Chloe Howell, for their enthusiasm for this project and for all their work in seeing the book through to publication. For support and encouragement along the way, Ben Jackson thanks Zofia Stemplowska and Edward, Jacqueline and Daniel Jackson; Robert Saunders thanks Andrew and Penny Saunders.

Our final debt of gratitude is both personal and intellectual. At different stages in our lives, we were privileged to work with the very distinguished Thatcher scholar, the late E. H. H. Green. Ewen was a much valued tutor, colleague and friend, whose scholarship made an enormous impact on the study of British Conservatism. We hope that he would have approved of this volume, and it is dedicated to his memory.

Abbreviations

CCO	Conservative Central Office
COSA	Colliery Officials and Staff Area
CPS	Centre for Policy Studies
CRD	Conservative Research Department
EEC	European Economic Community
EOC	Equal Opportunities Commission
ERG	Economic Reconstruction Group
ERM	Exchange Rate Mechanism
HC Deb.	House of Commons Debates
HL Deb.	House of Lords Debates
IEA	Institute of Economic Affairs
IMF	International Monetary Fund
INLA	Irish National Liberation Army
IRA	Irish Republican Army
LCC	Leader's Consultative Committee
LEA	Local Education Authority
MFGB	Miners' Federation of Great Britain
MPS	Mont Pèlerin Society
MTFS	Medium-Term Financial Strategy
MTFW	Margaret Thatcher Foundation website: www. margaretthatcher.org
NCB	National Coal Board
NEC	National Executive Committee
NUM	National Union of Mineworkers
NVALA	National Viewers' and Listeners' Association
PEB	Party Election Broadcast
PMQ	Prime Minister's Questions
PPS	Parliamentary Private Secretary
PSBR	Public Sector Borrowing Requirement
SDLP	Social Democratic and Labour Party
Thatcher CD-ROM	*Margaret Thatcher: Complete Public Statements, 1945–1990* (Oxford University Press, 1999)

TUC	Trade Unions Congress
UDA	Ulster Defence Association
UDM	Union of Democratic Mineworkers
UUP	Ulster Unionist Party

Citations from the Thatcher Foundation website are given in the following format: MTFW [unique document ID]. Documents can be found either by typing this number into the search box on the website, or by appending it to the URL www.margaretthatcher.org/document/. For example, MTFW 107590 can be found at www.margaretthatcher. org/document/107590.

Introduction: Varieties of Thatcherismplaceholder

Ben Jackson and Robert Saunders

Margaret Thatcher was one of the most controversial figures in modern British history. No Prime Minister since Gladstone aroused such powerful emotions, or stirred such equal measures of hatred and veneration. For her admirers, she was 'the greatest living Englishwoman',[1] a new Churchill who had reversed decline, defeated socialism and restored Britain's place in the world. For her critics, she was a small-minded bigot, who destroyed British industry, widened inequality and unleashed a new era of greed and rampant individualism.

Yet if commentary on the Thatcher years is often very polarised, the period itself offers a nest of contradictions. Thatcher was the first Prime Minister since the Great Reform Act to win three general elections in a row; but the first since Neville Chamberlain to be evicted by her own party. She was the only Prime Minister of the twentieth century to give her name to an ideology, but there is no agreement on what it was or who believed in it. In electoral terms, she was the most successful party leader of the modern era, but she won a smaller share of the vote than any Conservative government since 1922, and fewer votes in absolute terms than her successor, John Major.

The Thatcher years have inspired a substantial literature, drawn from every point on the political spectrum. There are at least twenty-five biographies of Margaret Thatcher, numerous documentaries and dramatisations, and an unusual array of diaries and memoirs. Journalists, economists and political scientists have all engaged closely with the period, as have sociologists, scholars of gender politics and historians of popular culture. Regional studies have begun to emerge, and there is a significant literature on the political legacies of Thatcherism.[2] The result has been a rich, diverse and often very impressive body of scholarship that is already more extensive than for any other government of modern times. Is there any need, then, for a further volume?

* We are grateful to Tim Bale and Matthew Grimley for helpful comments on an earlier version of this introduction.

1

This is not a new biography of Margaret Thatcher; nor is it a comprehensive survey of the Thatcher years. Instead, it offers a fresh perspective on the period from the viewpoint of the historian. As the 1980s recede in time, and as papers and archives become more readily available, 'Thatcherism' is emerging as a major field of historical research. Scholars such as E. H. H. Green, Brian Harrison and Richard Vinen have challenged the tendency to view the Thatcher era in 'splendid isolation', and have reconnected the period to the social, political and cultural history of the twentieth century as a whole.[3] This volume seeks to broaden and extend that engagement, by drawing together scholars from many different areas of historical enquiry. The approach is both historicist and comparative, locating the Thatcher era within a range of different contexts. The essays that follow explore the place of Thatcherism within the political, cultural and economic crises of the 1970s; they consider its relationship with Europe, the Commonwealth and the Atlantic world; and they assess the different experiences of the Thatcher governments for class, gender and regional identities. They restate the importance of the Cold War context and restore a 'four nations' approach to the history of the United Kingdom in the 1970s and 1980s. This introduction offers a framework for the chapters that follow, beginning with a brief overview of the Thatcher era, before proceeding to an analysis of the key themes that dominate existing scholarship on this period.

The grocer's daughter

Margaret Roberts was born in Grantham in 1925, the second child of Alfred and Beatrice Roberts. Her father was a grocer and Methodist lay preacher who rose to become mayor of Grantham, and he encouraged his daughters to take an interest in politics. Alfred took Margaret to meetings of the council, and she sat in the public gallery of the magistrates' court where her father served on the bench. There was a strong emphasis on discipline and self-improvement: as Margaret recalled years later, 'I always got the books I wanted. But no pleasures.'[4]

In 1943 Margaret won a scholarship to Oxford, where she studied Chemistry at Somerville. University life offered a welcome relaxation from the strict regimen of Grantham: she attended her first dance, smoked her first cigarette and tasted alcohol for the first time.[5] Though excluded by her gender from the Oxford Union, she joined the University Conservative Association and became only the third woman to hold the presidency.

Leaving Oxford in 1947, Margaret worked for a short period in industry as a research chemist. In 1950 she contested the safe Labour seat of Dartford for the Conservative Party, cutting the Labour majority by 6,000 votes; and, as the youngest Conservative candidate in the country, her campaign drew considerable attention from the media. It was in Dartford that she met two of the most important men in her life: Ted Heath, who would promote her to the Shadow Cabinet in 1967; and Denis Thatcher, whom she married in 1951. After a brief period away from active politics, in which she passed her Bar exams and gave birth to twins, she was elected in 1959 as Conservative MP for Finchley. She would hold the seat for almost thirty-three years.

Thatcher entered Parliament during the Conservative ascendancy of 1951–64, and quickly made an impression. In 1961 she was given her first ministerial post in the Department of Pensions and National Insurance, and six years later she was appointed to the Shadow Cabinet with responsibility for fuel and power. When the Conservatives returned to office in 1970, she became Secretary of State for Education. There she acquired the nickname 'Thatcher the Milk Snatcher', after withdrawing free school milk from children in primary education. *The Sun* labelled her 'The Most Unpopular Woman in Britain', and her decision attracted a torrent of public abuse.[6]

As the only woman in Heath's Cabinet, Thatcher acquired a significant public profile, but few would have tipped her for the leadership. As a woman whose origins lay in the provincial lower-middle class, she did not fit the mould of previous party leaders; and until 1975 the height of her ambitions appears to have been the Exchequer. Yet the culture of Conservative politics was undergoing a change, which opened up new possibilities for a woman of Thatcher's background. Defeat in 1964 had triggered a reaction within the Conservative Party against the patrician style of Harold Macmillan and Sir Alec Douglas-Home. Between 1965 and 1997, the party elected four leaders in succession from relatively humble backgrounds, each of whom could claim an authentic connection with the lives of 'ordinary' voters. This cultural shift was sharpened by changes in the party's internal procedures. Thatcher would never have achieved the premiership before 1964, when the leadership was in the gift of a 'magic circle' of party grandees; but the move to election by MPs gave greater scope to candidates who defined themselves against the party establishment.

Thatcher played little role in these developments, but she rode them expertly. Since leaving Grantham in 1943, Thatcher had played down her provincial background, acquiring the poise and accent of the Tory *grande dame*. She had rarely returned to Grantham after moving to Oxford, and references to her father were fairly scant before the 1970s. The tone of these remarks was sometimes ambivalent; and while she credited her father with stimulating her *interest* in politics, there was little sense as yet that its *substance* was derived from this source. The image of Thatcher as 'the grocer's daughter' was partly a media construction, fashioned by interviewers and political journalists eager to establish a creation myth for this new and interesting figure. Yet it was keenly embraced by Thatcher herself, for it allowed her to refashion her public profile in the image of the society she hoped to lead. By reactivating her provincial roots, Thatcher could soothe anxieties that the wife of a millionaire, living in a privileged metropolitan culture, would have difficulty appealing to a mass electorate.[7]

Heath had always known that he was likely to face a leadership election in 1975. His position had been weakened by successive electoral failures in 1974, and the Tory right was in rebellion over the alleged U-turns of 1972–3. The most likely challenger was Keith Joseph, but he destroyed his chances with an ill-judged speech at Edgbaston, which appeared to advocate eugenic policies.[8] Thatcher, who entered the leadership contest in his stead, was viewed primarily as a stalking horse, but her position was stronger than at first appeared. Given the fate of the Heath government, the fact that she had never held an economic portfolio, or played any obvious role in the decisive events of that ministry, could be turned to her advantage; and a strong result for Thatcher offered the only prospect of a second ballot in which other potential candidates could stand. After a skilful campaign, masterminded by Airey Neave, she caused a sensation by defeating Heath in the first ballot. Unexpectedly established as the front runner, she secured outright victory on the second ballot, becoming leader of the Conservative Party on 11 February 1975.

The party Thatcher inherited was in some disarray. By 1975, the Conservatives had lost four of the last five general elections, and the party was losing support in all parts of the United Kingdom. Its share of the vote had declined from almost 50 per cent in 1955 to 35.8 per cent in October 1974, and it was in third place behind the Liberals among first-time voters. The Conservatives' most recent period in government, the Heath administration of 1970–74, had collapsed into a chaos of recriminations after a protracted confrontation with the miners. The party, it seemed, could neither work effectively with the unions nor impose its authority upon them, raising questions about its capacity to govern at all in a modern corporatist state.

At a time when the Conservatives needed to broaden their appeal, and to prove that they could build a constructive relationship with organised labour, it was not at all clear that Thatcher was a sensible choice of leader. To her many critics, Thatcher was a suburban housewife with no experience of high office, who seemed neither willing nor able to expand the party's constituency. Her personal powerbase remained precarious, and she was outnumbered by Heathites even within the Shadow Cabinet. Her predecessor was openly hostile, and she operated throughout her period in opposition under the shadow of a Heathite restoration.

Had an election been called in 1978, the Conservatives might well have lost and Thatcher's leadership would almost certainly have come to an end. But the Labour Prime Minister, James Callaghan, delayed the election until 1979, ensuring that the country went to the polls under the shadow of industrial unrest. The public sector strikes of 1978–9 – the so-called 'Winter of Discontent' – destroyed Labour's claims to a superior governing competence, and handed the electoral advantage to the Conservatives. With 44 per cent of the popular vote, the Conservative Party won a majority of forty-three seats, with a lead over Labour of seventy MPs.

The first term (1979–83): back from the brink

The first term was dominated by economic policy. On public sector pay and reform of trade union law the government moved cautiously. Ministers accepted a raft of inflationary pay awards, while labour reforms focused on trade unions' internal procedures, rather than on the right to strike. In macro-economic policy, however, there was a radical change of direction. The new Chancellor of the Exchequer, Geoffrey Howe, cut the top rate of income tax from 83p to 60p in the pound, and the basic rate from 33p to 30p. To compensate, VAT was increased from 8 per cent to 15 per cent. To squeeze out inflation, interest rates rose to 17 per cent by the end of 1980. The government removed all controls over the exchange of foreign currency and ambitious targets were published for control of the money supply, embodied in the Medium-Term Financial Strategy of 1980.[9]

The effects were seismic. Between 1979 and 1981 the manufacturing sector contracted by 25 per cent, buffeted by a combination of high interest rates, tight monetary policy and a soaring exchange rate. GDP shrank by 2 per cent in 1980 and by a further 1.2 per cent in 1981, in a recession that was both deeper and longer than ministers had anticipated. Unemployment escalated from 1.3 million in 1979 to over

3 million in 1983, where it remained until 1987. Inflation – which had stood at 8.3 per cent in 1978 – hit 22 per cent over the Conservatives' first year in office, and did not fall below the 1978 level until 1983.

The pressure to change course was overwhelming. In a letter to *The Times* in March 1981, 364 university economists insisted that government policy had 'no basis in economic theory'. The monetarist experiment, they warned, would 'deepen the depression, erode the industrial base of our economy and threaten its social and political stability'.[10] As if to prove the point, riots broke out in Brixton, Southall and Moss Side. In June 1981, the government's approval ratings hit a record low of −43. For much of 1981 and 1982 the Conservatives occupied third place in the polls, trailing both Labour and the newly formed Liberal–SDP Alliance.

Slowly, however, the economy began to improve. Inflation fell from a yearly rate of 18 per cent in 1980 to 11.9 per cent in 1981. By 1982 it was 8.6 per cent, plunging to 4.6 per cent in 1983. Interest rates declined from 17 per cent to 9 per cent, while a fall in the value of the pound eased the pressure on exports. After two years of contraction, GDP grew by 2.2 per cent in 1982 and 3.7 per cent in 1983. How much credit the Thatcher government could take for all this remains contested, but its political significance cannot be doubted.[11] By standing firm against all opposition, Thatcher and Howe had exorcised the memory of the Heath U-turn; and, as the outlook brightened, they could claim vindication for their tough economic medicine.

Economic uplift coincided with a major foreign policy crisis. On 2 April 1982, Argentine forces landed in the Falkland Islands, a British colony since 1833. Sovereignty had been contested by Argentina for many years, and in 1978 the Callaghan government had sent naval reinforcements to the region to discourage an attack. The invasion was a humiliation that could well have destroyed the government. The Labour leader, Michael Foot, accused ministers of betraying the islanders, and challenged them to 'prove by deeds' that 'foul and brutal aggression does not succeed'.[12] The crisis was viewed as the supreme test of Thatcher's capacity to lead, and the recapture of the islands became one of the defining moments of the Thatcher premiership. Whether it proved decisive at the following election, as widely claimed, is doubtful;[13] but failure would probably have cost Thatcher the premiership and would have made it harder to deploy patriotic defence as an electoral weapon. Instead, it was the opposition that suffered the political fallout. Despite Foot's determined stand, the Labour Party was visibly divided over the war, establishing defence as a clear electoral advantage for the Conservatives.

By July 1982, Thatcher's personal approval ratings had reached 52 per cent – up by 27 points from the previous December. For most of the next two years the Conservatives rarely dipped below 40 per cent in the polls, as Labour dissolved into fratricidal conflict and the Alliance lost some of its early momentum. When Parliament was dissolved in June 1983, the Conservatives won a landslide. Though their share of the vote fell slightly from 1979 (from 44 per cent to 42.4 per cent), they won an overall majority of 144 seats. Labour only narrowly held onto second place in the share of the vote, beating the Alliance by 27.6 per cent to 25.4 per cent, but the new party was denied its breakthrough by the electoral system. While Labour achieved a roughly proportional result – winning 32 per cent of the seats on 27.6 per cent of the votes – the Alliance secured more than a quarter of votes cast, but a paltry 3.5 per cent of seats. The big winners were the Conservatives, who returned 61 per cent of MPs on 42.4 per cent of the vote.

The second term (1983–7): high Thatcherism

With their majority secure, the Conservatives continued the programme of radical reform. Privatisation, in particular, emerged as a central component of Thatcherite policy. The sale of council houses, initiated in the first term, was accelerated and expanded, while giants like British Telecom, British Gas, British Airways and Rolls-Royce were all transferred into private ownership. Revenues from privatisation, which had never exceeded £494 million a year in the first term, rose to more than £10 billion over the course of the Parliament, while the flow of North Sea oil revenue became a flood. In the five years from 1983 to 1987, government oil revenues totalled £41.6 billion – more than double the figure for the previous four years. Given that oil revenue had been a mere £25 million as recently as 1975, this was a substantial windfall. As well as paying off public debt, this allowed the new Chancellor, Nigel Lawson, to make further reductions in direct taxation. The main rate of corporation tax was cut from 50 per cent to 35 per cent, while the small business rate fell from 30 per cent to 25 per cent.[14] There were further cuts in the basic rate of income tax, which fell from 30 pence to 27 pence in the pound.

There were also curbs on union power and local government – both seen as bastions of the left. Union membership was banned at the government intelligence communications centre, GCHQ, while the 1984 Trade Union Act required secret ballots for union officers and removed legal immunity from unions that held strikes without balloting. Caps were imposed on local taxation, and the metropolitan councils and the

Greater London Council were abolished. The Anglo-Irish Agreement (1985) and Single European Act (1986) opened up new directions in European and Irish policy, while a deregulation of financial services in 1986, known as the 'Big Bang', transformed the City of London.

The main crisis of the Parliament was the miners' strike of 1984–5. The year-long strike, called in response to a national programme of pit closures, was one of the iconic events of the Thatcher era. It was only the second national coal strike since the 1920s, and the most recent shutdown had destroyed the Heath government in 1974. When a strike had seemed possible in 1981, the government had made concessions; but it used the time gained to build up coal reserves, improve strike planning and prepare for a future conflict.

As David Howell shows in Chapter 8 of this volume, the miners' defeat was not simply a case of Thatcherite resolution succeeding where Heathite prevarication had failed. The dispute in 1973–4 had been about pay, at a time when pay agreements were determined nationally, and this made it easier to achieve solidarity across the industry. That was harder to achieve when the issue was pit closures, for it required pits whose futures were apparently secure to strike in sympathy. The National Union of Mineworkers, led by Arthur Scargill, took the controversial step of striking without a national ballot, alienating public support and ultimately landing the union in court. Four nuclear power stations had opened since 1976, providing an alternative source of energy, while stockpiles of fuel and the increased supply of North Sea oil diminished the government's reliance on coal.

The political consequences of the strike were ambiguous. On the one hand, victory cemented Thatcher's authority and exorcised the demons of 1973–4. Norman Tebbit later said that it broke 'not just a strike, but a spell', re-establishing the authority of government over organised labour.[15] Yet the government's approval ratings sank dramatically after the miners returned to work, falling from 42 per cent at the beginning of the strike to just 23 per cent by August 1985.[16] Once beaten, the miners seemed more to be pitied than feared; and Thatcher's rhetoric appeared, to some voters, unduly triumphalist. The violent scenes in and around the strike may have persuaded many voters that the battle needed to be won, but they also entrenched a perception that Thatcherism was socially divisive. In so doing, they undermined any lingering pretensions the government may have had to the mantle of 'One Nation'.

The third term (1987–90): decline and fall

Nonetheless, when Parliament was dissolved in June 1987, the Conservatives won a second landslide victory. With 376 seats and 42.3

per cent of the vote, they had a parliamentary majority of 102, enabling them to undertake further radical reforms. The basic rate of income tax, reduced shortly before the election from 29p to 27p, was cut further to just 25p, while the top rate was slashed from 60p to 40p. New privatisation measures were introduced, and further reforms were signalled in local government. However, the economic climate was about to take a turn for the worse, with dramatic effects for the government's popularity.

The first warning came with a stock market crash in October 1987, in which the FTSE lost a quarter of its value. Though the so-called 'Lawson boom' triggered 5 per cent growth in 1988, inflation re-emerged in 1989, with a spike in the retail price index of 7.8 per cent. As interest rates climbed, reaching a high of 15 per cent, growth slowed to 2.3 per cent in 1989 and 0.8 per cent in 1990, before tipping back into recession in 1991. By 1989, the government's ratings were down to −36, their lowest since 1981, plunging to −42 in 1990. Though Thatcher remained more popular than her party, her own ratings reached −32 in June 1990.

As the climate worsened, old alliances began to fray. Howe was demoted in July 1989, removed from the Foreign Office to the less prestigious post of Leader of the House of Commons. Lawson resigned three months later, exasperated by the influence of Alan Walters as the Prime Minister's chief economic advisor. Thatcher was accused of an increasingly autocratic style and, in December 1989, she was challenged for the party leadership by Sir Anthony Meyer. Socially liberal and pro-European, Meyer was easily defeated; but the failure of 60 Conservative MPs to back Thatcher was a straw in the wind. His action broke – as it was intended to do – the taboo against challenging a serving Prime Minister, paving the way for the events of 1990.[17]

Two issues proved especially toxic for the government: the relationship between Britain and Europe, and local taxation. The Community Charge – or 'Poll Tax', as it was widely known – was introduced in England and Wales in April 1990, having been trialled in Scotland a year earlier. It was a flat-rate tax levied on all adults, and was intended to make local councils more accountable financially to their electorates. The tax was widely perceived as inequitable and, disastrously, initial bills proved higher for most households than the system it replaced. Opposition to the tax was widespread, and serious public disorder at an anti-Poll Tax demonstration in London in March 1990 encouraged a perception that the government was losing its grip.

The Prime Minister also took an increasingly hostile stance towards the European Community. Thatcher had warned in 1988 against 'a European super-state exercising a new dominance from Brussels';

and on 30 October 1990 she dismissed a whole series of proposals for Community reform, declaring robustly that 'we have surrendered enough'.[18] Two days later, Howe resigned from the government, accusing Thatcher of promoting a 'nightmare image' of 'a continent that is positively teeming with ill-intentioned people'. In an electrifying resignation speech, Howe openly invited a leadership challenge: 'The time has come for others to consider their own response to the tragic conflict of loyalties with which I have myself wrestled for perhaps too long.'[19]

His appeal was answered by Michael Heseltine, a Thatcher critic since his resignation from the Cabinet in January 1986. Though Thatcher won 204 votes in the first round of voting, 152 MPs voted for Heseltine, while 23 abstained or spoiled their papers. Thatcher's authority had been damaged beyond repair; and, under pressure from the Cabinet, she announced her resignation on 22 November 1990.

Thatcher's resignation prompted extraordinary reactions from both supporters and opponents. At Glasgow Airport the news was announced over the tannoy, drawing cheers from travellers and impromptu parties around the baggage conveyers.[20] The journalist Julie Burchill, by contrast, told *The Guardian* that it was 'a terrible day for this country, I feel as if somebody's banged me over the head with a mallet.'[21] At Peterhouse, in Cambridge, the historians Niall Ferguson and John Adamson drank away their misery in Ferguson's study, listening to 'The Death of Siegfried' from Wagner's *Götterdämmerung*. 'As far as I was concerned', Ferguson recalled, 'that was the night that Britain gave up any hope of seriously reforming its post-war institutions.'[22]

Such divergent reactions have also been reflected in commentary on the Thatcher era. Three themes in this commentary are of particular importance to the arguments developed in this book: an extraordinary emphasis on Thatcher as an individual; a preoccupation with the ideological claims asserted for her ministries; and a conviction that her governments had unusual historical significance. We will survey each of these in turn.

The Thatcher effect

One of Thatcher's most striking characteristics was her capacity to inflame the imagination. No other Prime Minister has made such an impact on popular culture, or achieved such notoriety in the pop charts.[23] For her critics, like the writer Hanif Kureishi, she embodied all 'that was most loathsome in the English character'. A. N. Wilson, by contrast, thought her 'truly magnificent on a human level'; her 'qualities of personal greatness outshone what you might think of as her "policies"'.[24] Critics routinely called her a 'fascist', and the satirical programme *Spitting Image* developed a running joke in which Thatcher took instructions from an elderly Adolf Hitler.

This emphasis on Thatcher as an individual owed much to her gender. Early profiles stressed her 'femininity' and 'sex appeal', and their incongruity with established models of authority.[25] Thatcher's femininity automatically set her apart from any of her predecessors. She had never worn uniform, or served her country in battle; she had never held high office, prior to the leadership; and she was poorly connected in Conservative clubland. By virtue of her sex, Thatcher was neither an officer nor a gentleman, and the models of authority invoked by male leaders were largely closed to her. It is easy to overlook the extent to which Thatcher had to create her own model of female leadership, while operating in an overwhelmingly male environment. Her ventures in this regard naturally captivated public attention, marking her out – regardless of policy – as a new and unique political phenomenon.

Thatcher was often described as a 'presidential' leader, though this understates the differences between a presidential and parliamentary system. Unlike her close contemporary, Ronald Reagan, Thatcher enjoyed an almost unlimited command over the legislature; but she had little power over the selection of MPs or civil servants. Ministerial appointments had to be drawn from a limited pool, with the result that she was often in a minority within her own Cabinet. The civil service could be supplemented with small numbers of political advisors, but Thatcher enjoyed none of the sweeping powers of patronage conferred upon the White House. This made it harder in Britain than in America to bring about a change of political culture. The corridors of Whitehall did not, like those on Capitol Hill, hum with energetic, young political staffers committed to a programme of reform.[26]

These constraints inevitably shaped Thatcher's governing style. Cabinet government was undesirable, because she could not rely on the consistent support of her ministerial colleagues. In the face of this disadvantage – and from a desire to distinguish her tenure from that of Heath – she cultivated her own highly personal model of leadership, combining courage and determination with an astute reading of the political space available to her. At the same time she relied, to a greater extent than any Prime Minister since Gladstone, on a network of supporters outside her institutional base in Parliament. From the moment she challenged Heath in 1975, Thatcher attracted a personal court, whose members proudly self-identified as 'Thatcherites'. The term was significant, for unlike the labels with which it is conventionally associated – 'neo-liberal', 'Conservative' or 'free marketeer' – it implied a personal, rather than doctrinal, allegiance. The term was first used in the 1975 leadership election, as an antonym to the 'Heathmen' loyal to the former Prime Minister. In this respect, it had an oppositional flavour from the outset; and that usage was to re-emerge after 1990, as a mark of allegiance to the deposed leader.

'Thatcher's people' were not so much a 'kitchen Cabinet' – a private, policy-making unit of the kind maintained by Harold Wilson – as a network of cheerleaders, with a strong, public allegiance to Thatcher as an individual. Geoffrey Howe likened the Prime Minister to 'Joan of Arc, invoking the authority of her "voices"'; but though their political influence was far from negligible, these were prophets, not policy-makers.[27] Their claim to articulate Thatcher's private opinions, sometimes in opposition to the actions of her government, gave them the flavour of a rebel movement, only loosely connected with the official Conservative Party. The result was to establish 'Thatcherism' as a public discourse independent of official Conservative policy. As such, it drew into the party's orbit a number of figures that did not self-identify as Conservatives, and it allowed Thatcher to act almost as a commentator upon her own ministry.

In this respect, Thatcher served as the focal point for a set of overlapping institutions and allegiances. Her fall in November 1990 broke the link pin, sending the various groups scattering across the political landscape. Her eviction was, of course, a symptom of that breakdown as much as its cause; but the rupture allowed for new political alignments in the 1990s. Just as importantly, it ensured that Conservative politics in that decade would not be marked by the loyalty and party discipline with which it has customarily been associated. As 'Thatcherites' first and Conservatives second, her followers established a new set of rules after her departure, with damaging consequences for her successor.

Thatcherism and hegemony

A second line of approach has focused neither on 'Thatcher' nor the 'Thatcher era', but on 'Thatcherism' as an ideological project. It has long been a cliché that Thatcher was the first Prime Minister to give her name to an ideology, yet talk of 'Thatcherism' obscures as much as it reveals.[28] Originally a pejorative term, the word was coined by the Labour Party and theorised by the Marxist left, before being adopted as a badge of honour by Thatcher and her associates.[29] It has been used as a receptacle for a dizzying array of ideas and never achieved a stable meaning, even among Thatcher's closest allies. Historians cannot simply abandon the word, for it was central to political discourse in the

1980s, but nor should they impose upon it a single, arbitrary definition. 'Thatcherism' should be viewed as a discourse to be interrogated, not as an explanatory tool for the actions of the Thatcher governments.

The first substantial discussion of 'Thatcherism' was found in the pages of *Marxism Today*, and emphasised both the scale of Thatcherism's ambitions and its place in a global movement of ideas. 'Thatcherism', for these writers, was reducible neither to the opinions and political style of Thatcher herself, nor to the actions of the governments she led. Instead, it stood as a local embodiment of a global revolution, making Thatcher the architect – to an extent unprecedented in British history – of an explicitly ideological reconfiguration of domestic politics. Though the journal had an obvious ideological leaning, the intellectual calibre of its contributors was extraordinarily high. Both right and left drew freely on its insights, establishing Stuart Hall and Andrew Gamble in particular as the most authoritative early commentators on the Thatcher phenomenon.[30]

It was no accident that the theoretical analysis of Thatcherism had its origins on the Marxist left. Influenced by the Italian Marxist, Antonio Gramsci, *Marxism Today* inclined naturally to a reading of ideology as conditioned by material interests, paying close attention to the historical forces that underpinned high political innovations. It located Thatcherism at the convergence of three long-running trends: economic decline, or a breakdown of 'Fordism'; the decay of the post-war social democratic consensus; and the beginning of a new phase in the Cold War.[31] Linking global economic turbulence to a crisis of authority within the bourgeois state, *Marxism Today* theorised Thatcherism both as an 'accumulation strategy' – based on free markets and liberal economics – and as a new 'hegemonic project', directed at the exercise of political and moral leadership. It saw Thatcherism as an attempt to recast the electoral politics, ideological premises and policy regime of British government in such a way as to subvert the social democratic assumptions of the post-war era and to restore the Conservatives as the leading party of the British state. Neo-liberal ideas – of the sort espoused by Friedrich Hayek and Milton Friedman – were said to have played a critical role in the formulation of this project. For this reason, *Marxism Today* privileged the affinities between Thatcherite Conservatism and the American 'New Right', while asserting a disjunction within British Conservatism before and after 1975.[32]

Jim Bulpitt, by contrast, located Thatcherism within a British tradition of Conservative statecraft. From the era of Salisbury onwards, Bulpitt argued, Conservatives had sought to insulate 'high politics' from the collision of class interests within the market. This was achieved, in part, by externalising responsibility for the economy to other agencies, so 'depoliticising' the issues most likely to undermine the 'governing competence' of Conservative governments. By the mid 1970s, however, the party had become trapped in a 'statecraft game' that Conservatives no longer believed they could win, since the basis of governing competence had become the successful management of corporatist bargaining. It was this, Bulpitt argued, that attracted Conservatives to neo-liberalism. The intellectual resources of the New Right were harvested by Thatcher and her allies because they offered a new technique for 'depoliticising' economic policy and therefore an alternative to the failures of Heathite statecraft. On this reading, ideology was instrumental – a new weapon to be mobilised behind the Conservative Party's longstanding instinct for power.[33]

For these and many other writers, the Thatcher administrations aspired to more than the efficient conduct of government. Instead, they sought to re-engineer the structural, ideological and cultural foundations of British politics, allowing them 'not merely to reflect the wishes of the electorate, but to *shape* that electorate'.[34] That view has also found an echo on the right, among those who supported and admired the Thatcher governments. Such writers have tended to define Thatcherism against some prior cultural authority, from the 'post-war consensus' and the 'permissive society' to ideological infections like 'declinism' or 'socialism'. Acknowledging the hegemonic aspirations of Thatcherism, they frame its ambitions in less pejorative terms. For Thatcher sympathisers, 'hegemony' could be understood as an attempt to restore the authority of Parliament, reasserting the institutions of the democratic state against unelected corporate interests. Shirley Robin Letwin has seen in Thatcherism a still more ambitious project to restore what she termed the 'vigorous virtues' to British society, undoing the moral corrosion of collectivist social democracy.[35] Thatcherite politicians often framed their case in moral terms, vowing to 'destroy socialism', end the culture of decline and restore the traditional values of Judeo-Christian civilisation.[36] As Thatcher herself told the *Sunday Times* in 1981, 'Economics are the method; the object is to change the heart and soul.'[37]

Legacies of Thatcherism

If Thatcherism is to be measured by the scale of its ambitions, can it be said to have achieved them? Some historians and political scientists have been sceptical of the transformative claims made for the Thatcher effect. This is not simply because statements and positions once thought radical have become orthodox; nor is it solely because, after the end of the Cold War, free market liberalism was in the ascendancy across the world. It is also linked to a broader perspective on the period, which puts some of the more extravagant claims for the Thatcher effect in a more sobering context. As Richard Vinen has noted, the period between 1975 and 1990 witnessed extraordinary changes across the globe, from the Iranian Revolution and the massacre at Tiananmen Square to the fall of the Berlin Wall and the dissolution of the Soviet empire. In such company, privatisation and the sale of council houses take on a less epoch-making hue.[38]

Like any government, the Thatcher administrations were often pragmatic, improvising their agenda in response to the pressures of office. The consequence was a sometimes confused and contradictory policy legacy.[39] For all the radicalism of Thatcher's rhetoric, the welfare state remained largely intact. Measured as a proportion of GDP, taxation actually *rose* over the Thatcher era, from 38.8 per cent in 1979 to 39.3 per cent in 1990; and in the financial year 1981–2, it rose as high as 43.7 per cent. Public expenditure increased throughout the first term, reaching 48.5 per cent of GDP in 1982–3. As late as 1984–5 – perhaps the peak of 'high Thatcherism' – it was as high as 48.1 per cent, before falling to 40 per cent in 1990–91. Proposals for radical welfare reform were largely ignored; and Thatcher continued to insist that 'the NHS is safe in our hands'.[40] Despite her moral conservatism, and willingness to use the premiership as a pulpit, Thatcher made little effort to legislate on matters of personal morality; and the government's response to the AIDS crisis focused on safer sex rather than abstention. In many respects, as Richard Vinen argues in Chapter 11 of this book, the most dramatic movement during the Thatcher era took place on the left. On foreign policy, defence and relations between Britain and Europe, it was *Labour* that abandoned the consensus, while Conservative positions remained broadly orthodox.

Nonetheless, the scale of the Thatcher legacy should not be understated. Between 1979 and 1990, the state withdrew almost entirely from the direct control of industry, while shrinking significantly the state provision of housing. If the overall tax burden remained static, there was a marked shift from direct to indirect taxation, with the percentage of revenue raised from income tax down from 43.5 per cent in 1978 to just 33.1 per cent in 1990. The top rate of income tax fell from 83p to just 40p, while the basic rate fell by 8p in the pound. This was accompanied by a sharp rise in economic inequality: the incomes of the poorest fifth of the British population rose by between 6 and 13 per cent from 1979 to 1993, while the incomes of the richest fifth rose by more than 60 per cent.[41] Public borrowing also fell: though the government ran deficits in all but two years of Thatcher's premiership, the national debt declined as a proportion of GDP from 49 per cent in 1979 to 39 per cent in 1990.

Perhaps the most dramatic change was the diminished power of organised labour, due to a combination of falling inflation, rising unemployment, the break-up of state monopolies and new trade union legislation. The number of days lost in strikes fell from 29 million in 1979 to just 761,000 in 1991, while union density in the workforce fell from 57 per cent to 42 per cent. Just as significant was a change in assumptions, in both industry and politics. Trade unions were never again viewed as partners in government; nor was governing competence measured by the capacity to work constructively with organised labour. By the time the Labour Party returned to office in 1997, it had accepted large parts of the Thatcher legacy. As for 'socialism', the word all but disappeared from British politics.

It would be churlish, then, to deny the impact of the Thatcher governments; yet three qualifications should be borne in mind. First, there is little evidence of the broader cultural change so often associated with the Thatcher era. Survey evidence does not support the emergence of more individualist popular attitudes, and the Conservative share of the vote actually declined in each election from 1979 to 1992. On this evidence, the British electorate was not significantly 'Thatcherised'; nor was it persuaded of the Thatcher governments' ideological claims in relation to full employment and the welfare state.[42] The political success of Thatcherism owed a considerable debt to the electoral system, and to a constitution that permitted radical policy change on the basis of 42–44 per cent of the popular vote.

Second, it is important to distinguish the impact of the Thatcher governments from those social, economic and generational changes that coincided with its period in office. The increasing opportunities for working mothers, the rise in teenage pregnancy, the decline of traditional manufacturing industry and the rise of the service sector – all these developments were in progress before Thatcher took office, and operated autonomously upon British society. Any government spanning a period from the late 1970s to the early 1990s would have experienced seismic changes. For all the power of 'Thatcherism' as an idea, it should not be made an explanatory tool for every social development.

Third, many of the changes associated with 'Thatcher's Britain' were not to the Prime Minister's liking. By 1990 divorce, abortion and teenage pregnancy were both more common and more socially acceptable. Church attendance continued to decline, while crime increased by an average of 5–7 per cent each year.[43] Despite Thatcher's own emphasis on thrift, personal borrowing escalated dramatically. In the decade after 1978, non-housing loans by UK banks rose from £4 billion to £28 billion, while housing loans increased more than tenfold to £63 billion.[44] The Conservatives had promised a manufacturing revival in 1979, but the number of workers employed in manufacturing industry fell by 42 per cent over the 1980s. Thatcherism had also promised to restore the Anglo-Scottish Union, after both major parties had flirted with devolution. Support for Scottish independence, however, rose from 14 per cent in 1979 to 33 per cent in 1987. If 'Thatcherism' aimed at the restoration of the traditional family, the reinvigoration of industry and the strengthening of the Anglo-Scottish Union, its success had been limited indeed.

Thatcherism in historical perspective

As the Thatcher era becomes the province of historians, new questions are being asked and new evidence assessed. The history of Thatcherism is still an emerging field, but two lines of inquiry have already become prominent: the place of Thatcherism within the Conservative tradition; and its emergence as a viable political project in the context of the 1970s.

Locating Thatcherism within the Conservative tradition is an especially vexed task, for it depends not only on one's view of the Thatcher decade but also on how one reads Conservative history. Nonetheless, several historians have sought to challenge the widespread perception of Thatcherism as an alien intrusion into a hitherto pragmatic creed.[45] The main tenets of Thatcherism, it is argued, are deeply embedded in Conservative history: from Burke's defence of the individual and Peel's free trade reforms to the deflationary politics of the inter-war period and the Conservative grassroots campaigns against inflation in the 1950s and 1960s.[46] From this perspective, it is the emollient Conservatism of the Macmillan era that appears exceptional. Among historians sympathetic to Thatcherism, this interpretation could lead to an indictment of the 'guilty men' in charge of the party after 1945. As Andrew Roberts put it: 'Instead of treating it as the freak result it was, an entire generation of Tory politicians was emasculated by the 1945 election result, especially over the issues of nationalisation, the growth of the State and trade union reform.'[47]

Others have doubted whether pre-1945 Conservatism can be mapped so easily on to Thatcherism. For Andrew Adonis, Conservative political strategy for most of the twentieth century involved accommodating the agenda of its opponents. After its traumatic, Edwardian confrontation with 'New Liberalism', inter-war Conservatism was cautious in its economics and conciliatory in its governing strategy, offering a rhetorically inclusive, progressive Conservatism as the best antidote to socialism. On this reading, Thatcherism marked a new development in the party's history: an attempt to win elections on the basis of an uninhibited liberal market prospectus and, ultimately, to remake the sociological foundations on which previous electoral strategy had been premised.[48]

The relationship between Thatcherism and the Conservative tradition is not simply of academic interest. It was keenly contested during the Thatcher era itself, for the claim that Thatcherism marked a radical disjunction in British Conservatism was not ideologically neutral. Rather, it was promoted by two distinct groups, each with a political purpose to serve. The first were those critics of Thatcher who had been frozen out of the party hierarchy, of whom the most articulate spokesman was Ian Gilmour. By extruding Thatcher from the Conservative tradition, and aligning themselves with an older, purportedly more authentic Conservatism, 'One Nation' Tories were able to legitimise their dissent and to hold out the promise of a future restoration.[49] Thatcher's cheerleaders, by contrast, presented the 'wets' as the alien intrusion, an accommodationist old pals battalion said to have dominated the party since 1945. Thatcherism could then be portrayed as 'the reversion to an older tradition' of Conservatism, in which 'the false lessons taught by the war have begun to be unlearned'. This allowed Thatcherites to distance themselves from the errors of the Heath government and the electoral failures of the period since 1959.[50] Historians have become increasingly sensitive to the political charge carried by these debates, viewing terms like 'One Nation' not as fixed camps on the party battlefield, but as contested terrain, to be fought over by political pugilists.[51]

A second line of enquiry focuses on how the Thatcherite approach became politically possible in the 1970s, a question addressed not only by historians, but by political scientists influenced by historicist methodologies.[52] Such an analysis locates the emergence of Thatcherism in the economic and political crises of the 1970s. In this respect it shares common ground with the writers of *Marxism Today*, though it focuses less on material change than on the capacity of the Conservatives to 'construct' or 'narrate' these crises through the shrewd use of ideological frames. This has encouraged a greater sensitivity to the ideological charge carried by narratives such as 'decline', and their role in structuring contemporary interpretations of crisis.[53] Such analyses have necessarily emphasised the contingency of Thatcherism, crediting its ascendancy as much to political agency as to structural economic change.

Making Thatcher's Britain

This book seeks to build on and extend the nascent historical interest in the Thatcher era, exploiting the thousands of documents published by the Thatcher Foundation and the rolling release of official papers under the 'thirty year rule'. The book also aims to broaden the focus of historical investigation, reaching beyond the traditional emphasis on statecraft and political economy. To this end, the volume explores issues of class, race and gender; sets Thatcherism within an international context; and pays attention to each of the 'four nations' that comprise the United Kingdom.

Part I examines the ideas and influences that shaped Thatcherism as it emerged in the 1970s. Robert Saunders opens this line of enquiry by investigating how Margaret Thatcher responded to the economic and political crises of the 1970s, showing how she reinterpreted them rhetorically in ways that widened the political space available to her. Ben Jackson then assesses the influence of the neo-liberal think-tanks that acquired ever greater ideological heft from the 1960s onwards, revealing how they mobilised both financial and intellectual resources to re-shape the outlook of British media and political elites. Jim Tomlinson gives an account of the politics of inflation in the 1970s, revealing the strategic, rather than strictly economic, thinking that governed Thatcherite policy prescriptions. Matthew Grimley explores the moral and religious dimensions of Thatcherism, locating it within a wider reaction against permissiveness in the 1970s. On this reading, Thatcherism was a response not only to economic crisis, but also to a perceived moral crisis. Camilla Schofield concludes this section by looking at the influence of Enoch Powell on Margaret Thatcher and her allies and finds a more complicated relationship than is commonly assumed. Powellism and Thatcherism, she notes, were separated by important ideological differences, particularly in relation to the status of the nation. Taken together, the chapters in Part I show how both the form and content of Thatcherism were shaped by its historical context, acted upon by a range of forces and issues that came to prominence in the 1970s. Yet Thatcherism was not simply a product of these contexts. Through rhetoric, strategy and policy formation, it responded to its environment in ways that expanded the terrain of the possible.

Part II turns to the impact of the Thatcher years on British society and political culture. Laura Beers analyses the differing reception of Thatcherism by men and women, focusing on Margaret Thatcher's appeal to female voters. Jon Lawrence and Florence Sutcliffe-Braithwaite show how Thatcherism recast the dominant social discourses of British public politics, substituting a language of 'ordinary working families' for the more familiar notions of class that had hitherto governed the post-war British political imagination. David Howell casts new light on the archetypal class conflict of the Thatcher years – the miners' strike – by demonstrating that commentators who focus on Thatcherite resolution have neglected the complex forces at work within mining trade unionism in this period. The National Union of Mineworkers was riven by significant internal disagreements and could not mount as powerful a collective response on closures as it had done in the 1970s on pay. Richard Finlay investigates why Thatcherism gained less traction in Scotland and Wales, arguing that Thatcher embraced a particular form of unitarianism that set her at odds with other unionist traditions. He shows why, in spite of their shared rejection of Thatcherite Conservatism, the politics of Scotland and Wales diverged from one another with respect to the strength of nationalist sentiment and popular commitment to some form of home rule. Marc Mulholland chronicles the complex evolution of the Irish question during Thatcher's time in office, and the dilemmas it posed for a government led by a Prime Minister so staunchly committed to a certain vision of British unionism. Overall, the chapters in Part II emphasise the diversity of the Thatcher effect across different classes, regions and social identities. As these chapters make clear, to ask 'What is Thatcherism?' or 'What is the Thatcher legacy?' evokes a further set of questions: where? when? and for whom?[54]

Part III places Thatcherism in an international context. Richard Vinen locates Thatcherism within the foreign and domestic policy debates surrounding the Cold War. He concludes that, in crucial respects, the Thatcher governments should be seen as upholders of the establishment consensus rather than radical challengers thereof. Andrew Gamble reconstructs Thatcherite perceptions of Europe and America during the 1970s and 1980s, culminating in the neo-Thatcherite orthodoxy of the 1990s: that a clear choice had to be made between closer integration with Europe and stronger relations with the United States. Stephen Howe takes up the question of empire, which sits alongside Europe and the United States as one of the three referents that have historically shaped Britain's role in the world. Howe surveys the legacy of empire in the Thatcher years, not only for foreign and domestic policy but also for the shaping of memory and national identity. The chapters in Part III therefore significantly widen the field of discussion of Thatcherism, recasting the Thatcher era as a consequential episode in the twentieth-century transformation of Britain's place in the world.

We do not pretend, in this volume, to undertake a comprehensive survey of the Thatcher era. Many important themes are under-represented; others are absent altogether. More could certainly be said about privatisation, policing and the welfare state; while environmentalism, the AIDS crisis and popular culture all deserve volumes of their own. By offering the case studies included in this volume, we aim simply to illustrate the varieties of Thatcherism and to offer a range of historical perspectives. We hope that this will encourage further scholarship in the historical study of Thatcherism, as archives and papers become more readily available, and we look forward to learning from the results.

Part I

Making Thatcherism

1 'Crisis? What crisis?' Thatcherism and the seventies*

Robert Saunders

More than any peacetime Prime Minister since 1931, Margaret Thatcher took office in 1979 amidst a mood of national crisis. The Conservative manifesto had described the recent contest as 'the most crucial election since the war', a 'last chance' to stave off national disaster; and Thatcher herself invoked the spirit of Pitt the Elder in 1756: 'I know that I can save this country and that no one else can.'[1] In office, appeals to the 'seventies crisis' proved a powerful rhetorical device, framing the actions of the Thatcher governments against a gallery of apocalyptic alternatives. The decade became a shorthand for a set of nightmare images, when 'the dead went unburied', 'rubbish piled up in the streets' and a British Chancellor went 'cap in hand' to the International Monetary Fund: 'a chronicle of the collapse of confidence which ensured the acceptance of the Thatcher revolution'.[2]

Yet Thatcher did not simply exploit a sense of crisis; she offered a specific interpretation of the seventies that privileged particular responses. As Colin Hay has argued, crises 'are above all public constructions', which 'need bear no direct correspondence with the symptoms they narrate'. This is not to say that they are false, or that the events they describe are not real and serious; but they require an active process of narration, in which the 'raw materials' of crisis are bound together and given meaning.[3] The diagnosis offered by the Thatcherites was far from the only reading in play, even within the Conservative Party. That it became the hegemonic narrative was Thatcher's first great achievement, and served as a foundation for all the others.

This chapter explores the evolution of that narrative after 1975, and its place in the rhetorical construction of 'Thatcherism'. As many commentators have noted, the Conservative manifesto in 1979 was remarkably light on policy, placing little emphasis on those phenomena, such as privatisation, that would define the Thatcher governments in office.

* I am grateful to Tim Bale, Ben Jackson, Glen O'Hara and the participants in the 2010 Oxford workshop for their comments on this chapter.

In so far as 'Thatcherism' had a clear public identity in the seventies, it was descriptive rather than prescriptive: a narrative that cleared the way for policy responses, rather than a policy programme in its own right. As such, it was directed not just against the Labour Party but against rival analyses within her own party, which favoured concili-ation of the unions, constitutional reform and/or the active pursuit of coalition. For Thatcher, these analyses were flawed intellectually and dangerous to her personally. She was not remotely plausible as a coali-tion leader, or as someone who could negotiate prices and incomes with union bosses, and her distaste for constitutional reform was well known. In this respect, 'Thatcherism' was forged not only in the electoral con-flict with Labour and the Liberals, but by pressures operating on and within the Conservative Party. It was no coincidence that the words 'Thatcherite' and 'Thatcherism' first appeared, not as ideological state-ments, but as markers of allegiance within Conservative politics, serv-ing as antipodes to 'Heathism' and 'the Heathites'.[4] It was not enough for Thatcher simply to encourage a sense of crisis; she had to imprint it with particular meanings, so that it spoke to her own purposes and not those of her opponents.

For this reason, the chapter privileges rhetoric over policy, and Thatcher personally over the 'New Right'. As Leader of the Opposition from 1975 to 1979, Thatcher was above all a public politician, strug-gling to impose her authority on a fractious party and to articulate a new vision of Conservative politics. For a constituency to whom the internal workings of politics are invisible, rhetoric forms the principal medium by which parties take on a wider public identity; and in this sense, as Philip Williamson has written, 'politicians *are* what they speak and publish'. Yet rhetoric is not simply a vehicle through which reality is mediated. The most successful rhetoricians engage in a creative dialogue with the world around them, narrating their context so as to reorder the scope for political action. 'It is by these means', writes Williamson, 'that a political "centre" or "consensus" may come into existence – not simply from the momentum of events or structural change, but by the constructive and collective efforts of successful politicians.'[5]

Thatcherism: ideas and ideology

The party Thatcher inherited was in a state of unusual intellectual fer-ment. Keith Joseph had recently concluded that he had never truly been a Conservative at all, and set out on a national campaign to stir up debate.[6] There was a proliferation of right-wing think-tanks and discus-sion groups, and a flurry of books appeared on the nature and identity of Conservatism.[7] This was by no means an academic exercise. By 1975, the party had suffered four defeats in the previous five elections, and had slipped into third place among first-time voters. The Conservative share of the vote in October 1974 was its lowest since 1918, and the party was losing ground in all parts of the United Kingdom. In Scotland, it had secured less than a quarter of the popular vote, and even its heartlands seemed under threat from a Liberal revival in rural England.[8]

The result was a crisis of confidence in the future of Conservative politics. For a political tradition rooted in church, Crown and colonies, the combined effect of the end of empire, the decline of religious authority and Britain's new identity within the European Community had been profoundly dislocating. The disintegration of the Heath government deepened the sense of a party that had lost its intellectual bearings. Even the historian Robert Blake, who was in many respects sympathetic to Edward Heath, thought in retrospect that he had become 'disorientated' by the 'lack of a guiding purpose'. It was 'hard to believe', Blake concluded, that a government with 'a firm doctrinal base, and an intellectually legitimate ideology … would have diverged quite so far from the principles which it had been proclaiming before it came back into power'.[9]

That mood accorded closely with Thatcher's own instincts. Accepting the leadership in 1975, she spoke of a widespread feeling that 'we have lost our vision for the future' and of a hunger among the public for 'more emphasis on principle'.[10] Though it is unlikely that she ever said 'We must have an ideology',[11] she described herself repeatedly as 'a conviction politician'[12] and told her first party conference as leader that 'policies and programmes should not be just a list of unrelated items. They are part of a total vision of the kind of life we want for our country and our children'.[13] To a greater extent than her predecessors, she used the leadership as a pulpit from which to impress her values upon the public.[14] She talked of 'the ideological battle against Socialism' and of her determination 'to create a wholly new attitude of mind' in the country.[15]

Underpinning all this was a deep suspicion of 'consensus'. Thatcher understood the necessity for compromise and had a good ear for what the public would accept, but she never saw 'consensus' as of value in itself. As early as 1968, she had defined it as 'an attempt to satisfy people holding no particular views about anything', and she found her one ministerial visit to the National Economic Development Council – the institutional embodiment of consensus politics – 'a total waste of time'.[16] 'The Old Testament Prophets', she told a rally, 'didn't go out into the highways saying, "Brothers, I want consensus". They said,

"This is my faith and my vision. This is what I passionately believe".'
'No one should be in politics', she thought, 'unless he has strong beliefs
and wants to see them translated into action.'[17]

It was in this context that Thatcher began to be spoken of as an 'ideological' politician, an exotic growth in Conservative politics. Labour
ministers warned that she would trigger a devastating confrontation
with the unions in pursuit of a dogmatic and implausible ideology, and
there were coded warnings from her own ranks, too.[18] Even a Tory academic such as Blake disliked talk of a 'Conservative philosophy', as suggesting a 'more exact set of beliefs and axioms than is natural to a party
like ours'. Only socialists, he thought, could 'talk plausibly about their
philosophy for they do genuinely think in terms of blue-prints for the
future'.[19]

This was a perennial difficulty for Tory leaders, but it bore particularly hard upon Thatcher. She had come to the leadership after the
failure of a Conservative government with an overtly modernising programme, whose leader had promised to 'change the course of history'
in his country. Heath was remembered, perhaps unfairly, for promising
to cut inflation 'at a stroke', and his legacy was a suspicion of grand
programmes for economic reconstruction. As Keith Joseph put it, the
party had lost faith in 'short cuts to Utopia' and 'well-meant but wrong-
headed drives for growth'.[20] In this respect, the pressures on Thatcher
were diametrically opposed to those on her predecessor a decade earlier. Heath had come to the leadership in the mid sixties, when the main
charge against the Conservatives was of aristocratic drift, and when the
electorate seemed captivated by the technocratic dynamism of Harold
Wilson. Thatcher operated in a world that was politically disillusioned,
in which constructive programmes were viewed with suspicion. As a
strategy document warned in 1978, 'people are fed up with *change*, and
with new systems that *don't* work'. Voters did not want 'radical upheaval,
based on promises of a Brave New World', and would 'no longer believe
politicians' promises of better times ahead'.[21]

Despite her later reputation, Thatcher broadly shared this suspicion of
'ideology' and rarely used the word except as a stick with which to beat
the Labour Party. Like other Conservatives, she condemned the notion
that the world could be reordered according to an ideological blueprint,
and she always denied that 'capitalism' or even 'Conservatism' were
meaningful analogues to 'socialism'. Even towards the end of her career, when most inclined to make grand claims for her achievements, she
repeatedly denied inventing an ideology. It was wrong, she told Russian
students in 1991, 'to see freedom and free enterprise as a system based on
an ideology – a system with the purpose of moulding man and shaping

society along some predetermined lines'. Democratic capitalism was 'not some kind of mirror image of Marxism', but 'a way of allowing people to live as they wish rather than as the state wishes'.[22]

The challenge was to distinguish 'ideas' from 'ideology'. In the ecclesiastical language that came naturally to many Conservatives, what they were seeking was not a blueprint but a creed: a set of beliefs *about* the world, rather than a constructive programme for remodelling it. This distinction between the man-made prescriptions of socialism and the timeless norms of Conservative politics had deep roots in the self-image of the Tory Party, and found a ready echo in Thatcher's own temperament.[23] Delivering the Iain Macleod Lecture in 1977, she claimed to stress 'vision, not blueprint; values and principles, not doctrines'.[24] As she put it several years later, 'These are not the panaceas of political theorists. They are ideas that have worked.'[25]

In this context, talk of 'Thatcherism' was dangerous rather than flattering. In an interview for the *Today* programme in 1977, she mocked the word as an 'ogre' invented by the Labour Party to frighten the electorate: 'Is it not ridiculous?'[26] When she did deploy the term, she slipped in an indefinite article, observing that 'To stand up for liberty is now called *a Thatcherism*.'[27] Phrased as such, it was relegated from an ideology to a precept, or the sort of thing that Margaret Thatcher might *say*. As leader, Thatcher was wary of any public association with foreign ideologues, however much she respected their ideas. Milton Friedman and Friedrich Hayek received only a single mention in the whole of the 1970s, both during visits to the United States.[28] Even in 1980, when Friedman took part in a seminar at Downing Street, Thatcher assured MPs that she had attended 'only briefly' and that Conservatives kept 'an open mind on these matters'.[29] She avoided words like 'monetarism', preferring to talk of 'sound' or 'honest money'.[30] Economists, she grumbled, 'clothe simple propositions with really rather extravagant jargon to make them sound very much cleverer than they are'.[31] It did 'not require A-level economics, or artificial labels like monetarism', to understand that one could not simply magic money out of the air.[32] This was not a prescription *for* the economy, but a statement *about* it. 'Monetarism' was 'not a new-fangled thing: it is as fundamental as the law of gravity, and you cannot avoid it'.[33] She applied a similar device to the problem of Enoch Powell. When challenged either to endorse or to condemn him, she treated the question as absurd. Her values were 'fundamental' and 'far older even than Mr Powell'.[34]

As Matthew Grimley shows in Chapter 4 of this volume, those values were often couched in moral terms, aligning the Conservative Party with the norms of Judeo-Christian civilisation. Expressed politically,

Thatcher's pretensions were no less extensive, equating her principles with freedom, democracy and the rule of law. These, of course, were the common currency of British politics; so if Thatcher was to offer more than windy rhetoric, she had, first, to imprint those values with her own definitions;[35] and, second, to establish that they were imperilled by her opponents. If the first was part of the constructive task of Thatcherism, the latter formed the core of its critical project, to which a party of opposition was peculiarly well suited. As an internal party paper on electoral 'Themes' observed in 1978, 'Fear is more potent than hope', so 'the first step' was 'to make clear the threat'.[36]

A 'crisis of socialism'

Apocalyptic expectations were not, of course, in short supply. The future Lord Chancellor, Lord Hailsham, proclaimed in 1976 that 'We are living in the City of Destruction, a dying country in a dying civilization.'[37] In a book commissioned by the BBC, Anthony King warned that Britain was entering 'the sort of "crisis of the regime"' that had not been seen 'since 1832, possibly not since the seventeenth century'; and 65 per cent of those questioned in an NOP poll in 1974 thought that there was either a 'serious threat' or 'some threat' to the survival of British democracy. Samuel Brittan and Peter Jay warned that democracy might be structurally incapable of controlling inflation, raising the possibility that it would 'pass away within the life-time of people now adult'.[38]

Thatcher thrived in such a climate, which played naturally to her own brand of eschatological politics. Britain, she repeatedly suggested, was experiencing catastrophic national decline, threatening the very 'survival of our laws, our institutions [and] our national character'.[39] As Brian Walden noted in 1977, her public appearances had a 'hectic and unusual' flavour which 'often startled her audiences'. 'Instead of the reassurance we've come to expect from Conservative leaders, Mrs Thatcher's conveyed a sense of imminent danger.'[40] The perception of crisis, however, did not automatically favour Thatcherite solutions. For some, what Britain was experiencing was a crisis of *capitalism*, requiring new methods of economic control. For others, it was a crisis of state authority, which meant 'recognising where industrial power lay and coming to terms with it'.[41] Talk of the 'economic contradictions of democracy' risked legitimising calls for a new political settlement, of the kind proclaimed by Labour in its 'Social Contract' between government and trade unions. Labour presented the Social Contract as a renegotiation of 'the democratic process', contrasting its actions with 'the authoritarian and bureaucratic' instincts of the Conservatives.[42]

Labour had come to office in 1974 on just 39 per cent of the vote, with an overall majority after the October election of only three MPs. No government since 1922 had won a majority on a smaller vote share; yet Labour enjoyed a lead of forty-three seats over the Conservatives and was able to push through an array of radical measures. Pessimistic about their own chances of wielding power, some Conservatives sought not to capture government but to constrain it, by means of proportional representation, devolution to Scotland and Wales, a written constitution and the incorporation of the European Convention on Human Rights into British law.[43] It was not only Tory 'wets' who took this stance: Keith Joseph advocated both a bill of rights and a constitutional limit on taxation – demands that enjoyed considerable support across the New Right.[44]

Joseph was the politician with whom Thatcher was most commonly associated in 1975, through their work at the Centre for Policy Studies. There were, in fact, important differences between Thatcher and her presumed mentor. She lacked his taste for the admission of error and was less inclined to indict the records of previous Conservative governments. Unlike Joseph, she saw no need to use the 'social market' as a euphemism for the 'free market', and she actively mocked the term towards the end of her career.[45] Nor did she share the anxieties of so many on the New Right about mass politics, or their enthusiasm for constitutional safeguards. Confident that the electorate shared her own political preferences, she showed no interest in constitutional mechanisms for constraining democracy, relying instead upon her capacity to lead it. Nonetheless, she agreed with Joseph's central insight: that the origins of the crisis lay in an accommodation with socialism. Like Joseph, Thatcher thought that there had been 'altogether too much Socialism' in British politics, and she echoed his warning that a nation could not endure 'half collectivist, half free'.[46]

Thatcher insisted that 'What we are seeing in Britain now is not a crisis of capitalism but a crisis of Socialism', and this became the organising principle of her rhetoric.[47] In a statement formally accepting the leadership, she warned that if 'the Socialists were to win again we would be set irretrievably on the path to the Socialist State'. Her first party political broadcast promised 'to lead the people of this country away from the quicksands of Socialism' and to 'rid the nation of this Socialist albatross'.[48] Visiting New York in September, she broke diplomatic convention by criticising the Labour government, telling reporters briskly that 'it's no part of my job to be a propagandist for a socialist society'.[49]

The case against 'socialism' was not primarily economic. Thatcher never doubted that socialism was wasteful and inefficient, or that high taxes were damaging productivity. Nonetheless, as she told a meeting in 1977, 'the real case against Socialism is not its economic inefficiency ... Much more fundamental is its basic immorality'.[50] She liked to remind the electorate that Nazism was an abbreviation of 'National Socialism', and she insisted that the National Front, too, was a 'Socialist' organisation.[51] Denying that there was any conceptual difference between socialism in Britain and the horrors of the Soviet bloc, she warned that:

Socialism is what socialists do, and socialists do more or less the same, as the opportunity permits. GULAG was the consequence of socialism ... It only happened because socialism demoralised the whole nation, replaced the individual conscience by the party, right and wrong by what was good for the revolution.[52]

Rallying her party before the election in 1979, Thatcher drew the challenge of defeating Labour in apocalyptic terms, twice quoting Burke's aphorism that 'All that is necessary for the triumph of evil ... is that good men do nothing.'[53]

For Thatcher, the task was not simply to defeat the Labour Party at the polls; it was to delegitimise socialism as a moral position. In Thatcher's view, socialism stripped individuals of personal responsibility. By passing their charitable obligations over to the state, individuals felt absolved of the need to help others themselves.[54] The result was a process of moral ossification, which would ultimately 'dry up ... the milk of human kindness'.[55] According to Thatcher, it was not 'compassion' that was driving the expansion of the state – 'Not a bit of it!' – but a lust for power over other people's lives.[56] The generous, sacrificial giving of individuals was repeatedly set against the cold bureaucracy of state welfare. As she mused, in one of her periodic reflections upon the Bible, 'I wonder whether the State services would have done as much for the man who fell among thieves as the Good Samaritan did for him?'[57]

Likening class prejudice to racial discrimination, Thatcher redefined socialism as the 'political organisation of hatred'. Conservatives, she acknowledged, had no monopoly on virtue. 'But we don't preach hatred and we are not a party of envy.'[58] On this reading, socialism was disintegrative as well as demoralising. Inflation forced workers into a constant battle to maintain their pay and conditions, a struggle in which only 'the hyenas of economic life' could profit.[59] Corporatism, too, set groups in perpetual competition. As a CPS pamphlet argued in 1975:

The more governments have intervened to remove economic decisions out of the market and into the political arena, the more they have set group against group, class against class, and sectional interests against the public interest. The politicisation of so wide an area of the country's economic activities has set up strains which are threatening its social cohesion.[60]

By lowering inflation, dismantling the corporate state and ending the rhetoric of class war, Thatcherism promised healing and reconciliation. Her famous prayer on the steps of Downing Street in 1979 – 'Where there is discord, may we bring harmony' – was in this respect wholly characteristic. 'My purpose in politics', she declared in 1976, 'is … the creation of One Nation.'[61]

Anti-socialism had been a theme of Conservative rhetoric throughout the twentieth century, but no previous leader had made it so central to their message, or talked so confidently of the elimination of socialism from British politics. This was rooted in Thatcher's own convictions, but it also served a political purpose. With its long history in the party, anti-socialism could be presented as authentically Conservative – a relearning of ancient truths in which the '*old* consensus is in the process of being re-established'.[62] Its sense of mission was especially appealing to radicals and younger voters, while Thatcher's tough language towards the Soviets – and their obliging coronation of Thatcher as the 'Iron Lady' of the West – helped to establish her as a strong leader. It may also have encouraged the drift to Conservatism from the anti-Soviet left, while establishing for Thatcher an international profile.

Thatcher constantly resisted demands to 'Tell us what you mean by Socialism'.[63] As an organising principle for a precarious political project, the ambiguity of the term was part of its attraction. It satisfied the need laid out in the 'Stepping Stones' report 'to see *all* our problems as part of a single pattern';[64] and, by polarising politics between 'socialism' and 'the defence of freedom', it squeezed the space for the Liberals. The Liberal surge in 1974 had cost Heath the premiership, propelling the Liberals into second place in 42 per cent of Tory seats.[65] By emphasising the threat, anti-socialism placed sanctions on the exercise of a 'wasted' vote, while claiming for the Conservatives the mantle of 'freedom'. It also provided an intellectual case against coalitionism – the position with which Heath was increasingly associated. As Thatcher told the party conference in 1981, socialism could not be 'half stopped, least of all by those who for years helped to nurture and support [it]'.[66]

There was no guarantee, of course, that voters would accept this critique, either as a description of socialism in the abstract or as a meaningful analysis of the Labour Party. Given that Labour had governed for long stretches in the past, without visiting upon Britain the horrors of the Gulag, Thatcher had to show that the threat in her own day was qualitatively different. A crucial role was played here by Labour defectors, who were drawn to Thatcher in remarkable numbers. Some were instinctive rebels, transferring their allegiance to a new rebel project; others were strongly anti-Soviet; while many were essentially libertarians, who now thought union power the chief menace to freedom.[67] In a series of speeches and articles, men like Paul Johnson, Reg Prentice and Lord Chalfont warned that 'The nature of the Left has changed.' Labour, they insisted, was now a collection of 'hardline, dogmatic Marxists', who would 'use the instruments of parliamentary democracy ... to destroy our existing political system'. As Prentice put it, this was 'no longer the Labour party of Ernest Bevin and Hugh Gaitskell. Neither will it be the party of Jim Callaghan – for what that is worth – much longer. It will be the party of Tony Benn, and others even further to the left.'[68] Thatcher herself described the Labour programme as 'frankly and unashamedly Marxist', aspiring 'towards a Britain modelled on Eastern Europe'.[69]

For the Conservatives, the charge against Labour was threefold. In the first instance, its nationalisation programme, punitive tax regime and closed-shop legislation were endangering the freedom of individual citizens to work, spend and save as they chose. Even freedom of speech was said to be at risk from the proposed extension of the closed shop into journalism.[70] This framed the case against union power in broad moral terms, as a defence not of profits but of people. While Thatcher steered clear in public of bodies like the Institute of Economic Affairs, she was much happier to be linked with the National Association for Freedom, even attending its inaugural subscription dinner in 1977.[71] Second, democracy was said to be in jeopardy, as Labour strove to bring 'the Iron Curtain down on the Mother of Parliaments'.[72] As its Commons majority shrivelled, Labour was accused of sidelining Parliament by the suspension of standing orders and the guillotining of debate. Thatcher charged ministers with 'a contempt of Parliament unprecedented in our whole history', while party literature accused ministers of adopting 'the Reichstag method' of government.[73] The 'Social Contract', too, was denounced as a 'blatant violation of the Constitution', an arrangement 'under which the TUC ... became almost an organ of government – or vice versa'.[74] This allowed Thatcher to promise not a new constitutional departure, but a *return* to parliamentary government as traditionally understood. As she told Conservative trade unionists in 1976, 'We are not in the business of handing over the Government of this country to any group, however important, which has not been elected to govern. It is Parliament and no other body, which is elected to run the affairs of this country.'[75]

Third, Labour stood accused of sponsoring law-breaking, and of lifting its trade union allies beyond the reach of the courts. 'For the first time in my life', Thatcher warned in 1976, the rule of law was 'at hazard in Britain'.[76] Thatcher never forgave the left for bringing down the 1971 Industrial Relations Act, or its support for the rebel councillors at Clay Cross.[77] As the *Campaign Guide* pointed out in 1977, no fewer than three Labour ministers had fallen foul of the courts, and it drew particular attention to Foot's attacks upon the judiciary.[78] This, Joseph argued, was not simply the high-handed language of a single minister, but the natural animus of the left towards any barrier to socialist transformation. Since the entire legal system was founded upon individual property rights, he noted, it was hardly surprising that socialists should hold it in contempt.[79]

Freedom, democracy and the rule of law were reassuringly conservative principles, rooting Thatcher's rhetoric in some of the core values of British political thought. Yet all this depended upon a particular political vocabulary, in which words like 'freedom' and 'democracy' took on a peculiarly Thatcherite hue. The language of freedom was unapologetically individualist, framed around freedom from state intervention. As Keith Joseph put it, 'Every new power to government is a new restriction on individuals and corporations.'[80] For Thatcher, too, freedom was usually equated with market choice. In an article for the *Sunday Express* in 1975, headed 'It's Your Freedom They Hate', she insisted that 'Without choice, no one is free.' Under capitalism, the consumer was 'Free to take it or leave it, whatever it may be. Socialism says, "Take it and lump it".'[81]

That gave a new importance to private property as 'the essence of a free economy', for 'on that freedom all our other freedoms depend'.[82] Joseph, too, thought the right to own property 'even more important politically' than economically, for it made citizens independent of the overmighty state.[83] This stood in contrast to the notion of 'public ownership', in which property was diffused to all citizens through the democratic state. In 1973 Lawson had urged his party to avoid this 'emotively favourable phrase', and Thatcher herself mocked the term as 'a misnomer': 'the moment things are taken into public ownership is the moment when the public ceases to have control, consideration or choice'.[84] It was in this context that Thatcher began to trumpet the democratising power of the market as a complement to strictly political institutions:

the democracy of the ballot box, important though it is, is only one form of democracy. In a truly free society, and a society of truly free men, it must be reinforced by the democracy of the market, in which people can cast their vote, not once every four years or so, but every day as they go about their daily business.[85]

This was a common idea on the New Right, and drew a warm response from Thatcher's supporters. As David Howell put it, the extension of property ownership would make 'a reality of democratic rights in a way that socialist theory could never hope to provide'.[86]

Narrating the crisis

Thatcher had evolved a critique of Labour as a menace to the very existence of a free society. The danger was that this would appear hysterical as Labour tacked back towards the centre ground, especially once Callaghan had replaced Wilson as Labour leader in 1976. Privately, the Tory leadership thought Callaghan 'a twister', but they recognised that his sunny demeanour and conscious anti-intellectualism made him scarcely plausible as an extremist.[87] With a modest economic recovery in progress, Labour could trumpet its pragmatic economic management as well as the benefits of its Social Contract with the unions. The nightmare, for the Conservatives, was that the electorate would reward Labour with another term in office, or credit the Liberals for their moderating influence within the Lib–Lab Pact.[88]

In this context, it was imperative 'to destroy the Labour proposition that it is mild and moderate under benign Callaghan'. If the Prime Minister could not be made out to be an extremist, he should be presented as 'a temporary, expendable front-man', behind whom lurked 'the Socialist reality' of 'contempt for the Law, the Constitution and the rights of the individual'.[89] He was commonly contrasted with Hugh Gaitskell, Labour leader from 1955 to 1963, who had fought a series of memorable battles within his party. As Gilmour put it:

When Gaitskell had to deal with Labour's Left-wing, he fought and fought again ... This lot just trim and trim again. The history of the Labour Party since Gaitskell's death is the history of one surrender after another by the Labour moderates.[90]

The contrast between a courageous champion of the centre ground and his pliable, easy-going successor was heightened by Callaghan's reputation as a union man. As Thatcher reminded the party in 1978, it was Callaghan who had led Cabinet opposition to *In Place of Strife*, Barbara Castle's proposed trade union reforms in 1969. 'The unions did not like it', she recalled, so 'Mr Callaghan saw it straight into the waste paper basket.' The way to unbridled union power 'was opened in 1969 by Mr Callaghan'.[91]

For the Conservatives, the economic recovery after 1976 was attributable neither to Callaghan nor to his Liberal allies, but to a combination of IMF supervision, the loss of Labour's majority and the need to disguise its socialist intentions before facing the polls. The implication was that victory in the coming election would herald a quite different Labour government, with an independent majority at its back and North Sea oil wealth at its disposal. As Prentice warned, the IMF straitjacket had secured Labour moderation for a time; but 'a new Labour government, with a working majority, would soon sweep this away. It would probably sweep Mr Callaghan away as well.'[92]

This was important in fending off the threat of coalitionism, for it suggested that there was no real common ground between the parties on which to build. But the Conservatives still had to show that they could govern alone, which meant addressing their relationship with organised labour. Thatcher nursed a deep suspicion of unions, which she saw as unconscionable restraints upon personal freedom. She abhorred secondary picketing and professed a particular aversion to the closed shop. Yet the pressure to reach an accommodation was still strong; and with nearly half the working population unionised, 'trade unionists' were simply too large a constituency to be antagonised en masse. Despite her suspicion of the union leadership, Thatcher made considerable efforts to reach out to ordinary members. As leader, she increased funding for the almost moribund Conservative Trade Union Association and made a point of addressing its annual conference. As she reminded a party meeting in December 1978, 'We Conservatives count millions of trade unionists among our political supporters and an increasing number among the active workers for our cause. It is neither our purpose nor our interest to damage these institutions.'[93] She praised the work of 'Conservative trade unionists, Conservative negotiators and shop stewards', and repeatedly urged Conservatives to join their union and to become active in its affairs.[94]

Thatcher trod carefully around the economic functions of trade unions, distinguishing their legitimate role as participants in collective bargaining from a wholly inappropriate place as special partners in government. This was a political, rather than economic critique. Labour's 'Social Contract', she alleged, had 'allowed a handful of trade union leaders to dictate to the Government' across the spectrum of public policy. 'And I am bound to say to them: "With great respect, that is not your job. It is Parliament's."'[95] This allowed Thatcher to present her policy not as an assault upon organised labour, but as a return to the demarcation observed by Bevin, Morrison and the 'great leaders of the past', who 'were careful not to involve their unions in either running the government or becoming mere agencies of government'.[96] In this context, claims that the unions would actively seek to destroy a Conservative administration were not entirely unhelpful, for they enabled Thatcher to frame the issue as a conflict between the democratic authority of Parliament and a protection racket run by Labour and its union paymasters.[97]

This was partly why Thatcher was so hostile to a statutory incomes policy, for it blurred the divide between 'economic' and 'political' activity. Yet this position threw up problems of its own. Without significant proposals to curb union power in the market, the Tory policy of restoring free collective bargaining seemed to imply that the party was giving up on industrial relations altogether. This raised the spectre of a union 'free-for-all' and a return to industrial chaos. The most plausible response – that monetary policy would enforce wage discipline by driving up unemployment – was politically unsayable, not least when the Conservatives were attacking Labour for rising unemployment. This made it hard for the Conservatives to capitalise on Labour's own problems towards the end of 1978. The Labour Party Conference had seen a rebellion against the leadership by the union vote, which rejected the 5 per cent pay policy and demanded a minimum wage of £60 a week for public sector workers. Though Callaghan's biographer thought this a 'disaster', the perception from the Conservative camp was subtly different.[98] The collision between the Labour leadership and the unions, followed by a powerful speech from Callaghan restating the dangers of inflation, helped to project a sense of distance between the government and organised labour, and a determination to stand up to union militancy. With Heath offering cross-party support, this opened up a potentially dangerous contrast with Thatcher. As Alfred Sherman warned in a memorandum, 'Callaghan and Heath gave the impression of somehow standing up to the unions and producing some framework for economic stability, whereas we simply said: remove the brakes, let it rip.' Ironically, 'We appeared to be associating ourselves with the most unpopular institution in Britain today, the trade unions and their rampage.'[99] The Conservatives fell five and a half points behind in the polls, indicating even to Thatcher 'that the public wanted us to back the Government against the unions'.[100]

From this perspective, the 'Winter of Discontent' could hardly have been better timed. It destroyed the argument that Labour could resolve industrial conflict and refocused attention on the political critique of unionism. The perception that this was a strike against the *public* established what Colin Hay has called 'the near hegemonic' perception of 'a beleaguered state held to ransom by the union movement'.[101] Above all, it exposed the inflated claims associated with the 'Social Contract'. As David Marsh has argued, the Social Contract after 1976 was in practice little more than an incomes policy, demanding levels of wage restraint that the unions could not in the long term deliver.[102] For this reason, it was probably always doomed to failure; and, since it weighed most heavily upon the public sector, it was always likely to end in a *levée en masse* by public sector workers. Yet the Social Contract had been presented as a new form of government, a recasting of 'the democratic process'. That was important in selling the Contract, both to the unions and to the Labour left, and in persuading the electorate that Labour could build a durable relationship with organised labour. The unintended by-product was that when it collapsed in the winter of 1978–9, it appeared not simply to be a failure of incomes policy but the collapse of a governing system. That cleared the way for a new political settlement and a paradigm shift in the assumptions of British statecraft.

The 'Winter of Discontent' made a reality of the aspiration set out in 'Stepping Stones', transforming 'the unions from Labour's secret weapon into its major electoral liability'.[103] It was hard to believe in the moral superiority of socialism when vital operations were under threat and pensioners were starved of heat and light.[104] With Callaghan apparently in denial, it was left to Thatcher to articulate the sense of crisis and to propose a way out of it.[105] Yet the 'Winter of Discontent' not only damaged the Labour Party and created a mood of revulsion against the unions; it also helped to resolve the incoherence within the Conservatives' own union policy. Thatcher seized the opportunity to make a unilateral shift in policy, announcing on television that she would legislate to restrict secondary picketing and reform the 'closed shop'. This made it more difficult to argue that, by abandoning incomes policy, the Conservatives were opening up a 'free-for-all'. Joseph had warned in 1975 that 'Monetarism is not enough', and the 'Winter of Discontent' enabled Thatcher to take up its necessary complement in a way that had not been politically possible before. Thatcher herself later acknowledged that 'had we fought an October general election the manifesto would have included no significant measures on union reform'. As she put it in her memoirs, 'Appalling as the scenes of the winter of 1978–9 turned out to be, without them and without their exposure of the true nature of socialism, it would have been far more difficult to achieve what was done in the 1980s.'[106]

Conclusion

As a public doctrine, Thatcherism in the 1970s was essentially a negative body of ideas, defined more by what it was against than by a specific set of policies. The challenge after 1979 was to turn what had been a highly effective oppositional creed into a positive programme for government. That Thatcherism was diagnostic, rather than creative, was not in itself a disadvantage. Thanks to the CPS, the IEA and, most importantly, the Conservatives' own policy-making machinery, proposals for implementing Thatcher's agenda were not in short supply. Thatcherism supplied the cohering narrative and the resolution to carry those ideas into practice.

That was never better displayed than in the famous proclamation of October 1980, that 'the lady's not for turning'.[107] With interest rates at 17 per cent, inflation at 18 per cent and unemployment nearing two and a half million, the pressure on Thatcher to change course was overwhelming. Her reluctance to do so was not solely the product of extraordinary courage, or even the memory of the Heath government. Rather, it reflected an ordering of priorities, evident throughout the 1970s, that marked her out from her immediate predecessors. For Thatcher, the goal was not to engineer a short-term improvement in the economy, but to eliminate socialism from British political culture. This is not to say that she was oblivious to economic hardship: only that she disbelieved in the possibility of recovery without this prior cultural change. For Thatcher, as for Joseph, growth was 'like happiness': attainable only as 'a by-product of other policies'.[108] As she had put it in 1975, 'Our aim is to build a flourishing society – not an economic system'.[109]

From this perspective, Thatcher's strategy for recovery was not fundamentally about economics at all. Her economic thought was uncompromisingly individualist, allowing almost no constructive role for government beyond the maintenance of sound money. She showed little interest in infrastructure or broader economic conditions and, as Andrew Marr has noted, barely mentioned North Sea oil in her memoirs.[110] Her analysis of British economic history was almost entirely psychological, founded upon a collapse of personal responsibility and the corrosive moral effects of socialism.[111] The Victorians had prospered because they believed in the virtue of hard work; socialism, by contrast, had weakened the national character and created a culture of 'something for nothing'.[112] In this respect, Thatcherism could not be refuted by trade statistics or growth rates. The evidence that mattered was of a resurgence of character, with new businesses starting up and a 'new attitude' in industry.[113] Against the anxieties of the 'wets' and the protests of organised labour, Thatcher mobilised the superior authority of British history. Past experience *proved* that the British people would respond to the stimulus of free enterprise: 'in view of our history it would be surprising if it were otherwise ... it is that freedom on which the advance of civilised societies is based, a freedom that for us goes back to Runnymede'.[114]

This gave Thatcherism a peculiar strength in the face of adversity; yet it was always vulnerable to a change in conditions. By 1990, most of the enemies Thatcher had fought against since the seventies were slain. Trade union power was broken, corporatism was a thing of the past and Labour had commenced its long march away from socialism. With the fall of the Soviet Union, Thatcher stood triumphant over every foe: 'As Socialism goes down all over Europe', she exulted, 'so it will be in Britain. And tomorrow, as today, will be ours.'[115] For Thatcher herself, however, that hope was swiftly disappointed. Stripped of the unions, the Soviets and, from December 1990, Margaret Thatcher herself, 'Thatcherism' in the nineties lacked coherence. 'Democracy' was not a rallying cry when it no longer seemed at threat, and 'freedom' no longer resonated as a battle-cry against the unions. In so far as Thatcherism retained its oppositional flavour, it was compelled to reorient itself against a different, more contentious set of enemies: from Euro-federalism and the reunified Germany to the lack of competition within public services.

In consequence, the resonance of Thatcherism began to change. With the waning of the socialist threat, Thatcherism lost some of its moral and strategic purpose. That left it reliant on a programmatic content – more privatisation, lower public spending and tax cuts – that increasingly resembled ends, rather than means. This rendered the party's appeal more narrowly economistic, weakening the sense that Thatcherism had any higher purpose beyond the creation of wealth, and leaving it vulnerable to a decline in the fortunes of the economy. As the party pushed for greater private sector involvement in welfare provision, its policies increasingly resembled those grand constructive programmes for change that Thatcherism had disclaimed two decades earlier – rolling the market *forward*, rather than pushing the state *back*.

All this caused considerable difficulties for Thatcher's successor. Harassed by her personal devotees, John Major was compelled to prove his 'Thatcherite' credentials without any of the targets against which his predecessor had defined her identity. He could not make speeches attacking the Soviet Union, tame the leviathan of organised labour, or shield the country from the onset of communism. Instead, he was measured against a set of policy tests – on Post Office privatisation, educational reform and anti-Europeanism – that Thatcher herself would not, as Prime Minister, have passed. In this respect, Thatcherism was a creature of the 'long 1970s', a response to crisis politics which abolished the conditions of its own success. In the 1990s, it was 'Thatcherism' and not Britain that was in crisis: with devastating consequences for the party that Thatcher had led.

2 The think-tank archipelago: Thatcherism and neo-liberalism*

Ben Jackson

In 1959, the Mont Pèlerin Society (MPS) met in Oxford, the first occasion on which the Society had held one of its regular conferences in Britain. Friedrich Hayek, Wilhelm Röpke, James Buchanan and other eminent figures gathered in Christ Church to debate, once again, the principles and practice of economic freedom. The Society had been founded by Hayek in 1947 as an international discussion group, composed of invited academics and a few select journalists and business-people. It devoted itself to the advancement of what would subsequently be dubbed 'neo-liberalism'. The Oxford meeting covered familiar terrain for MPS veterans – employment policy, monopoly, the values of a free society – but it also included a session on a fresh topic – 'Strategy and Tactics' – which featured, among other contributions, a paper by Ralph Harris and Arthur Seldon.

Harris and Seldon were the two young men recently entrusted with running the new British free market 'think-tank', the Institute of Economic Affairs (IEA). Harris had been taught by the MPS member Stanley Dennison at Cambridge, had worked for the Conservative Party for a time, and before taking up his post at the IEA had been employed as a leader writer on the *Glasgow Herald*. Seldon had been involved in Liberal politics in the 1930s and 1940s, having been educated at the LSE, where, he said, 'I was turned away from the Conservatives by Lionel Robbins who taught me that they were doing more damage than Labour in the 1930s by socialising in the name of capitalism.'[1] In their paper to the MPS, Harris and Seldon reflected on the obstacles to popularising free market ideas that they had encountered since beginning to work for the IEA.[2] These obstacles, they argued, did not stem

* For comments on an earlier version of this chapter I am grateful to Philip Booth, Gilles Christoph, Glen O'Hara, Robert Saunders, Zofia Stemplowska and the participants at the Oxford workshop in September 2010. The Leverhulme Trust provided much-appreciated financial support during the research and writing of the chapter. The Institute of Economic Affairs and Jan Martel kindly granted permission to quote from private papers.

43

from public opinion, but 'from the opposition of established interests to unavoidable and desirable change, from the preference of weak politicians for following short-sighted public opinion rather than leading and from the skill of anti-liberal intellectuals in developing their new mythologies'. In short, they envisaged their principal task as influencing elite opinion – business, politicians and, most of all, 'teachers, journalists, broadcasters, lecturers and others who function as retailers and wholesalers of ideas'. In spite of the formidable task in front of them, Harris and Seldon detected significant 'chinks in the enemies' armour': 'rising incomes and the human spirit are on our side: there is a new groping towards independence: dependence on the state is a passing phase'. Indeed, by 'rejecting the free market, the non-liberals are *spurning the consumer*'. Above all, 'non-liberal' opponents could now be judged on 'their record: they can no longer confine the debate to theoretical idealism: the utopia has been seen at close quarters'.[3]

In retrospect, these remarks appear to outline core elements of what would become the Thatcherite critique of British social democracy. Certainly, the role played by neo-liberal intellectuals and think-tanks in winning the battle of ideas in British politics has long been a fertile approach to the analysis of Thatcherism.[4] Yet there has also been a nagging worry that this genre of Thatcher commentary has accepted at face value the self-lauding accounts of individuals and institutions that had a vested interest in promoting their own importance.[5] This chapter explores the relationship between neo-liberalism and Thatcherism by giving a historical account of the way in which neo-liberal ideas were disseminated into British politics. In particular, it cautions against too ready an acceptance of the self-image of the neo-liberal pioneers as a marginalised group of intellectuals who succeeded through the sheer force of their ideas. This image, I will argue, has obscured a more complex story about the sources of support for neo-liberalism and the political strategy of its advocates.

My approach in this chapter will be premised on two assumptions. First, as Harris and Seldon argued to the 1959 MPS meeting, the aim of the popularisers of neo-liberalism was not to convert public opinion but to influence elites. Their strategy drew on the pioneering analysis of Hayek, who thought the boundaries of political feasibility were determined by a conventional wisdom that was itself the product of 'second-hand dealers in ideas': journalists, academics, teachers, publicists, public intellectuals, novelists, political advisors and so on. These individuals – who usually had no particular claim to expertise themselves – drew upon what they took to be the most fashionable expert opinions and broadcast them to a wider audience. The key to changing policy, Hayek argued, was therefore to change the minds of this opinion-forming stratum. This was why the think-tank became such an important weapon for neo-liberals: it was a crucial instrument for changing the climate of opinion by persuading journalists, commentators and politicians that what they had previously regarded as out-of-date and intellectually unfashionable was, on the contrary, at the cutting edge of political thinking.[6]

As recent scholars of neo-liberalism have stressed, however, this 'battle of ideas' should not be analysed in purely idealist terms. Free market ideas did not obtain political prominence solely because of the incisive writing and thinking of great minds, but because of a concerted effort, sponsored by sympathetic business elites, to disseminate these ideas through a complex international network of institutions. This think-tank archipelago, which sprang up in Britain and many other nations during the post-war boom, drummed up the business sponsorship required to translate the abstract and uncompromising academic thinking produced by members of the MPS into a more digestible form. Thus, as Harris and Seldon had stressed in 1959, neo-liberal activists like themselves worked as brokers who mobilised and connected four important elite groups: business, sympathetic intellectuals, journalists and politicians.[7]

My second assumption is about sources: considerable archival evidence has yet to be fully exploited by historians or political scientists. These unpublished sources give an insight into the back channels and informal networks that were established in the 1960s and 1970s and which underpinned the publications that were the public face of neo-liberal proselytising. These sources have previously been explored by Richard Cockett in his path-breaking *Thinking the Unthinkable*. But in spite of the considerable achievement of Cockett's book, it should not be taken as the final word on this subject. My own investigation of the archives of the MPS and the IEA has led me to differ from Cockett in important respects.[8]

The chapter proceeds in two stages: first, I will examine the critical role played by the IEA and later by its allies in mobilising two crucial resources for the dissemination of neo-liberal ideas: financial support from the business community and the patronage and scholarly output of sympathetic intellectuals. Second, I will illustrate how these resources were used to shape elite opinion in Britain during the 1960s and 1970s, focusing in particular on the links between the IEA, the British media and the Thatcherite fraction of the Conservative Party.

Mobilising resources

Business

One of the great advantages of capitalism, thought Milton Friedman, was that inequality of wealth – and the patronage it facilitated – helped to preserve political freedom. 'In a capitalist society', he wrote, 'it is only necessary to convince a few wealthy people to get funds to launch any idea, however strange, and there are many such persons, many independent foci of support.'[9] As Friedman knew, neo-liberal theorists and think-tanks were themselves beneficiaries of such patronage. The financing of free market ideas in the United States has been widely discussed,[10] but there has been a curious silence on the relationship between such ideas in Britain and their business sponsors. Yet the IEA – and later sister institutes such as the Centre for Policy Studies (CPS; established in 1974) and the Adam Smith Institute (ASI; established in 1977) – were only able to operate successfully because of donations from business. Other sources of revenue, for example from the sale of publications, were never sufficient to cover costs.

This point has been mentioned by certain commentators, but they do not analyse its implications.[11] Such reticence, however, obscures an important aspect of the work of the IEA and its sister organisations: not the straightforward materialist point that the payer of the piper calls the tune, but that the influence between these think-tanks and their funders worked in both directions. Fundraising by neo-liberal advocates was simultaneously an exercise in harvesting much-needed financial and political support (which inevitably conditioned the nature of the work they subsequently undertook) *and* in teaching the business community what sort of economy and society was in their own best interests. As Mirowski has put it:

It was not that disgruntled conservative philosophers and corporate movers and shakers knew precisely what sort of political economy would prove to coincide with their interests; rather, they had to be taught what it was they wanted. Here lies a lesson for all explanations rooted in self-interest.[12]

Harris and Seldon made a similar point to the 1959 MPS Conference. They stressed the necessity of persuading self-interested 'businessmen', 'who wish to contract out of competition when it suits them', that they should stick to a more principled free market position. 'Sometimes', they noted, 'the worst enemies of the free market are businessmen.'[13]

The IEA was itself founded by a businessman, Antony Fisher, who had made his fortune by introducing the battery-farming of hens to Britain. Influenced by a meeting with Hayek, it was Fisher who employed Harris and Seldon to realise his vision of 'a scholarly research organisation to supply intellectuals in universities, schools, journalism and broadcasting with authoritative studies of the economic theory of markets and its application to practical affairs'.[14] Fisher, a member of the MPS and the Conservative Party, was an early and true believer in the message of Hayek and his colleagues. He provided the start-up funds for the IEA and maintained oversight of its activities as chair of its trustees. But as the IEA evolved and gathered strength over the course of the 1960s and 1970s, Fisher's funding was quickly displaced, and exceeded, by a large number of annual corporate donations. These were recruited through an indefatigable fundraising regimen spear-headed by Ralph Harris and John Wood, a veteran of the Conservative Research Department, sometime City financier, and eventually the IEA's deputy director from 1969. The number of corporate donors to the IEA increased rapidly during the 1960s, from 110 in 1962 to 299 in 1968.[15] Thereafter the number of corporate donors fluctuated around the 250–300 level throughout the 1970s and early 1980s. The consistent donors to the IEA represented a fair cross-section of the business community: major companies such as BAT, BP, IBM, John Lewis, Marks and Spencer, Procter & Gamble, ICI, Shell, Tate and Lyle, and Unilever; the high street banks (Barclays, Lloyds, Midland, NatWest, as well as their Scottish equivalents); media outlets (the *Daily Telegraph*, the *Financial Times*, IPC Newspapers); the City (Lazard Brothers, British Assets Trust, Cayzer Irvine, Prudential); and the odd state-sponsored wild-card such as the Bank of England and the nationalised British Steel Corporation.[16]

Uniquely among British institutions, the IEA found the 1970s a time of financial promise. In spite of rising inflation and other adverse economic circumstances, revenue from corporate donors increased in real terms. 'Between ourselves', Harris told Milton Friedman in 1977, 'the Institute is now having no difficulty in keeping income ahead of inflation.'[17] It operated with a tiered system of contributions, ranging from small annual contributions of £100 or less up to annual contributions of £5000 or more. The game-plan was to recruit new donors to replace those who cancelled or reduced their annual donation, while persuading existing donors to give more each year. Harris, Wood and their colleagues were very successful at this. Annual donations brought in £47,264 to the IEA in 1968; by 1981 the equivalent figure was £267,040, a nominal increase of 565 per cent. In the same period, income from the sale of publications rose from £13,926 to £38,320 (a nominal increase of 275 per cent).[18] Perhaps unsurprisingly, the most dramatic nominal rises in corporate income seem to have been after 1974, with donations rising from £76,574 in 1974, to £112,979 in 1975, to £161,979 in 1977, to £210,343 in 1979.[19] In real terms, the increases were much less spectacular, but the fact that the IEA was able to register real increases in income in this period was itself a significant achievement.

The broader political and economic environment of the 1960s and 1970s was an important driver of business support for the IEA, especially after the Conservative fiasco of 1974, though it was of course necessary for the IEA's team to capitalise on this opportunity. The IEA represented one conduit for business to express its unease about the tumults of this period, though it was by no means the only one – the more directly political lobby group, Aims of Industry, had around 4,000 corporate subscribers in 1974.[20] But the organisation's ability to serve as one vehicle for the mobilisation of business interests was itself due to the IEA's efforts to persuade businesses that the promotion of neo-liberal ideology represented one potent way of improving the economic outlook of enterprises who felt besieged by inflation, low profits and obstreperous unions. As Sir Nicholas Cayzer put it, an evening with the IEA had impressed on him that, since the left-wing output of universities was providing ammunition for the unions, the IEA was an important source of bullets for business. Cayzer's company, Cayzer, Irvine and Company, duly subscribed at the level of £250, eventually increasing to the level of £8,000 a year by 1989.[21]

In such approaches, the IEA presented itself as practical – 'we do not represent a batch of eggheads in the academic clouds' – and oriented towards the problems of British business. The IEA, potential donors were told, understood the mistrust business felt towards economists, 'many of whom are ignorant of and often hostile to commercial enterprise', and sought to correct the balance of economic debate by putting the case for 'individual effort, market pricing, competition and the profit motive'.[22] By the mid 1970s, the tone of these appeals had become more politicised: the IEA promised to engage with the successive economic failures of Labour and Conservative governments and claimed credit for Keith Joseph's outspoken 1974 speeches, as well as the economic journalism of Samuel Brittan, Peter Jay and Patrick Hutber. The IEA's task was to 'deploy many of the world's leading economists to analyse the error and unrealism of dominant economic theories and practice'. The most fundamental of these errors, Harris told one potential donor, 'has been to exaggerate the capacity of government action to solve every problem'.[23] This was a message disseminated not only in the IEA's publications, which were of course distributed to IEA donors, but also, perhaps more powerfully, through sociability, at the convivial lunches, dinners and meetings that the IEA hosted and which mixed together corporate donors or prospects with sympathetic economists, academics, journalists and politicians.

A similar, and complementary, fundraising strategy was pursued by the CPS. Founded by Keith Joseph, the CPS consulted Harris and his colleagues about fundraising, and the two organisations cooperated to ensure a mutually beneficial relationship. Harris sent Joseph a list of potential donors and enlisted Joseph's help in raising funds for the IEA and for Harris's own pet project of establishing a private university (eventually realised in the shape of Buckingham University).[24] Joseph envisaged that about £100,000 would be needed to run the CPS and aimed to attract annual donations from between forty and sixty companies to raise this sum.[25]

The IEA's message – and that of neo-liberalism – evolved between the 1950s and 1980s. In the 1950s, as Harris and Seldon argued in their 1959 MPS paper, part of the IEA's brief was to oppose anti-competitive business practices as well as ill-advised state interventions. In this sense, they initially sought to educate those in business about free market principles. But by the 1970s and 1980s, it was the problems of government that occupied the IEA's attention and formed the core of their fundraising appeal. The IEA no longer criticised business, but sought to defend it from the clumsy attentions of politicians, civil servants and unions. The shift was subtle, but palpable, and surely reflected the complicated relationship between ideas and interests that had developed at the IEA's offices since the 1950s.

Intellectuals

While the money and contacts available from business represented one crucial resource for the advancement of neo-liberalism, the second indispensable ingredient was the intellectual authority of leading neo-liberal scholars. These included the string of Nobel Prize-winning economists who were members of the MPS: Hayek, Milton Friedman, George Stigler, James Buchanan and (more peripherally) Ronald Coase. With the exception of Hayek and Coase, they were all from the United States, and Hayek and Coase were both based there from 1950–62 and from 1951 respectively. No British figures of comparable academic prestige allied themselves to neo-liberal ideas, with the partial exception of Lionel Robbins. However, Robbins was not a consistent ally of the neo-liberal crusade, adopting a sympathetic but sceptical pose towards its ideology.[26] Other British economists contributed to the work of the IEA and the CPS – figures such as John Jewkes, Peter Bauer, Alan Peacock, Alan Walters, Graham Hutton and Arthur Shenfield – but although important as supporting characters, and in Walters's case as an economic advisor in government, these British economists would not have made the same impact without the ideas and eminence of their overseas allies.

The closeness of the connection between the IEA and the pre-eminent neo-liberal scholars is easily underestimated. The generation of American academics from which Friedman and Buchanan were drawn was still one that regarded British history, politics and economics as of central cultural significance. Indeed, Britain had a particular resonance for economists because their discipline had been fundamentally shaped both by the Scottish Enlightenment and by the Cambridge of the 1930s. They accordingly welcomed opportunities to visit, and publish in, Britain, and were well informed about British politics. Friedman even spent an early sabbatical year in Cambridge in 1953–4, during which he gave supervisions to an undergraduate called Samuel Brittan.[27]

The MPS was a crucial conduit for the import of neo-liberal ideas into British politics. In the 1960s and 1970s, Harris, Seldon and another IEA stalwart, Arthur Shenfield, were key players in the life of the MPS. They were regular attendees and assiduous networkers at its events: social network analysis by Dieter Plehwe has revealed them to be among the most frequent participants at MPS meetings. Harris served as the Society's secretary (1967–76) and president (1982–4); Shenfield was also president in 1972–4.[28] Seldon first met Friedman at the 1960 MPS meeting at Kassel, Harris sometime before that. Both grew close to Friedman during the 1960s and 1970s.[29] Indeed, Friedman later paid tribute to Fisher, Harris, Seldon and the IEA as 'pillars of strength, a near invincible legion, in the battle that so many of us have fought to limit the depredations of bureaucratic control and extend the area of human and economic freedom'.[30]

The IEA's relationship with Hayek and Buchanan is less easy to date precisely, but Hayek had been connected to the IEA from its inception (Shenfield was a particularly close collaborator), and Buchanan was a regular participant at the MPS during the 1960s. Buchanan spent time in London in 1965, frequently visiting and lunching at the IEA.[31] Buchanan's long-time collaborator, Gordon Tullock, also made regular visits to London in the 1970s, when he was usually entertained at the IEA, and drawn into fundraising lunches.[32]

What ideas did British neo-liberals draw from their intellectual mentors? Neo-liberals subscribed to the view that the continual expansion of social democratic institutions and policies in the Western democracies was eroding both individual liberty and economic efficiency. This progressive widening of the domain of democratic collective choice, they argued, entailed greater powers for collective agencies, especially the state and unions, at the expense of the free exchange between individuals promoted by markets. They therefore sought to reduce the power of such collective agencies in order to grant individuals greater liberty and to improve economic performance. The decentralised and pluralistic allocation of resources by market transactions, neo-liberals maintained, was preferable to the uniformity and coercion inherent in the political allocation of resources through democratic votes. In short, neo-liberals diagnosed the fundamental problem as an excess of politics – by which they meant democratically authorised state coercion – over economics – by which they meant the use of the price mechanism to coordinate commercial activity in a non-coercive and maximally productive fashion.[33]

This general analysis generated three more specific strands of political argument that the IEA, the CPS and their allies promoted in Britain. First, they maintained that government economic policy should focus on reducing inflation rather than unemployment, and that the key to reducing inflation was to be found in the use of monetary rather than fiscal policy, specifically in the control of the money supply. On the neo-liberal analysis, the pursuit of full employment by successive governments was an example of the state trying to do too much, undermining market price signals and generating inflation. Indeed, on the grounds that government expansion of demand led to an increase in inflationary expectations, neo-liberals dismissed as quixotic the notion that it was possible to trade-off higher inflation for lower unemployment, as famously embodied in the Phillips Curve. On the contrary, they said, it was only by means of a socially disastrous acceleration of inflation that unemployment could be artificially driven below its 'natural' rate. This line of argument was often presented as a rejection of the broadly 'Keynesian' norms of the post-war era in favour of a 'monetarist' approach.[34]

Second, neo-liberals thought the welfare state offered a model of state monopoly provision that inhibited innovation, denied individuals any meaningful control over service provision, and exacted efficiency-sapping levels of taxation. Furthermore, these institutions had been designed to serve an egalitarian political morality that mandated envy of the rich and deprived individuals of responsibility for their own lives. Neo-liberals supported instead a residualised welfare safety-net to take care of the poor, alongside the introduction of user charges, private insurance, and vouchers to break-up monopolies such as the NHS and the school system and make them more responsive to individual choice.[35]

Third, neo-liberals portrayed democratic collective agencies, notably political parties, the state and unions, as primarily self-interested, concealing their own sectarian agendas with rhetoric about the public interest. In the state, bureaucrats and politicians sought to expand their own power rather than serving the public, while, in the economy, producer interest groups privileged themselves at the expense of the consumer. Unions, in particular, were to blame for creating unemployment and pressuring governments to undertake an inflationary expansion of the money supply. On some accounts, this analysis mandated further constitutional constraints on the power wielded by legislative assemblies, as a means of reducing the reach of democratic collective action.[36]

Shaping elite opinion

Media

Such were the principal resources available to British neo-liberal activists: money and contacts from business; and a powerful body of economic analysis sanctioned by leading economists from the United States. How did they plan to mobilise these resources? One answer, given by the IEA itself and often accepted at face value, is that they aimed to bombard university students, school teachers and university lecturers with publications, in a bid to shape the teaching of economics and politics to the next generation.[37] While this does indeed seem to have been the intention of its founders, the IEA was not in fact particularly successful in shifting educationalists to the right. As Brian Harrison has shown, support for the Conservative Party among university lecturers declined between 1964 and 1992, falling from a high of 35 per cent to a low of 14 per cent.[38] In practice, however, the IEA, the CPS and the ASI stumbled on a more effective alternative: directly influencing the views of the small metropolitan media and political elite that shaped policy debate in Britain. In other words, they narrowed their sights on a subset of the 'second-hand dealers in ideas' that Hayek had identified in the 1940s. The 1970s yielded considerable success for this strategy.

The circumstances of the 1970s were, of course, propitious for such efforts. The economic trajectory of the decade delegitimised existing policy norms, opening a profitable market for fresh ideas.[39] Neo-liberal ideology possessed a peculiar attraction for certain journalists and politicians because it offered a coherent and systematic account of the various economic problems of the decade as symptoms of a larger crisis of Keynesian social democracy.[40] It also prescribed an agenda for public policy that was congruent with the interests of the Conservative Party and the British press. For the Conservatives, neo-liberalism legitimised a counter-inflationary strategy that did not require painful negotiations about incomes policy with the trade unions. It also provided authoritative warrant for public expenditure cuts and established that the state should not be held responsible for unemployment.[41]

While this relationship between neo-liberalism and Conservative politics is well known, the way in which neo-liberal ideas resonated with the interests of the British press requires further explanation. The mid 1970s, particularly the years 1973–4, was a period of industrial crisis for the British newspaper business: advertising revenues plummeted, the cost of newsprint doubled, and production costs remained high because of existing wage agreements with the unions. Newspaper executives and journalists felt besieged by the power of the print unions, a feeling compounded by the debates surrounding Labour's introduction of the closed shop to journalism in 1974–6. For some commentators, union control over the printing presses and entry to the journalistic profession threatened the very existence of free expression.[42] In these circumstances it is perhaps not surprising that proprietors, editors and journalists were receptive to neo-liberal analysis, particularly those columnists whose professional identity was similar to that of self-employed skilled workers and who accordingly felt disconnected from the collective workplace identities fostered by the labour movement.[43]

The neo-liberal message was skilfully disseminated to political and media audiences by the IEA (and others) in numerous publications but also through extensive public relations drives. The IEA organised high-profile and media-friendly visits to the UK by Friedman, Hayek and other leading figures, during which journalists, politicians and other opinion-formers were invited to meet the great man in more intimate – often social – settings. The assistant editor of *The Sun*, for example, wrote to express his thanks to the IEA for convening an invigorating evening at which he met Hayek.[44] 'Monday evening was marvellous; I enjoyed every minute', Margaret Thatcher reportedly wrote to Harris after a private dinner with Friedman, Harris and Seldon. In return, Friedman told Harris that he found Thatcher 'a very attractive and interesting lady', though he was uncertain 'whether she has the capacities that Britain so badly needs at this time'.[45]

A seminal occasion was Milton Friedman's delivery of the first Wincott Memorial Lecture in 1970 (sponsored by the IEA), which began the process of seriously marketing monetarist ideas in Britain.[46] On another visit in 1974, Friedman packed in a press conference, a seminar at the IEA, and an appearance on the BBC2 programme *Controversy*, in which Friedman took on four sceptical British economists to defend the proposition that 'inflation is created by government and by no one else'.[47] Outside of such visits, Harris, Seldon and their colleagues built relationships with leading journalists and editors and used these relationships to garner sympathetic coverage. Sociability was once again a key weapon, with lunches, dinners and seminars freely deployed: journalists were included alongside academics, businessmen and politicians, while special events were held to woo specific news outlets.

As has been widely noted, however, a relatively novel form of economic journalism took a pre-eminent role in the 1970s. A new sort of policy-focused economic journalism had emerged in the post-war period, in place of the more traditional focus on commercial news and stock market tips. The professionalisation of economics had led to a growing distance between academic economists and the public sphere. While the former focused on specialised debates in professional journals, public debate on broader issues of political economy came to be conducted by a group of heavyweight broadsheet journalists who were able to mediate between academic and policy debates. While the earliest exponents of this style, such as Andrew Shonfield, broadly adhered to the social democratic policy norms of the post-war settlement, the late 1960s and 1970s saw a transition in this group towards a more neo-liberal outlook.[48]

Famously, at the leading edge of this transition were the economic commentators of two British newspapers which in the 1970s exercised an extraordinary grip on elite opinion: Peter Jay in *The Times* and Samuel Brittan in the *Financial Times*. Brittan had returned to the *Financial Times* as economics editor in 1966 after a chastening interlude as a civil servant in the Department of Economic Affairs; his columns began to manifest an increasing sympathy with the free market right from about 1969 onwards. Jay was also a former civil servant, with close family connections to the Labour Party, who joined *The Times* as economics editor in 1967. Although he was initially sceptical about monetarism, by 1974 Jay's economic commentary had adopted significant elements of neo-liberalism. Unusually, Brittan and Jay were well connected to the American economics profession and began to be interested in Friedman and his monetarist ideas without prompting from neo-liberal activists. Their conversion to a broadly neo-liberal economic analysis – although welcomed by the IEA – was not a result of the efforts of Harris, Seldon, *et al.*, but rather emerged from reading neo-liberal writings, particularly Friedman's famous 1967 Presidential Address to the American

Economics Association, through the prism of the failures of British Keynesianism in the late 1960s and early 1970s.[49] However, after their respective conversions from Keynesianism, they granted high-profile and positive coverage to IEA publications and regularly cited and recommended the analysis of Friedman, Hayek and other like-minded economists. Their use of such ideas was not restricted to the monetarist approach to inflation. A neo-liberal (indeed Hayekian) analysis of trade unions and of the dangers posed by the over-extension of government were also key features of their public advocacy (perhaps reflecting their experience as civil servants).[50]

Although the most celebrated examples, Brittan and Jay were only part of a broader penetration of the British press by neo-liberal ideas in the early 1970s. *The Times* threw its considerable authority behind monetarism with the conversion of the paper's editor, William Rees-Mogg, partially under the influence of Jay. Other *Times* journalists were also enthusiastic supporters: the paper's political columnist Ronald Butt, for example, and a young Tim Congdon, later a leading advocate of Thatcherite policy in the 1980s, who started out as an economic journalist on the paper between 1973 and 1976.[51] The *Financial Times*'s editorial line was also increasingly neo-liberal from the mid 1970s.[52] At the *Telegraph*, the editorship of Maurice Green (1964–74) was marked by a decisive shift towards neo-liberal analysis in the paper's leaders and coverage. Green had a background in economic journalism and was sympathetic to free market thinking. This sympathy was bolstered by like-minded journalists on the paper, notably two members of the MPS who occupied key editorial positions: Colin Welch, the deputy editor from 1964 to 1980, and John O'Sullivan (who was later a political advisor to Margaret Thatcher in government). Among other benefits, the link with Welch enabled Seldon to emerge as a frequent contributor to the *Telegraph*'s editorial pages.[53] The City editor of the *Sunday Telegraph* between 1966 and 1979, Patrick Hutber, was a close associate of the IEA and a regular fixture at their events. The *Telegraph* was therefore the paper with the closest links to the IEA and the one where the IEA's work made the greatest impact on its editorial line.

Harris and Seldon maintained a friendly dialogue with Alastair Burnet, editor of *The Economist*. *The Economist* was comparatively late to the neo-liberal party, retaining a broadly Keynesian line until Burnet's replacement by Andrew Knight in October 1974.[54] Nonetheless, there was common ground between Burnet and the IEA. In 1970, for example, Harris reported that Burnet was dissatisfied with left-wing staff members 'agitating for "staff participation", complaining about the current editorial policy for example, on "standing up to the unions"'. Burnet,

Harris continued, was open to IEA suggestions about candidates for freelance work.[55]

The right-wing press broadly coalesced around neo-liberalism in the early 1970s. This meant that were, say, a leading Conservative politician to offer a full-throated endorsement of the neo-liberal agenda after the Conservatives left power in 1974, substantial support would be forthcoming from these newspapers. When Keith Joseph duly entered the fray with his iconoclastic series of speeches in 1974, he was rewarded with substantial support from this section of the press, particularly *The Times*, which used Joseph's speech at Preston as the platform for a searching debate about post-war economic policy.[56]

Broadcast journalism was another area in which the IEA was active, albeit in more defensive mode. The chairman of the BBC's Governors, Michael Swann, lunched at the IEA and corresponded with Harris and Seldon on what they saw as the BBC's left-wing bias and resistance to free market ideas. Harris complained to Swann about the 'partisan presentation' of A. H. Halsey as the Reith lecturer in 1978, and, more generally, Seldon argued that 'the BBC ... still reflects minority elitist fashion'.[57] The BBC's broadcasting of J. K. Galbraith's TV series, *Age of Uncertainty*, provoked condemnation from the IEA and senior Conservative politicians.[58] Although Milton Friedman's own TV series, *Free to Choose*, was itself broadcast on the BBC in 1980, a powerful rhetoric took shape about broadcasters out of step with the times: 'the producers, aged around 45 to 50, who decide programmes and choose the people who appear in them are largely the product of the post-war academic consensus dominated by Keynes and Beveridge and have yet to accommodate themselves to the change in economic opinion'.[59] The marketing of neo-liberalism to the media as superseding earlier, now outdated social democratic economic theories represented an important gambit in the shaping of elite opinion.

Politics

As a charity, the IEA styled itself as unaligned to any political party. This claim was central to its identity and its mission: the loyalty of the IEA was to a set of ideas and it sought to ensure those ideas were taken up across the political spectrum. It characterised its mission as social scientific, bringing into public view insights drawn from the academic study of economics. This approach fostered some unlikely alliances. The Duke of Edinburgh was assiduously wooed by the IEA in 1977, after venting his frustration about the economic culture of Britain in a controversial interview.[60] Harris and Seldon wrote to express their solidarity, enclosing IEA publications, which demonstrated 'the formidable academic support for your views'. The Duke attended dinners at the IEA in 1978 and 1981, at which about a dozen IEA stalwarts (academics, journalists and businessmen) were assembled to convey the IEA perspective (at the 1978 dinner Lionel Robbins, John Jewkes, John O'Sullivan and Patrick Hutber, among others, were mobilised alongside Harris, Seldon and Wood). In the briefing that Harris sent the attendees before the first of these dinners, Harris noted that 'Prince Philip broadly shares the IEA critique of "utopian" post-war policies'; thus, the purpose of the dinner was to give him 'a stronger impression both of the intellectual ancestry and validity of our ideas and of the growing impact the IEA is making'. Having perused some IEA literature, the Duke himself expressed relief at finding others who shared his outlook. Contact was maintained throughout the 1980s, and Harris was invited to private dinner parties at Buckingham Palace with the Duke in 1977 and on subsequent occasions.[61]

One of the more unlikely lunch guests at the IEA was the hard-left Labour MP Eric Heffer – 'both Ralph and I are working-class lads', Seldon pointed out in his follow-up letter – and he emphasised to Heffer the shared anxiety of both the socialist left and New Right 'about the over-powerful state and its resistance to decentralisation of power – public or private'.[62]

But the non-partisan positioning of the IEA was to some extent misleading, since the Institute clearly supported an agenda that was opposed to the basic assumptions of the Labour Party and the trade unions. While Peter Jay was seen as a possible harbinger of a form of Labour monetarism, a feeling to some extent confirmed by the economic policy of the Labour government 1974–9, neo-liberal activists were ultimately dismissive of the potential of the Labour Party to take up their agenda with any seriousness. Although Seldon personally still felt some affection for the Liberal Party, it was the Conservative Party that represented the neo-liberals' only realistic hope of significant influence. Contacts were accordingly developed with a number of Conservative MPs. A clue to the politicians who were most closely connected to the neo-liberal network is given by the membership list of the MPS. Only a few British politicians were invited to join the Society in the 1960s and 1970s: Enoch Powell, Geoffrey Howe, John Biffen and Rhodes Boyson (the first three all joined in the 1960s). Other politicians, for example Keith Joseph, David Howell and Jo Grimond, attended meetings as guests.[63] Although it is intriguing that Keith Joseph was not invited to join the MPS, the three most important politicians who were closely associated with the IEA were unquestionably Powell, Howe and Joseph.

Powell was a particular favourite of the neo-liberals: they admired his intelligence, principles and willingness to stand against conventional wisdom. Friedman wrote to the American Conservative luminary, William F. Buckley, to contest a critical column Buckley had written on Powell in the strongest possible terms:

I have met, talked with, and participated in meetings with Enoch Powell on a number of different occasions. He has a better and deeper understanding of economic principles, and a clearer conception of the relation between economic and personal freedom, than any other major political figure I have ever met. And even this is to put it too mildly. Broaden the field as widely as you want, and I have met few men who have as sophisticated an intelligence on these matters as Powell.[64]

The IEA had hoped that Powell might offer them a gateway to political influence. They worked closely with him in the 1960s, giving him a copy of Hayek's *Constitution of Liberty* in 1960 as he re-entered government 'before the Ministry of Health civil servants could get at him'. Later that year Harris and Seldon introduced him to Hayek over lunch at the Reform Club.[65] But however highly they esteemed him, by the 1970s Powell's idiosyncratic career path had placed him far from the heart of political influence. He was not destined to be the bearer of their ideas into government.

Howe was a different proposition: a politician on the rise, who shared with Seldon an interest in the critique of the welfare state. Howe worked closely with Seldon and the IEA in the 1960s and early 1970s on issues such as private medical insurance and industrial relations, and they remained in contact as Howe ascended the political ladder.[66]

As I have hinted, the position of Keith Joseph was ambiguous. Seldon and his colleagues invested a lot of energy in advising Joseph in the late 1960s and early 1970s and were less than delighted by the results. Seldon had voted Conservative for the first time in his life in 1970 and vowed never to do so again after the trajectory of the Heath government became apparent; Harris joined Powell in voting Labour in February 1974.[67]

When Joseph returned to the IEA on 14 March 1974, it was to a frosty reception. He had already been upbraided by his sometime speechwriter Alfred Sherman and the monetarist economist Alan Walters when he attempted to renew his acquaintance with them after leaving government.[68] Harris recorded the gist of the IEA meeting in a memo to Seldon and Wood. Joseph asked Harris for help in undertaking 'a new "crusade" for private enterprise':

I opened up by asking whether it would really be helpful to the Conservative Party or to the IEA, in view of all that had happened over the last three years ... Most engagingly he responded by acknowledging 'guilt' for all that had gone wrong.

As a quid pro quo, Joseph undertook to help the IEA with its fundraising, while the IEA would provide a list of businesses that might help him establish the CPS; contacts with economists close to the IEA; and some reading material to guide his research.[69] Joseph subsequently sent an exuberant hand-written note to Harris from his summer holidays, indicating that he had been reading Hayek's *Constitution of Liberty*; works by Friedman; and a number of IEA pamphlets.[70]

The fruit of Joseph's change of direction was revealed in the important series of speeches he delivered from June 1974 to 1976, offering a critique of the post-war settlement that was heavily indebted to neo-liberal analysis (as well as to the drafting skills of Alfred Sherman). His September 1974 speech at Preston, 'Inflation Is Caused by Governments', offered a punchy exposition of the monetarist case. It had been written by Sherman with assistance from Alan Walters and Samuel Brittan. As we have seen, influential media figures were now highly receptive to this message, and played an important role in amplifying it: the speech was printed verbatim in *The Times*, with a sympathetic editorial.[71] But Joseph's message ranged wider than the control of the money supply. Taken as a whole, his speeches popularised the neo-liberal message that 'most of the failures in our economy are due not to failings of the market, but to government interference with the market'. As he argued:

For the past 30 years in our party competitive efforts to improve life, we have overburdened the economy. We have overestimated the power of government to do more and more for more and more people, to re-shape the economy and indeed human society, according to blueprints.[72]

The place of Margaret Thatcher in the think-tank archipelago is more difficult to discern. Although contacts were made between her and the IEA before 1974, she was not a close interlocutor in the style of Howe or Joseph. Leaving aside the almost certainly mythological anecdotes about her intellectual interests recounted after the fact, there is little archival evidence of the Thatcher of the 1970s as a neo-liberal ideologue.[73] But in the 1980s, as political space opened up before her, she embraced the identity of a crusader for free markets and offered valuable patronage to the IEA and the CPS, initially by giving Harris a peerage shortly after she became Prime Minister. Whether she herself read or was even influenced by specifically neo-liberal ideas is hard to judge. More important is the fact that key advisors and ministers – Joseph, Howe, Alan Walters and so on – were connected to the broader neo-liberal network, and that neo-liberal activists were so successful at projecting their ideas as dynamic and innovative that eventually even a Prime Minister felt she could bolster her authority by associating herself with them.

This raises a further point about the reception of neo-liberalism in the Thatcher-era Conservative Party. Thatcherism as it evolved in government drew ideological sustenance from neo-liberalism, but was not co-extensive with it. Two differences in particular should be highlighted. First, as Robert Saunders suggests in Chapter 1, Margaret Thatcher and her associates acquired much greater confidence in free market economics as democratic statecraft than was ever espoused by neo-liberal theorists. Having developed their thinking during the years of social democratic state expansion, neo-liberals were pessimistic about whether free market ideas could win elections. Instead, they favoured constitutional limitations on the reach of democratic government in order to contain the inexorable pressure to increase the power of the state which they regarded as inherent in the democratic process. In this sense, Thatcherite Conservatives were far more comfortable with majoritarian democracy than their neo-liberal allies.

Second, neo-liberals regarded a comprehensive restructuring of the welfare state, particularly the NHS and the education system, as a key priority, perhaps even more important than tackling union power or altering macro-economic policy: private health insurance and vouchers were the two great reforms urged on their political allies. To their enduring disappointment, however, there was no fundamental shift in the size and role of the welfare state during the Thatcher government.[74] This was not because politicians lacked ideological sympathy: both Joseph and Howe, for example, were attracted to these proposals at various times.[75] In this respect, political judgement and the defence of middle-class interests trumped ideology.

Conclusion

Funding from leading British companies; sympathetic coverage in the editorial pages of *The Times* and *The Telegraph*; lunch with the chairman of the BBC Governors; dinner with Prince Philip: none of this suggests a movement that was exactly marginalised by the British establishment. While it may have been useful to the IEA and British neo-liberal activists to present themselves as maverick outsiders, this claim is overstated. A more precise characterisation of their position would be that neo-liberals had only a marginal presence in British universities, were a small minority among intellectuals, and lacked significant support from the British economics profession.[76] Their heavy intellectual artillery therefore had to be imported from overseas, but there was significant indigenous support for their endeavours from business, the media and, eventually, influential politicians. In this sense, neo-liberal activists were insufficiently faithful to their own creed in publicly emphasising the importance of intellectual conversion to their cause. In a politics dominated by private interests, it was skilful marketing that was crucial to securing a dominant position in the marketplace of ideas.

3 Thatcher, monetarism and the politics of inflation

Jim Tomlinson

In her memoirs, Margaret Thatcher stresses that in the years between 1975 and 1979 'the foremost issue was how to deal with inflation'.[1] In retrospect, 'dealing with inflation' can indeed be seen as central to Thatcherite economic ideas and policy, and for three reasons. Most generally, the central strategic thrust of the Conservatives from 1975 was to treat all economic problems not as the result of conjunctural events or specific policy failings, but as symptoms of a profound, long-term malaise in the British economy and British society.[2] In this 'declinist' approach, the inflation of the 1970s was not a contingent or transient problem, but a crucial part of the evidence of a national pathology, requiring a complete rethink in the approach to economic issues.[3] Hence inflation was central to the Thatcherite claim that only a radical new start could save Britain from ever-worsening decline.

Second, inflation was crucial to the debate about monetarism. The precise meaning of this much-contested term is returned to below, but there is no doubt that what made emphasis on monetary issues central to Thatcherite economic policy was its link to the priority accorded to reducing inflation. Without the rapid inflation of the 1970s, monetarism would not have become the centrepiece of debate.

Third, inflation was crucial because in Conservative thinking it was linked directly to the question of the role of trade unions. Traditionally Conservatives grounded much of their hostility to unions on their alleged impact on inflation. The rapid inflation of the 1970s, and the Labour government's 'Social Contract' aimed to reduce that inflation, when combined with the 'monetarism' debate, brought this traditional approach to the unions very much to the centre of Conservative economic policy arguments.

In examining inflation and Thatcherite thinking this chapter focuses largely on the period in opposition, 1975–9. These were the years when new economic policy positions were being hammered out by the Conservatives, and they were constructing the approach which they would carry into government. Of course, policy after 1979 is not reducible to the implementation of a blueprint worked out in the years of opposition. Nevertheless, crucial battles were fought out before 1979, and much that followed was predicated on the outcomes of those battles.

The chapter is divided into three unequal parts. The first part contextualises the arguments of the 1970s, both in respect of preceding Conservative approaches to inflation and the broad right-wing doctrinal approaches to the issue which developed especially in the early 1970s. The second part looks in detail at the inflation debate in Conservative circles from the accession of Thatcher to the leadership of her party down to the beginning of her premiership. The concluding part assesses how these issues played out in the years of Thatcher government after 1979.

Conservatives and inflation

Concern with inflation was not of course new to Conservative politics in 1975. Historically that concern was based on a range of beliefs about the dangers of inflation, with different elements coming into prominence at different times. The key components were that inflation redistributed wealth away from the party's natural supporters, penalised savers, and damaged Britain's standing in the world.

Attacks on post-First World War inflation helped the modern Conservative Party construct the electorally highly successful 'Labour versus the public' narrative in the inter-war years.[4] In the 1940s, Conservatives (and others) were worried that promises of 'full employment' would shift bargaining power in the labour market in such a manner as to bring a permanent threat of wage-driven inflation. In office after 1951, the Conservatives saw inflation as a major problem, especially because of the threat it posed to the fixed exchange rate regime for sterling established at Bretton Woods.[5] In 1958, disputes about how high a priority to give inflation, and the appropriate means to combat it, were a central cause of the resignations of the Chancellor and other ministers.[6] Part of the problem for the Conservatives was disagreement about how far monetary policy should be used to hold price rises in check. Prior to the 1958 crisis, the Conservative government had already established the Council on Prices, Productivity and Incomes, which strongly linked inflation to wage bargaining. In the early 1960s the Conservative government was driven into an incomes policy as a way of trying to combat inflation.[7] By contrast, the 'rebels' of 1958 had wanted more emphasis on monetary policy.

Inflation in Britain, which had fluctuated without a clear trend through the 1950s and most of the 1960s, rose rapidly after the 1967 devaluation, and when the Conservatives fought the 1970 election they put a lot of emphasis on reducing it, especially by reductions in taxation, while repudiating Labour's 'compulsory wage control'.[8] In 1972, the 'U-turn' in policy involved boosting demand in the economy, but seeking to avoid the inflationary consequences of this by introducing an unsuccessful incomes policy, which ultimately fed into the election defeat of February 1974. This policy U-turn infuriated many Conservatives who believed in the central role of monetary growth in inflation.[9]

In sum, Conservatives before Thatcher took on the leadership already gave a high priority to defeating inflation, but had not developed a coherent doctrine about its causes or how to combat it. The predominant policy response was based on the view that union wage pressure in the context of full employment was the central issue, but one strand in thinking had always been to regard monetary restraint as at least part of the solution, and that view gained in strength in the late 1960s. Discussion of inflation in Conservative circles up to the 1970s largely rested on the belief that it was an important problem because it threatened both the international value of the currency (a value freighted with all sorts of 'great power' beliefs about Britain, as well as direct economic significance) and to bring about undesirable income redistributions.

Economic policy is always formed out of a complex interplay of doctrinal assumptions and political calculation. Thatcherite policy is not distinct in that respect, and we return to that issue below.[10] Equally importantly, right-wing doctrine on inflation as it had evolved by the mid 1970s must not be reduced to positions taken on the causes and cures of inflation and the development of views about the relationship between monetary growth and price movements. At least as important was the development of positions about the *effects* of inflation. Taking their cue from an oft-quoted line attributed by Keynes to Lenin – 'that the best way to destroy the capitalist system is to debauch the currency'[11] – writers such as Lionel Robbins and Friedrich Hayek argued that rapid inflation was incompatible with the functioning of free market economies and democracy.

Robbins was a long-term critic of what he saw as inflationary policies driven by excess demand, and by 1972 was linking Lenin's 'statement' to the view, common in certain circles in the early 1970s, that current experience in Latin America reinforced the message that 'Democracy certainly stands to be undermined by inflation, and what is even more fundamental, the free society itself.'[12] Ironically, one of the key figures in applying Keynes's analysis to Britain in the 1970s was Keynes's sharpest critic, Hayek. Hayek's economic theories emphasised the damage done by inflation's impact on relative prices, but more broadly he emphasised the social and political harms.[13] The political tone of some of his 1970s writing (which was not untypical of the times) is captured by his allegation in the mid 1970s that 'the present inflation has been deliberately brought about by governments on the advice of economists. The British Labour Party planned it that way as early as 1957.'[14] Against the background of much higher inflation across much of the world in the early 1970s, even prior to the quadrupling of oil prices in 1973/4 (OPEC1), this argument about the dangers of inflation became part of the *grande peur* among sections of the political class which was a feature of this period as 'important sections of the middle classes did lose confidence. For the first time parts of the Establishment began seriously to consider alternatives to our present form of parliamentary democracy.'[15] Typical of that climate was *The Banker*'s claim in March 1974, in a commentary headed 'The Last Chance', that unless inflation were dealt with the last opportunity would have been lost 'for the parliamentary system to cope with Britain's economic problems'.[16] The following year *The Economist* claimed 'Britannia's dream of apocalypse is horribly close to coming true.'[17]

Claims about this alleged link between inflation and the breakdown of capitalism are most evident in British public debate in the early 1970s in the response to the 1973 coup in Chile. In *Times* editorials, William Rees-Mogg supported the coup (which led to up to 50,000 dead and a million Chileans in exile) on the grounds that it was a reasonable price to be paid for defeating inflation. Thatcher, as is well known, was also a keen supporter of the leader of the coup, Pinochet, the 'Butcher of Santiago'.[18] Thus for right-wing thinkers inflation was never just an 'economic' problem, but one of such profundity that it could be used to justify the most radical measures, up to and including political violence.

Doctrine, strategy and tactics

Internal Conservative Party discussions in the mid 1970s understandably focused primarily on how to reduce inflation rather than on its effects.[19] That it was harmful was taken as read. Occasional references to a 'Weimar' situation may be found, implying that, as in Germany in the 1920s, high inflation would shift the allegiance of the middle classes from conservatism to fascism.[20] After inflation began to fall in 1976 some party strategists thought it important to continue to stress its dangers.[21] In public speeches the most apocalyptic vision of the effects of inflation tended to be offered by Keith Joseph after his

Damascene conversion to economic liberalism around 1974. Following this conversion, and prior to the election of Thatcher as leader, he had asserted that 'Inflation is threatening to destroy our society. It is threatening to destroy not just the relative prosperity to which most of us have become accustomed ... but ... it will lead to catastrophe ... and to the end of freedom.'[22]

But such language was not confined to the insurgent economic liberals in the party. In a paper in May 1975, the quintessential 'Cabinet wet', James Prior, asserted that 'the measures that the Government contemplate will be unlikely to stem more than temporarily the holocaust to come'.[23] Thatcher echoed some of this rhetoric. In Glasgow in March 1975 she averred that 'rampant inflation, if unchecked, could destroy the whole fabric of our society'.[24] A little later in the House of Commons she cited Thomas Mann: 'a severe inflation is the worst kind of revolution ... only the most powerful, the most resourceful and unscrupulous, the hyenas of economic life, can come through unscathed'.[25] The following month she argued that 'the extremists welcome inflation' because it undermines enterprise and self-reliance, and expands the role of the state.[26]

While recognising the visceral dislike of inflation that Thatcher espoused as a genuine feeling, we need to ask what strategic purpose this hyperbole supported. First, as Green suggests, it fitted with the desire to play down the relative importance of reducing unemployment, at a time when almost everyone assumed there was a trade-off between lower unemployment and higher inflation.[27] Stressing the damage caused by inflation went along with attempts to redefine and play down the significance of unemployment, a process briefly considered but rejected in 1958, pursued albeit tentatively under the Heath government, and a staple part of the 'New Right' agenda in the 1970s. Of course, playing down the damage caused by unemployment in think-tank publications was accompanied by continuing emphasis on the unemployment problem while the Labour government was in power, including the famous 'Labour Isn't Working' election posters of 1979.[28]

Underlying much Conservative rhetoric on the effects of inflation was its alleged redistributive consequences. These were sometimes portrayed as random, but often as hitting particularly hard at 'middle Britain' and the middle class: both Thatcher and Joseph were forthright in asserting this. In a speech in Chicago in 1975, Thatcher said: 'No democracy has survived a rate of inflation consistently higher than 20 per cent. When money can no longer be counted on as a store of value, savings and investment are undermined, the basis of contracts is distorted, and the professional and middle class citizen, the backbone of all societies is disaffected.'[29] Or, as she put it earlier: 'It is cruel beyond words for the poor and thrifty, and it destroys the middle class.'[30]

Finally, the corollary of this claim that the middle classes were the biggest losers from inflation (with potentially disastrous political consequences) was that trade unionists, or at least some of them, would be the biggest gainers. The whole relationship between trade unions and inflation was absolutely central to Conservative debates in the mid 1970s, and is returned to in detail below, but it is important to note that one version of this relationship might be characterised as inverting the commonplace view that unions cause inflation to 'inflation causes trade unions'. This was most explicitly argued by Joseph in 1979. Inflation, in this account, leads to a scramble for resources, and collective action by trade unions appears to many as the most effective way of joining this scramble.[31] Given the strength of Conservative hostility to unions, inflation could be rationally anathemised for strengthening their position.

If Conservatives believed the effects of inflation went well beyond narrowly economic consequences, many also believed that its acceleration in the 1970s was not only a culmination of long-term inflationary pressures, but also a symptom of deeper failings. In these accounts, inflation was a serious problem in its own right, but also symptomatic of wider pathologies of 'decline'. Thus in her broad-ranging speech in Chicago in 1975, Thatcher presented inflation as the consequence of the errors of the 'last thirty years', and in Zurich in 1977 she told a similar story of inflation as an inevitable consequence of socialism, where socialism was defined in a Hayekian, all-embracing way as the tendency of all British governments since the Second World War.[32]

To put this point in another way, Conservatives were very keen to present inflation as much more than just conjunctural – it was instead a culmination of past mistakes, and was both a contributor to, and a result of, 'decline'. In Nigel Lawson's words: 'The economic weakness we set out to cure went far deeper than the state of the conjuncture in May 1979 ... what worried me more than the 1979 conjuncture was the long-term decline of the British economy, and the climate of defeatism this engendered.'[33]

Academic narratives of pathological long-run decline had not yet become well known,[34] but the notion was well entrenched in Conservative thinking by the mid 1970s. That Labour had failed to reverse long-running decline was a staple of Thatcher's speeches: 'If we are to halt and then to reverse the long years of our country's economic decline, fundamental changes of policy and of attitude are required at almost every level.'[35] Keith Joseph was unusual in stretching this story of decline back before the 'age of consensus', inaugurated in the 1940s, to 'over a century ago when our lead and our national initiative began to falter'.[36] At the core of the radical 'Stepping Stones' strategy put forward by John Hoskyns was the argument that decline was the central issue to be faced, and Thatcher backed this view, though the scale of decline and emphasis upon it was disputed by some 'wets'.[37]

Inflation functioned especially well in its role as evidence of underlying decline before the rate of price increase peaked in August 1975, but after that, as Alfred Sherman warned Joseph, with inflation now down to 13 per cent, and 'Industry ... no longer on the verge of collapse', the story became less clear. But right up to the 1979 election, Conservatives were keen to assert that inflation was being suppressed and masked, its underlying causes neglected, and its recurrence inevitable.[38] In January 1979 Joseph was asserting that Britain was 'top of the Western league for inflation, bottom of the league for growth' (neither of which was true).[39]

The public rhetoric of Conservatism in the 1970s presented inflation as a profound problem, potentially disastrous in its own right, but also evidence of a deep malaise in the British economy and society. In their private discussions Conservatives paid much less attention to the effects and significance of inflation, but a huge amount to how to reduce it. Thatcher's memoirs present the problem from her point of view as largely one of her preferred solution, tight money, not being accepted by many of her Shadow Cabinet colleagues, and only the Winter of Discontent making possible the necessary shift in party sentiment to make 'monetarism' possible. She notes the tactical problems posed for policy formation by having to respond to the Labour government's initiatives on inflation, but beyond that the struggle is presented as one between truth and error, with the former triumphing only after three to four years of internecine debate.[40]

Debate on policy in senior Conservative circles there certainly was, but we may perhaps get a better handle on what was at stake here by largely setting aside doctrinal struggles posed in terms of monetarism and its enemies, and focus instead on the *political* dilemmas of countering inflation faced by the Conservatives in this period. Jim Bulpitt has argued that we should see monetarism as an answer to problems of 'statecraft' faced by the Conservatives in the 1970s. An attention to statecraft does not mean simply focusing upon pragmatism and expediency, but sees politics as 'concerned primarily to resolve the electoral and governing problems facing a party at any particular time'. This involves addressing issues of party management, electoral strategy, 'political argument hegemony' and governing competence.[41] This broad approach to the debates of the years 1975–9 has much to commend it.

Some of the political dilemmas facing the Conservatives from 1975 were tactical. If inflation followed growth of the money supply with an eighteen-month/two-year lag, as contemporary monetarism and its adherents in the Conservative Party asserted, then the inflation of 1974–5 could be laid at the door of the Heath government. While Thatcher and Joseph were keen to distance themselves from that government, the assertion that its policies had led to the mid-decade inflation with its allegedly disastrous results was not a comfortable conclusion. Howe was keen to avoid any such linkage, by stressing that the 1975 level of inflation was wholly the Labour government's fault because of its attitude to wage and tax increases.[42]

But while such tactical issues can never be set aside in looking at policy development, 'monetarism' involved far deeper strategic issues for the Conservatives than simply the 'blame game' over the mid-1970s level of inflation.

Four strategic issues may be discerned. Most important was the question of trade unions, linked to the issue of the state's role in wage negotiations. Second was the issue of unemployment. Third, there was the problem of public spending and borrowing. Finally, there was the question of how monetary policy related to the issue of housing.

Traditional Conservative hostility to trade unions fitted in many respects with an analysis of inflation which saw it as primarily the result of union pressure. The strategic problem of the 1970s was how to deal with the conclusion of the monetarist argument that 'inflation is always and everywhere a monetary phenomenon', and the implication of this that unions were not to blame for the 'wage–price spiral'.[43]

Of course such a dilemma existed solely because of what can only be described as a visceral distaste for unions, long evident on the Conservative back benches, but much enhanced by 'New Right' thinking in the 1970s, and reinforced by a desire to seek revenge for the humiliating election defeat of February 1974. Thatcher had long adhered to such views.[44] This depth of hostility meant that anti-unionism had to be a key part of the party's platform.[45] Paradoxically, the evidence suggests increasing hostility to trade unions among the public in Britain in the 1970s, especially because of the belief that they were major contributors to inflation, precisely at a time when the Conservatives wanted to absolve them of that particular fault.[46]

A key way of dealing with this dilemma was to link the critique of unions to *decline*, where blame could be attached to their activities without challenging monetarist doctrine. Thus in a speech in 1979 Joseph analysed the response of unions 'to an inflation which they did *not* originally create', but wanted to set the union problem 'in the context of our economic decline rather than at the centre of today's crisis'.[47] One of the appeals of declinism was the way it allowed every political tendency to blame their favourite *bête noire*, and for the New Right a major 'usual suspect' was the unions.

Previous attempts at linking unions to inflation had led Conservative as well as Labour governments down the path to incomes policy. Conservatives had tried this in 1962 and again in 1972. While such an approach was congenial to some, as it clearly suggested unions were at least in part the cause of inflation, the corollary was less happy. To secure deals on incomes involved some degree of compromise with unions in order to try and obtain at least their acquiescence in such policies. In both 1962 and 1972 the Conservatives had tried, albeit unsuccessfully, to achieve such agreement. For monetarists this was precisely the problem with incomes policies: not only did they offend doctrinal dictates about the causes of inflation, but they had disastrous political consequences in reinforcing the political role of unions as 'partners in the state'. Thus in the 1970s, when Labour had pushed such government–union deals to the stage of the 'Social Contract', attacking incomes policy because of the way they encouraged unions' political role was just as important for Conservatives as direct attacks on unions' economic impact.

Here Bulpitt's analysis of the politics of monetarism is especially pertinent. He argues that the monetarist rejection of incomes policy was a key part of the central aim of Conservative statecraft, the greater insulation of central policy-making from 'interests' – a reversal of the quasi-corporatism which he sees emerging from the time of Macmillan's attempts to modernise the economy from 1962 onwards.[48] Hence the thrust of Conservative attacks on incomes policies was not only to claim that they were ineffective against inflation, but that, much worse, they strengthened the unions. In addition, incomes policies with their national norms and codifications of wages necessarily cut across the proper functioning of the labour market, namely to allocate workers in accordance with market forces. Thus monetarist analysis of inflation underpinned a 'retreat of the state' not only from dealing with unions in the context of incomes policies, but also from interventions in wage issues. In an ideal monetarist world governments would set the monetary framework, and within that framework market forces would quickly bring 'reality' home to union bargainers.[49]

The logic of this degree of hostility to incomes policies was spelt out by Adam Ridley of the Conservative Research Department in 1978, when he argued that such policies should be rejected *irrespective* of any success they might have had in reducing inflation. Their embrace, he argued, would be disastrous for the Conservatives, involving 'an open confession of pessimism and failure'.[50]

This wholesale rejection of incomes policies was not readily accepted by many Conservatives in the 1970s. Partly this was a tactical issue: if the Labour government was putting forward such policies to combat inflation, should the opposition simply oppose these initiatives? This was a continuing dilemma for the leadership.[51]

But beyond the short-run tactical issues around incomes policies was a major and longer-running problem: how far were such policies desirable not to reduce inflation (which monetarist doctrine said was not possible), but to reduce the consequences of tight monetary policy for unemployment? Posed in this way it is clear that even a full-hearted believer in the monetary causes of inflation could rationally make a case for at least temporary incomes policies in order to avert the electoral disaster that many expected would follow from a rapid rise in unemployment brought about by deflationary policies.

Debates about how far incomes policies should be used to manage inflationary expectations were in part related to doctrinal divisions within monetarism about how rapidly expectations about inflation would be changed by a shift in monetary policy, and therefore how long any fall in output and employment would be sustained.[52] Even prior to the 'rational expectations' revolution in economics, which hugely strengthened (at least among economists) the view that private agents would react very quickly to tight money, the issue was recognised as politically hugely important.

In 1975 the Economic Reconstruction Group (ERG) distinguished the 'gradualist' from the 'dramatic' monetary approach.[53] The former would involve aiming for a monetary slowdown over four to five years, while the latter would mean an abrupt halt to monetary growth. The Group opined that the former would involve heavy unemployment for four or five years, would hit private confidence and investment, and 'the need to sustain the policy throughout the life of a parliament would raise obvious political difficulties'. A 'dramatic' policy would be even worse – it would be 'politically impossible' but also do lasting and probably unacceptable damage to the economy by dislocating the public sector and causing simultaneous crises in financial institutions, the stock exchange and productive industry. Hence the Group called for an 'Ideal Programme' which would combine monetary restraint with, among other things, a total wage freeze for a year.[54]

These views were controversial within the Conservative Party. The chair of the group discussing the ERG's report asserted that 'the differences of opinion within the group on the possible use of incomes policy should be seen as a reflection of the views of the intellectual community'.[55] No doubt this was true in part – the 'gradual' versus dramatic view was an important debate in academic economics at this time. Joseph, for example, took a 'rational expectations' view that the way to change expectations was to rely on bargainers quickly adjusting to realities: 'For though it is said that expectations can be modified by incomes policy, they are more surely modified by experience.'[56]

But many senior Conservatives were less sanguine, and feared that the transition to lower inflationary expectations would be slow, with disastrous effects on unemployment. As Ridley put the point in 1976: 'There are policy issues of considerable importance when we ask ourselves what obstacles there are to increasing the maximum sustainable level of unemployment.'[57] Everyone in the Conservative Party expected some unemployment as a result of monetary tightening, and everyone assumed that if this took on massive proportions it would be electorally disastrous. 'Whatever approach [to inflation] was adopted significant and by post war standards unprecedented deflation is inevitable in the short run.'[58] Even Joseph urged caution on this issue when he suggested restraint in attacking the Labour government's job subsidies, lest such attacks opened the Conservatives to the charge that they favoured high unemployment.[59] One response, as noted above, was to try to reduce the electoral sensitivity of unemployment by redefining much of it as voluntary. Joseph was keen to get John Wood, who had written the IEA pamphlets on this issue, involved in policy.[60] More important was to link it to the trade union question.

Monetarism involved a clear political message on unemployment: it could not be solved by government, but only by reforms to the labour market, especially the weakening of trade unions. This followed from what in the literature of economics was called the 'reassignment' argument. Where traditionally post-war governments had accepted responsibility for employment and output levels, and the level of inflation was seen as the result of wage bargaining, in monetarist thinking this was reversed. Governments, and only governments, were responsible for inflation levels, while wage bargaining determined the level of unemployment within this macro-economic framework. For Conservatives this doctrine had the happy result of reassigning political responsibility for unemployment from government to the trade unions.[61]

Bulpitt's statecraft approach to monetarism suggests that the common focus on the 1970s as a period of transition from Keynesianism to monetarism is unhelpful. As he suggests, 'in statecraft terms there is precious little difference between monetarism and the politics of Keynes' demand management'.[62] His key point is that both involve the manipulation of centralised policy levers in ways that avoid any direct state involvement in decisions about price-setting or the allocation of resources. This is an important argument, and in general he is right that this alleged doctrinal transition is not the best way to approach economic debates in these years. But we should not, of course, use scepticism about the helpfulness of this particular doctrinal difference to reject the importance of doctrine altogether. One component of statecraft is 'political argument hegemony', and economic doctrine was clearly a component (though certainly not a determining) part of political argument in the 1970s. As Bulpitt suggests, 'economic theory is best viewed within a perspective which looks at statecraft'.[63]

The simple proposition that inflation is related to monetary growth, and that therefore government should contain monetary growth, had become a doctrinal commonplace by the 1970s (albeit still contested by some). But academic adherents of such a view were heavily divided on how that monetary restriction was to be achieved, and this doctrinal difference had major 'statecraft' implications.

Central to Conservative economic policy discussions in the 1970s was the desire to roll back the state. The grounds for this were the traditional ones derived from belief in private enterprise and low taxes, beefed up in the 1970s by a newly invigorated economic liberalism, drawing on the tradition of a certain interpretation of Adam Smith, much reinforced by writers such as Friedman and Hayek.[64] Also important at the time were 'crowding out' arguments, in which public sector borrowing drove up interest rates and discouraged private sector investment, though Lawson later acknowledged that such a mechanism was implausible in an internationalised capital market.[65] The expanding role of the state under the Labour government of the 1970s provided the basis for Conservatives to tell both declinist accounts of the long-run significance of such expansion, and apocalyptic stories of what would happen if this expansion were not reversed.[66]

But how did the defeat of inflation by monetarist means fit with this priority of 'rolling back the state'? The politically tempting answer was to link the growth of public spending and public borrowing directly to monetary growth, and generate the happy conclusion that reducing the role of the state would lead straightforwardly to monetary continence and the reduction of inflation.[67] All roads would lead to the Promised Land. The attractions of this approach to 'monetarism' were made clear by Howe when he argued that the party should stress 'the prime importance of the money supply (without much attempt to popularise this unintelligible proposition – except by arguing the case against big public spending, and big borrowing by the government and internationally)'.[68]

Unfortunately for the Conservatives, this direct linkage was not accepted by many monetarists, above all Milton Friedman. He argued that neither government spending nor borrowing levels had a necessary relationship with monetary growth. In particular, he ridiculed the idea that controlling government borrowing was the best way to reduce monetary growth. For him the relationship between these two variables was contingent and indirect. Instead he favoured direct control of monetary growth, or what became known as Monetary Base Control.[69]

The records of internal discussion in the Conservative Party in the 1970s support the view of Nigel Lawson that the issue of the mechanisms of monetary control was neglected in the years of opposition.[70] Partly this was because attention was focused on the bigger battle to gain acceptance that monetary growth was indeed the key to defeating inflation. But linking that growth, and the menace of inflation, to reducing the role of the state, and directly to government borrowing (what had come to be designated the Public Sector Borrowing Requirement (PSBR)), was too tempting politically to be set aside for any niceties of doctrine.

The final strategic issue facing the Conservatives arising from the focus on defeating inflation by monetary means was that of housing. Gordon Pepper, who acted as an informal advisor to Thatcher, in answer to the question 'whether Mrs Thatcher was a monetarist', said:

Firstly Mrs Thatcher hated inflation. Inflation erodes the real value of people's hard-earned savings and she thought this immoral. Secondly she accepted the general proposition that excessive monetary growth in due course leads to a rise in inflation. Because she accepted this she attached great importance to preventing excessive monetary growth and, in this sense, was a monetarist.

However, he goes on to note that 'she hated high interest rates because of their effect on the housing market and her vision of the property-owning democracy'.[71]

Pepper is undoubtedly right to emphasise Thatcher's commitment to the property-owning democracy, especially as this related to housing.[72] It was a common reference point in her speeches, often linked back to previous Conservative leaders, especially Anthony Eden, to emphasise how far this was a traditional Conservative goal.[73] Her devotion to this cause was demonstrated when she chaired the Conservative policy group on housing in the run-up to the October 1974 general election, when, alongside a commitment to abolish domestic rates, she got the party committed to a maximum interest rate of 9.5 per cent on mortgages in perpetuity.[74]

In the debates after 1975 this tension between the desire for monetary stringency, which was bound to lead to higher interest rates, and the desire to encourage home ownership, led to frequent discussions about dual interest rates, and the idea that the homeowner could and should be insulated from rate rises elsewhere in the markets. But no detailed scheme for such a dual interest rate system ever emerged, and it would be difficult to see how one compatible with a broad commitment to economic liberalism would have been possible. It became all the more unlikely with the abolition of exchange controls in 1979.

The Conservatives in power

In office after 1979 the Conservatives' success in combating inflation was episodic, with surges of price rises in 1980 (to 18 per cent), and again at the end of the 1980s (to 9.5 per cent). Part of the reason for this only qualified success, according to Nigel Lawson, was Thatcher's devotion to the homeowner, which was at odds with the needs of anti-inflationary policy: 'Her detestation of inflation was genuine enough; but while willing the end, she was repeatedly reluctant to embrace the means.'[75] Enthusiasm for the property-owning democracy led to council house sales, an exceedingly effective electoral strategy, with council houses sold at huge discounts to sitting tenants.[76] The desire to encourage such ownership, coupled with financial deregulation, led to an unsustainable housing boom between 1985 and 1988, a precursor of future events.[77]

The failure to get an effective grip on inflation can be ascribed to the failings of monetary policy after 1979, when the idea that the money supply was directly linked to public borrowing was embodied in the Medium-Term Financial Strategy (MTFS) of 1980. This failure came despite the warnings of Friedman. The MTFS in its own terms was a failure, as it was widely recognised inside and outside the government that the money supply data used in this strategy were entirely misleading, and that there was no direct relationship between public borrowing and monetary growth.[78] Inflation did fall after 1980–81, but this owed a great deal to the impact of high interest rates on the exchange rate, something seemingly hardly thought of in Tory circles before 1979.[79]

However, in other terms the MTFS worked. Its formulation was wholly around monetary variables, with no element of output and/or employment targeting. This emphasised the economic but also political 'reassignment' of responsibility for unemployment noted previously. In pursuing the MTFS the budget of 1981 was *politically* crucial. In the face of the slump, the government stuck to its macro-economic policy, even though the evidence suggested that monetary policy was not working as the Strategy suggested, in order to emphasise that the responsibilities of government were limited, and that policy would not be diverted by what was happening to real output and employment.

As Bulpitt points out, Conservative economic discussions before 1979 showed striking neglect of the international context within which policy was pursued, though Howe, like Lawson later, favoured entry to the ERM. Yet the most important macro-economic force in the initial period of the Thatcher government was the unprecedented rise in the real exchange rate.[80] This was unplanned but enormous in its effects: by driving large parts of the tradable sector of the economy into uncompetitiveness it brought about the collapse of much manufacturing industry in particular, and a leap in unemployment.[81] But it turned out that this scale of unemployment was not necessarily electorally disastrous, as the election of 1983 showed. There were of course contingent factors, most importantly the Falklands War, but the attempt to 'reassign' responsibility for unemployment to trade unions must be given some weight. Analysis of opinion poll evidence suggests that while unemployment was important to electors in 1983, and the Labour Party was favoured on this issue, Labour's claim to be able to achieve a rapid reduction in its level was not believed. As Ivor Crewe noted: 'What was in doubt was not Labour's greater concern about unemployment, but its superior ability to do much about it.' In Bulpitt's terms, while the Conservatives had not achieved 'political argument hegemony' on the unemployment issue, they had significantly reduced Labour's electoral benefit from being seen as best on that issue. The corollary of this was that while inflation was deemed less important by the electorate in 1983 than in 1979, the Conservative lead on this issue was enormous, at 40 per cent.[82]

The biggest success in terms of 'political argument hegemony' secured prior to 1979 was in relation to the unions. Here considerable weight must be given to Conservative propaganda, but the biggest impact came when this success was greatly reinforced by their effective framing of the Winter of Discontent as evidence of the damage caused by the unions.[83] This crisis not only undermined support for unions, but also the whole idea of a state role in wage bargaining.

In the early 1980s, then, 'monetarism' as an economic policy failed; the government did not find a way to effectively control monetary growth and inflation showed no permanent reduction. This was to remain a major problem for the Conservatives throughout their period of office, and led, of course, to the departure of Lawson as Chancellor when Thatcher resisted his plan to use the exchange rate as a key target in anti-inflationary strategy. But while these disputes mattered, and not only to monetary economists, they should not hide the bigger truth that, in the crucial respect of statecraft, monetarism succeeded admirably from a Conservative point of view. The key aim of 'monetarism' identified by Bulpitt – to disentangle the central state from 'interests' – was substantially achieved.

As suggested in the introduction to this chapter, the 1970s inflation was a crucial condition of the rise of monetarism, and this in turn made possible the narrowing of state responsibility and the de-legitimisation of unions that accompanied monetarism's triumphs. But inflation was also deployed very effectively by the Conservatives to make the declinist case for a radical reversal of policy. Partly, this was done by telling a story of inflation as the result of cumulative socialist error: while the direct cause of inflation was excessive monetary growth, the underlying cause was state expansion, a link made despite the fact that there was little doctrinal warrant for suggesting any direct relationship between state expansion and monetary expansion. Unhelpful suggestions about the absence of such a direct relationship, even by such monetarist gurus as Friedman, had to be set aside to sustain this key political narrative. Apocalyptic stories about the effects of inflation had to be accompanied by accounts of how this inflation was the inescapable consequence of the post-war consensus if the battle for hegemony was to be won.

4   Thatcherism, morality and religion[*]

Matthew Grimley

> Look at the scale of the opposing forces. On the one side, the whole
> of the new establishment with their sharp words and sneers poised.
> Against them stood this one middle-aged woman. Today her name
> is a household word, made famous by the very assaults on her by her
> enemies.[1]

The object of Keith Joseph's admiration in this 1974 speech was
not Margaret Thatcher, but another 'middle-aged woman', Mary
Whitehouse. But Joseph could just as well have been talking about
Thatcher. As we shall see, both women identified and amplified disen-
chantment with the permissive society in the 1970s. Both were popu-
lists, presenting themselves as ordinary women taking on an effete or
decadent establishment. Both sought to renew Britain as a Christian
nation. Each encouraged the other in her endeavours. For Margaret
Thatcher, a crisis of values was an important part of the broader crisis she diagnosed in the 1970s, and the remoralisation of society was
among the medicines she prescribed. Where she encountered some difficulty was in explaining who or what would drive this remoralisation.
Her belief in the inadequacy of state action presented a problem; if the
state could not remoralise society, then what could?

The moral and religious dimensions of Thatcherism have been over-
looked in existing accounts, which have tended to concentrate on what
Thatcherism *achieved*, in terms of concrete policy, rather than on what
it *represented*. Because the main policy manifestations of Thatcherism
were economic, historians have tended to view it as primarily an

[*] I am grateful, for suggested improvements, to audiences in Bournemouth and
Birmingham and to participants in the Thatcher conference in Oxford in September
2010. I am also grateful to Ferdinand Mount for patiently answering my enquir-
ies, and to archivists at Royal Holloway, University of London; the University of
Essex; Lambeth Palace Library; the Churchill Archives Centre, Cambridge; and the
Bodleian Library, Oxford. This chapter was completed before I had the chance to
read Liza Filby, 'God and Mrs Thatcher: Religion and Politics in 1980s Britain',
unpublished PhD thesis, University of Warwick, 2010, which offers a fuller account
of the relationship between Thatcher and the churches.

economic phenomenon. Anna Marie Smith bewailed this in her 1994 book on Thatcherism, race and sexuality, but despite the appearance of some very distinguished contributions on Thatcherism since then, economistic readings of Thatcherism continue to predominate.[2]

Of course, it is true that economics *were* central to Thatcherite policy. It is also true that, as Prime Minister, Margaret Thatcher did little to legislate on morality and the family. The permissive reforms of the 1960s were left intact, and the only Conservative attempts at legislating on morality were Section 28 of the 1988 Local Government Act, which banned the promotion of homosexuality in schools, and the clauses of the 1988 Education Reform Act that stipulated the teaching of Christianity in schools (both of which were the result of backbench Lords amendments). But the fact that Thatcher did not legislate to reverse permissiveness does not mean that anti-permissiveness was an unimportant part of her ideology. My argument in this chapter is that there was more to Thatcherism than the laws it enacted; looking at its fruits does not necessarily tell us about its roots. In order to explore its appeal, we need to look at language as well as legislation – at the words Margaret Thatcher and her associates used. We might usefully borrow here from the work of Philip Williamson, who has demonstrated how, in the inter-war period, Stanley Baldwin used his speeches to expound a moralised rhetoric, offering a vision of society that did not necessarily directly correlate with policy.[3]

Some contemporary commentators on Thatcherism did emphasise its moral dimensions. Stuart Hall argued that it was important to explore 'the moral discourses of Thatcherism ... They are the site for the mobilisation of social identities and, by appropriating them, Thatcherism has put down deep roots in the traditional, conventional social culture of English society.'[4] Hall also noted the sense of crisis that was so central to Thatcherism, a crisis 'experienced at the popular level in the universal, depoliticised, experiential language of popular morality'.[5] From a radically different political perspective, Shirley Robin Letwin argued in her book *The Anatomy of Thatcherism* that Thatcherism tapped into 'a distinctive but unidentified British morality'.[6] David Marquand also emphasised the paradox that Thatcherism was 'at one and the same time a revenge for, and a paradoxical continuation of, the cultural revolution of the 1960s, of the so-called permissive society'.[7]

All these interpretations are suggestive, but all were made close to the events they described. With the benefit of distance (and readier access to Thatcher's public statements), we can pinpoint Thatcherism more precisely as part of a wider reaction against permissiveness in 1970s Britain. Thatcher and her associates were tapping into an existing protest against aspects of the permissive society that had emerged at the end of the 1960s, in Mary Whitehouse's National Viewers' and Listeners' Association (NVALA), in the Black Papers on education, and in the adverse reaction to student disturbances in some universities.[8] They were also drawing on, and contributing to, a more diffuse anxiety about moral decline that accompanied the economic decline of the 1970s, as well as a rejection of the materialism manifested in high wage demands. What Ferdinand Mount called Thatcher's 'direct, unabashed appeal to morality' was essential to her freshness and attractiveness as a politician in the 1970s.[9] Later, morality receded somewhat as a theme in Thatcherite rhetoric, but as we shall see, it continued to offer an explanatory framework for Conservative policies after 1979.

Against permissiveness

As an opposition MP in 1967, Margaret Thatcher had voted for two of the most famous pieces of 'permissive' legislation, the Medical Termination of Pregnancy Act and the Sexual Offences Act (though not for the Divorce Reform Act two years later).[10] At this time, she seems to have followed the distinction drawn by the 1957 Wolfenden Report, and subsequently by the legal philosopher H. L. A. Hart, between public and private morality.[11] In her 1995 memoir, Thatcher explained this stance, while also expressing contrition:

> Knowing how things turned out, would I have voted differently on any of these matters? I now see that we viewed them too narrowly. As a lawyer and indeed as a politician who believed so strongly in the rule of law, I felt that the prime considerations were that the law should be enforceable and its application fair to those who might run foul of it. But laws also have a symbolic significance; they are signposts to the way society is developing – and the way the legislators of society envisage that it should develop. Moreover, taking all of the 'liberal' reforms of the 1960s together they amount to more than their individual parts. They came to be seen as providing a radically new framework within which the younger generation would be expected to behave.[12]

This emphasis on the 'symbolic significance' of law marked a shift from Hart's position to that espoused by Sir Patrick Devlin in the two men's celebrated controversy over the Wolfenden Report.[13]

But Thatcher had expressed unease at the unintended consequences of the permissive reforms as early as 1970. Asked by the *Finchley Press* the question 'What Lies Ahead in the Seventies?' in January 1970, she listed as the first change that she would like to see – ahead of the conquest of inflation – 'a reversal of the permissive society'.[14] For

Thatcher, the term permissive society had particular connotations. 'I think perhaps its deeper meaning seems to imply to most of us that a certain amount of self-discipline has broken down, that things have gone beyond the usual moderation and that the Permissive Society seems to some extent to be undermining family life and the family as a unit of society', she said on *Women's Hour* in April 1970. She was at pains to separate specific permissive reforms like homosexual and abortion law reform from a more general ambience of licence. In distinguishing between different types of permissiveness, she still espoused Hart's public/private distinction: while *private* behaviour was tolerable, it was its *public* manifestations that were unacceptable, especially where these could influence children. 'Homosexual offences and abortion, of course, are part of the Permissive Society, but only a very small part', she told *Woman's Hour*. 'I think that what the average woman would really mean by it is rather more – a good deal more sexual licence, now, fear of one's children going on drugs. Often how exactly does one guide one's teenage son and daughter as to how they should behave in this kind of society?' She addressed this question as a *woman* and as a *mother*, still quite a novel perspective for a professional politician in 1970. The other aspect of the permissive society singled out for criticism was pornography, and here too she spoke as a parent. 'Many of us parents are really quite worried about the thought of literature, either that comes through the letterbox or which you do see on the newspaper stalls, and this is also a very powerful aspect of the permissive society.'[15]

Thatcher's presentation of herself as an ordinary woman in 1970 was strikingly similar to that employed by Mary Whitehouse at the same time. During the 1970 election, the morality campaigner warned in a letter to the main regional papers that:

Many women are deeply concerned about the dangers of the 'permissive society' … The women's vote could be decisive in this election. Let us make sure that we return to power candidates who will reverse the current trend of permissive legislation and who will revitalise those moral and spiritual values which has [sic] made Britain great in the past.

In her letter Whitehouse also complained about 'the political one-upmanship which keeps the eyes of the electorate fixed on purely material issues'. There was, she warned, 'a far greater danger to the future of our country than the much discussed economic state of the nation': namely, 'the drift towards moral anarchy which is seen in so many areas of our society'.[16]

Morality and the 1970s crisis

Whitehouse was not the first person to bewail the fixation of politicians on the material at the expense of the moral. The Conservative politician Angus Maude had already done so in a 1969 book, *The Common Problem*.[17] Significantly, given his later role as one of Thatcher's advisors, he framed his argument in opposition to consensus politics:

> The present political 'consensus' derives from the primacy of economics, which has usurped almost the entire field of politics. On the efficient functioning of the economy the *whole* of the 'good life' for the individual is deemed to depend, with the result that what we now call 'government' has become largely preoccupied with the conditioning or regulation of the economy.[18]

Maude's was a lonely Conservative voice in the late 1960s (though it was strangely in tune with the wider counter-culture), but after the Heath government's second defeat in 1974, the contention that the Conservatives had made a mistake by over-emphasising the economic became more compelling. This was the argument Keith Joseph pursued in the October 1974 speech with which this chapter began.[19] 'This economics first approach', he warned, 'has aggravated unhappiness and social conflict.' Instead, he urged that it was 'better to approach the public, who know that economics is not everything, as whole men rather than economic men'. This would involve concentrating on issues like 'respect for other people and for law, the welfare of young people, the state of family life, the moral welfare of all the people, cultural values, public-spiritedness or its lack, national defence, the tone of national life'. It was these issues, he said, which 'are at the centre of the public's concern'. Identifying the family and 'civilised values' as the bases of the nation, Joseph warned that 'if we cannot restore them to health, our nation can be utterly ruined, whatever economic policies we might try to follow, for economics is deeply shaped by values, by the attitude towards work, thrift, ethics, public spirit'. He ended with a call to 'remoralise our national life'.[20]

At the end of this speech, almost in passing, Joseph made the notorious comments, advocating contraception to prevent working-class girls from breeding, which ended his chances of becoming party leader and paved the way for Margaret Thatcher to challenge Ted Heath. Thatcher was later critical of Joseph's speech, which she felt had been an unhelpful piece of freelancing.[21] But once she became leader, she continued her mentor's argument that economic recovery was doomed without moral regeneration. 'We believe that man needs more than material things', she told the Conservative Central Council in March 1975, a month after becoming leader. 'Our aim is to build a flourishing society – not an economic system.' In the same speech, she argued that there had been a concerted attack on traditional virtues. 'For many years there has been a subtle erosion of the essential virtues of the free. Self-reliance has been sneered at as if it were an absurd suburban pretension. Thrift has been denigrated as if it were greed. The desire of parents to choose and to struggle for what they themselves regarded as the best possible education for their children has been scorned.'[22]

In the later 1970s, Thatcher developed her theme that permissiveness involved a deliberate attack on traditional morality by intellectuals and the professions. 'Never have our basic values, the Christian values which rest on Hebrew and Hellenic foundations, been so menaced as they are today', she told an audience in Houston, Texas in 1977. 'Family life, the innocence of children, public decency, respect for the law, pride in good work, patriotism, democracy – all are under attack.'[23] Addressing the Scottish Conservatives in May 1978, Thatcher complained that 'we have come through a strange period – a period when traditional and tested values were set aside in favour of sociological theories divorced from experience. Twenty years of social analysis and woolly political theory' had led to a situation where 'the older language of morality and legality, of right and wrong, is conveniently forgotten'.[24] Her advisor, Alfred Sherman, ascribed this change in a 1979 memorandum to 'an incoherent philosophy containing Rousseauism, Pelagianism, materialistic determinism, moral relativism … which ends by rejecting not only the idea of personal responsibility but the idea of good and evil which is inseparable from it'.[25] Other Conservatives made a similar charge. Lord Hailsham blamed a '*trahison des clercs*, the moral betrayal by those who ought to be the upholders of the traditional virtues, qualities and institutions'.[26]

For Thatcher, the intellectuals' betrayal lay in encouraging people to depend on the state, thus reducing their capacity for individual responsibility. Not only could the state not remoralise people, it could actually *de*moralise them. She developed this theme at length in her St Lawrence Jewry speech in 1978, arguing that there were 'grave moral dangers … in letting people get away with the idea that they can delegate all their responsibilities to public officials and institutions'. She went on:

Once you give people the idea that all this can be done by the state, and that it is somehow second-best or even degrading to leave it to private people (it is sometimes referred to as 'cold charity') then you will begin to deprive human beings of one of the essential ingredients of humanity – personal responsibility. You will in effect dry up in them the milk of human kindness.[27]

Thatcher owed this line of argument partly to Maude, who had argued in 1969 that the decline of traditional forms of authority was leaving a dangerous vacuum, into which was coming the impersonal idea of 'society', a sort of 'all-embracing super-family'. Society, said Maude, robbed people of their agency and responsibility, forcing them to conform to an 'imaginary norm'. As a result, 'the bewildered individual, seeking lost authority, certainty and standards, is reduced to social conformism'.[28] In her speeches in the 1970s, Thatcher tended to blame the 'state' rather than 'society', but her point was essentially the same, and she later picked up Maude's criticism of society as a meaningless abstraction in her notorious 1987 claim that there was 'no such thing as society'.[29]

The idea of a moral crisis was an important part of what Colin Hay has called the Thatcherites' 'discursive construction' of crisis in the 1979 election.[30] Throughout the campaign, Thatcher deliberately conflated the moral and economic crises, blaming Labour for both. In her adoption speech at Finchley in 1979 she argued that:

economic ills are only half – and possibly in the long run not the more important half – of the lost years of Labour government. Everywhere there has been a loosening of national standards, a weakening of the bonds which hold us together as a people, a decline of manners, of morals, of shared beliefs.

Significantly, given her later association with Victorian values, she insisted that the answer to this decline was 'not an overnight return to what (a little unjustly) people call Victorian discipline', but rather a recognition that 'every one of us has a choice between good and evil from which nothing can absolve us'.[31] Her election address included a passage, reiterated in several campaign speeches, which also stressed the importance of instilling a sense of right and wrong in the young: 'I want a Britain where children are taught that there is a real and absolute difference between right and wrong, and that there are certain acts which by their very nature are invariably wrong and must be outlawed by society.'[32]

Thatcher was not the only party leader in 1979 to exploit the anti-permissive backlash. James Callaghan, who like Thatcher had been brought up as a Nonconformist, had famously promised to 'call a halt to the rising tide of permissiveness' as Home Secretary in 1969. The head of his Policy Unit, Bernard Donoughue, recalled how, soon after becoming Prime Minister in 1976, Callaghan asked him to produce a paper about restoring 'responsible values' to society, and how he had expressed enthusiasm for this as a potential theme for his speeches.[33] Callaghan and Thatcher shared both a morally conservative outlook and good antennae for trends in public opinion. When Callaghan was likened to Moses by his son-in-law, Peter Jay, Thatcher replied with the famous put-down, 'My message to Moses is this. Keep taking the tablets.'[34] At a 1979 campaign rally in Callaghan's own stamping-ground, Cardiff, she claimed the prophetic mantle for herself, declaring that 'the Old Testament prophets didn't go out into the highways saying, "Brothers, I want consensus." They said, "This is my faith and my vision! This is what I passionately believe!" And they preached it.'[35]

But Thatcher's invocation of religion was more frequent and insistent than Callaghan's. That morality could only come from religion was a stock theme in her speeches at this time; morality without religion, she would say, was like a flower cut off from its roots.[36] She also emphasised the Christian origins of national life, telling the Bow Group in May 1978 that:

We cannot claim that our society is entirely a Christian one ... But we are the heirs of a society whose religion and whose way of life has been Christian for century on century. Most of us whether Christian or not are thus inspired directly or indirectly by the absolute value which Christianity – derived in part from the Old Testament and Greek philosophy – gives to the individual soul, and hence to man's innate responsibility for his own actions and omissions, and his duty to treat other men as he would have them treat him.[37]

A key source for this Christian rhetoric was Alfred Sherman, who wrote speeches for both Margaret Thatcher and Keith Joseph. On the face of it this was surprising, as Sherman was Jewish, but he believed that many of Britain's economic and social problems were a consequence of the 'de-Christianisation of social and political thought in this country'.[38] When he wrote parts of Keith Joseph's ill-fated Birmingham speech, Sherman had been re-reading *Moralise Public Life*, by the inter-war Italian politician-priest, Don Luigi Sturzo.[39] When Thatcher became party leader, Sherman encouraged her to talk about her religious faith in a series of speeches and interviews, the most famous of which was her speech at St Lawrence Jewry Church in London in 1978.[40]

Thatcher and her associates were also picking up on the recent activities of pressure groups that sought to defend traditional morality against permissiveness, such as Whitehouse's NVALA, and the Nationwide Festival of Light (NFOL), a predominantly, though not exclusively, evangelical campaign group with which Whitehouse was also associated.[41] In 1973, NVALA and NFOL submitted a 1,350,000-signature joint petition for public decency to Number 10, which argued that 'moral issues cannot be separated from the other problems which vex the government and the country. The truth, as we see it, is that our ability as a nation to accept limitations in human desire in the economic sphere is inseparable from our willingness to set limits on "freedom" in the realm of personal morality.'[42] In a similar vein the Archbishop of Canterbury, Donald Coggan, broadcast a 'Call to the Nation' in 1975, which argued that economic regeneration had to be accompanied by moral regeneration:

Many are realising that a materialistic answer is no real answer at all. There are moral and spiritual issues at stake. The truth is that we in Britain are without anchors. We are drifting. A common enemy in two world wars drew us together in united action – and we defeated him. Another enemy is at the gates today, and we keep silence.[43]

Coggan's 'Call' prompted 27,000 letters from the public, some of which were later reproduced in a book. In the introduction, the Archbishop noted that 'I touched a raw nerve when I suggested that the individual feels that he doesn't count as he should in our mass society. Evidently the frustration in our national life is acute at this point, almost bordering on despair.'[44] The other concerns that loomed large in the published letters to Coggan were unemployment, inflation, big business, trade unions, bureaucracy, the moral impact of the welfare state and the permissive society. There were close links between the Conservative Party and Coggan's 'Call to the Nation', which had been instigated by two Tory MPs, Michael Alison (an NVALA supporter, and later Thatcher's PPS) and Richard Wood, who had asked for 'a call to prayer and repentance'.[45] Thatcher quoted several times from Coggan's postbag in a major speech in 1977.[46]

During the 1979 election, Mary Whitehouse asked the party leaders to reply to four questions on broadcasting, obscenity and religious and sex education. In her reply to Whitehouse, Thatcher promised that she would introduce new legislation on indecency and resist any erosion of the Christian content of religious education, but it was her insistence 'that education about sex should be based on Christian principles' that delighted Whitehouse most. She hailed Thatcher's words as 'one of the most radical statements made during the whole campaign. The implementation of it would revolutionise sex education and indeed the whole quality of human relationships in our society.'[47] This was tantamount to an NVALA endorsement for the Conservatives, for which Whitehouse was duly rewarded with a CBE in 1980.

How much did Thatcher's invocation of Christian morality actually contribute to her victory in 1979? As Alfred Sherman explained in his memoirs, his attempts to get her to speak about Christianity did not go entirely to plan. When she delivered her address at St Lawrence Jewry,

Things went wrong. The *Daily Telegraph* sent a reporter to cover the speech, but for whatever reason failed to publish it. *The Times* had gone on strike. So the initiative was lost. Mrs Thatcher's colleagues were lukewarm or worse. They preferred leaving religion to the clergy, not noticing that the church had become increasingly hostile.[48]

Certainly there were Conservatives who objected to Thatcher's invocation of religion. When the draft Conservative manifesto for the 1979 election included a quotation from Archbishop William Temple, an official in the Conservative Research Department warned that the reference would be obscure to some and unpopular with those who held the bishops in low esteem.[49] There was a strong tradition in the Conservative Party of reticence in talking about religion, which Thatcher herself shared, deliberately discussing religion in a measured, rather than fervent, tone. But the distaste of some Conservatives for discussion of religion also reflected an ambiguity within the party about how to react to what they saw as the secularisation of Britain. While some, like Thatcher herself, felt that it was precisely *because* Britain was becoming more secular that it was necessary for the government to keep religious values alive, others argued that the Conservative Party should acknowledge secularisation by avoiding reference to religion. The Conservative historian (and Michael Portillo's old tutor) Maurice Cowling argued in 1978 that de-Christianisation had already gone so far that it was impossible to make religious rhetoric work. 'Today, in spite of a Christian monarchy and an established Church, England is not a Christian country', he argued. 'It is a very long way from being one and will require long-term preparation if it is to become one. Until it gets this ... neither Mrs Thatcher nor anyone else is likely to make Christianity stick politically.'[50]

But appeals to religion and morality *did* fit into Conservative strategy in the late 1970s. They provided a spine that linked different economic and social policies, giving them coherence. Part of the Conservative project in the late 1970s was, as a 1978 Shadow Cabinet memorandum put it, to 'jump the class barrier' and create a cross-class alliance of voters; reviving old discourses of respectability was one way of doing this.[51] In another policy document circulated in 1978, Angus Maude, Norman Tebbit, Nigel Lawson and others had singled out particular 'Themes' that would benefit the Tories. One of these was 'let's return to common sense'. Another theme was 'nostalgia ... for a settled, civilised life ... The change that people want today is much more a change *back* to known standards than a leap forward into the unknown.' A third theme was 'the nation, not the state'. The authors had been inspired by the 'orderliness' and 'unity' of the Silver Jubilee celebrations in 1977, arguing that 'people passionately welcomed an occasion for national pride and national unity, when both had seemed to be at a discount'.[52] All three themes could be pursued by appealing to traditional morality and to the idea of a Christian nation. Emphasising the nation's Christian heritage may also have been a discreet way of addressing concerns about immigration. Though Thatcher rarely addressed immigration in opposition, aside from her notorious reference to 'swamping' in 1978, this did not mean that it was absent from her appeal to the electorate.[53] Talking about the Christian nation may have carried a subliminal message.

Thatcher also used Christianity as a rhetorical counterpoint to Marxism. Rather as 1920s Conservatives had stigmatised Labour and the trade unions as 'Bolshevist', so Thatcher's 'Marxism' was a conflation of various strains of socialism, statism and 1960s expressive individualism. One way of giving definition to this rather baggy idea of Marxism was to contrast it with Christianity. She wrote in the *Daily Telegraph* in May 1978 that 'the denial of the morality of personal choice, the reduction of history to a predetermined conflict between classes wholly shaped (as Marxists contend) by their role in the economic process – these are an outright denial of the Christian faith'.[54] Giving the Iain Macleod Memorial Lecture in July 1977, she proclaimed that 'because we see man as a spiritual being, we utterly reject the Marxist view, which gives pride of place to economics'.[55]

Morality and government, 1979–90

'The mission of this government is much more than the promotion of economic progress', the new Prime Minister told the Conservative Political Centre Summer School soon after the 1979 election. 'It is to renew the spirit and the solidarity of the nation.'[56] As Prime Minister, she continued to use moralised language in her public rhetoric, particularly on the economy. During the 1981 recession she described inflation as 'in my view, a moral issue not just an economic one', and wage restraint as 'a moral responsibility'.[57] Or, as she told the *Sunday Times* in 1981, 'economics are the method; the object is to change the soul'.[58] As Raphael Samuel pointed out, her habit of 'translating policy issues into "moral economy"' was 'one of Mrs Thatcher's strengths, and not the least of the reasons why she was able so frequently to wrong-foot her opponents'.[59]

What the Thatcher governments did not do, though, was to reverse any of the permissive legislation of the 1960s. Nor, despite a rhetoric of promoting family values, did they legislate to recreate the traditional family. True, the Family Policy Group, established in 1982 and largely the brainchild of Ferdinand Mount, sought to promote family life by espousing policies like parental choice in education and the right to buy, but it was never anti-permissive in intent.[60] Those pieces of family legislation that were passed by the Thatcher government were largely pragmatic rather than ideological, and the government refused the entreaties of pressure groups to legislate against abortion or birth control.[61] Thatcher's reluctance to pass laws to reverse permissiveness was, however, entirely consistent with her belief that 'you cannot make people good by legislation'.[62] This belief had always set her apart from moralists like Mary Whitehouse, who were sometimes frustrated by Thatcher's refusal to legislate against moral ills.[63] Thatcher's own conception of morality was strongly individualised. In a set of notes for her conference speech in October 1979, she reflected that 'morality is personal. There is no such thing as a collective conscience, collective kindness, collective gentleness, collective freedom ... You can't delegate personal responsibility to your country. You are your country.'[64] This was not quite as atomistic as it sounded; as Florence Sutcliffe-Braithwaite has rightly pointed out, 'when Thatcherites talked of "the individual" what they really meant was "the family"'.[65] But what was true was that there was little role for government in promoting morality. Shirley Robin Letwin pointed out that Thatcherism rejected 'the usual paradigm for political action. For "the government" cannot be expected to "do something" about the condition of individuals and families in a modern liberal state.'[66]

But there was one area – religious education – in which Thatcher believed the state *could* promote morality. She had argued for this exception in a newspaper article in 1978:

There is one sphere in which the state has a positive role. As a nation, we are heirs to a Christian culture and a Christian moral condition. I still believe that the vast majority of parents want their children to enter into that inheritance. Accordingly, I hold it to be the business of government to ensure (though with proper respect for the consciences of all who dissent or who belong to another religion) that our schools shall be places in which Christian belief and morality are taught. This is not indoctrination, merely a practical recognition of the truth that, while a mature person may reject the faith in which he has been brought up, a child will find it difficult to acquire any faith at all without some instruction in the discipline of belief and practice.[67]

There were pragmatic grounds for allowing the state a particular role in religious education. One of Mary Whitehouse's crotchets during the 1970s was a 'Save Religious Education' campaign, and the Conservatives were able to exploit the fact that some Labour activists had been campaigning against religious education. Thatcher repeatedly spoke in defence of religious education in 1978, declaring herself 'passionate for it'.[68] Her emphasis on religious education helps explain why, a decade later, she was ready to accept amendments to the 1988 Education Reform Act defending Christian religious education (though, as with Section 28 of the Local Government Act, a desire to curb 'loony left' councils was also important).

In the late 1980s Thatcher began once again to address religious themes more explicitly in her speeches. She had done this less in her early years in government, partly because of the sidelining of Sherman as a speechwriter, partly because of the truth of Mario Cuomo's dictum that 'we campaign in poetry, we govern in prose'. In her memoirs, she recorded that 'near the end of my time as Prime Minister, I became increasingly conscious of and interested in the relationship between Christianity and economic and social policy'.[69] Most famously, she offered her own highly coloured rendering of the Gospels in her address to the General Assembly of the Church of Scotland in 1988, the notorious 'Sermon on the Mound'.[70] She also asked Michael Alison and Brian Griffiths, then head of the Policy Unit, to initiate a dialogue (including non-Tories) about Christianity and Conservatism, and contributed a foreword to the ensuing volume of essays.[71] Her renewed interest in theology may have been prompted by the loss of other familiar coordinates, once the battles against socialism and the trade unions had largely been won, but she may also have had a personal desire to reconnect with the religion of her youth. In 1989, she resolved to read the entire Old Testament, giving her staff daily updates on her progress.[72]

Throughout her leadership, Thatcher's reading of Christianity was partial and idiosyncratic.[73] She drew her homilies from an odd melange of spiritual authorities – St Paul, C. S. Lewis, hymns she had learned at chapel as a girl. Clergy objected that this was a travesty of Christianity. But in a sense that did not matter. In the 1970s and 1980s Thatcher was appealing, not to clergy, but to a lay public that was itself often hazy about Christian theology, and was thus open to her over-simplifications. Her half-remembered, 'Sunday School' Christianity resonated with voters whose own religion was increasingly only a half-remembered relict of childhood.

The duties of churches

Thatcher's belief that the state could not, in general, legislate for morality placed a special responsibility on religious groups. As Sherman put it in a draft speech for Margaret Thatcher in 1978, 'values cannot be given by the state or politicians. Only religion has proved able to

impart them.'[74] Thatcher's advisors had seen the Church of England
as a potential source of support in the 1970s. A policy document by
Sir Keith Joseph entitled 'draft questions for Mrs Thatcher' included
the question 'How can Mrs T help bring the Church back into a helpful influence?' and the Conservatives were initially optimistic that
this was possible.[75] Although some bishops, like Mervyn Stockwood
of Southwark, were already hostile to the Conservatives in the 1970s,
others seemed sympathetic. Coggan's 'Call to the Nation' had raised
many of the same concerns about moral decline as Margaret Thatcher.
Graham Leonard, Bishop of Truro and chairman of the influential
Board of Social Responsibility, spoke in support of Thatcher's call for
immigration controls in 1978, saying 'I am thankful that Mrs Thatcher
has raised the issue at the present time.'[76] It was not until Thatcher's
clash with Archbishop Robert Runcie over the commemoration of
the Falklands War in 1982, and reports like *The Church and the Bomb*
(1982) and *Faith in the City* (1985), that the *Kulturkampf* between the
Thatcherites and the Anglican episcopate really began. In background,
many of Thatcher's antagonists on the bishops' bench – John Habgood
(Eton and King's), Stanley Booth-Clibborn (Highgate, the Royal
Artillery and Oriel) and David Sheppard (Sherborne, Trinity Hall
and the England cricket captaincy) – resembled the wets who opposed
her from within the Cabinet. Runcie (who had been in the Oxford
University Conservative Association with Thatcher) was much closer
to her grammar-school background, but (like Michael Heseltine) had
acquired a patrician patina through service in the Guards.[77]

Hugo Young described the attitude of many Conservatives to the
church as one of 'affronted disappointment', and this is a very good
description of Margaret Thatcher's own attitude in the 1980s.[78] In a
1987 interview with *Woman's Own*, during a discussion of the AIDS
crisis, she complained that the churches had neglected their duties as a
guardian of morals:

I think one is entitled to say to the great institutions of life, because I mean
Parliament is not the only institute [*sic*] of life, your churches are your very
great institutions, your great voluntary institutions or your great voluntary
associations ... you are also, I think, entitled to look to them, to say: 'Look.
There are certain standards, and if you undermine fundamentally these standards, you will be changing our way of life!'
It is when sometimes the authority of those institutions is undermined
because they have not been so forthright that then people turn too much to
the State.[79]

As Ewen Green has argued, Thatcherites, like Conservatives earlier
in the twentieth century, were inclined to judge organs of civil society by whether or not they were performing a 'valuable and effective

social role'. According to this criterion, the Church of England was increasingly found wanting in the 1980s.[80] Thatcher unfavourably contrasted the established church with religious groups that *did* perform a valuable role. She sometimes found this comparison in her own Methodist tradition, extolling Wesley as the archetype of a religious leader.[81] She liked to quote those sayings of Wesley's that did not condemn wealth accumulation, such as 'gain all you can, save all you can, give all you can', and 'the fault does not lie in money but in them that use it'.[82] Such sloganising ignored both the complexity of Wesley's own social teaching and the trenchant criticism of Thatcherism offered by Methodist leaders like Donald Soper and Leslie Griffiths.

The other religion that she contrasted with Anglicanism was Judaism, which embodied similar virtues of hard work and self-help. Years as MP for Finchley meant that she had had closer contact than her Conservative predecessors with the Jewish community (and was notably more willing to promote talented Jewish MPs to the front bench). At Sherman's prompting, she had also endeavoured to win Jewish recruits to the Conservatives in the 1970s.[83] She often described the values she extolled as coming from the 'Judaeo-Christian' or 'Judaic-Christian' tradition, thus deliberately including Jews and emphasising the contribution of the Old Testament.[84] As Prime Minister, Thatcher was particularly drawn to the Chief Rabbi, Immanuel Jakobovits; like her, he was a defender of traditional family life and an advocate of self-help who criticised the *Faith in the City* report.[85] Jakobovits increasingly became Thatcher's 'ideal-type' of what a senior cleric should be, and she rewarded him first with a knighthood and then with a peerage (the first rabbi to be ennobled). Her reading of Judaism, like Methodism, was monolithic and contestable; as Chief Rabbi, Jakobovits represented only one wing of British Jewry, and many Jews opposed Thatcher's policies. It is notable that she did not extol Islamic values in the same way as Christian and Jewish ones, though in ignoring Muslims she was typical of politicians of all parties in the years before the *Satanic Verses* controversy began in 1989.

Thatcher's enfolding of different religious traditions was only possible at a particular conjuncture in late twentieth-century British religious history. As a Methodist-turned-Anglican, she was herself a product of the decline of Nonconformity after the First World War, and of its assumption into a more generic common Protestantism.[86] But the 'Nonconformist Conscience' was still within living memory in the 1970s and 80s; when she invoked Wesley, Thatcher could be confident that her audience had at least a vague idea who she was talking about. Likewise, her singling-out of Judeo-Christian virtues would have been possible neither in the anti-semitic political culture at the start of the twentieth century, nor in the more inclusively multi-faith Britain at its end. Above all, Thatcher's appeal to religion was to a 'silent majority' who no longer attended church, but who considered themselves Christians, who had some folk memory of religious stories and symbols, and who remained susceptible to appeals to Christian morality. Declining observance meant that this was a large constituency in the final decades of the twentieth century.[87] That it had fallen away from churchgoing was partly a result of the declining authority of the clergy, and Thatcher was able to exploit this. Just as she presented herself as the embodiment of the frustrations of the ordinary citizen with 'the government', so she could embody the disappointment of ordinary Christians with their clergy. In both cases, she argued, ordinary people had been let down by a *trahison des clercs*. In this interpretation, clerical condemnation could even be sported as a badge of honour. Writing to congratulate Thatcher on her Church of Scotland speech in 1988, Mary Whitehouse reassured her that 'the very fact that you received so much "flak" from certain quarters indicated how effective your words were and I am sure were echoed in the hearts of countless people throughout the land, many of whom never go to Church'.[88] Thatcherism, then, drew on the survival of what Callum Brown has called 'discursive Christianity' long after the 1960s (when Brown claims it vanished). But it also benefited from, and contributed to, the decline of religious authority. Thatcher showed scant respect for the remaining vestiges of 'Christian Britain', as her unsuccessful attempt to deregulate Sunday shopping in 1985–6, which cost her some evangelical support, demonstrated.[89]

Conclusion

'The central paradox of Thatcherism', John Campbell has remarked, 'is that Mrs Thatcher presided over and celebrated a culture of rampant materialism – "fun, greed and money" – fundamentally at odds with her own values which were essentially conservative, old-fashioned and puritanical.' For Campbell, 'Margaret Thatcher is the link between two utterly opposed moral systems which reflect not only the ambivalence of her own personality but the story of Britain in the twentieth century: Alfred Roberts to Mark Thatcher in three generations.'[90] But while this paradox may have been inherent in the variegated nature of Thatcherism, it was not until the consequences of Thatcher's economic policies became apparent in the 1980s that commentators began to notice it.[91] Recognising this is important, because it reminds us that Thatcher's invocations of morality did not seem as preposterous, or as replete with ironies, in the 1970s as they did by 1990. When she arrived on the doorstep of Downing Street on 4 May 1979, and intoned the Prayer of St Francis of Assisi, her promise to bring harmony, truth, faith and hope resonated with many of her hearers.[92] But it resonated precisely because it recalled the promise of moral regeneration that she had first made several years before, a promise that had been instrumental in smoothing her 'path to power'.

5 'A nation or no nation?' Enoch Powell and Thatcherism

Camilla Schofield

[The Conservative] is more conscious than anyone else of the delicacy and vulnerability of that which sustains society … That the web of understood relationships which sustains society is an object, to a degree, of veneration as something which cannot be without danger tampered with, which arguably once injured may not be capable of being restored.[1]

If one looks at Thatcherism through the prism of Enoch Powell, it becomes clear what Thatcherism is not: it is not a conservative philosophy of the nation. For Powell, the nation-state was the 'ultimate political reality'. There was 'no political reality beyond it'.[2] In an effort to salvage that reality, Powell in 1963 argued for what he called a 'new patriotism' – oriented towards entrepreneurship and a post-imperial national pride.[3] Five years later, it was again 'the nation' that took precedence, when he spoke of future national disintegration due to the supposedly unbreachable divide of racism. For Powell, civil society once 'lost' could not be found. In contrast, for Margaret Thatcher, Britain's 'reawakening' was beyond itself, a reawakening of 'the values and traditions on which Western civilization, and prosperity, are based'.[4] Britain or Britishness came to be synonymous not with that fragile 'web of understood relationships' but with a set of values – with the 'spirit of trade' and self-reliance.[5] Yet Thatcherism was a situational, strategic ideology. The question still unanswered in the 1970s for the ideological makers of Thatcherism was *who* would commit to this 'enterprise culture' – the Asian and West Indian middle classes or Powell's disillusioned working-class supporters (who tended, the polls found, to have 'weak class identifiers')?[6]

There is no doubt that Powellism helped to produce Thatcherism, or that Powell contributed both to the New Right's political and economic thinking and to Thatcher's rhetorical style. As Andrew Gamble put it in 1974, Powell aired new grievances, new alliances and a new 'politics of power'[7] that could be harnessed in support of Thatcher. But, as this chapter argues, this coherence between Powell and Thatcherism was contingent and incomplete. Powell himself replied, when it was remarked that Thatcher was a convert to Powell's monetarist policies, that it was 'A pity she did not understand them!'[8] For Powell, monetarism was not a moral endeavour: it was a necessity of national economic independence. Powell's insistence on the need to untether market relations in British society from the constraints of economic planning was less an effort to remake the social order than a sign of his overriding concerns about sovereignty in the context of American global power. Fiscal conservatism was, like an independent military and a loyal and unified 'people', an essential component of national independence. Thatcher and Powell were, in a sense, fighting different wars – with the same weapons but against different enemies. For Powell, this was a struggle, like the Second World War, to preserve the 'unique structure of power' of English rule.[9] For Thatcher, this was a larger war, an ideological and moral war. Thatcher's war, both inside and outside Britain, was the Cold War.[10] While Powellism gave political meaning to the 'crisis' of the late 1960s and 1970s, with apocalyptic visions of racial violence and national disintegration, Thatcherism offered a solution: the world remade in her own likeness.

In 1988, David Marquand, a former Labour MP and founding member of the Social Democratic Party, claimed that, for the Conservative, '[b]etween the state and the citizen there lies, and there ought to lie, a mass of intermediate institutions which protect the individual from arbitrary power'. Wider society is a 'mosaic of small collectivities' in which civility, order, deference, political responsibility and freedom are learnt. He cites, here, Edmund Burke's famous line: 'To be attached to the subdivision, to love the little platoon we belong to in society, is the first principle (the germ as it were) of public affection.'[11] Critically, Thatcherism as a political project lacked a sensitivity to what Powell called 'the delicacy and vulnerability that sustains society'; it proved to have little reluctance to transform or 'tamper with' and 'injure' British communities and institutions.[12] In fact, Thatcherism launched a fervent attack on these 'nurseries of civility' in the 1980s – on local authorities, on the trade unions, on the BBC, on universities, and at times even on the Church of England.[13] A 'healthy society' is counterposed in the Thatcherite project to a society of encroaching socialism and collectivism.[14] As will be discussed in this chapter, economics was treated as instrumental in the speeches and policy papers of the New Right on the remaking of a conservative moral order. In Thatcher's speeches, Britishness appears as an antidote. Britain and 'true' Britishness appear, then, as Cold War belief.

Powell had, for decades, refused the dominant logic of pro-capitalist government spending, maintaining a 'far right' commitment to 'sound money'. In this, he was self-consciously an anachronism, who held dear to his heart the old truths of pre-war conservatism. This was a language that Thatcherites also sometimes deployed. Nigel Lawson, for example, told an audience in 1980 that Britain had to find a prior, truer self, unlearning the false lessons inculcated during and after the Second World War. Calling for the return of an 'old consensus', to the 'golden age' of Disraeli and Gladstone, Lawson proclaimed the 'reversion to an older tradition' of sound money. New conservatism was, therefore, truly conservative.[15] However, through Powell, we see in Thatcherism not such a stark disavowal of post-war 'moral' economics. Thatcherism's effort to morally transform Britain via economic policy appears, rather, as a continuation and development of liberal post-war ideas of social and economic planning.

But Powell was anachronistic in another way too. Despite the Second World War, a war that proved to many that ideas or values were the real substance of war and politics, Powell retained another unpopular truth. Shared values and shared belief, such as those within the New Commonwealth, could not produce a political community – that was, rather, the function of war and patriotic allegiance. Similarly, 'Britishness' was not a liberal project but a definition of allegiance. Powell refused the political logic, then, of the post-war world: the new internationalism of the United Nations, human rights and nuclear defence remained for Powell throughout his career infringements on national sovereignty, on the truly 'political'. By 1980, Powell had spent his life refusing to join what he regarded as America's liberal war. In this way, Powell serves as a peculiar link in the history of popular Conservatism.

Preparing the way, 1968–74

Enoch Powell is sometimes credited as an economic influence on Thatcherism because of his early arguments that control of the money supply would decrease inflation. Some of Powell's economic disciples – such as Geoffrey Howe, John Biffen, Nicholas Ridley, John Nott and Ian Gow – would go on to serve as Thatcher's ministers.[16] According to E. H. H. Green, however, Powell was 'articulating, rather than leading an important body of Conservative opinion', acting as the voice of an emergent middle-class perspective in the Conservative Party. Green notes a transformation in the make-up of the rank and file of the party – a turn to more salaried, middle-class members who were 'almost a ready-made conservative audience for the Thatcherite agenda'. He also notes a transformation in British society as a whole, towards growth demographically and economically in the south and south-east, toward 'embourgeoisement', towards 'non-unionised' 'service-sector activity' and 'a greater degree of "economic instrumentalism" in voting allegiance'.[17] Here Thatcherism appears to represent an inevitable transformation and Powell happens to be along for the ride.

Thatcherism was not one discourse but 'a field of discourses' at work on the terrain of popular ideology in the 1970s.[18] Powell's historic role in the making of Thatcherism is, likewise, multifaceted. One frame by which to understand Thatcher, at least, is via the strength of her anti-communist convictions. For Thatcher, it was in many ways communism, both within and without Britain – as terrorism, in the unions, in popular culture, within the state bureaucracy, in local government, and also, simply, as Soviet military aggression – that stood against 'the survival of our way of life'.[19] A revival of the 'Anglo-Saxon heritage' and 'the remarkable qualities of the British people' promised, in Thatcher's schema, to save Britain from state collectivism and consequent moral decay. Though at times explicitly racial, the concept of Britain found here is less a fragile entity facing an existential crisis than it is an ideological orientation. 'Britain' was, for Thatcher, less the divinely ordained and ritualised order of Tory tradition than the exportable, missionary nation. Still, Enoch Powell's particular vision of Britain's existential crisis – and the mass support that this vision produced – worked to endow some British people's experiences of unrest and uncertainty in these years with radical political meaning. As one political analyst put it, Powellism played an essential 'preparatory role' in making the electorate more receptive to radical politics, 'to positions outside the mainstream of British politics'.[20] Powellism made Britain ready, in other words, for Thatcher's crusade.

The name Enoch Powell is now synonymous with a picture of Britain 'foaming with much blood', due to the immigration of black people from the New Commonwealth.[21] In 1968 and consistently thereafter, Powell prophesied a future race war in Britain. The racism of Powell's speeches on immigration is not merely symptomatic of an emerging race politics. Powell's words in 1968, as Gamble emphasised in 1974, constructed new political formations. Britain faced at this time what Stuart Hall has persuasively called an 'organic crisis'. The post-war promises of affluence, consensus and an ever-enlarging middle class were exposed in the 1960s and 1970s as unemployment rose, wages did not, and the social and political norms of the consensus were shattered by a new 'permissive society'.[22] In this context, immigration was offered by Powell as a sign of the state prioritising past international (post-imperial) obligations over the protection of the working classes – over the 'defence' of the nation. The immigrant was drawn, in these terms, as a scrounger, an embodiment of all that is wrong with the (undemocratic and authoritarian) state.

Powell's populist patriotism questioned the trustworthiness of state bureaucracy. The Home Office itself, charged by Powell with lying about the numbers of New Commonwealth immigrants, became the 'enemy within'. The white working class are redrawn, here, as *victims* of a traitorous state. This is a populism that skilfully dismantles the fusion within social democracy of state and people. As Hall's work emphasises, Powellism enabled the crises of the 1970s and the threat of 'anarchy' to be 'largely thematised through race'. Via Powell, an economic crisis became a crisis of identity. 'Race [became] the prism through which the British people are called upon to live through, then to understand, and then to deal with the growing crisis.'[23]

My own research into Powellism has shown the enduring significance of the Second World War in Powell's patriotic appeal.[24] With the aid of Powell's papers and the thousands of letters he received from the public after his 'rivers of blood' speech, this work reveals the crucial ways in which Powell and his supporters explicitly used memories of the Second World War to rewrite its meaning within British political discourse. The war, which had served as the foundation for the moral justification of social democracy, state power and Britain's alliance with America's Cold War crusade, was re-made, via Powellism, into a myth of Britain permanently under siege. The myth of the heroic sacrifice of 'the people' – a sacrifice that worked to resolve the contradictions of a classed society and legitimise the peace of 1945 – matured, with Powell's help, into a myth of white sacrifice and victimisation.

Powell associated the Establishment – and especially the economic consensus of the Middle Way – with the appeasers of the 1930s. Here, Powell married nationalism and anti-Keynesianism. The People's War was, by 1968, retold not as a resolution of the class war of the interwar years, but as an assertion of self-reliance – 'the people' against the liberal state. In an interview with the *Sunday Times* that year, Powell explained that he viewed his political role as being a representative in the Burkean sense, rather than as merely a delegate whose job it was to voice the people's sentiments. The politician at his best gave voice and meaning to an unarticulated feeling.[25] To name it – to act as the prophet of the 'River Tiber foaming with much blood' – was itself a creative act.[26] Resentment against immigrants was given meaning through Powell's Churchillian language of war, appeasement and invasion. Powell's metaphors in his speeches on immigration were violent and militaristic: with phrases such as an 'invasion of our body politic', 'alien territory', 'whole areas, towns … occupied', 'detachments from … the West Indies or India or Pakistan encamped in certain areas in England', 'whip hand', 'throwing a match on to gunpowder', 'much blood', and 'impending disaster'.[27] This resonated in deep and unexpected ways with his supporters. Letters flooded in with references to Winston Churchill and intimate histories of wartime service, sacrifice and post-war deprivation.

Powell externalised, or politicised, social violence.[28] He explained mugging by West Indians in the 1970s, and later the Brixton and Liverpool riots of 1981, as signs of political alienation. The black Briton did not and could not, in Powell's mind, identify with the political order. British citizens were, in this way, placed outside the nation – they were the 'enemy within'. The same goes for those who sought to break the government with labour unrest and those who violently opposed Unionist domination in Northern Ireland. As a Unionist MP for South Down from 1974 to 1987, Powell sought complete integration of Northern Ireland into the British Parliament. He regarded republican prisoners as enemies of the British state and believed that the difficulties in Northern Ireland were exacerbated by US defence interests.[29] Strikes against nationalised industries, similarly, were not economic, but political: 'The railwaymen, like the miners, are not negotiating with the Railways Board – that is merely a façade – but with the Government. Nor are the railwaymen and the Government negotiating about things economic. They are negotiating about things political.'[30] In other words, for Powell, this was political opposition intimately linked to questions of state sovereignty and its declining authority. Thatcher deployed a similar language, but annexed to it an ideological component that was quite absent from Powell's thought. There was an 'enemy within' but that enemy was consistently socialist. Anti-racism, for instance, was most threatening, for Thatcher, when wedded to a critique of capitalism.[31] Further, within Thatcherism, authority promised, at least in these instances, to whip the body politic into the right shape. Black criminality is not political but a consequence of family structure and environment; a strong police force is therefore offered as one component in a 'total system of social control'.[32] Likewise, the IRA prisoner is 'criminalised', and thereby (unsuccessfully) made non-political and invisible.

The Powellism of the late 1960s has been read as an early sign of the coming social dislocation of the 1970s: the 'decade of dealignment', or the loosening of post-war political loyalties based on class status, and the emerging influence of issue voting.[33] The letters from Powell's supporters in favour of greater immigration restrictions, which number over 100,000, are steeped in racism; yet they also reveal the experience of profound social and economic uncertainty and serve as testaments to social changes unrelated to immigration. Powell's letter-writers speak of student protests, labour unrest, but most of all they speak of the indignities of declining welfare provision – filled hospital beds and unavailable council houses.[34] In this sense, via the repatriation of immigrants, Powell called for a reversal of history, a return to a certain world. According to electoral studies, Powellism initially found its support with the alienated voter – with the 'weak class identifier'. But soon, according to political analyst Douglas Schoen, Powellism became more diffuse. It evolved into a wider coalition of those dissatisfied with the political system, serving as a major catalyst in the growth of support for extreme right-wing groups, such as the National Front and the Immigration Control Association.[35] Despite the preponderance of working-class letter-writers, Powell's most active supporters were distinctly middle and upper-middle class – their influence was felt, too, in local government, on school boards, in housing associations. The activities of the Young Conservatives, the Monday Club, and particularly the association Powellight, served as hubs of this middle-class base.[36]

Heath sacked Powell from his position as Shadow Minister of Defence just days after his 'rivers of blood' speech, and Powell would never again return to the centre of political power. Still, the party's relatively tough stand on immigration contributed to the Conservatives' surprise election victory in 1970. The next year, Heath's Conservative government passed an Immigration Act that introduced a 'patrial' clause into British immigration law; this resulted in the further restriction of black immigration into Britain. This did not, however, erase Powellism. Powell left the Conservative Party in 1974 over Britain's continued membership of the EEC, only to join the Ulster Unionists that same year. Race hardly surfaced as an issue in the two general elections of 1974. The miners' strike and Powell's defection to the Unionists focused attention away from immigration. The Conservative loss did, however, seem to have a racial dimension. The Community Relations Commission produced a report showing that thirteen of the seventeen seats Labour gained in the October 1974 election were won with a majority that was smaller than the non-white population of that constituency.[37] Meanwhile, Conservatives collected just 19 per cent of the Asian vote, to Labour's 73 per cent.[38] The party alienated the non-white voter at its peril.

A public doctrine, 1974–9

Keith Joseph joined Powell in warning of social decay in 1974, asking: 'Are we to move towards moral decline reflected and intensified by economic decline, by the corrosive effects of inflation? Or can we remoralise our national life, of which the economy is an integral part?'[39] Joseph's answer, then, was social engineering – not solely in terms of class but in reconstructing a conservative moral order. Degeneration was not just economic: he claimed that 'our human stock is threatened', and called for greater access to birth control for unfit mothers. This eugenic line lost him the leadership of the party. It also begged the question, who would be included in this remoralised Britain? Crucially, for Thatcher and her ministers, 'transformism' was accepted as necessary because British society had taken a wrong historical turn.[40] The 'corrosive effects' of inflation had set in: saving and prudence were under threat. Likewise, the bastions of 'civility' – such as the church, the voluntary sector and the press – no longer offered lessons in economic and political self-reliance. Thanks to post-war corporatism, 'the people' did not know the moral rules of the game. 'Socialist encouragement of class hatred of the existing order', as one policy discussion paper explained, 'is easily translated into exemption from obeying society's laws.'[41] For Powell, it was not the politician's role, but the role of the 'moralist' to work against public sins, like lack of prudence – or even explicit racism. In response to Joseph's speech, Powell warned that politicians should not preach, as they had little effect on public morals.[42] But it was 'beliefs, not the people', argued Joseph, that were 'the poison on our economic life. We are trapped by them.'[43] As John Casey put it in 1978, conservative philosophy required 'the largest imaginative leap' in order to grasp the 'decay in customs and patterns of behaviour', which signalled 'a profound change in the consciousness of the age'.[44]

In the autumn of 1977, the ex-army officer and businessman John Hoskyns and another businessman named Norman Strauss prepared a Centre for Policy Studies document entitled 'Stepping Stones'. This now legendary document was distributed and discussed in the Shadow Cabinet, and Hoskyns later became the head of Thatcher's Policy Unit from 1979 to 1982. 'Stepping Stones' viewed the unions as the key stumbling block to economic recovery, and recommended modifying, rather than confronting, the beliefs of union members. Here we see something of the intellectual work involved in producing a new moral hegemony. Hoskyns and Strauss discuss the social introduction of 'discontinuity' – 'breaking constraints which we had assumed were unbreakable'. These constraints had previously been considered 'unalterable "facts of life'" – in other words, the stuff of common sense and culture. The report called for a special working party on the 'Mind Set' of union members. There we see the recognition that union life is a major aspect of a union member's identity – in other words, the nationalised industries and the unions are part of Britain's 'little platoons'. The 'individual worker and his union are closely linked' such that 'Exile would be like banishment to Siberia':

Between him and the terrors of being on his own in a society which, as yet, offers fairly unequal opportunity, stands his union – that is, his tribe, his clan, his own small society. Inside it he is warm, and to a large extent, safe. Outside, he is nothing. If he is to desert Labour – and thus by close connection, qualify his loyalty to his union – it must be for something better and equally reassuring.

This is an extreme vision – outside, the union member is nothing: not parishioner, not father, not hobbyist, not consumer. The appendix 'Union Behaviour Change Strategy' warned that 'we cannot ask the unions, or their members, to give up their current feelings of comradeship, protectiveness and group strength if we do not guarantee them similar feelings of strength, togetherness and security under any new arrangement'. This is true 'transformism': the unionist must be stripped down to 'the terrors of being on his own' and then re-made as a non-union man with, they propose, 'a minority stake on the Board of a company, share-owning, or a controlling role in a local authority'.[45]

Powell's response to efforts to produce a 'national revival' with economic policy is particularly revealing. When in the autumn of 1966 Ray Gunter, then Minister of Labour, blamed Britain's economic ills on the 'dishonesty' and 'thriftlessness' of the nation at large, on a collective irresponsibility, Powell received a pile of letters for and against the nation. He viewed this as a sign of how much the idea of the state controlling peoples' lives had affected those writing to him. It was neither his job nor the job of the National Economic Development Council, but a 'job for moralists', to work on the nation's moral ills.

For the purposes of politics, human nature, including the human nature of the nation concerned, must be treated as constant, something given and assumed, a starting point. The politician's business is with the environment in which human nature is placed.[46]

Like Michael Oakeshott, Powell was sceptical of 'rationalism' in politics and the supposed perfectability of man. While politics and the politician may be 'the nation's psychiatrist' when they create and recreate myths that legitimise their authority,[47] they cannot dramatically change that organic evolutionary entity, the habits and expectations of a community. Instead, the politician is employed by society to dramatise the inevitabilities of the world so as to make them 'appear human, explicable, and amenable to management'.[48] This was Powell's essential critique of Keynesian social democracy and the corporate state.[49]

Importantly, we see the same criticism appearing later against Thatcherism. In response to Chancellor Geoffrey Howe's first budget in 1979, Powell spoke out against the notion that economic policy could transform the moral order. The 1979 budget shifted £2.5 billion onto indirect taxation. As he had done in the past, Powell argued in support of income tax, against indirect taxation.[50] He rejected the argument that income tax cuts motivated individuals to work harder. It is worth quoting Powell at length, for in this we see the fundamental divide between Powell and Thatcherism on economics and the nation:

[I]t is necessary not to treat people of any walk of life as automata, nor the economy as a kind of marionette, which Governments and Chancellors of the Exchequer can operate by lifting a leg here and depressing an arm there, through the alterations in the tax system ... The proposition that people will work harder or longer for 3p off the standard rate of income tax, let alone that they will work more effectively – which is what we are talking about – betrays a crass misunderstanding of human nature, individual and social. The reasons why people address themselves collectively and individually to their activities, and the reasons why at one phase of a nation's history they direct them in one way rather than another, are far deeper, more complex and more subtle than can be reached by a remission of income tax.

Powell then went on to critique Thatcherism's historical mission:

I profoundly reject that conception and modes of thought which assert that there has been either a relative – if we are compared to our Continental neighbours – or an absolute decline in the quality of life in this country. If it has occurred – and a case could be made that in certain aspects of our life there has been a deterioration – it would be in aspects which are not measured or measurable by GNP ... If we are failing, if the sum total of our pride and satisfaction and achievement is diminishing, I do not believe that it is in the power of Governments, through Budgets, to alter that course of events. Some say that this is a secular decline which has been going on for a century. If it has been going on for a century, so much the more profound, so much the more fated, must be the causes that lie behind it. What certainly will not turn a nation again is to be told to measure itself, to measure what it achieves, against an objective, mechanical, material standard by which its [European] neighbours are also measured; nor to inform it that it will be given opportunity for renewed and wider achievement by a minor adjustment of the relationship between gross and net income. If a Government were to tell a nation that and the nation were indeed in a state of moral and physical decline, it would only encourage it upon that course. I do not believe that the nation reacts to the sort of stimuli in which the Government apparently believe; and if the Government address the nation in the terms in which this Budget speaks, so much the less will the nation listen.[51]

The consistency of Powell's critique, against both Keynesian and Thatcherite economics, offers another perspective on the New Right. Thatcher and Powell both spoke in the late sixties and seventies against the notion that redistributive taxes could be 'moral'. Charity and altruism had no meaning when applied to taxation by a public authority, either for the welfare state or international development aid. They agreed that morality was individual: the Good Samaritan cannot be forced to be good. As Powell put it in 1965, it was an 'inherent absurdity' to imagine a state behaving charitably, for 'it is collective advantage that governs how a state acts'.[52] However, through Powell, we see in Thatcherism a less stark disavowal of post-war 'moral' economics. Rather, Thatcherism may be read in this way as a continuation and development of liberal ideas on social and economic planning. Economics remained the method: the object was to police the heart and soul.[53]

Powell's insistence that politics, both at the domestic and international level, had no logical bridge to 'the assertions of Christianity' stands in contrast, then, to Thatcherism.[54] By 1977, Thatcher had made clear that her party was Christian (as opposed to a party of the established church).[55] It was, under Thatcher, a party concerned not with ritual obedience, but individual salvation. As Paul Rich explains, this neo-liberal concern for the individual 'acted as a considerable brake on the emergence of a full-blown Tory organicism which, allied [to] a theory of racial nationalism, would have taken the party's intellectual right a good way towards British fascist ideology'.[56] Instead, on race and immigration, Thatcherism remained ambiguous.

Immigration was, according to Thatcher's assistant in 1976, 'always' the most popular subject in Margaret Thatcher's postbag. In the first six months of 1976, for instance, it was the focus of 25 per cent of all mail that Thatcher received from the public.[57] The Malawi Asian crisis of that year and the passing of the Race Relations Act (which the Conservative Party did not oppose) had produced a renewed opposition to black immigration at both the party and popular level. Enoch Powell's release of details of a secret document which alleged widespread evasion of immigration restrictions and fraud in 1976, too, further heated the public debate. In the lead-up to the Race Relations Bill, Airey Neave wrote that 'strong comments' were made within the party chairman's management committee of the need for new 'party policy' on immigration. Neave feared that Willie Whitelaw's statements seemed to be 'adopting an "elitist" attitude which ignored the opinions of reasonable residents of the reception areas for immigrants, who found their neighbourhoods literally taken over'.[58] At the party conference, Whitelaw promised an end to 'immigration as we have seen it in the post-war years'. That same year, however, with recognition that Asian and West Indian voters were electorally significant in marginal seats, in the Midlands, Greater London, Yorkshire and Lancashire, the Central Office set up a new Central Office Department of Community Affairs, which in turn funded two new national organisations: the Anglo-Asian Conservative Society and the Anglo-West Indian Conservative Society.[59] These attempted to recruit businessmen, doctors, accountants and other middle-class professionals into their ranks. Thatcher was made honorary president of the Anglo-Asian Conservative Society. Still, there were limits to this (classed) anti-racism.

When party members were invited to participate in the Joint Committee Against Racialism in 1977 (together with the Labour and Liberal parties, the British Council of Churches, the Board of Deputies of British Jews, the National Union of Students, the British Youth Council and leading immigrant groups, such as the Indian Workers Association), Thatcher vetoed the appointment of John Moore MP as joint chairman. She was apparently 'appalled' when she discovered that the party might be involved in activities with far-left groups.[60] Instead, Mrs Shelagh Roberts, who was not a Member of Parliament, took up the post.

Thatcher's remark on television in 1978 that the people are afraid that 'this country might be rather swamped by people with a different culture' was a political calculation.[61] The popular presence of the National Front was at its peak in these years, winning 120,000 votes in the 1977 elections to the Greater London Council. Just days after her 'swamped' comment, Thatcher spoke, too, of Britain's sick society: 'a state that is responsible for just about everything' and 'a society in which the individual feels responsible for nothing' was a reason why 'prisons are full to bursting; vandalism is growing; in some areas people are afraid to answer their doors at night'. Not only was the state producing discord, it could not be trusted. Here, like Powell, race came in. Thatcher spoke of 'Smokescreen Socialism', a 'cloud of excuses, explanations and justification' – and here, at this point, she linked the state, socialism and the unknown 'numbers' of immigrants. She promised to remove 'the doubts on numbers' and 'the doubts on commitments' and respect 'the genuine fears and concerns of many of our citizens'.[62] Thatcher's people, here, are white *victims*. Thatcher promised to hear and speak for the fears of 'the people'. Like Powell, she received a deluge of letters in support. The *Daily Telegraph* maintained that Thatcher's 'swamped' remark had struck a popular chord, claiming that 58 per cent of Labour supporters, 71 per cent of Liberals and 84 per cent of Conservatives endorsed Thatcher's words.[63] These words all but destroyed the National Front in the 1979 general election. Though immigration was not a big election issue in 1979, there were still massive swings to the Conservatives in Islington through to the East End and Dagenham – areas where the National Front had been most active. As Powell put it on Thatcher's populism: 'People hearing her are convinced that she shares the same frustrations and nurtures the same ambition', which was, 'in a single word ... "nation".'[64]

Thatcher in power

Powell refused to believe that indirect taxation could transform Britain, but war was another thing entirely. After the Falklands War in June 1982, Powell experienced a changed Britain: 'A change has come about in Britain. I do not need opinion polls ... to tell me that. I have the evidence of my own senses as I go about the country.'[65] Powell was not alone in this view. According to an *Economist* editorial the week before, 'Britain has said something to itself', and produced 'some restoration of the idea that Britain can do things well'. 'Britain had long needed its own sort of cultural revolution', the article went on, shaking off the 'malaise' of the immediate post-war and Vietnam generation, with its tendency to view 'military values and men as out-of-date jokes'. Now a younger generation could look upon soldiers who were 'men a bit more handsome and heroic than Mr David Bowie'.[66] This gendered understanding of the value of war in society echoes the words of Powell and his supporters, who viewed the 1968 generation as decadent without the experience of war. Anthony Barnett's near-contemporary portrayal of the politics surrounding the Falklands War speaks at length about how memories of the Second World War, when Britain 'knew itself', worked to legitimate military action.[67] Thatcher's Churchillian rhetoric famously came home, too, when she spoke at a Conservative rally at Cheltenham: 'We have to see that the spirit of the South Atlantic – the real spirit of Britain – is kindled not only by war but can now be fired by peace.' Now it was time, she argued, 'for management to lift its sights and to lead with the professionalism and effectiveness it knows is possible'. Now was the time for the railwayman to stand for 'true solidarity', not with his union on strike the following day, but by putting 'his family, his comrades, and his country first'.[68] According to Thatcher, it was war, then, which bore Britain's revival: finding that prior, truer self in memories not of 1945, but of 1940.

Though Thatcher had shown her mettle on the Falklands, protecting British interests, she tellingly failed to do so when American marines invaded Grenada in October 1983. Friendship with the United States had failed to prevent the Grenada invasion; this confirmed for Powell, as Simon Heffer put it, that 'America's loyalty to her British ally [was] a sham.' This was of particular significance at a time when the US was about to station nuclear weapons on British soil. Thatcher's commitment to the Anglo-American alliance, her willingness to bind Britain to the nuclear deterrence policy of the United States against Soviet power and her use of the language of 'freedom' and 'Western Civilization' against communism were signs, Powell thought, of an 'American view of the world'. This view he described as, 'in the strictest terms, Manichean. It divides the world into two monoliths – the goodies and the baddies, the East and the West, even the free and the enslaved. It is a nightmarish distortion of reality.'[69] It was, in other words, a view of the world without a need to protect the conservative nation. To depend on the United States or the continent of Europe for British arms was, as he put it in 1989, 'suicide'.[70] Thatcher's political rhetoric was highly patriotic; she often talked of British greatness, but – as Richard Vinen has found – she said very little about English nationalism.[71] Similarly, Thatcher's approach to Europe might be read, by her Bruges speech of 1988, as nationalistic, but the underlying argument in that speech remains: 'We have not successfully rolled back the frontiers of the state in Britain, only to see them re-imposed at a European level, with a European super-state exercising a new dominance from Brussels.'[72] Through the prism of Powell, it appears to be less sovereignty than the nature of political and economic order that remains Thatcher's concern.

While Powell viewed the Brixton and Liverpool riots of 1981 as the beginnings of an inevitable civil war between those who identified with and those who were alienated from the state, Thatcher's government – after the Scarman Report – turned to support the structures of social authority in Britain's minority communities. A. Sivanandan refers to this as the 'culturalism' or 'ethnicism' of the Thatcher period and views it as an attempt to contain black power politics. The report's discussion of the black community in Brixton begins by pathologising family life in the Brixton community.[73] It eschews the charge that the riots were caused by high unemployment or widespread institutionalised racism. It was, rather, the 'racial disadvantage' of certain groups, 'the cure being to pour money into ethnic projects and strengthening ethnic cultures'.[74] The fight against racism was reduced, Sivanandan argues, to 'a fight for culture'. In fact, as David Feldman has emphasised, the formalised recognition of ethnic difference as a means of ordering society was in no way a new phenomenon in the history of British governance.[75] This 'ethnicism' can be seen, too, as a continuation of Thatcher's war for British (middle-class) values. The cohesion of families in Asian communities – and their 'innate conservatism' – increasingly appealed to some Conservative politicians in the 1980s as a possible source of middle-class authority in the inner city. As Cowling put it in 1978: 'If there *is* a class war – and there is – it is important that it should be handled with subtlety and skill.'[76]

In an analysis of the British Nationality Act of 1981, David Dixon has argued that Enoch Powell was the 'immediate progenitor of Thatcherism' and that 'their ideologies of race and nation are fundamentally the same'.[77] But Thatcherism was a changeable entity. The Powellite nature of the British Nationality Act does not give a complete picture of Thatcher's views on race and nationality. The message on a Conservative political campaign poster of 1983 (which was produced to generate electoral support for the Act) is yet another strategic approach to nationality within Thatcherism; and it certainly breaks with a Powellite vision of the nation. The poster, which came in two varieties, presents a photograph of a black man or an Asian man in a suit, with the line: 'Labour says he's Black, Tories say he's British.'[78] For Powell, race in Britain in the 1970s and 1980s produced an insurmountable identity politics. As a solution, this poster promises to wash away history and identity. In Powellite fashion, it argues in fine print against the treatment of a non-white Briton as a 'special case' to fight discrimination. The poster provoked resentment, because 'it misunderstood the wish of many to retain their own identity, to be both British *and* black'.[79] But the poster also nicely reflects on what it means to be British within Thatcherism. Britishness is expressed in their shared suit. The man, as Paul Gilroy has noted, looks ready for a job interview: 'isolated and shorn of the mugger's key icons – a tea-cosy and the dreadlocks of Rastafari – he is redeemed by his suit, the signifier of British civilisation'.[80] Here, the Manichean world, the inside and outside of the nation, seems to be defined by one's orientation towards capital.

Conclusion

To mark the revival of the Conservative Philosophy Group in 2007, John Casey recounted an interaction between Margaret Thatcher and Enoch Powell at a meeting of the group shortly before the Falklands War. The discussion turned to nuclear weapons, which Thatcher defended as a safeguard for 'Western values'. Powell's reply, though filtered through the long memory of John Casey, offers a key insight into the ambiguities of a 'nationalist' politics: 'No, we do not fight for values. I would fight for this country even if it had a communist government.' 'Nonsense, Enoch', Thatcher retorted. 'If I send British troops abroad, it will be to defend our values.' To this Powell replied: 'No, Prime Minister, values exist in a transcendental realm, beyond space and time. They can neither be fought for, nor destroyed.' Thatcher, apparently, looked on at Powell 'baffled'.[81] If values cannot be 'fought for', perhaps Powell was no revolutionary. This disagreement, on the eve of the Falklands War, suggests Powell's refusal to become a genuine member of Britain's Thatcherite revolution.

Thatcherism did not seek to conserve the fragile web of understood relationships – the 'little platoons' of affection – that make up the conservative nation. There was no alternative; traditional industrial communities and the mediation of local governance could not survive. As one analysis put it: 'Thatcherism enjoyed negative success as the corrosive agent which broke down the certainties of old forms of social life.'[82] If we look at Thatcher's record, we see less a concern with the protection of particular institutions between the state and the individual, and more a sense that certain cultural and social forms enable a healthy market order. According to Powell, the life of the British nation was evolutionary. Its progress was *slow*. Powell argued for the political status quo. He believed the sovereignty of British parliamentary democracy and the social order that recognised its sovereignty were in jeopardy due to post-war international realities. Ironically, Powell failed to see that his commitment to the free market was, essentially, a commitment to a revolutionary force that would, under Margaret Thatcher's governments, raze the web of understood relationships and the nature of the political order far more effectively than non-white immigration, labour unrest, Irish republicanism, or even European integration.

Part II

Thatcher's Britain

6   Thatcher and the women's vote

Laura Beers

Throughout Margaret Thatcher's term as Prime Minister, women continued to prefer the Conservative Party to Labour in greater numbers than their male counterparts. This fact in itself was not surprising. While the differentials between male and female voting had varied as long as polling data had been available, the so-called 'gender gap' had always favoured the Conservatives. Only in 2005 did women begin to show a stronger preference than men for the Labour Party. However, the persistence of an aggregate gender gap masked significant class and generational trends within women's support for the Conservative Party in the 1980s. Young women grew more pro-Labour over the course of the decade. After an initial flirtation with Thatcherism, women trade unionists also shifted to the Labour Party at the end of the decade. In contrast, middle-aged women barely waned in their support for the Conservatives, while older women remained a bulwark of Tory support. Ultimately, the swing to the left among younger women was stronger than the countervailing movement among older women, causing the gender gap to shrink considerably over the course of Thatcher's premiership.

Scholars have devoted significant attention to the fall-off in Conservative support among women, arguing variously that the turn away from Thatcherism reflected the disillusionment of working women with Thatcher's policies on women in the workforce; the betrayal felt by 'Thatcher's children', both male and female, at the failure of the market economy to deliver for their generation; women's support for the peace movement; and, finally, a long-term secular trend towards greater progressivism among women born after the Second World War. The continued appeal of Conservatism to a large section of British women, particularly middle-aged and older women, has, in contrast, received only slight attention.

This chapter begins with a survey of the existing literature on gender and party preference in Britain. It then considers Thatcher and the Conservative Party's appeal to women voters in the 1980s, before examining the efficacy of those appeals, as revealed through opinion polling on gender and party preference carried out by Market & Opinion Research International (MORI), most of it at the behest of the Labour Party. The MORI data should not be read as definitive, and much research remains to be done on the reasons for Thatcher's continued appeal to middle-aged women in particular. However, polling reveals several distinctions between how men and women viewed Thatcher and why members of each group supported the Conservatives. According to the data, women were more likely to vote Conservative because of personal support for Margaret Thatcher; they were more likely to share Thatcher's economic worldview; and they were more likely both to accord a high importance to education, and to support Thatcher's education policies. While feminists viewed Thatcher as an enemy of women's liberation, on average women voters were less likely to view Thatcher as anti-feminist. Such aggregate figures necessarily obscure significant variation among individual responses to Thatcherism. However, they suggest that a significant percentage of women in the 1980s both admired and agreed with Margaret Thatcher, and that their support was crucial to her political success.

The gender gap in British politics

Fifteen years ago, Ina Zweiniger-Bargielowska wrote that 'gender differences in voting behaviour have been virtually ignored by mainstream psephology and electoral sociology'.[1] Since then, David Jarvis's work on the inter-war years, and Zweiniger-Bargielowska's research into the gender gap in the age of affluence and austerity have shed light on the success of the Conservative Party, and the concomitant failure of Labour, in appealing to women in these two periods.[2] More recently, Rosie Campbell has explored gendered differences in political preference during the New Labour era.[3] However, there has as yet been little investigation into the reasons behind the persistent gender gap during the Thatcher years.

This is arguably because the gender gap narrowed appreciably in the 1980s. Joni Lovenduski and Pippa Norris suggest that there was only a slight gender gap in 1979, and no gender gap in the 1980s. According to their statistics, in 1979, 48 per cent of women and 45 per cent of men voted Tory. In 1983 that number was 45 per cent for both sexes, and in 1987 it was 44 per cent.[4] Labour Party strategists, on the other hand, did not accept that the gender gap had disappeared. For one thing, the party tended to rely on MORI polls, not the Gallup polls cited by Norris and Lovenduski. MORI had 46 per cent of women voting Conservative in 1983, compared with only 42 per cent of men.[5] While statistically the gap might not be significant, the MORI numbers appeared more damning for Labour. More importantly, MORI measured the gender gap not in terms of the percentage of the Conservative vote recruited from women as opposed to men, but by the Conservative lead over Labour in each demographic. On this measure, a gender gap persisted throughout Thatcher's term in office. In October 1974, when Wilson's Labour Party edged out Heath's Conservatives on an aggregate vote of 40 per cent to 37 per cent, MORI's gender breakdown of voting showed women favouring the Conservatives by 1 per cent, while men preferred Labour by 11 per cent, yielding a gender gap of 12 per cent. This figure declined slightly in 1979, although Labour's fortunes suffered with both men and women. In that year, Labour trailed the Tories by only 3 per cent among male voters, but by 12 per cent among female voters. In 1983, the gap shrank to 8 per cent. Only in 1987 did it almost completely disappear.[6] The ITN/Harris polls show a slightly different picture. While ITN/Harris record a smaller gender gap than MORI in 1979 and 1983, in 1987 their recorded gender gap remained at 4 per cent, essentially unchanged from four years earlier.[7]

While the poll numbers vary, they all show that the gender gap was shrinking throughout the 1980s. Political scientists working on gender and politics in this period have thus focused not on the persistence of gender variations in voting, but on the phenomenon of 'gender dealignment'.[8] To the Labour opposition, however, the 'gender gap' took on increased importance in the 1980s. This was, in part, because political science studies in the United States, where women were more likely than men to vote Democrat, threw into relief the continued conservatism of British women.[9] It was also because of the seeming absurdity of women supporting Thatcher. The Iron Lady championed and pursued policies that were hostile to working women and single mothers, neglectful of child welfare and generally bad for women and families, and yet women continued to vote for her in larger numbers than men.[10] Joyce Gould, Labour's Chief Women's Officer from 1975 to 1985, and subsequently Director of Organisation, was particularly keen to understand what she perceived to be deviant behaviour on the part of many women voters.[11]

One aspect of the polling results that particularly struck Gould and others was the differential attitude of women of different age brackets towards the two principal political parties. While older women seemed lost to Labour, young women (aged 18 to 24) appeared to be drifting back to Labour in the 1980s. Pippa Norris has argued that these contradictory trends among older and younger women problematise the dealignment school's argument that gender is no longer a factor in modern voting. Instead, she has identified a generational divide wherein women born before 1945 are more conservative than their male counterparts, and post-war women more progressive. The explanation proposed is that women raised under the welfare state have a greater appreciation of the value of activist government. Her research suggests a reversal in the gender gap that should manifest itself in a gradual realignment of the British electorate to the left as older women pass away and are replaced by their more progressive daughters and granddaughters. However, while the youngest group of female voters, those aged 18–24, were the most pro-Labour demographic in the 1987 election, a plurality of women aged 25–45 continued to support the Conservative Party, suggesting a limit to the process of radicalisation identified by Norris.[12]

Norris's research has highlighted the persistence of gender distinctions in voting behaviour among generational cohorts, even when aggregate figures suggest that sex is not a useful indicator of party preference. More recently, Rosie Campbell has argued that, even when both sexes support a party in equal proportions, 'there may be a *motivational* gender gap in vote choice, where men and women vote for the same party for different reasons'.[13] Women, she argues, were more likely to vote for New Labour because of their policies on health and education, whereas men preferred the party principally for its economic policies. This notion of a motivational gender gap also informs Beatrix Campbell's *Iron Ladies: Why Do Women Vote Tory?*, which remains a fundamental text for understanding the relationship between Thatcher and the female electorate in the 1980s.[14] Despite its title, Campbell's book focuses equally on the question of why many women, and particularly younger women, had become disenchanted with the Conservative Party by 1987. Here, she identifies employment policies, and particularly the Thatcher government's hostility towards European directives on equal pay and family leave, and its promotion of women's part-time work without securing pay or benefits to part-time workers, as crucial in alienating the female electorate. She also points to women's (particularly younger women's) greater opposition to the government's Trident cruise missile programme, as compared to their male counterparts, as a reason for the narrowing of the gender gap. While Campbell admits that the trends she observes are more moves away from the Conservative Party than moves towards Labour, the book is written as a call to arms for the left. Its intent was to expose the chinks in the Thatcherite armour, in the hope that Labour would take the hint and go after these disaffected women.

In so far as Campbell discusses women's reasons for supporting the Conservative Party, she focuses on the hard-line morality of Conservative women activists. She argues that it was in large part the 'women's agenda' within the party rank and file, an agenda 'almost entirely expressed in the language of law and order ... debates which punctuated women's conferences from the late 1930s [onwards]' which propelled the 'emergence of the new right, anti-modernist axis which became Thatcherism'.[15] The 'hang 'em and flog 'em' lobby, she argues, was fuelled by a highly sexualised and racist fear which extended from the question of public safety to encompass a broader anxiety about moral decline. Thatcherism's deployment of moralistic arguments about the decline of British society in the debates over education reform are discussed below. In that context, questions about the decline of standards and values in modern society certainly came into play. What is notable, looking at the polling data, is how little crime and policing appear to rate as a priority among any group other than the elderly.

Thatcher's bid for female support

Margaret Thatcher was, by her own admission, no feminist.[16] During the 1979 general election, the Conservatives produced an election poster that read:

It was a Conservative – Mrs Pankhurst – who first led the fight for votes for women.

It was the Conservatives who first gave all women the vote 50 years ago.

It was a Conservative who was the first woman to sit in Parliament.

It was the Conservatives who elected the first woman party leader.

It only leaves one thing for a woman to do.

Vote Conservative.[17]

But the blatant appeal to women to vote for Thatcher qua woman was exceptional, and was not repeated in subsequent elections. As she said in a press conference in 1979: 'I like people who have ability, who don't run the feminist ticket too hard, after all I reckon if you get anywhere it's because of your ability as a person. It's not because of your sex.'[18] When in 1986 the Labour Party announced plans to establish a Ministry for Women if returned to power, Thatcher denounced it as a place for 'dungarees only, no skirts allowed' – a jibe at the supposedly unfeminine appearance of the 'strident' feminists behind the proposal.[19] Her lack of support for a women's ministry mirrored her lukewarm tolerance for the Equal Opportunities Commission (EOC) set up in 1976 – she told a reporter for *Cosmopolitan* magazine that the main purpose of the EOC was symbolic, 'to remin[d] certain parts of the country that women in some areas do not quite have equal opportunities'.[20] She did little to encourage women's participation in the workplace. She was unsupportive of the equal rights legislation generated by the European Commission. Pay differentials between men and women remained greater in Britain than in the rest of Europe, and access to childcare and maternity and parental leave more restricted. Her government changed eligibility for unemployment benefit so as to exclude women who could not prove that they had adequate childcare arrangements in place if they were to be offered employment. Those women who did enter the workforce in the 1980s did so primarily as part-time workers, with lower pay and weaker access to benefits than men doing comparable jobs. All of these realities profoundly alienated many feminists from the Conservative Party in the 1980s, and led Campbell and Lovenduski to write in 1987 that 'all the main parties except the Tories have developed a women's agenda'.[21]

But Thatcher's failure to use activist government to support the cause of working women did not mean that she did not have a 'women's agenda'. Throughout her political career, Thatcher worked to valorise housewives in British society, and to facilitate, as she perceived it, a woman's ability to balance work and family. She appealed to women primarily as homemakers, often targeting women through media traditionally seen as outside the purview of politics – such as *Cosmopolitan*, or *Woman's Own*, to which she famously pronounced that 'there is no such thing as society', or mid-morning radio programmes, consumed primarily by housewives.[22] Thatcher made explicit her appreciation of the central role of women's magazines in politics at a speech to a group of magazine editors, when she said that: '[W]e always read, every week in my home *Woman's Weekly* and I must tell you it upheld excellent standards, it really did, and it had quite an influence over what people believed in this country and what were the acceptable standards.'[23] Her party's appreciation of the political potential of women's magazines can be seen in a 1979 election poster in which the case for Conservatism was outlined through the medium of a *Cosmo* quiz.[24]

The case for Conservatism, as outlined in the quiz, centred on the importance of choice in education, the arguments for free enterprise and low taxation, crime and the cost of living. Notably, education was presented as a women's issue, or rather a mothers' issue, but it was the last theme that most explicitly appealed to gender solidarity. The quiz asked readers which of these people was more likely to know what it was like to do the family shopping.

a. James Callaghan
b. Your husband
c. Mrs Thatcher

Again and again throughout her premiership, Thatcher emphasised that she was Mrs Thatcher first and foremost, a housewife and a mother, and that as a wife and mother she was able to understand the concerns of ordinary women. One such concern, particularly in the 1970s and the early 1980s, was the cost of living, and the housewife's ability to manage the family budget. As she said in a BBC interview in 1979: 'housewives ... know I know from experience the sort of thing which they encounter daily'; they 'know I know what it is like to be a working wife as well as running a home'.[25]

Elsewhere in this volume, Jon Lawrence and Florence Sutcliffe-Braithwaite emphasise the ways in which Thatcher used the rhetoric of the family to counter Labour's appeals to broader class or social solidarity. However, it is important to emphasise the extent to which Thatcher perceived the family in distinctly gendered terms: as the primary sphere in which women's lives achieved value and purpose. In a press conference in 1979, Thatcher responded to a question from a female journalist on women's 'right to work' by saying that:

Look, look I do believe *passionately* that many women take the view, and quite rightly, that when their children are young their first duty is to look after the children and keep the family together. I wasn't a Member of Parliament until after my children were six ... And I do say this to you very seriously indeed: it is every bit as worthy an objective and an ambition to stay at home and look after the family as it is to go out to work. And you must not in *any way* make young women feel guilty because they don't go out to work ... *That must not be* ... It's not for us to lay down how they should choose, and I will not have them criticised in any way for doing perhaps one of the most important jobs in the world, which is keeping family life together.[26]

Thatcher reiterated similar sentiments throughout her premiership, particularly in support of her government's unwillingness to regulate more heavily the part-time labour market. Whereas for feminists loosely regulated part-time labour represented a reversion towards the sweated industries of the nineteenth and early twentieth centuries, in Thatcher's rhetoric fostering the creation of such jobs meant improving opportunities for many women. As she said in June 1986: '[W]hat is wrong with having a part-time job? Many women like a part-time job ... It suits them. It raises the standard of living of their family and then they go out and spend what they have earned or part of it and then they spend it on other things.' A few months later, her language was again defensive: 'What is wrong with working part-time? Many women like it. It suits the pattern of running the house. Often it suits the pattern of being home with the children for some part of the day ... It also means that the family has a higher standard of living and there-fore can spend on other things and perhaps bring into existence other jobs full-time.'[27] Thatcher simply ignored the single mothers, and wives of unemployed men, who worked part-time from necessity, but would have preferred the higher pay and greater job security that came from full-time employment.

Women's central role as the guardians of the family also made them particularly sensitive to issues such as education. Thatcher's education policy focused on the importance of choice, and the dangers of bur-eaucratisation and homogenisation in education. As such, it built on earlier Conservative critiques of one-size-fits-all comprehensive educa-tion. What differentiated Thatcher's approach to education policy was her focus on its impact on individual children and families. Here again the family replaced 'society' as the principal social unit, and within the family unit, it was the mother to whom Thatcher's policies were most clearly directed.

Having established Thatcher's appeal to the female electorate, the rest of this chapter uses polling data to look first at the ways in which some women responded to Thatcher as a female role model, before exploring female reactions to Thatcher's economic and social policies.

Women and Thatcherism: a view from the polls

Margaret Thatcher and the Conservative Party could, and did, seek to shape women's perceptions of their policies, but how women responded to Thatcher and Thatcherism was ultimately outside the control of the leader and her party. One fact that the Conservative Party could spin, but not ultimately change, was Thatcher's sex. Going into the 1979 election, in particular, it was unclear how Thatcher's sex would play with her fellow women. Would they feel a special affinity to her because of her sex? Or were women particularly suspicious of other women?

As long as women had been involved in politics, it has been suggested that women's hostility towards fellow members of their sex would work against female candidates.[28] After Thatcher's victory in the leadership contest in 1975, the BBC reported 'some Labour MPs, who can be pretty conservative themselves about these things, are much enjoying themselves taunting [the] Tories with the fear that a woman leader will frighten off women voters and keep Labour in office for ever more – one of those common beliefs for which there seems to be no evidence at all'.[29] Yet Thatcher herself admitted that women had been the biggest obstacles to her selection as a candidate in the 1950s.[30] Curiosity about the effect of Thatcher's gender on female voters served as an initial spur for both the Labour Party and the *Sunday Times* to commission polling from MORI on the difference between men's and women's attitudes towards the Tory leader in April 1979. What they found was that, contrary to conventional wisdom, women professed to be more sympathetic than men both to female leaders in general, and to Thatcher in particular.

Now, here women's responses need to be read with a grain of salt. We should not automatically infer that women's professed support both for Thatcher and for women in leadership roles more generally indicates a hitherto unappreciated support for feminism among British women. Studies of opinion polling have long appreciated that people lie to pollsters.[31] In 1970s Britain, when even non-self-professed feminists would have found it difficult to escape the international enthusiasm generated by the Conservatives' election of a female leader, women may have felt it was 'right' to profess support for Thatcher. On the other hand, men who may have secretly admired Thatcher as a strong woman might have been ashamed to own up to their admiration, either to themselves or to a pollster. Further, women's stated reasons for liking Margaret Thatcher, which were most frequently put in terms of her strength of character, need not have had a feminist origin.

Women were particularly prevalent among the grassroots soldiers of the New Right, and it is conceivable that such Conservative women would have admired a strong male leader to an equal extent. However, the evidence suggests that at least some women liked Thatcher for being a strong female role model. While Thatcher herself denied being a feminist, it does not follow that those who voted for her did not do so for feminist reasons. Even women who professed to disdain the feminist movement as much as Thatcher might well have felt her success to be a victory for their sex and liked her for it. Randall and Lovenduski note: 'Surely, the very fact of her occupation of the supreme political office, and of the confidence and authority with which she carried out its duties, had some effect. She must have made it seem more possible for women to be powerful, to succeed in a "man's world".'[32] Lovenduski and Norris again implicitly endorse this view when they describe Thatcher as 'an important component of the party's positive feminine image'.[33] And Campbell owns that 'Part of many women's pleasure in Thatcher's power is everything to do with her gender:

Thatcher is more powerful than all the men around her, she bosses them around.'[34]

While such statements may seem so obvious as to be self-evident, Thatcher's appeal to women qua women has hitherto been given little consideration by historians or political scientists, partially owing to the fact that feminist scholars of Thatcher rejected the notion of her as a feminist role model, and Thatcherite sympathisers were too disdainful of feminists to consider Thatcher in that context. As Heather Nunn has written:

Thatcher's political presence highlighted a taboo area of feminist analyses: woman's engagement with structures of political power and discourse that aggressively asserted nationhood, militarism and state authority. Thatcher constituted a problem ... [in that h]er authority seemed to derive from both her movement across gender identities, troubling the binaries of sexual difference, and also through the way she endorsed an unequal gender divide by locating women within the domestic and moral sphere and placing men as active political subjects.[35]

On 25 April 1979, MORI gave a private polling presentation to the Labour Party on the results of a poll commissioned for the *Sunday Times* in which members of both sexes were asked whether they would prefer a man or a woman to serve in various leadership and professional roles. A majority of all respondents expressed a preference for a man in each of the six categories surveyed: to work for; as Prime Minister; as Member of Parliament; as a doctor; as a magistrate; and as a trade union official. However, with the exception of 'as a magistrate', for which women actually preferred a man in greater numbers than men, women's preference for a male representative was comparatively weak.[36]

In the same presentation, MORI's founder Bob Worcester and his team produced the results of a private poll conducted for the party in which they named a list of personality traits and asked respondents whether they felt that men or women were more likely to exhibit such traits, and also whether they felt that either Callaghan or Thatcher exhibited each trait. The results were given both as aggregates of all respondents and separately for women only. With a few exceptions, women were less harsh on their own sex than men; and more likely to associate positive traits with Thatcher, to disassociate negative traits from her, and to associate negative traits with Callaghan. Women were appreciably less likely to believe that men were more rational than women, and more likely to think that men were more unreliable than women. While more men thought that women were the more devious sex, women were inclined to believe men more devious than women. In reference to the particular man and woman under question, women

were appreciably less likely to perceive Thatcher as devious, less likely
to see Thatcher as snobbish or emotional, and more likely to view her
as both compassionate and intelligent. They were also much less likely
than men to view Callaghan as intelligent. Overall, the two polls suggested, first, that being a woman was not going to hurt Thatcher with
other women, and, second, that women perceived Thatcher in a more
positive light than did men.[37]

Women's more sympathetic attitudes towards women in professional
and leadership roles, on the one hand, and to Margaret Thatcher, on
the other, were likely reflective of the partial but nonetheless significant
shift in attitudes towards women's work since the Second World War.
While half of the female population remained outside the workforce in
the 1980s, the other half were working either full- or part-time.[38] The
rising number of women in the workforce did not, however, signify a
flight from domesticity. A 1985 MORI survey of 1,001 women found
that 89 per cent believed a woman's first priority should be to her mar-
riage and her children, with only 1 per cent believing her first priority
should be to her job.[39] Yet, as Dolly Wilson has shown, post-war women
increasingly viewed paid work outside the home as defensible on the
grounds that it helped to provide for their children and give them a better life.[40] Of the women surveyed by MORI, 86 per cent felt that women
with children should work outside the home if they wished to do so. Over
half of those surveyed agreed that women could successfully combine a
full-time job with running a family; and, whereas only two years earlier a significant majority had expressed a preference for working for a
man over a woman, only 26 per cent professed to believe that men made
better bosses than women, as opposed to 54 per cent who disagreed.
Yet, when asked whether women had the same career options open to
them as men, less than a third agreed. According to the polling report,
'there was a considerable degree of resentment over this – two in three
(62 per cent) of those who felt their career choices were not the same as
men said they thought this was unfair'. Older women were more likely
to perceive this inequality than younger women, and it was notably the
oldest age groups surveyed (45+) who were most likely to feel that it was
important that there should be more women in Parliament.

On one level, the support that these women expressed for wom-
en's equality and the right of women to work outside the home seems
unlikely to have translated into support for Thatcher. Yet, however
paradoxical it might seem to some feminists, many women were still
able to view Thatcher as a role model, even as both her actions and
her rhetoric revealed her at best limited support for career women and
her contempt for women's liberation. By presenting herself, however

disingenuously, as a housewife who also happened to lead one of the world's most powerful democracies, Thatcher forged a bond between herself and 'ordinary' British women.[41] Her self-presentation struck a chord in a country where women were increasingly working outside the home, but where the vast majority still held conservative views about the gender order.

In the same survey in which 89 per cent said that a woman should prioritise caring for her children above her career, three-quarters of respondents (over half of whom were working women) agreed that 'children should be looked after by their mother rather than a childminder, crèche or other relative'. As the MORI analysts wrote:

> These figures suggest that sexual equality has made few strides against traditional views in the field of employment, and this is further underlined by the fact that, asked who if husband and wife both work, should take time off work when the children are sick, 71 per cent unequivocally said 'the wife' with only 28 per cent saying 'either' or 'it depends'. To some extent this reflects economic reality, as the wife is likely to earn less than the husband, but it is still a strong vote for tradition.[42]

In a world in which the majority of women may have resented the limited opportunities open to women, but still embraced the traditional gender order, Thatcher's self-presentation as the housewife Prime Minister could be viewed as striking an admirable and enviable balance between family and career. Early in her career as party leader, Patrick Cosgrave concluded that Thatcher had the potential to make 'a particularly important electoral appeal' to 'young or youngish married working women whose husbands were Labour voters with old-fashioned views on the place of women. These ladies ... had been touched by the Women's Movement to the extent of feeling some discontent with their lives, but they were not radical feminists.' He felt that Thatcher, as a career woman with traditional views about family life, 'might strike a particular chord with them'.[43] While it is not clear whether younger women married to Labour voters in particular took to Thatcher's brand of domesticated professionalism, MORI polling repeatedly reaffirmed feminine admiration for Thatcher, particularly in the early years of her premiership.

An exploration of MORI polling from the 1980s – both that produced for the commercial press and private polling for the Labour Party – sheds further light on some of the issues driving the gender gap. Starting with the run-up to the 1983 election, the Labour Party commissioned numerous investigations into the roots of Thatcher's popularity among women voters. These polls continued to show a comparatively strong *liking* of Thatcher by women. In May 1983, MORI reported: 'One of the most striking differences found between men and women is in reasons *why* people support the Conservatives. Among women, nearly half again as many women as men are attracted to support the Conservative Party by Mrs Thatcher's stronger character and personality.' 'For women, by far the most important reason for voting Conservative is Mrs Thatcher's own strength of character.' While Tory men did not own to voting Conservative for this reason, male Liberal and Labour supporters were most likely to attribute Thatcher's support to her strength of character – perhaps supposing that this was a particular draw to women voters.[44] Two years later, a survey asked women what woman they most admired. Margaret Thatcher won hands down, as the choice of 21 per cent of respondents, followed by the Queen with 12 per cent, Princess Diana with 11 per cent and the Queen Mother also with 11 per cent. The Prime Minister won by an even larger margin among ABC1 women, where she garnered 29 per cent of all votes. Thatcher's personal popularity among women persisted through her third general election victory. A 5 June 1987 memorandum from MORI to the Labour Party noted: 'when respondents are forced to choose' whom they would prefer as Prime Minister, men chose Thatcher by a margin of 1 per cent, whereas women preferred Thatcher by 13 per cent.[45]

It should not be inferred from this, however, that women voted Conservative merely to keep a woman Prime Minister in Number 10. Three-quarters of women said that, whatever their feelings about the benefits of more women MPs, they would not break party ties to vote for a female candidate.[46] In 1987, a series of MORI surveys asking whether various politicians made voters more or less likely to vote for the Labour Party yielded consistently double-digit net positives for Denis Healey, and high net positives for Bryan Gould. Barbara Castle and Harriet Harman, on the other hand, had almost the same number of detractors as supporters, whereas those that mentioned Jo Richardson and Joan Ruddock said that they made them less likely to vote Labour.[47] While these survey results were not broken down by gender, the uniform hostility to Labour's most high-profile feminist candidates suggests that feminism was not a winning proposition with most voters, male or female. While MORI only surveyed attitudes towards Labour candidates, a 1981 *Times* article on the co-founder of the SDP, Shirley Williams, presented her as the 'woman politician most women like and positively trust', arguing that her appeal lay in being 'never less than feminine' without ever 'seem[ing] to work at it'. Williams was the daughter of a famous inter-war feminist, but like Thatcher she did not wear her feminism on her sleeve, a trait that was apparently attractive to many female voters. Beatrix Campbell describes one Thatcherite Tory councillor whom she interviewed for *Iron Ladies* as, 'like many of her ilk', 'believ[ing] in equality without recognising inequality'.[48] By simultaneously being an exceptional political woman, and downplaying the extent of her own exceptionalism, Thatcher earned the solidarity of a group of women who respected successful women but would not have self-identified as feminists.

Thatcher and domestic Chancellors of the Exchequer

A strategic component of Thatcher's self-presentation as the home-maker-Prime Minister was her often-repeated characterisation of the national economy in domestic terms, a characterisation that she defended in the face of accusations that it intentionally over-simplified the complexities of national and international finance. As she claimed in November 1982: 'Some say I preach merely the homilies of housekeeping or the parables of the parlour. But I do not repent. Those parables would have saved many a financier from failure and many a country from crisis.'[49] Thatcher frequently used analogies to the domestic economy in order to counter the left's Keynesian arguments about the value of counter-cyclical spending to create jobs and boost the British economy out of recession, contending, disingenuously, that 'international economics work just the same as home economics'.[50] While her rhetoric of 'commonsense economics' was directed towards both men and women, polling showed that women related more readily to arguments framed in terms of the domestic economy.

Even as women entered the work place in ever greater numbers, they remained primarily responsible for the domestic economy. A MORI survey from 1985 found that a third of women reported that their husbands always helped them with the shopping. However, 14 per cent did all the family's shopping themselves, and a further 40 per cent said that their husband helped with the shopping only sometimes.[51] As the family's primary consumers, women could be assumed to be more sympathetic to the logic that, as families did best if they succeeded in living within their means, so too did nations. This is borne out by a 1983 survey of men's and women's attitudes towards deficit spending. Over two-thirds of both men and women supported increased public spending to create new jobs, free nursery education and increased house-building. Both men and women rated job creation through increased public spending as the highest priority facing government. Women were, however, more likely to rate education and the NHS as important election issues. These trends held throughout Thatcher's premiership. However, only

45 per cent of women (compared to 61 per cent of men) accepted that it was appropriate for the government to 'borrow money to invest in the future'. When the question was rephrased to ask whether, 'like a household, the government shouldn't spend more money than it earns', a majority of both men and women agreed that it should not, although women again professed a greater adherence to fiscal rectitude.[52] Here, 'Mrs Thatcher's "good housewife" mentality', a modern-day equivalent of the 'domestic chancellor of the exchequer' rhetoric that Stanley Baldwin used in the 1930s to attract female support for the National Government's austerity measures, appeared to hold the same sway fifty years later.[53]

The success of Thatcher's rhetorical appeal to home economics becomes more evident when one considers that women, in the abstract, were less hostile to state intervention in the economy than men. In 1983, 79 per cent of women (10 per cent more than men) believed that the government should intervene in the market to institute price controls, and women remained more supportive of state intervention to control prices throughout the decade. Further, women were theoretically more supportive of social welfare initiatives than men.[54] However, they appeared to be unwilling to accept that the government could afford to accomplish the things that they wanted to see done. A 27 May poll (not disaggregated by gender) found that 'on the key issue of credibility', 37 per cent felt that Labour was 'making promises the country can't afford' versus only 19 per cent who felt the same way about the Tories. Writing in 1989, the Labour Party strategists Patricia Hewitt and Deborah Mattinson identified this anxiety as a crucial stumbling block to uniting women behind Labour's social programmes, as they 'dislike any idea of "throwing money at problems"' and need to be convinced that such social expenditure is in fact an investment that will reap long-term rewards.[55] Women's reluctance to believe that Britain's social problems could be solved by throwing money at them arguably limited their sympathy for Labour assertions in 1987 that the British school system's problems were best addressed by increases in state funding.

Education

In the run-up to the 1987 election, Thatcher's government turned its attention to education. Education is generally an issue in which women take a greater interest than men, due to their position as the primary carers in the majority of households.[56] This was seemingly confirmed by MORI's surveys in 1983, which saw 35 per cent of women identifying schools/education as an issue that 'will be important in helping them to decide which party to vote for at the General Election', compared to only 21 per cent of men.[57] By January 1985, interest in education had decreased, with only 11 per cent of women identifying education as an 'important issue facing Britain today', compared to only 6 per cent of men. However, the low aggregate figures masked a continued interest among women at an age likely to have young children. When those responses were broken down by age, one-quarter of women aged 35–44 identified education as an important issue, placing it far ahead of prices and inflation and law and order, and on a par with disarmament and nuclear weapons. The only issue identified as considerably more important was unemployment, a perennial first choice among men and women of all age groups in the 1980s.[58] As the data were not broken down by parental or even marital status, the link between the 35–44-year-old women's greater interest in education and the likely higher incidence of motherhood in this age group can only be inferred. However, a recent US study on 'parenthood and the gender gap' found a greater jump in interest in education and health care between mothers and non-mothers than between fathers and non-fathers, and concluded that 'because women are, on the whole, more responsible for attending to their children's education and health care needs, the more pronounced parental effects on those issues for women are not surprising'.[59]

The extent of maternal frustration with the educational system was revealed in a June 1987 MORI poll asking potential voters whether they would support a return to the system of selection based on the 11+ exam. Net approval for the suggestion was significantly higher among women (+13 per cent) than among men (+4 per cent). Among the age group most likely to have school-aged children, the 35–54-year-olds, there was an 18 per cent net approval for the suggestion. The net approval figures mask a large percentage of respondents who answered that they did not know, or had no opinion. Even among 35–45-year-old women, barely more than half supported a return to the 11+.[60] Nonetheless, it appears that such a proposal would not have been without traction had it been seriously proposed in 1987.

Labour came out early on education in the 1987 campaign, criticising the government for cutting education spending by over 10 per cent in real terms since coming to power. The party took the side of the teachers' unions in their ongoing dispute with the government, and argued that budget cuts were to blame for the falling performance in Britain's schools.[61] The Conservatives countered Labour's criticism by blaming declining student performance not on shortfalls in school funding, but on self-interested teachers and left-wing education authorities that prioritised touchy-feely, liberal curricula over maths, science and applied skills. The Conservatives' 1987 manifesto asserted: 'Parents want schools to provide their children with the knowledge, training and character that will fit them for today's world. They want them to be taught basic educational skills. They want schools that will encourage moral values: honesty, hard work and responsibility. And they should have the right to choose those schools which do these things for their children.'[62] As mentioned earlier, Thatcher's framing of education reform in terms of 'moral' as well as intellectual decline was arguably coded to appeal particularly to mothers. The Conservative proposals also played to mothers in their emphasis on the human face of educational decline. As Hewitt and Mattinson impressed upon their Labour Party colleagues: 'Extensive qualitative research suggests that women are preoccupied with the issues that concern themselves and their families directly.'[63] Whereas Labour pointed to abstract budgetary shortfalls, the Conservatives spoke in terms of individual 'consumers' of education, and promised proactive parents an opportunity to improve their particular child's circumstances.

A principal target of the government's education reforms was the teachers' unions. The continued teachers' strikes in 1987 were an issue that divided men and women. When polled in June 1987, half of male respondents agreed that 'teachers are justified on balance' in striking, whereas only 42 per cent disagreed. Women, in contrast, 'clearly oppose strike actions', with only one-third saying that they were justified.[64] The government's other principal target was the alleged mismanagement of LEAs. Their manifesto proposals ranged from creating a national curriculum to encouraging the creation of independently run and partially privately financed city academies, to increasing 'consumer choice' over schools, to 'liberating' schools from the yoke of LEAs. MORI polling on the proposal to allow schools to opt out of LEA control showed nearly half of all respondents approved of the proposal, with only one-third opposed. 'Again women are keener on the idea than men ... while 25–44-year-old women are the most enthusiastic group of all the demographic sub-groups.'[65]

Women between 25 and 55 were perceived as a key target group going into the 1987 election. In 1983, the gender gap had been widest in this age group, at 14 per cent among 25–34-year-olds, and 9 per cent among 34–54-year-olds.[66] As Campbell's work has highlighted, polling revealed these women to be the most hostile to the government's defence and nuclear policies, seemingly creating an opening for Labour. The Conservative onslaught against the education system appealed to them on grounds more propitious to the government. Brian Harrison describes the Conservatives' crusade against the Department

of Education as 'wielding populism and publicity as its weapons'.[67] The
success of the Conservatives' attempts to put education policy on the
agenda can be seen in the increased number of voters who identified
education as an issue that politicians should be talking about in the
weeks leading up to the election. While on 12 May that number was
only 22 per cent (27 per cent of women), by 2 June it had risen to 34 per
cent (40 per cent of women). Among women in that crucial 25–44 age
group, over half felt that education should be a campaign issue.[68] By 2
June 1987, polling revealed the public to be evenly divided over which
party had the best policies on education.[69] This marked an improvement for the Tories, as earlier polling had revealed net positives for
public opinion on Labour's education policy. As Worcester pointed out
in a memorandum to the Labour Party polls committee, '[one] policy
worth commenting on is education. Yesterday's poll found education to
be of particular importance among women generally, 25–44-year-old
women specifically and switchers. It is disappointing to see that women
generally are 7 points less likely to say that the Labour policy on education is good than men.'[70] In a memorandum on marginal constituencies, MORI reported that 'women in general are more concerned about
education (37 per cent to men's 29 per cent) … This doesn't necessarily
work well for Labour, as women tend to agree with Mrs Thatcher's views
on education.'[71] The Labour Party's attempts to shift the debate back
to the issue of funding were thwarted by the Conservative-dominated
popular press, which kept 'the education issue … well-contained', with
the emphasis on the 'left-wing domination of schools'.[72] While the
extent to which education policy influenced mothers' voting decisions is
unknown, it is significant that Labour's revival between 1983 and 1987
was weakest among women aged 35–54, and that even working-class
women in this age group remained evenly split between Labour and the
Conservatives in 1987.[73]

Conclusion

This chapter has sought to use polling data to shed light on under-
appreciated aspects of Thatcher's appeal to women voters in the 1980s.
Economics, education and Thatcher's position as a role model were
obviously not the only reasons that women supported the Conservative
Party in the 1980s. Like men, many women voted for (and against)
the Conservatives because of their policies on defence, council housing and trade unions. Further, as Campbell emphasised in *Iron Ladies*,
Thatcher's tough stance on crime clearly appealed to many women,
particularly older women. Yet, without discounting the value of

Campbell's work, this chapter suggests that her emphasis on the centrality of 'law and order' has been overstated, and has obscured other aspects of Thatcher's appeal to women voters.

In the lead-up to the 1983 election, the only group interviewed by MORI to rank 'Law and Order/Riots' among the top three issues that would 'be important in helping them to decide which party to vote for at the next General Election' was those aged 55 and over. In a 1985 poll, this time disaggregated by sex, only women aged 55+ ranked law and order as one of their top three priorities. While two-thirds of women surveyed in 1984 supported increased spending on law and order, less than one-quarter strongly supported this as a policy priority. Further, the high profile given to the issues of robbery, petty theft and juvenile delinquency by the government may arguably have worked against the Conservatives among older voters. A 1987 poll found that, while all segments of the population overwhelmingly thought the Tories to be the stronger party on law and order, pensioners were slightly more likely to prefer the opposition parties on this issue – an expression of dissatisfaction with the status quo that Labour sought to play on in its campaign propaganda.[74] The importance of fear among elderly women should not be discounted as a reason for their support for the Conservative Party, but we need to look beyond crime and punishment to explain why Thatcher maintained a plurality of supporters among all but the youngest and most industrially well-organised female voters throughout her premiership.

Extrapolating too broadly from opinion polls is always risky. It is impossible to know for certain, first, whether respondents answered pollsters' questions honestly, and, second, what motivated their responses. Further, polling figures are by definition aggregates and averages. Nonetheless, a close reading of polling data can tell us much about the way in which political constituencies are constructed and held together over time. Thatcher's image as Britain's most powerful housewife, and her presentation of her fiscal and education policies as a logical outgrowth of her commonsense approach to governing household and country were important components of her appeal to many women voters in the 1980s.

7 Margaret Thatcher and the decline of class politics

Jon Lawrence and Florence Sutcliffe-Braithwaite

Ditching the class baggage

When Margaret Thatcher became leader of the Conservative Party in 1975, British public discourse remained heavily stamped by the impress of social class. Indeed, arguably 'languages of class' were more ubiquitous in the 1970s than they had been a decade earlier. In the 1960s, Wilson's shrewd campaign against the Conservatives' 'thirteen wasted years' had traded heavily on a classless populism. In the anti-establishment rhetoric of Wilson's proposed technocratic revolution, the rule of the privileged 'classes' was to give way to a new meritocracy capable of reversing Britain's relative economic decline.[1] Reworking earlier tropes about the unity of workers 'by hand and by brain', Labour tapped into the new managerial, 'technicist' strand in post-war thinking to proclaim that a 'New Britain' could be built from a production-centred alliance of planners, technicians and workers.[2] The political rhetoric of the mid 1970s was very different. Left-wingers like Michael Meacher looked forward to 'the coming class struggle' and argued that only 'class politics' could deliver the 'radical political change' that Britain needed.[3] Writing in December 1976, Robert Kilroy-Silk (of all people) declared 'there must be no truce in the class war'; 'the Labour Party', he insisted, 'is a class party. God help us when it ceases to be so. It is a class party because it was formed by and for the working class to protect and advance its interests.'[4] True, more mainstream Labour figures generally avoided such explicit appeals to class feeling, but the tone of their pronouncements was nonetheless more conflictual than a decade earlier. Not only did the two election manifestos of 1974 place the defence of workers' rights and interests centre-stage, but during the February campaign Denis Healey famously declared that the party would 'squeeze property speculators until the pips squeak' (that political mythology quickly translated this into the more generalised pledge to 'squeeze the rich' tells us much about the febrile social and political context in which Thatcher emerged as Conservative Party leader).[5]

With the media awash with talk of private armies, coups and the breakdown of ordered government, right-wing polemicists warned of 'the decline and fall of the middle class', and sought to whip up organised, middle-class resistance to the incoming Labour government and its trade union allies.[6] Polls in the mid 1970s consistently found that almost two-thirds of Britons believed there to be 'a class struggle in this country', double the level recorded at the start of the decade.[7] And after October 1974, as their party slumped to its fourth defeat in five elections (registering a then record low poll of 35.8 per cent), pessimistic Conservatives began to debate whether their party was doomed to permanent minority status – driven back to its 'south-eastern laager'.[8] Indeed, many portrayed Thatcher's candidacy for the Conservative leadership as just another symptom of the party's malaise. Thatcher, it was argued, 'represents, by image, by class, by geography and by attitude, all that is narrowest in modern Conservatism' – indeed one *Daily Express* columnist proclaimed her to be 'totally out of touch with anybody but carefully corseted, middle-class, middle-aged ladies'. Thatcher, it was alleged, 'would turn the party into a sort of middle-class pressure group', sealing its fate as a rump party of suburban protest.[9]

In short, Thatcher herself was stamped by class in the mid 1970s. Critics and supporters alike saw her as a symbol of middle-class resistance to big government, to social liberalism, and even to social change itself. But no Conservative leader could afford to become the figurehead of a Poujadist reactionary spasm, and Thatcher was careful not to fall into that trap.[10] Instead, she sought to construct a broad-based appeal which neutralised the perceived disadvantages of her southern, middle-class image. Contemporaries noted how Thatcher sought to ditch her class baggage through a personal makeover of voice, wardrobe and life story,[11] and through populist appeals to cross-cutting issues such as law and order.[12] Historians have recognised these activities, but have underestimated their significance. Like Ewen Green, most have seen this as 'covering fire', used to disguise an essentially middle-class agenda.[13]

David Cannadine insists that Thatcher 'genuinely believed that "the great middle mass of the British" was the repository of all the virtues she most admired', observing that she looked down on both 'the languid, appeasing, privileged aristocracy' and 'the traditional working class, especially organised labour'.[14] But he is too quick to conclude that 'Thatcher never projected a fully coherent social vision' and that 'she offered up no new vision of the social structure'.[15] Thatcherite political language was more creative than this suggests, though its creativity was born of necessity, not prescience.[16] Thatcher's hatred of class politics ran deep, but it was the need to play down her own class image that most urgently pressed her to minimise this theme in favour of a more positive vision of a new popular constituency that bridged the fault-lines of class.

Behind the scenes the Thatcherites were clear that they hoped to explode once and for all the Marxist/socialist model of class. The Thatcher papers bulge with articles, briefing notes and speech drafts, including some by Alfred Sherman, her trusted guru at the Centre for Policy Studies (CPS), rejecting the socialist view of class as wrong-headed propaganda. The term 'working class', for example, was dismissed as 'a Marxist term which has no meaning in any non-Marxist schema', while the 'class war' was simply a 'divisive and de-stabilising thesis' perpetuated by dogmatic partisans. Since 'class' had no objective meaning, the 'classless society' was a 'Marxist chimera'. Thatcherites planned something very different: a completely new popular constituency.[17]

Rarely in the late 1970s did Thatcher give vent to her full vitriolic feelings about class publicly. Instead, the principal line of attack was to redefine who belonged to 'the great middle mass' of British society – who constituted 'our people'. In imagining this new popular constituency Thatcher explicitly denied the salience of conventional distinctions between 'working' and 'middle' class. 'Ordinary working families', rather than 'the workers' or 'working class', occupied centre-stage. A diffuse, mutable language of 'ordinariness', hard-working respectability and family-centred individualism was mobilised to describe these people. Thatcher consistently argued that the values she stood for – values which her critics within and without the party claimed were sectional and 'middle-class' – were in fact near-universal values rooted deep in the national psyche. This shift in rhetoric was not another example of a Conservative politician mobilising the nostalgic language of 'community', or the patriotic language of 'nation', to mask potentially divisive class antagonisms. For sure, Thatcher was not averse to patriotic, 'One Nation' rhetoric,[18] but deep down her politics was about *remaking* Britain, on her terms, as 'One Nation', not about celebrating existing sources of putative national unity. Nor was it less divisive than the 'out-dated' class politics Thatcherites despised. Thatcherite populism simply depended on an alternative set of oppositions: between the people and the (liberal) 'Establishment', between the industrious and the idle, between private and public sectors. As such it could never become truly universal, or even 'hegemonic', but it could (and did) transform British politics. In this sense, the so-called 'death of class' was largely a political, not a sociological phenomenon in Britain.[19]

Later, others would call this constituency 'Middle Britain' (or later still the 'squeezed middle') and see wooing it away from Conservatism as the central objective of their New Labour projects[20] but, after a few outings in early summer 1975, Thatcher herself eschewed this slippery terminology. In May 1975, Thatcher used 'Middle Britain' narrowly to refer to 'wealth creators who are harried by taxation', but in June and July she deployed the intriguing phrase 'the masses of middle Britain' (in both cases referring to the victims of rampant price inflation).[21] But while this awkward, 'massified' formulation did not catch on, we should not assume that Thatcher and her allies therefore abandoned the political vision that it implied – namely of a broad mass of 'ordinary people' who supposedly already shared the Conservatives' 'commonsense' social and political values. Instead, they developed more subtle ways of constructing their imagined constituency. Had Thatcherites shared the reflexive, postmodern sensibilities of their New Labour successors they might have termed this their 'project'. In many respects they embraced a much bolder, more genuinely transformative political vision than Blair, Brown and company in the 1990s: the Thatcherite project meant recasting the dominant social discourses of British public politics.

Prospects for a new politics

Political scientists and historians have frequently argued that in the late 1970s Thatcher merely came into a long-maturing Tory inheritance. The manual 'working class' was shrinking, as well as becoming more prosperous; population growth was already concentrated in southern, 'Tory' England; home ownership levels had been rising for decades, and education, social mobility and television were loosening old 'tribal' social and political identities. According to Vernon Bogdanor, even the industrial militancy of the 1970s reflected the tide of consumerism and possessive individualism that was eroding Labour's core constituency.[22] But it is hard to overestimate how differently Thatcherites viewed the social and cultural changes of the late 1970s. Not only did most share (and often fuel) the near-apocalyptic mood of media crisis-mongers, they also believed that militancy, social liberalism and state dependency were sapping the 'vigorous virtues' that had made Britain great.[23] They saw themselves as locked in a battle of ideas and values in which 'socialism' appeared to be gaining the upper hand across *all social classes* in the 1970s. The contours of this paranoia will be explored in greater detail below.

Nor did wider public culture offer many reasons to think that a radical project to recast the language of politics was likely to prosper. British popular culture frequently pedalled a manifestly anachronistic view of society, peopled by crude class stereotypes. On television, *Coronation Street* (Britain's long-running northern soap opera) brought an implausibly broad range of classes together in its friendly corner shop and pub. Indeed, the Street developed its own vaudeville version of the 'class struggle' in 1976 when Jag-driving, self-made Cockney businessman Mike Baldwin took over the local clothing factory. At the same time, anachronistic comic creations from the 1960s, such as the 'poor but loyal' working-class Tories Albert Steptoe (*Steptoe and Son*, 1962–5 and 1970–74) and Alf Garnett (*Till Death Us Do Part*, 1965–8 and 1972–5), continued to draw large audiences.

Such popular representations of social class remained strongly influenced by the legacy of social realist literature and cinema from the late 1950s and early 1960s – works like Alan Sillitoe's *Saturday Night and Sunday Morning* (1958, film 1960) and Stan Barstow's *A Kind of Loving* (1960, film 1962). They lionised manly working-class heroes who had either resisted, or simply missed out on, the supposedly 'feminising' effects of post-war affluence.[24] Along with more sociological accounts of 'traditional' working-class life by writers such as Norman Dennis, Richard Hoggart and Michael Young, the 'angry young men' of the 1950s and 1960s breathed new life into old cultural stereotypes about working-classness – stereotypes that remained prominent well into the 1970s: that poverty and deprivation were primary markers of class, that the working class lived almost wholly for the moment, and (for some at least) that only men could be wholly and authentically 'working-class'.[25] In 1964, when Michael Apted and Granada TV set out to explore the effects of the British class system on children's life chances in the landmark documentary *Seven Up!*, they ignored contemporaneous sociological controversies about 'affluence' to paint a stark picture of the indelible marks of class on children's lives. Their subjects were drawn overwhelmingly from the quintessential extremes of rich and poor. This stark polarisation remained the programme's dominant focus in the 1970s, when it revisited the children at ages 14 and 21.[26]

Mainstream social science also appeared determined to reassert the primacy of class as the unbridgeable fault-line of British society in the 1960s and 70s. For some this meant ensuring that the poor did not become 'the forgotten Englishmen'.[27] Building on Richard Titmuss's pioneering work, Peter Townsend, Brian Abel-Smith, Ken Coates and others reminded the public that poverty had not been vanquished, and that millions of their fellow Britons still lived impoverished lives far removed from the comforts of the so-called affluent society.[28] Others, such as Brian Jackson and Jeremy Seabrook, followed Hoggart and the social realist writers of the 1950s in search of their own 'authentic' working class (though like Hoggart, Seabrook sounded notes of alarm about consumerism and social mobility erasing 'traditional' working-class communities).[29] In 1964 John Westergaard suggested that talk of affluence and the 'death of class' among sociologists was a diversion fuelled by right-wing propaganda,[30] but the most influential restatement of traditional sociological models of class came on the cusp of the 1970s with John Goldthorpe's and David Lockwood's sustained critique of the theory of working-class *embourgeoisement* – that key plank in the Labour revisionists' case for rethinking traditional socialism and 'class politics'. *Embourgeoisement* held that workers who had benefited from increased affluence had become middle-class in lifestyle and values, as well as in income.[31] Determined to undermine this heresy, Goldthorpe and Lockwood used a study of archetypal affluent manual workers in Luton to argue that they did not share values with the middle class, socialise with middle-class people, or aspire to be seen as 'middle-class'.[32] Affluence, they argued, might be replacing workers' supposedly 'traditional' communal culture with one that was more instrumental and privatised, but it was not instilling middle-class values. The social and cultural gulf between manual and non-manual workers remained undiminished – at most one could talk of 'normative convergence' in lifestyle and consumption patterns.[33] They downplayed changes – including the significance of 'normative convergence' – in order to argue that class remained fundamental to British society and politics. Goldthorpe and Lockwood swiftly became a staple authority for anti-revisionist Labourites who argued that after the reversals of Wilson's second government Labour must become a more unapologetic champion of 'working-class interests'.[34] Structural problems within the Labour Party crippled its dynamism in the 1970s, and the revisionism of the 1960s now appeared to many to be a disastrous mistake.[35] The political space that Wilson had exploited with his 'classless populism' became wide open for Thatcherite colonisation.

Had they thought to look, the Thatcherites might have found a few pointers towards a new politics in British popular culture. At the same time as the BBC revived the comic caricatures of both *Steptoe and Son* and *Till Death Us Do Part*, it also revived Dick Clement and Ian Le Frenais's social realist comedy *The Likely Lads* (1964–6) as *Whatever Happened to the Likely Lads?* (1973–4). The final episode was a Christmas special screened just weeks before Thatcher became leader of the Conservative Party, but it was 'The Shape of Things to Come', the final regular episode, which best summed up the programme's latent Thatcherite message. As so often, the two Geordie 'Likely Lads', Bob and Terry, argued about 'class' – specifically Bob's right still to call himself 'working-class' though he was now 'white-collar' and buying a house. Bob is shown as determined to hold on to his historic class identity for personal reasons, but his comment underscores the scope for a new popular politics of plebeian prosperity – of 'getting on'. He tells Terry: 'I went to the same school, grew up on the same streets, lived in the same draughty houses. But that's my point. You still want to live like that, you like the old working-class struggle against the odds. What you won't realise is that some of us won the struggle and it's nothing to be ashamed of.'[36]

To later commentators, sociological work from this period also offers hints that the 1970s might offer the opportunity for a new politics of individualism and aspiration. This was not about the emergence of new aspirational groupings, such as those conjured up in the 1980s stereotypes of the 'yuppy' or 'Loadsamoney'; rather older currents in popular culture were refracted in new ways as the rising expectations of the post-war era stalled in the deteriorating economic climate (and labour relations) of the 1970s. As Mike Savage has shown in his re-analysis of survey data from the 1960s and 1970s, among British workers 'class was often associated with personal characteristics such as being ordinary, natural and authentic'.[37] Affluent manual workers, such as those studied by Goldthorpe and Lockwood in Luton, proved especially keen to deny that class impinged on their everyday lives, either at home or at work, and absolutely denied the salience of the supposed gulf between manual and non-manual labour. But Savage has also found evidence of an idiosyncratic view of 'class' among supposedly 'traditional' manual workers. Tyneside shipyard workers tended to contrast themselves not with conventional 'middle-class' figures from their own experience, but with caricatured representations of the 'upper class' such as the 'idle rich', the landed classes or the 'establishment'.[38] Savage has identified a deep-rooted 'rugged individualism' running through British working-class culture. Down to the 1970s it characteristically found expression in *collective* strategies for defending autonomy and self-esteem within the workplace, but there was always potential for it to find expression via less solidaristic outlets.[39] Ray Pahl drew similar conclusions from his famous study of gender and work on the Isle of Sheppey, *Divisions of Labour* (1984), which began in early 1978. Pahl stressed the deep historical roots of specifically *English* individualism, and argued that for most workers collectivism had never been more than an instrumental strategy for maximising family well-being.[40] He found that employers 'were seen by many as better-paid workers, whose job it is to provide the means of getting money for other workers', and argued strongly for the emergence of a large 'middle mass' of British workers – perhaps two-thirds of the population – strongly orientated towards 'privatised', family-centred consumption strategies.[41] Looking back on his research in 1988, Pahl reflected how closely Thatcher's 'national political statements' echoed the 'archetypal "respectable" values' and 'the home-centred values of Sheppey'.[42]

The contours of a new language

The work of Savage and Pahl helps to explain why the Thatcherite project could work in late 1970s Britain, but these powerful interpretations of workers' values, aspirations and individualistic culture were unavailable to the Thatcherites as they planned their Conservative 'counter-revolution'. It was not a culture to which Thatcher, as an Oxford Young Conservative and then a millionaire's wife, had had much exposure since her time as a grocer's daughter in Grantham (and nor had many of her associates). But if orthodox opinion continued to assert the centrality of class to British life and politics, Thatcherites did have access to at least one self-consciously heterodox voice. In 1976 the proto-Thatcherite CPS published Ferdynand Zweig's extended essay, *The New Acquisitive Society*. Zweig's impressionistic, 'gentlemanly' approach to sociology had long been out of favour among academic social scientists,[43] but this did not prevent him from capturing the attention of the Thatcherite inner circle. Ignoring the extent to which the Luton study had been constructed to disprove his own version of the *embourgoisement* thesis,[44] Zweig proclaimed Goldthorpe and Lockwood's 'normative convergence' to be just another way of conceptualising rapid social changes which were blurring the distinction between manual and non-manual labour.[45] Zweig argued not only that the proportion of manual workers self-identifying as 'working-class' was in secular decline, but that there was an ambivalence and 'emotional flatness' in workers' attitudes to 'class'. 'The idea of class', he concluded, 'seems to be relegated, in the workers' minds, to something unimportant.'[46]

In his foreword to the book, John Vaizey, himself a renegade from the left, like so many of those associated with the CPS, highlighted Zweig's argument that Britain was witnessing 'the end of the old working class and the reciprocal of this – that is, the end of the old middle class'.[47] Vaizey identified both opportunity and threat in this transformation. He welcomed the growth of home ownership, real wages, savings and education as evidence that, as Zweig put it, 'the real ambition of the working class ... the abolition of itself *qua* class', had 'to a considerable extent ... been achieved'.[48] On the other hand, he stressed the inherent dangers of 'a radical shift in the structure of middle-class values' caused by upward social mobility, growing reliance on big public services provided by socialist governments, and the adoption of 'militant trade union attitudes by middle-class people'.[49] The *embourgeoisement* thesis had been a child of 1950s optimism about material and social progress, even if its birth coincided with the first pangs of 'declinist' doubt.[50] By the mid 1970s 'declinism' had become a national disease, and its grip was nowhere stronger than on the Conservative right (even if this was partly tactical: Thatcher certainly endorsed the view that, electorally, the Conservatives' best hope lay with talking up 'the *national decline theme*').[51] In this context, the threat of middle-class '*de-bourgeoisement*' seemed at least as great as the opportunity of working-class *embourgeoisement*.

Sir Keith Joseph had been frank about the ambition to change popular culture during the course of his famous series of speeches rethinking Conservatism in 1974–5.[52] Addressing the Economic Research Council in early 1975, Joseph declared that 'the objective of our lifetime, as I have come to see it, is *embourgeoisement*'. 'Bourgeois' to Joseph indicated a set of cultural attributes which the middle class had historically been more likely to cultivate, but which were not inherently linked to any one section of society ('middle-class' itself he saw as a sociological descriptor of dubious value). *Embourgeoisement* did not mean creating a 'classless society', but rather a society based on 'a common value system' – one in which it would be possible to declare 'we are all bourgeois now'.[53] Suspicious of attempts to mould behaviour by legislation, the New Right hoped, in Joseph's words, to 're-create the conditions under which the values we cherish can form the cement of our society. Our job is to re-create conditions which will again permit the forward march of *embourgeoisement*.' For *embourgeoisement* appeared no less 'halted' than the forward march of labour in 1970s Britain. Joseph, like Vaizey, feared the march of 'universal proletarianisation' – the very survival of 'bourgeois' values was in doubt.[54] Thatcher concurred. Reading a summary of Patrick Hutber's alarmist *Decline and Fall of the Middle Class* in 1976, Thatcher highlighted a section calling for the '*embourgeoisement of the majority of the population*' (not, note, the *whole* population: just one of many indications that Thatcherites were unconcerned about the fact that some would fail to be part of their brave new world; this was not a major problem, given Britain's first-past-the-post voting system).[55] The Conservatives' task was to decontaminate the middle classes of collectivism and socialism, while persuading aspirational workers that restoring small government and free markets would create the conditions in which they, and their families, could 'get on'. Thus at the heart of the Thatcherite project lay a culture war. Thatcherites still used conventional, occupation-based demarcations of class (hence their concern to understand social change within 'middle' and 'work-ing'-class groups): these were, after all, deeply ingrained in public discourse and had a basic usefulness. But they already considered culture more important than socio-economic structures.

How were cultures to be changed, when human nature meant that people could not be coerced by legislation to be good? First, governments could set rational frameworks which rewarded productive effort and responsible decisions. This understanding drove decisions on taxes, benefits, council house sales and privatisation – of which more later. But Thatcher was also aware that her boundless conviction in her own rhetoric was itself a powerful tool for change. Whatever anxieties Thatcher might have felt about social trends, in public she was careful (unlike Joseph) to speak as though it was self-evident that the vast majority of 'ordinary' Britons shared her decent, 'commonsense' values. Thatcher consistently argued, first, that old class labels were pernicious and out of date, and, second, that the values others labelled 'middle-class' (or 'bourgeois') were, in truth, universal 'British' values shared by 'ordinary', 'decent' people whatever their social background. Speaking on the eve of the 1975 leadership contest, Thatcher argued that 'the income groups have got all muddled up these days ... if several of us went along to a cinema together from totally different backgrounds and sat there watching, you couldn't label us from looking at us, either from looking at us in appearance or from what we did'. Underscoring her 'anti-class' message, she proclaimed, 'I hate these labels, I really hate them. I simply don't understand why you can't look at a person quite apart from their social background for what they are, for what they can do, for what contributions they can make.' In the same ITV interview, she then proceeded to counter the argument that her appeal was narrowly class-based: 'I see Britain as having an entirely what you would call a middle-class approach. I call it a fundamentally conservative approach with a small c.'[56] Similarly, in 1977 she rejected the relevance of class in politics, declaring '[p]eople no longer think that way. Many of the typical classifications ... are totally out of date.'[57]

In May 1977 we find Thatcher telling *Sunday Telegraph* readers that it was 'insulting' to assert that her 'derided "middle-class" values' were not 'instinctively held by a majority of working people'.[58] In her adoption speech as candidate for Finchley in 1979, Thatcher termed her core constituency the 'quiet majority', adding, in a revealing annotation, that its defining qualities were: 'Hard work, pay their taxes, live within their means, don't demonstrate, don't strike, who are law-abiding citizens.'[59] Time and again, Thatcher sought to present the

Conservatives as a 'party of ordinary, commonsense, hardworking freedom loving people'.[60] Never afraid to mobilise a platitude, Thatcher repeatedly stressed the theme of 'ordinariness' to construct a bond between herself and the aspirational electorate she hoped to win for Conservatism and 'bourgeois values'. She spoke of '[h]onest, loyal and decent people – ordinary working men and women' who had become victims of the closed shop, and claimed to understand that 'the ordinary person wants really to be independent, doesn't like being dependent on the State'.[61] She rehabilitated her own modest upbringing (which previous PR had largely smothered) to sustain this claim to 'ordinariness', insisting that her credo was 'borne out by the development in my own life going to an ordinary state school, having no privileges at all', and that 'I had a very ordinary background – probably a lot more ordinary than many of their own [Labour's] front bench'.[62] Thatcher used the terms 'ordinary people' or 'ordinary working people' at 175 different public events between 1975 and 1990.[63]

Her 'ordinary people' were hard-working, independent, family-centred and determined to 'get on'. She insisted that only the free market could secure 'the dignity and independence of the worker': it would cast off the shackles of both government and union bosses. Sometimes she spoke in 'traditionally' gendered terms of defending 'the average working man and his family' against Labour misrule.[64] But more often she was careful to recognise that 'hard-working families' now relied heavily on women's as well as men's paid employment. In many of her powerful pleas for lower direct taxation she used gender-neutral terms, such as: 'People don't go out to work for the Chancellor of the Exchequer. They go out to work for their family, for their children, to help look after their parents.'[65] Appealing for the votes of moderate trade unionists in 1979, Thatcher argued, 'Trade union members, whether they vote for us or not, are not a thing apart. They're first and foremost, members of families, *mothers, fathers, sons and daughters* who share our values and who want to see once more a healthy Britain.'[66] But then, as John Vaizey had stressed in 1976, one of the hallmarks of the so-called 'new' working class was 'the increased tendency of working-class women to work, so that most families are now two-income families'.[67] Opponents and historians alike have been too quick to assume that the Thatcherites' social conservatism made them hostile to such trends:[68] rather it predisposed them to envisage women's increased economic independence (like men's) as bounded within (and subservient to) stable, nuclear families.[69]

Thatcher's attempt to construct a new social constituency drew strength from a populist idiom which sought to present the 'establishment', *bête noire* of 1960s radicals, as a left-socialist oligarchy restraining the natural acquisitiveness of 'free-born' Britons. Thatcher denounced what she called 'the class structure of Socialism ... more rigid than anything experienced in the nineteenth century', under which 'there are only two classes – those who have power and those who do not'.[70] According to Thatcher, the socialist denial of free choice 'does not produce a classless society; on the contrary it produces the most stratified of all societies, divided into two classes: the powerful and the powerless; the party-bureaucratic elite and the manipulated masses'.[71] The overthrow of this politicised 'class' system was central to Thatcher's distinctive version of 'One Nation' politics. She tapped into widespread suspicion of a politicised, interventionist state in order to restore popular faith in the comparative neutrality of markets as arbiters of people's fortunes. As in the nineteenth century, the success of the strategy depended on popular mistrust of politicians' disinterestedness, and a strong residual strain of 'rugged individualism'.[72] In this sense, 'declinism' shaped the reception of Thatcherism as much as its construction; no less than Wilson's earlier populism, it fed off – and fed – contempt for a discredited 'establishment'.[73] Thatcher proclaimed a vision of 'hard-working families' held back by a meddling and incompetent political elite which wanted to keep people 'in their place' every bit as much as any Victorian squire.

Forging a new constituency

In the run-up to the 1979 election two policies embodied the Conservatives' appeal to popular individualism: selling council houses to their tenants and cutting income tax. In 1975 Thatcher highlighted a passage in a Conservative Research Department (CRD) paper on housing calling for 'the extension of choice: – *80 per cent home ownership in the 1980s* ... is not necessarily an impossible dream'.[74] Accelerating the sale of council houses was seen as the quickest and simplest way to move towards this goal, though Thatcher famously baulked at the idea of simply giving the houses to their sitting tenants for fear of offending 'our people' – i.e. those already paying mortgages.[75] Crucially, the policy was also seen as a vital means of sidelining class division. In 1978, Thatcher declared that 'Council housing ... does more than any other single factor to stress class divisions in the community' and that the Conservatives' goal must be 'a Nation in which only a small minority of the population live as municipal tenants'.[76] The objective of reverse social engineering could hardly have been more explicit; nor could the limits to Thatcher's 'One Nation' ambitions.

On tax, Thatcher was equally clear. Quizzed about her message for this 'predominantly working-class' region on Tyne-Tees TV in 1977, Thatcher replied: 'we've got to have more incentives for those people who work jolly hard ... Sometimes when they do they get not only extra tax, which cuts down their pay packet, but they also get complications with the way the extra £6 on Phase 1 operated.'[77] Here high taxes and government incomes policies were presented as twin evils of an over-zealous state which stopped workers and their families from 'getting on' (though she was also playing on workers' fears about state intervention eroding customary 'differentials'). Thatcher was unapologetic about her support for 'a return to free collective bargaining' in the private sector, and in 1979 the Conservative election campaign focused remorselessly on the erosion of specifically *working-class* living standards under Labour.[78] Television viewers were repeatedly told that, since 1945 'the average industrial worker's real take-home pay has gone up nearly four-and-a-half times more' under Conservative governments, and that 'the British working man has been weighed down by more and more tax. More direct taxes, like income tax. In fact more tax on almost everything you earn.'[79] Behind the scenes, the development of taxation policy was closely linked to concern that perverse interactions between the tax and benefit systems created a 'poverty trap', or, more pejoratively, the 'why work?' syndrome. Here too Thatcherites desperately worked to find a method of reverse social engineering which would leave the poor with no option but to take 'responsible' decisions to look after their families.[80] It is commonly assumed that neo-liberal governments have used incentives and structures to encourage and reward particular behaviours because it is cheaper (and less politically exposed) than big government projects and interventionism (e.g. incomes policies). But we should perhaps take seriously Thatcher's testimony that a particular understanding of 'human nature' lay at the heart of this early 'nudge' approach to public policy.[81]

Although at other times 'morals' and 'values' were placed ahead of economics in the Thatcherite pantheon,[82] there was no place for such purism in a close-fought election. Even key Thatcherite advisors such as John Hoskyns were clear that the 1979 campaign must focus on Labour's failure to raise living standards and its crippling marginal tax rates for 'average' earners.[83] The appeal to acquisitiveness was explicit in the 1979 election broadcasts. The country was told, 'We will give people back their ambitions and drive. Make it possible for people to earn more so that they can buy more.' Thatcher ended the same broadcast by repeating the homily that people 'don't work for the Chancellor of the Exchequer, they work for their families. So we've got to cut the tax on earnings and the tax on skill.'[84] Four days later, she ended another election broadcast by personalising the theme of incentives: 'If we leave you with more of your own money by cutting tax, it will be worthwhile to work harder. Will be worthwhile to do the extra overtime. Will be worthwhile to acquire an extra skill.'[85] There are hints of a subtle, but significant, mismatch between the public face of the 1979 campaign and what core Thatcherites thought about crude appeals to affluence: John Hoskyns and Norman Strauss's 'Stepping Stones' strategy document warned that *'The promise of material improvement is not enough.'*[86] The sentence had been highlighted by Thatcher.

Lack of confidence led Thatcher and her allies to compromise their deepest beliefs in 1979. They were as yet not *sure* that their social vision would find a fertile reception among aspirational workers willing to take their chances with the free market. They wanted to construct a cross-class popular appeal around battle cries about 'freedom,' 'self-reliance' and 'enterprise', but as yet they lacked the assurance to ignore the calls of pollsters and media experts for a crude materialist appeal to familiar class groups, particularly the so-called 'C2' skilled working class. Hence the mobilisation, in the election broadcasts of 1979, of hackneyed images of 'typical' skilled manual workers in denim overalls complaining of 'years of training going unrewarded'; hence, too, the determination to assert that Conservatives, rather than Labour, were now 'the party of the working man'.[87] We know that Thatcher's speech-writing team felt Saatchi & Saatchi's campaign was 'inappropriate' and that 'the wrong theme [was] being struck', but we also know that in 1979 Thatcher ultimately sided with the media professionals.[88]

Things were very different in 1983. The party election broadcast on 9 June displayed no evidence of the old class stereotypes. Instead, 'ordinary' members of the public were now shown praising Thatcher's achievements as the architect of national renewal in snappy, vox pop street interviews. None of those interviewed could be placed easily in class terms. Most were filmed as 'talking heads', offering few visual clues to occupation or income level, and they spoke in accents ranging from mildly regional to mildly posh (remarkably, all appeared to be southern English accents: Thatcherites could now afford to be more comfortable conflating 'Britain' with England, more specifically southern England, a tension that had dogged Thatcherite rhetoric throughout the later 1970s). Thatcher herself now conveyed the aspirational, class-blind call to 'ordinary people' that had remained muted during the 1979 campaign. She declared:

I offer the certainty of liberty and the chance of property ownership ... That people should be able to own their own homes is deep at the heart of Conservative philosophy ... Never mind about public ownership – in practice that gives nobody anything – but personal ownership that rightly rewards the efforts of ordinary people ... That they should acquire property, which brings with it security and independence, is the very essence of what I am in politics to accomplish.[89]

The battle for what Thatcherites were willing, at least when speaking to sympathetic ears, to call 'bourgeois' values was now in full swing. A new political language was being born.

During the 1980s, Thatcherites wielded the power of office to weaken bastions of class discourse. One institution which came under attack was the discipline of sociology. The budget of the research council responsible for social sciences was cut by half, and, as a some-time Conservative advisor and professor of demography put it, the Thatcherites 'effectively ignore[d] British sociology'.[90] In 1982 Keith Joseph attempted to engineer the dissolution of the Social Sciences Research Council. Throughout the 1970s Joseph had still felt that some subjects might usefully be subjected to sociological analysis,[91] but the sociologists' determined defence of class analysis ultimately made them *persona non grata* in Thatcherite Britain. Sociologists insisted on economically and occupationally based definitions of class, and on the importance of class in structuring lifestyles and life chances: the very propositions Thatcherites denied. The attack on sociology was intended to sideline elements which might challenge the new Thatcherite understandings of society centred on individuals and families.

The unexpectedly enthusiastic public response to the flotation of British Telecom in 1984 added a new dimension to the emerging Thatcherite social politics. When the government sought to privatise British Gas two years later they sanctioned the demotic 'Tell Sid' (not Sidney) publicity campaign. It seemed designed as much to promote the idea of 'popular capitalism' as to sell shares in a utility company.[92] By the 1987 election Thatcher was proclaiming 'popular capitalism is on the march', and promising that by the end of a third Conservative term 'there will be still more families owning more property. More homes, more shares, more second pensions and more savings.'[93] By now Thatcher was openly triumphalist; the direction of history had been reversed:

Today, it is Socialism which is in retreat and Conservatism which is advancing ... people are finding that what we stand for is in tune with their own hopes and dreams. It doesn't strike them as a political dogma, but simple commonsense, that people should want to buy their own home, set aside something for their old age, have shares in companies they work for or buy from, and do the best for their children.[94]

It would take almost another decade for Labour to stake out its own rival claim to this imagined 'Middle Britain' of property-owning, 'hard-working families'.

Necessity, as much as vision, may have driven Thatcher to reach out to a new constituency in the mid 1970s, but that should not lead us to underestimate the transformation she wrought in the language of British politics. With hindsight, sociologists and political scientists have been attracted to a neat story which has the Thatcherites riding a wave of independent socio-economic change in the 1970s. Returning to examine what Thatcherites thought during their difficult years in opposition suggests that they were less riding a wave than fighting a desperate rearguard action against powerful trends which appeared to be entrenching socialist collectivism. It also throws into question the idea of discrete social changes which can be divorced from the rhetoric of the victors of history.

8   Defiant dominoes: working miners and the 1984–5 strike

David Howell

It's them blessed Yorkshire an' Welsh colliers as does it ... It's a union strike this is, not a men's strike.

(Mrs Bower, February 1912)[1]

We are not dealing with niceties here. We shall not be constitutional-ised out of a defence of our jobs. Area by Area will decide, and in my opinion it will have a domino effect.

(Michael McGahey, March 1984)[2]

In March 1984, Yorkshire pickets made the short motorway journey south to the Nottinghamshire coalfield. They sought solidarity against pit closures. Most Nottinghamshire miners rejected the call and con-tinued to work, protected when necessary by large numbers of police, both local and imported. In the months that followed, the reputed soli-darity of these mining communities was often expressed not in oppos-ition to employer or government but against their own trade union. On May Day, working and striking miners each demonstrated outside the Mansfield headquarters of the Nottinghamshire Area of the National Union of Mineworkers. Their officials were themselves divided in their vehement responses to the passions of the divided and massive demon-stration. The working majority in the county gained the public approval of Margaret Thatcher.[3] Litigation by miners opposed to the strike led eventually to the sequestration of the assets of the National Union of Mineworkers. Eventually the divisions and animosities of the year-long dispute produced a breakaway union.

The images vividly portray organised labour's most decisive defeat of the Thatcher years – the sense of a movement in disarray and incap-able of responding effectively to a concerted and distinctive political challenge. The divisions of 1984 contrasted with a decade earlier, when the second miners' strike within two years had provoked the Heath government into calling an election. The result was a defeat that was narrow, but definitive. Heath's eviction fed myths about the industrial and potential political strength of miners that sustained the victors and aggrieved the vanquished. The reversal a decade later was not a simple matter of Heathite irresolution succeeded by Thatcherite determination. The later victory owed much to the complexities of mining trade unionism. Understanding of the Thatcher years can be developed by analysis of a major adversary.

Cultures of mining unionism

An understanding of the working and the litigious miner requires consideration of the diverse cultures and traditions of mining trade unionism. The use of the plural here is significant. Miners have often been portrayed as expressing an industrial and political solidarity rarely found among other groups of industrial workers. Yet such belief in solidarity expressed at best an aspiration and arguably meant the embracing of a myth that could be a poor guide to effective strategy.

The National Union of Mineworkers, born on New Year's Day 1945, was the successor to the Miners' Federation of Great Britain (MFGB). The earlier organisation had been described accurately by its title. It was precisely a federation of district trade unions, each with its own organisational structure, its own rule book and enjoying a large amount of autonomy. Yet against such local priorities there were pressures for federation in order to secure national standards of wages and conditions. The memory of depression and the experience of wartime state control together led to the reform of the MFGB. It became the NUM.[4]

The remaking was limited. The District unions became Constituent Associations of the NUM, defined as Areas within the national rules. Each remained an independent trade union with its own rules and distinctive practices. Most funding stayed in the Areas to resource bureaucracies that, in the optimistic first decade of nationalisation, could support large numbers of full-time officials. In contrast, the National Union had only two full-time officials: the president and a general secretary. Essentially the NUM remained a de facto federation. The Areas were diverse in both size and function. In some coalfields the craftsmen had their own organisations. There were separate Areas for white-collar workers (the Colliery Officials and Staff Area, COSA), and for the cokemen. In some districts in the midlands, some craftsmen were organised into a separate Power Group.[5]

Such diversities rested on, but were not determined by, contrasting economic experiences. Coalfields varied in their geology, their costs of production, the profitability of markets and, under private ownership, the flexibility of colliery companies. Miners had contrasting expectations about security, levels of payment and the reasonableness of managers and employers. Often they lived in communities connected to a specific colliery; but sometimes, as in parts of Lancashire, Nottinghamshire and Staffordshire, they were one element within cities or large towns. All these factors had helped to shape the cultures of particular coalfields. Some, like Durham, Yorkshire and Nottinghamshire, were industrially cautious and stood politically on the Labour right. In contrast, South Wales and Scotland were by the 1940s firmly on the left, with a significant communist influence among the Area officials and the active members. Area identities were a result of economic environment, working conditions, expectations and memories, producing a culture that became for many the common sense of their particular coalfield.[6]

Such identities fuelled debates within the institutions of the National Union. For several years the potential for fragmentation was kept in check by a solid right-wing majority.[7] By 1970 this dominance was coming under increasing pressure. The massive closures of the 1960s had made the Yorkshire Area numerically the largest Area, and by 1972 Yorkshire had moved to the left.[8] Radical expectations were raised by the successful strikes of 1972 and 1974. The national president, Joe Gormley, effectively protected the position of the right by exploiting the complexities and ambiguities of the national rule book. When he retired in 1981, the weakness of the right at the leadership level was all too evident. Arthur Scargill, formerly president of the Yorkshire NUM, stood as the agreed left-wing candidate against three unpersuasive claimants to Gormley's legacy. His thorough victory, with over 70 per cent of the vote, testified to his campaigning skills and to the limitations of each of his opponents. Scargill's election was complemented by a shift to the left in the national conference and by a bare majority on the executive.[9] For the first time, the left controlled the institutions of the National Union.

This ascendancy was achieved just as the implications of the Thatcher government's policy on the mining industry became evident. The Coal Industry Act 1980 set the objective of an industry self-funding and free of subsidies by 1983–84. Economic recession reduced demand for coal and stocks mounted at pitheads. The drive for more efficient production compelled the Coal Board to concentrate investment in productive pits with strong markets and to cut back on units characterised as peripheral. Between May 1979 and the end of March 1984 thirty-six collieries closed, a reduction of 24 per cent, while the number employed in the industry fell by 23 per cent. As miners witnessed the decline in local manufacturing, optimism about a job outside the industry withered. The report on the industry by the Monopolies and Mergers Commission published in mid 1983 recommended a 10 per cent cut in capacity and emphasised the loss-making productivity problems of the peripheral Areas. In some coalfields, notably in Scotland, Area directors responded to the cost-cutting imperative by more assertive management that challenged long-established practices.[10]

NUM officials and activists frequently emphasised the need for an effective response to this predicament, but rhetoric and the passing of resolutions were misleading indicators of their members' sentiments once faced with an individual ballot. The union had never succeeded in mounting a credible action against closures. The mass retrenchment between 1957 and 1970 had produced only pessimism. Attempts to mobilise nationally against individual closures in Derbyshire and Nottinghamshire in 1976 and 1979 had only demonstrated the difficulty of achieving effective solidarity among the many to safeguard in the first instance the jobs of a few.[11] The impressive solidarity of miners in the 1972 and 1974 strikes was born of specific circumstances. The development of a uniform wage structure under the National Power Loading Agreement of 1966 had spread discontent over wage levels across the industry, as miners in relatively well-paid Areas such as Nottinghamshire marked time in order that other Areas could catch up. The solidarity evident in these strikes was always vulnerable to demands for a reversion to incentive payments from historically better-paid Areas and from management keen to raise productivity and to fragment wage-based militancy. Gormley and his allies introduced Area incentive schemes in the winter of 1977–8 through a series of constitutional manoeuvres abetted by the judiciary.[12] The resulting fragmentation of wage standards between coalfields meant that the wage-based solidarity of 1972 and 1974 was no longer feasible.

Closures and the road to 1984

In February 1981 the National Coal Board announced the closure of twenty-three pits and the prospect of up to fifty closures over the next five years. Many miners in the more left-wing Areas went on strike and the formal closure proposals were withdrawn. This could seem like one more victory for the NUM over a Conservative government, but the scepticism of some on the NEC was justified. One by one the twenty-three pits ceased production, with relatively generous redundancy terms lubricating the agreement of NUM branches.[13] Subsequent ballots on wages and closures in late 1982 and on the closure of Tymawr Lewis Merthyr in South Wales in March 1983 encapsulated the problem. In the second ballot the pro-strike vote was only 31 per cent.

The NUM leadership responded to a wage offer and the threat of closures in autumn 1983 not with another ballot campaign but by calling an overtime ban. This option did not require an individual ballot. By preventing weekend maintenance work, production would be cut during the week, and the consequential conflict could radicalise and encourage solidarity among members, preparing them for a strike ballot at a time of the union's choosing. An overtime ban had preceded the 1974 strike, but from the beginning in 1983 there was evidence of disunity. The Nottinghamshire Area Council had backed the ban only by sixteen votes to fifteen. Ray Chadburn, the Area president, emphasised the potentially misleading character of the message offered by this support. The decision had come from branch meetings – 'about 5 per cent of the Nottinghamshire miners'.[14] As the ban made an impact, so acrimony grew. In Scotland, the flooding of Bogside colliery was blamed by the Board on the ban. When Polmaise colliery was declared closed, the branch decided to go it alone and went on strike on 21 February 1984.[15] In retrospect, although it was not obvious at the time, this local refusal was the beginning of the strike.

When the National Executive met on 8 March it faced a request from the Scottish Area for an Area strike in support of Polmaise to be declared official. This request was accompanied by one from the Yorkshire Area, asking for the same sanction to be given to an Area stoppage in support of Cortonwood. This closure had been presented by the Area director to the Yorkshire NUM as unambiguously based on economic grounds. Given the opposition of both Area and National Union to such a closure, the challenge was difficult to ignore. The NEC agreed to both requests for the proposed stoppages to be declared official under National Rule 41. This stipulated the procedure for the NEC's authorisation of an official strike at Area or branch level.[16]

Some on the NEC suspected that the use of Rule 41 was designed to circumvent the necessity for a national strike ballot as ordained by National Rule 43.[17] These suspicions were fuelled by the extension of the resolution to cover any other Area that might decide to take the same route as Scotland and Yorkshire. Yet a move to require a national ballot found only three supporters at the NEC meeting. The right within the NEC was disorientated and, given union policy, it was difficult to sideline the two requests. Scotland and Yorkshire were on official strike, but extension of the strike beyond these Areas proved difficult. The dominoes were reluctant to fall.[18]

The Yorkshire Area could point to a 1981 Area ballot that had returned a vote of over 85 per cent in support of the principle of strike action to support a threatened colliery. In Yorkshire, well-attended branch meetings showed strong support for the stoppage, although there was some variation, which reflected the traditions of different sections of the

Table 8.1 *Area ballots on strike action March 1984; pro-strike percentage (compared with March 1983 ballot)*

Cumberland	22 (42)	Nottinghamshire	27 (19)
Derbyshire	49.8 (38)	North Wales	32 (23)
Leicestershire	11 (18)	Northumberland	52 (35)
Durham enginemen	15 (16)	Lancashire	41 (39)
South Derbyshire	16 (12)	Midlands	27 (21)

coalfield. In Scotland, there was resistance to the stoppage at Bilston Glen near Edinburgh. In South Wales – another left-wing stronghold – the lodges initially voted fifteen to six against striking, but picketing on Monday 12 March by pro-strike lodges brought solidarity. In Durham, where lodges voted eight to three to work, the dissident majority was picketed out. These four coalfields provided the basis for a strike; only in Yorkshire had there been a ballot and that had been three years previously.[19]

Elsewhere, the discussions on the NEC were retold to Area Executives and Conferences who were sometimes critical of the Rule 41 strategy and more often sensitive to the difficulties that its zealous pursuit by outside pickets would precipitate in their own Areas. The frequent response was to hold an immediate Area ballot. In all cases except one, strike action was rejected; and in that case, the majority was insufficient under the 55 per cent requirement (see Table 8.1).

Several of these Areas were numerically small and historically aligned with the NUM right. Derbyshire, finely balanced between left and right and the base of the newly elected national general secretary Peter Heathfield, rapidly called an official strike. So did Northumberland. Lancashire, after much confusion, became a preponderantly striking coalfield. In each case, support for the stoppage proved solid for some months. Elsewhere, the fact of the ballot result proved decisive. Coalfields divided or, in Leicestershire and South Derbyshire, became united in working on with only handfuls of strikers.

Initially, given this balance, the strike seemed provisional. A stoppage seemed unsustainable on the basis of a divided workforce. Several Areas continued to demand a national ballot and it was widely believed that a small majority on the NEC was committed to this initiative.[20] But on 12 April, whatever pro-ballot majority there was on the NEC was outflanked and divided by Scargill, who ruled that the matter had been decided the previous month and could not be reopened. A vote on a point of procedure allowed some NEC members representing pro-ballot Areas to in effect back their own, and different, preference. Instead, final responsibility for the substantive decision went to a National Delegate Conference a week later. The arguments had been well rehearsed and altered nothing. The voting gave a steady if small majority against all proposals for a ballot. The issue within the National Union's institutions was dead. A majority backed the strategy based on Rule 41 and called on all Areas to join the strike.[21]

Nottinghamshire

These Conference decisions still had to face the fact of Areas that had decisively rejected strike action and where a majority clearly wished to work on in the absence of a national ballot. Numerically, the most significant of these was Nottinghamshire. The coalfield was widely perceived as distinctive. Its miners earned high wages and believed themselves to be under little threat from closures. From other Areas, especially neighbouring Yorkshire, they could be dismissed as endemic scabs, unwilling to take action in solidarity with miners elsewhere who were threatened by closure. The more historically minded could recall the collapse of the Nottinghamshire resistance in the 1926 lockout and the subsequent formation of the Nottinghamshire Miners' Industrial Union, the 'Spencer' Union. Reunification with the official body in 1937 had been relatively favourable to the breakaway union and, for some critics, a residual culture of 'Spencerism' still influenced the politics of the coalfield. The Nottinghamshire Area's minutes appeared regularly under the Area motto 'United We Stand for Union Is Strength'. But the desired unity often seemed that of the Area rather than any wider solidarity and was expressed in a pit culture of cooperation with management in pursuit of high productivity and high earnings, unhindered by what many Nottinghamshire men dismissed as the restrictive and archaic customs of other, less-productive Areas.[22]

Yet there was another side. The Nottinghamshire involvement in the disputes of the 1920s had been in support of less-favoured districts. After 1966, Nottinghamshire miners had accepted the National Power Loading Agreement, despite the consequential limitation on their earnings. Conditions across the coalfield varied. The relatively new and productive pits in the Dukeries contrasted with the remnants of mining in the Erewash Valley. The Leen Valley and Mansfield district collieries had varying expectations of profitability. Many Nottinghamshire miners, especially in the newer pits, had moved from the north-east and Scotland during the mass closures of the 1960s. Overarching this diversity there was a shared industrial culture, which could not be attributed simply to geology and economics. Adjacent collieries in Yorkshire were characterised by similar geological conditions and there the industrial tradition was very different.[23]

The left was not without influence in Nottinghamshire. Joe Whelan, the previous general secretary, had combined Communist Party membership with fierce advocacy of local economic priorities. His successor, Henry Richardson, was a supporter of Scargill.[24] Elected narrowly late in 1982, Richardson sat as an Area representative on the NEC along with the president, Ray Chadburn. The latter was a typical representative of the Area's culture, an outlook also articulated by the two other full-time officials, Roy Lynk and David Prendergast. Within the Area Council there had emerged a minority sympathetic to the left.

The Area Executive responded rapidly to the NEC decision by calling an Area ballot on strike action, a decision endorsed by the Area Council.[25] The arrival of Yorkshire pickets in the north of the Area led to divided responses by local miners. The arrival of large numbers of police raised the temperature. Scuffles between pickets and both police and local miners culminated in the death of a picket outside Ollerton Colliery.[26] The Area Executive responded by calling a stoppage until the ballot had been held. The result was unequivocal: every branch voted against a strike. The Area response was to respect this decision and to lobby the NEC for a national ballot.[27] The situation remained volatile in part because of those Nottinghamshire miners who supported the national decision. These included a minority on the Area Council and several branch committee men. After the declaration of the Nottinghamshire result, pickets flooded back into the county, while police responded with an even greater presence, insulating working miners from pickets. Stories of picket line violence mushroomed. They were often sensationalised, but working miners could claim to be victims of intimidation in their role as upholders of a democratic decision. They could argue that abrasive picketing had strengthened the opposition to the strike call. This claim, however, is unpersuasive.[28] Area support for a strike had grown since March 1983, when there had been no pickets.

The Area Executive responded to the national decisions of 19 April by noting that anyone on strike was on strike officially and had the right to picket, and a week later by instructing branch officials and committee men to accept the national policy. Proposals were made for the production of official posters and badges.[29] Such initiatives were unrealistic. The instruction to branches had been opposed by two members of the Executive who were both full-time officials, Lynk and Prendergast.

They were increasingly at odds with Chadburn and Richardson who, as president and general secretary, faced an intractable dilemma. As Nottinghamshire officials they were bound by the ballot result; as members of the NEC they were obliged to follow its policy. Richardson, although sensitive to his Area's sentiments, was sympathetic to the national strategy, Chadburn less so, but he had endorsed the 19 April decisions. The rifts within the Area at every level – full-time officials, branch committees and members – were dramatically revealed on 1 May. Pro- and anti-strike miners demonstrated outside the Area's Mansfield headquarters separated by police. The conflict between the officials was stark as Chadburn and Lynk shouted to the crowd, one urging support for the strike, the other emphasising that he would support their decision to work in the absence of a national ballot.[30]

For a few weeks the Area Executive continued to express the views of its pro-strike majority. On 10 May, the NEC decided that Area elections due in June be suspended until the end of the strike.[31] Opponents of the strike in Nottinghamshire objected to this postponement and, early in June, the Area Executive decided on the basis of legal advice to hold the elections. The result was an almost complete removal of pro-strike representatives. Only one remained on the Area Executive, while their number on the Area Council fell from twelve to two. One calculation suggests that of 310 places on branch committees and as branch officials, only four were subsequently held by strikers.[32] The Nottinghamshire NUM had become effectively a union for working miners. Chadburn and Richardson still retained their positions, but their power increasingly shifted to Lynk and Prendergast. The small group of Nottinghamshire strikers became increasingly isolated from their union. By June, Nottinghamshire was effectively in the position that some small Areas had been in since March. Leicestershire and South Derbyshire had worked throughout, with the seventeen strikers in the latter paralleled by the Leicestershire 'Dirty Thirty'.[33] This Midlands trio formed a block with other largely working collieries, such as Daw Mill in Warwickshire, Agecroft in Lancashire and Point of Ayr in North Wales.

Where opposition to the strike had been largely uncontested, Areas carried on business as usual within their own institutions and in their dealings with the National Union. Their representatives attended the NEC and national conferences. In Leicestershire, South Derbyshire and COSA this response meant that working miners still remained firmly within the NUM because their own Areas had reflected throughout the views of the majority. Nottinghamshire was different. Its size, the early conflicts and the significant initial presence of pro-strikers within the Area's institutions meant that the revolt against the strike came not from the Area officials and institutions but from unofficial organisation among the members. Meetings began circumspectly in a Stanton Hill pub in April, and the May Day clash outside the Area offices showed the potential power of a working miners' movement. Shortly afterwards, the Nottinghamshire Working Miners' Committee was born. Its active core combined seasoned members of the Area's traditional right, such as Colin Clarke, with the previously inactive, such as the Bevercotes blacksmith, Chris Butcher. Widely lionised in the right-wing press as 'Silver Birch', Butcher was an assiduous net-worker with working miners in other coalfields. The Area elections in late June were a triumph for the Committee. In effect they had taken over the Area.[34]

Lawsuits and divisions

Success was the prelude to mistrust. For many, the purpose of the elec-tions had been achieved. Nottinghamshire, like Leicestershire and South Derbyshire, was now controlled by those who expressed the majority view. Their case rested on fidelity to the rule book and a con-viction that such rectitude must be maintained. Thus, it was only in the last weeks of the strike that the Area responded to pressure from branches and ended the overtime ban. This emphasis on procedural propriety led to criticism of some, whose agenda seemed to extend to wider political matters. Colin Bottomore, the Bentinck branch sec-retary, emphasised the limits of his and many Nottinghamshire min-ers' agenda. There was no longer any need for a Working Miners' Committee: 'They're continuing it because their aim is to defeat the strike … and to bring the union to its knees. That's not my aim'.[35] Elsewhere, working miners felt a need for organisation. Jim Lord, the Agecroft branch secretary, travelled to Nottinghamshire and met that Area's anti-strike officials. He was subsequently involved in forming a Lancashire Working Miners' Committee, a focus for those who had been effectively excluded from that Area's deliberations. Yet Lord, like many in Nottinghamshire, balked at any association with an August initiative, the National Working Miners' Committee. He was a member of the Labour Party and believed, rightly, that the National Working Miners' Committee was linked to and funded by business interests and Conservative members and sympathisers, whose objectives went far beyond the procedures of the NUM.[36]

The National Working Miners' Committee had links with the polit-ical right from the beginning, personified by the attendance of Tim Bell of Saatchi & Saatchi and David Hart. A wealthy and self-proclaimed libertarian, Hart was an occasional *Times* columnist who became heavily involved in the back-to-work movement in Derbyshire and claimed access to both Margaret Thatcher and Ian MacGregor. Colin Clarke became the Committee's president and another participant, the Sherwood branch secretary John Liptrot, subsequently attracted criticism from within the Area Council. The National Committee's most decisive contribution was probably its support for miners who wished to take legal action against their Areas.[37]

Such initiatives recalled the action taken by Walter Osborne against the Amalgamated Society of Railway Servants that had culminated in the Lords' judgement of 1909. The image of the little man battling against the powerful and unrepresentative union oligarchs harmonised with the rhetoric of the Thatcher years. Yet these interventions owed nothing to the trade union legislation introduced by the Thatcher government. The key actions were taken under common law and involved claims that union rules had been broken.[38] Clarke and Liptrot were parties to an action in May that the decision of the Nottinghamshire Executive that the strike was official following the national conference of 19 April was illegal. Their success on 25 May was the first of several victories by working plaintiffs. These actions were overshadowed late in 1984 by the case that had the most far-reaching impact on the union.[39]

Robert Taylor and Ken Foulstone were members of the NUM Yorkshire Area's Manton branch. They had been picketed out in March 1984 and had not worked since. Within the Yorkshire Area, Manton and its neighbour Shireoaks were anomalies. The pits were in Nottinghamshire where many of the miners lived. The Manton branch had been notable within the Yorkshire Area for the hostility shown to the strike call in March 1984. Their claims were against both the NUM Yorkshire Area and the National Union. The plaintiffs argued that the strike was invalid in the absence of a national ballot and that the Yorkshire Area had failed in their obligation to hold branch elections and branch committee meetings. In addition, restraint was sought against any attempt by the NUM to implement a new disciplinary procedure. The proposed action was the subject of an appeal by Sir Hector Laing, chair of United Biscuits, to around one hundred business men: 'They are in the front line fighting for what we believe in and they need to know they have friends.' Thirty thousand pounds rapidly came into a Miners' Ballot Fund administered by Taylor and Foulstone's solicitors. This firm, Hodgkinson and Tallents of Newark, had connections with the Conservative Party.[40] Mr Justice Nicholls found against the union on all counts, desisting only from a request that the NUM be ordered to hold a national ballot.[41] The judgement was of a piece with earlier ones, and the refusal of the NUM to abide by this outcome led to the sequestration of the union's assets. Clarke and fifteen other members of the National Working Committee went to court to call for the NEC members to be personally liable for the consequential fine, and for the national officials to be replaced as trustees by a court-appointed receiver. It was in this climate that the Nottinghamshire Area Council voted to dissociate the area publicly from the National Working Miners' Committee.[42]

Despite the declared limited ambitions of the Area leadership, by the end of 1984 Nottinghamshire had moved closer to a decisive break with the NUM. The origin of this polarisation lay in the National Union's attempt, in July 1984, to amend its rules, to allow for a disciplinary procedure against members who sought to harm the union. The newly elected anti-strike majority on the Nottinghamshire Executive and Council predictably saw the proposed procedure as one that could be directed at them. Neither body, however, had the chance to formally declare its opposition. Striking Nottinghamshire miners sat in at the Area offices and prevented the scheduled meetings. Clarke and sixteen others obtained an order restraining the NUM from proposing, debating and voting on any rule change since the Nottinghamshire Area had been prevented from mandating its delegates. Subsequently the High Court ruled that the rule changes carried by the national conference were void.[43] After this contretemps, Nottinghamshire rarely sent a delegation to any national conference, justifying its absences on the basis of legal advice. Once again, its position was distinctive from that of other working areas.

When the National Union decided to formulate new model rules, Nottinghamshire moved a step closer to separation. An Area Council meeting in December decided to remove Rule 30 from the Area rule book, thereby expunging the requirement that in matters of dispute Area rules were subordinate to national ones. The proposal to expunge Rule 30 had come from Clarke's branch, Pye Hill.[44] The Area leadership and the luminaries of the National Working Miners' Committee might have had their differences, but they could cooperate in defence of the Area's autonomy. With the removal of Rule 30 the Nottinghamshire Area was in violation of a condition of membership of the National Union. The Area deepened the rift by ending the overtime ban, exploring the prospect of a separate post-strike wage settlement with the National Coal Board (NCB) and eventually removing Chadburn and Richardson from their posts.[45] By mid 1985 all the permanent officials – Lynk, Prendergast and a newly elected colleague, Neil Greatrex – were thorough critics of the national leadership. In July, a rules revision conference of the NUM discussed and passed new model rules including the controversial disciplinary procedure. The Nottinghamshire delegation left the discussion at an early stage, and the Area leadership rapidly moved to separate from the NUM.[46] The break raised legal complications and involved covert discussions between the NCB and the Nottinghamshire officials.[47] By mid October 1985, the Area's miners had voted by 72 per cent to secede.

The Union of Democratic Mineworkers

The Union of Democratic Mineworkers (UDM) was a product of the industrial culture of the Nottinghamshire coalfield and the trauma of the previous eighteen months. After the strike, the ambitions of both the Nottinghamshire leaders and the NCB expanded. The Nottinghamshire Executive met its counterparts from Leicestershire and South Derbyshire in March 1985 to discuss concerted action – at this stage, explicitly within the NUM.[48] However, once moves had begun to separate from the NUM, an Executive meeting in August explored the basis for a wider organisation. The South Derbyshire Area sent representatives, as did the Colliery Trade and Allied Workers' Association – a Durham-based group of craftsmen who had become disenchanted with the NUM. Branch officials from Daw Mill in Warwickshire were also present. The meeting considered draft rules and chose provisional officials.[49] Following the Nottinghamshire ballot and support in ballots by South Derbyshire and the Colliery Trades and Allied Workers' Association (CTAWA), the UDM could embark on an agenda for expansion backed by a sympathetic NCB.

Yet, as with the strike mobilisation in March 1984, decisive dominoes refused to fall. Leicestershire had been thoroughly opposed to the strike and there was considerable optimism that the Area would join the UDM. Yet Leicestershire had not been represented at the August planning meeting. The Area secretary Jack Jones – a dedicated opponent of Scargill – argued for staying within the NUM rather than fragmenting the workforce further, a process that could only aid the NCB. A Leicestershire ballot was held early in 1986, preceded by an acrimonious campaign in which advocates for the UDM were presented as divisive. Jones's advocacy helped to produce a 64 per cent vote for the NUM. Although the Area was small, this unexpected result damaged the UDM. Opposition to the strike did not necessarily translate into support for an alternative union. The Leicestershire experience was paralleled in North Wales, where miners at the largely anti-strike Point of Ayr colliery rejected the UDM. Similarly, at Agecroft initial enthusiasm for the new union was stifled by appeals for unity and effective use of the Lancashire rule book by pro-NUM elements. Some individuals who had worked through the strike joined the UDM, but this could only be a symbolic shift.[50] Where the NUM remained the majority union it retained recognition, but in Nottinghamshire it lost all negotiating rights.

Legacies

The division within the union had an impact on Nottinghamshire politics, although it is difficult to separate this from broader trends. The county's coalfield constituencies, particularly Ashfield and Mansfield, displayed the Labour strength characteristic of mining seats elsewhere until the late 1970s.[51] The Conservatives captured Ashfield in a 1977 by-election. Although the seat was regained in the 1979 election, the Labour vote there and in Mansfield was significantly down on the two 1974 contests.[52] The same trend was evident in 1983, when Labour's majority in Mansfield slipped to just over 2,000. More sensationally, the newly created Sherwood constituency, which included ten collieries, narrowly returned a Conservative, Andy Stewart. His cause had been helped by the choice of Labour candidate. The NUM nominee, a local branch official, had been rejected in favour of a Westminster and Oxbridge-educated barrister, who could seem an outsider against the claims of a local, albeit Scottish, farmer.[53] The personal contrast might have been decisive in a close contest, but before the strike the familiar political solidarity was already declining, with a growth in support not just for the Conservatives but also for the Liberal-Social Democratic alternative.[54]

Stewart became a forceful champion of the county's working miners. He eulogised them as defenders of democracy, whose high productivity and consensual industrial relations offered the prospect of a low-cost and competitive coal industry. When he discussed conditions in the coalfield with the Prime Minister in September 1984, she immediately penned a supportive note – 'A Personal Message to the Nottinghamshire Miners' – copies of which were displayed on colliery notice boards. 'Andy has been to see me to-day and let me know your views. May I say how greatly I and most other people appreciate what you are doing. You are an example to us all.'[55]

Such an initiative contrasted with the elegiac image of miners presented by Harold Macmillan, speaking for the first time in the Lords as Earl Stockton in November 1984. His reference was not just to working miners but simply to miners, 'the best men in the world. They beat the Kaiser's army and they beat Hitler's army. They never gave in.'[56] Such romantic social Toryism was one strand in his attack on the Thatcher government's policies and style.

Inevitably the strike presented a problem for NUM-sponsored MPs in predominantly working coalfields. The Ashfield MP, Frank Haynes, adopted a low profile, but his Mansfield colleague, Don Concannon, supported the working majority. The result was criticism within the local party and a threat of de-selection, which Concannon threatened to resist before a car accident forced his retirement.[57] The 1987 Mansfield election was acrimonious. The new Labour candidate Alan Meale was identified with the left and indeed with Scargill. He was opposed by a 'Moderate Labour' candidate who was a UDM branch official and a former councillor. The latter attempted to identify official Labour with the strikers and was backed by Prendergast and Concannon.[58] More significantly, on a higher poll the Conservative vote increased by 3,122 and Labour's majority fell to fifty-six. The Conservative candidate later claimed that the legacy of the strike had won him votes:

The night before polling day I went into the Mansfield miners' welfare club where the steward on the door immediately took the rosette off my lapel because he wanted to wear it. We had to send out for extra "Vote Hendy" badges. When the Labour candidate turned up, he was asked to leave because he had supported the National Union of Mineworkers during the strike.[59]

The strike's legacy was also evident in the Sherwood contest, where Stewart faced the same Labour candidate as in 1983. His robust advocacy of the working miners' case increased his vote by 5,221 and his share of the poll by almost 5 per cent. Haynes experienced a much smaller swing to the Conservatives in Ashfield. While the Mansfield and Sherwood results showed that the dispute's passions could produce singular outcomes, the benefit for the Conservatives was limited. Another Nottinghamshire Conservative MP, Jim Lester, was appropriately sceptical. 'The Nottinghamshire Miners are not Tories ... [they] have not supported the Tory Party against the National Executive. They have supported their own deep instincts for democracy, for the rule book and for their union.'[60] The limited Conservative advance was nevertheless better than the Liberal-Social Democratic Alliance's slight decline from their 1983 vote. The latter's hope that trade unionists disenchanted with the Labour Party's support for the strike would shift to them proved barren.

More broadly, the Labour Party's response to the problems posed by the UDM was pragmatic. The Mansfield fracas proved atypical.

Affiliation of the union was out of the question; the UDM had been refused affiliation by the Trades Union Congress. But in local parties, UDM members and NUM opponents of the strike continued as individual members. The sentiment was similar to that which kept a significant number of working miners within the NUM. When the NUM held its political fund ballot as required by the Thatcher government's 1984 Act, the majority in favour was over 90 per cent on a 76 per cent poll. The ballot held in March 1986 followed the formation of the UDM, but for those of diverse views who remained within the NUM, solidarity on this issue was intact.

There could be no such restoration in industrial relations. Although the UDM's ambitions had not been realised, the NUM found itself seriously weakened both in individual collieries and as a national actor. Weakness inevitably deepened internal divisions. Beyond these squabbles, the weakening of the market for coal meant a rapid contraction of the industry, intensified by the privatisation of electricity generation and the industry's subsequent freedom to buy coal more cheaply on the international market.

Nottinghamshire was exposed heavily to the contraction of demand from the power generation industry. Closures produced claims that the working miners had been betrayed by the Conservative government. Stewart's optimism that low-cost output would safeguard jobs was shattered by the challenge of cheaper imports. By 1989 he acknowledged that 'the threat posed to Nottinghamshire by imported coal is potentially catastrophic'.[61] His plea for a five-year honeymoon to allow the county's collieries to improve their productivity still further proved unsuccessful. In the April 1992 election, the Nottinghamshire coalfield swung heavily against the government and Stewart lost his seat.[62] Six months later the announcement of thirty-one more closures produced opposition that went far beyond the organised labour movement. Several of the remaining Nottinghamshire collieries were included on the closure list. Roy Lynk sat in unavailingly at the threatened Silverhill Colliery. Collective protests proved equally ineffective. The critics had arguments but few resources.

Privatisation and the fragmentation of the union accorded with Thatcherite ambitions but the route by which they came about did not follow a preconceived agenda. Probably no one in government and the NCB expected a year-long strike in March 1984. The strategy of incremental closure without serious confrontation was working effectively. NUM branches had responded with verbal opposition to specific closure proposals followed by acquiescence. In this context the response of the majority of NUM members to the strike call was remarkable for its solidarity and longevity. It cannot be reduced to the imposed priorities of Scargill and his supporters. The motivations of the strikers were complex: loyalty to union and community; a desire to protect a way of life in an increasingly insecure world; an appeal to some sense of moral economy against the destructiveness of the market. Such sentiments left unclear what could count as an acceptable settlement for the strikers. For the government, there were several acceptable outcomes. An early end to the dispute would have meant a return to the strategy of incremental closures faced by a chastened union. In the event, it obtained a much more thorough victory.

The government's bargaining position was strengthened by the commitment of many NUM members to continue working, whether on constitutional grounds or because the ballot argument offered a more principled justification than the robust pursuit of a locally defined self-interest. The roots of the NUM's defeat lay not in the limitations of its leaders so much as in the structure and culture of mining trade unionism, which in turn was shaped by the character of the industry. The NUM was in reality far removed from the solidarity and radicalism of left-wing legend and right-wing paranoia. A collective response on closures was unlikely, and this mattered more than Scargillite inflexibility or Thatcherite determination.

Thatcherism, unionism and nationalism:
      a comparative study of Scotland and Wales

Richard Finlay

This chapter assesses why the experience of Thatcherism produced such different outcomes in Scotland and Wales in terms of promoting nationalism and some form of self-government.[1] Although the experience of Conservative rule was cited by supporters of home rule in both countries as a factor in turning many to the policy of devolution, the fact remains that this gained more momentum in Scotland. While a degree of ambivalence about self-government haunted Wales, in Scotland it was confidently asserted as the 'settled will of the people'.[2]

This chapter will focus on three themes. First, it will examine the role of unionism in Scotland and Wales and show that it had less of a pedigree in Wales and was not so central to Welsh Conservatism.[3] Unionism had been integral to Scottish political culture in the twentieth century and the 'peculiarities' of the Scots had long been taken for granted by both Conservative and Labour politicians. Scottish Tories had come to believe that they were *the* party of the Union, and a unionist tradition that encapsulated both Scotland and Ireland had been part and parcel of Scottish Conservative identity throughout the twentieth century. Nonetheless, both Labour and the Tory parties had banged the Scottish nationalist drum for their own ends on occasion when political expediency dictated.[4] In many respects, Toryism was more ideologically suited to utilising Scottish patriotism as part of a wider British nationalism than Labour, which was duty bound to stress the significance of class. As Iain Hutchison has noted, Scottish Tories actually became more aristocratic and rural in the period after the Second World War and, although anachronistic and stereotypical, the party was still identifiably Scottish.[5] Welsh Conservatism, on the other hand, did not have as distinctive a Welsh tradition.[6] Thatcher, however, had a limited and flawed understanding of unionism in Scotland, and conflated *unionism* with *unitarianism*.[7] Many of her dealings and problems with Scotland can be explained by this basic failure to grasp the historic role of unionism in Scottish political culture.[8] More to blame are Scottish Thatcherites, who had even less of an appreciation or understanding either of the party's traditions or of its association with unionism. Indeed, if Thatcherism can be seen as a form of ideological updating of the Conservative Party, it conspicuously failed to update unionism. Arguably, the lack of a similarly prominent role for Welsh unionism undermined the distinctive *national* dimension in Wales.

The second theme is that opposition to Thatcherism in both Scotland and Wales was undoubtedly based on class interests that were sharpened in an era of profound socio-economic change.[9] Arguably, whereas working-class identity in Wales remained strong, in Scotland this class identity became increasingly conflated with national identity.[10] A central issue to be addressed is why class appeal remained strong in Wales, but in Scotland was perceived as being soft to nationalist overtures that were increasingly appeased by Labour. Class will also be examined as a factor in the rise of the centre, especially in Scotland, where centre parties rather than nationalists were the prime beneficiaries of anti-Toryism. Indeed, the chapter will argue that there is too much of a tendency to equate the decline of the Conservative Party in the 1980s with the growth of small-'n' nationalism. In many respects, this was a post hoc explanation which minimises socio-economic change as the underlying cause of Thatcher's unpopularity. Part of the answer, it will be suggested, lies in the tendency of recent historiography to focus too much on the leading protagonists of the home rule movement and not enough on the features associated with socio-economic change.[11]

Finally, the chapter will examine the differing social structure of Wales and Scotland with respect to the growth of 'civic' nationalism. It has been argued that Scotland had a stronger 'civil society' based around national institutions, which rejected the selfish individualism of Thatcherism and led the campaign for self-government.[12] This chapter will question that assumption and point out that the experience of socio-economic transformation was fundamental to the decline of Conservatism in both Scotland and Wales. While Scotland enjoys greater territorial insularity than Wales, the decision of the opposition parties in Scotland to enthusiastically and unanimously endorse home rule was driven largely by practical political and electoral considerations, rather than principle. Furthermore, it was a convenient way for the old corporatist groupings of the post-war consensus to reinvent themselves at a time when their influence was in decline both from the Thatcherite onslaught, and also from social and economic structural change.[13] The same considerations of practical and electoral politics, likewise, account for the limited enthusiasm in Wales for devolution where nationalism was seen to pose less of a threat.

Unionism in Scotland and Wales

For some historians, the decline of unionism as a central ideological plank of the Conservative Party is fundamental to explaining why the Scottish Tory Party began to lose its distinctive Scottish dimension in the 1960s. This, it is argued, may have been a factor in its declining electoral appeal after 1965.[14] Dropping the 'unionist' tag was part of a process to modernise the party, but was largely unpopular with the rank and file.[15] In the 1950s, Scottish Tories had made great play of Labour's threat to Scottish national identity, warning that centralisation and nationalisation would mean greater London control north of the border. Such an appeal chimed with a historic sense of distinctive Scottish identity within the Union, which could hark back to the days of empire and global pre-eminence. By the 1960s, however, as empire declined, the welfare state was increasingly identified in the popular imagination as the fundamental British institution that cemented Scottish loyalty to the Union. This worked to the benefit of the Labour Party, rather than the Conservatives, whose organisation, image and electoral message struggled to present itself as modern and relevant to Scottish needs, particularly in the field of socio-economic regeneration.[16]

Although the electoral fortunes of the Conservative Party in Scotland show a linear decline since 1964, there has been a tendency in the historiography to tie this in with the collapse under Thatcher and project it backwards. In fact, while not enjoying as good a performance as Labour in Scotland, a closer examination of Conservative voting between 1964 and 1979 shows roughly the same rate of decline in terms of the popular vote as Labour.[17] Vote efficiency was the key factor in Labour's better performance.[18] The real period of Conservative decline in Scotland began in 1987, after the worst of the economic recession. Paradoxically, as the socio-economic profile of Scotland moved closer to England, its electorate displayed a greater aversion to Conservatism.[19]

In Wales, there is a slightly different pattern. The Union did not occupy such a central position in Welsh Conservative thought.[20] Wales lacked the widespread Irish immigration which, north of the border, added a frisson of sectarianism to Scottish unionism.[21] The Welsh Union was largely a nineteenth-century invention to bring Wales into line with the Scottish and Irish experience.[22] The Welsh did not have a formal treaty that they could moan about from time to time. Labour's share of the vote declined from the mid 1960s until 1987, though it remained the dominant party, while the Conservatives won a higher share of the popular vote throughout the Thatcher era than in the 1960s and 70s. Again vote efficiency is a factor in explaining the tendency of Labour to win proportionally more seats than the Tories. One point to stress is the effect of the first-past-the-post electoral system in exaggerating the extent of Conservative decline in both Scotland and Wales. In the latter, the Conservative Party secured just under a third of the vote in 1979, declining by about 1 per cent in each subsequent election until 1992. Yet the result was an overall drop in seats from eleven to six. Although the Scottish share of the popular vote was smaller, the same effect was observed. There is probably a complex mathematical relationship in a four-party electoral context in which, below a certain threshold, the decline in overall percentage share of the vote yields an inversely higher proportion of seats lost. Certainly, after 1987 the appearance in both Scotland and Wales was that the Conservative Party and Thatcherism had been decisively rejected.[23]

The extent to which this was a 'nationalist' rebellion against Thatcher is questionable, although it could not but help invite comment that the minority nations of the United Kingdom were out of kilter with the English. Paradoxically, for such a committed unionist, Thatcher had a poor understanding of unionism. It might be suggested that her uncompromising stance against the IRA coloured her assumptions and that any concession towards national distinctiveness or an acknowledgement that there was a 'territorial' dimension to United Kingdom politics went against the 'no surrender' mentality that characterised many of her dealings with Northern Ireland.[24] The connections between Scottish, Welsh and Northern Irish unionist policy in the Thatcher era is an area that has yet to be explored by historians.[25] Thatcher had little understanding of the historical dynamic that had characterised the development of unionism in both Scotland and Wales. In the postwar era, it had been axiomatic that national distinctiveness would and should be accommodated within the Union and that Scottish and Welsh patriotism could go hand in hand with a wider British patriotism. Thatcher, however, was particularly insensitive to the nuances of unionism. Instead, she was an advocate of unitarianism.

Although Thatcher did make an effort, particularly in Scotland, to appeal to a form of Scottish historic identity, she had little success. In the early years of her leadership, she undertook tours and made much, at conference speeches, of what could be described as traditional Scottish attributes, such as hard work, inventiveness and entrepreneurial skill. Yet the most committed Thatcherites in Scotland had an even more limited appreciation of the complexities of unionism than she did. The Scottish Conservative Party, as David Torrance rightly notes, was divided by a 'class war' in which Thatcherite comprehensive boys fought for ascendancy against traditionalist 'toffs' and 'wets'.[26] In many ways, Scottish Thatcherites were more unitarianist than Thatcher, with a profound hostility to anything that smacked of Scottish nationalism. As unionism had been understood in the past, they were committed anti-unionists who attempted to hijack the concept to one that stood for British uniformity and sameness.[27] This left no room for traditional Scottish Tory patriotism, or that other great Tory tradition of pragmatism. The traditionalists or 'wets' who managed to hold on to key government positions did their best to ensure that government subsidies were maintained. The same process was also evident during the period of Peter Walker's Secretaryship in Wales.[28] If Margaret Thatcher did not always 'get' Scotland, part of the problem must surely be laid squarely at the feet of the Scottish party itself, as it frequently pulled in different directions.

In the period after the Second World War, the Union had been reinvented in Scotland and Wales largely through the creation of institutions associated with state intervention, developing specific agencies to implement the corporatist agenda. In both countries, the role of the British state in socio-economic regeneration was regarded as a major boon of the Union and was the principal argument used by Labour against home rule in the 1960s and 70s. Furthermore, it was argued that political devolution might obstruct regional development. The Thatcherite onslaught against state intervention had a particular resonance in both Scotland and Wales, because the state played a significantly greater role in socio-economic life than was the case for England as a whole, although its role was arguably higher in some English regions. The attack on state agencies was easy to portray as an attack on the people of Scotland and Wales per se, especially as state intervention enjoyed so much public support in these areas. It is worth pointing out that, by 1985, about a fifth of the population in both countries were over the age of 65 and had memories of the 'hungry thirties'. Thatcher's riposte – that she was offering 'true devolution' by 'dispersing power from government to the individual'[29] – effectively amounted to the dismantling of the traditional props of the Union, without offering anything tangible as a means of replacement.[30] Unionism, by its very nature and historical evolution, was a flexible doctrine that certainly had the potential to be adapted to the particular circumstances of Thatcherism. Yet, this was not achieved.

The idea that Scottishness and Welshness could be accommodated within Britishness was not developed, and Thatcher was accused of crass insensitivity when it came to dealing with the Scots and the Welsh. Her claim that Thatcherism was invented in Scotland, by Adam Smith, was treated with widespread scepticism.[31] Likewise, the appointment of

Englishmen as Welsh Secretaries of State was described as colonial and Malcolm Rifkind, normally a consummate diplomat, made the unfortunate gaffe of calling the role of Scottish Secretary of State a type of 'colonial governorship'.[32] This inability to engage with sub-British nationality beyond tokenism contributed to making Thatcherism seem alien and even un-British. Similarly, the destruction of traditional heavy industry was described by trade unionists in both Scotland and Wales in the early 1980s as an attack on their British inheritance and way of life.[33] The same probably holds true for the north of England. A major weakness of Thatcherism was the inability to project itself as a genuinely British phenomenon and not, as many critics claimed, one that was purely a southern English movement.[34] A key element of unionism had always been an acknowledgement of, and an accommodation with, sub-British nationality. Yet one major criticism of both the Scottish and Welsh Conservative parties was their chronic inability to engage with the national question, or to align Thatcherism with a unionist position that took account of distinctive national characteristics. Rather, both Scottish and Welsh Tories developed a dependency culture, in which they relied on the English vote to get them into government, while doing their best to keep expenditure high.

The most plausible defence of the Union was to make the case that the net subsidy to Scotland and Wales would be in danger from nationalism, or to link higher welfare payments with the Union. Yet the period after 1987 witnessed an increased attack on Celtic 'subsidy junkies', which exposed a tension in Conservative thinking towards Scotland and Wales.[35] While, on the one hand, wishing to set the people free and end the culture of 'lame ducks', Scottish and Welsh Conservatives increasingly used the argument of higher public spending – often, it has to be said, as a direct result of economic failure – as the first line of defence for the Union.[36] The claim that Thatcherism represented real devolution by giving power to the people and limiting the influence of the state suffered from the difficulty of calculating, in real terms, the benefits compared to the losses of reduced state intervention. Fear of unemployment remained the single biggest issue for Scottish and Welsh voters until after Thatcher's premiership. The new jobs created, which featured in the annual litany of Conservative Party Conferences, were often low-paid, part-time and unskilled.[37] Safe in the knowledge that they could rely on English seats to secure a government majority, the only potential constitutional threat worth considering was the unlikely scenario that the nationalists would secure a mandate for independence. This had the effect of polarising the debate between take-it-or-leave-it unionism or complete-nation-state independence, a polarity which Conservatives hoped would take the wind out of the sails of the growing devolutionist sentiment in both countries. It was neither a particularly imaginative nor a successful policy. Indeed, other unionist parties alleged that Conservative intransigence was the main threat to the integrity of the United Kingdom.[38]

The Conservatives' failure to engage with the national question left the Labour Party and the Liberal Democrats as the champions of the Union, in the sense that most Scots and Welsh would understand it. By endorsing devolution, it was possible to adapt the Union in a way that would take account of national differences and compensate for what was seen as the 'democratic deficit' in that Tory England was too powerful. This phenomenon was undoubtedly stronger in Scotland than Wales for a number of reasons. First, Scotland enjoyed greater territorial integrity, for there was no porous border area that witnessed widespread English immigration as in Wales. Nor was Scotland divided geographically by a linguistic tendency to vote Nationalist that was confined to a Celtic heartland. The language issue remained remarkably unpoliticised in Scotland. The border was also sealed intellectually in Scotland by the existence of its separate legal system. Second, there was a wider range of institutions, such as the Scottish TUC, the Scottish Church, independent media and various organisations that were distinctively Scottish. Third, government institutions had developed, particularly after 1954, that gave the appearance of a separate Scottish polity. Similar points can be made for Wales, but they were neither as historically grounded nor as well developed. So when the Conservatives were thrashed in 1987, it was widely assumed that a 'national' dimension was at work.[39]

Socio-economic change and the decline of Conservatism in Scotland and Wales

The decline of the Conservative Party in Scotland and Wales did not automatically condition support for devolution, nor is it necessarily the case that the two phenomena were related. First, the dramatic decline of Conservative fortunes in 1987 did not feature much debate surrounding political nationalism or devolution in either Scotland or Wales.[40] There was, however, a tendency among political commentators to apply the issues of devolution and small-'n' nationalism retrospectively to 1979, as a way of legitimising the claims made in the late 1980s.[41] Second, it is commonly assumed that tactical voting came into play to specifically target the Tories. The evidence for this is slight and it may be nothing more than serendipity.[42] Third, in reconstructing the past, we tend to look to the memoirs and writings of the leading advocates of devolution and take at face value the connections asserted between anti-Conservatism and home rule. Finally, because the creation of a Scottish Parliament and a Welsh Assembly has come to be seen as the most significant development in the politics of Scotland and Wales in the last quarter of a century, there is a danger of seeing past events through this prism and relating all development towards this end. One consequence of this has been to downplay the role of economic and social turmoil in generating hostility to Thatcherism. In other words, class was critical.

Both Scotland and Wales witnessed a period of de-industrialisation during the 1980s that was unparalleled before the 1990s. Coal, shipping, steel and the traditional heavy industry that characterised much of their economies went to the wall in quick succession. In both societies, unemployment levels returned to those of the 1930s. Youth unemployment reached about a quarter and was not just experienced by the working class. The spectre of unemployment persisted until the late 1980s, even when the worst of the recession was past, while employment was maintained by longer working hours and growing female unskilled work. Since heavy industry tended to dominate communities, the impact of the downturn was communal and affected those dependent on servicing such communities. The Proclaimers' song, 'Letter from America', with its evocation of 'Bathgate no more, Linwood no more, Methil no more, Locharber, no more' captured this populist mood.[43] The sluggish performance of the economy meant that opportunities for new business start-ups, services and social mobility were largely absent in Wales and Scotland. If anything, dependence on the state for social mobility increased. In Scotland, in particular, middle-class voters increasingly turned away from the Tories, especially as many were employed in the public sector.[44]

Just as Thatcher was uncompromising on the issue of national concessions, she was adamant that there was no alternative to economic restructuring, despite the social pain it caused. Welsh and Scottish conference speeches expressed a blind faith that the collapse of the old industries was inevitable, heralding a new prosperous beginning.[45] The litany of new investments, jobs created and new companies formed was like a mantra to be repeated to show that the economy was coming right. Again, crass insensitivity was much in evidence. Thatcherism took no account of the psychological impact of economic restructuring. Shipbuilding and heavy engineering were arguably as much the fabric of Scottish national identity as tartan and heather.[46] The same could be said for mining and steel in Wales. Nor was this simply self-interest on the part of Scottish and Welsh workers, determined to keep their outdated industries going. In what might be termed 'popular political economy', there was a genuine belief that a nation that did not export or make things could not be prosperous. The invisible or service economy made no sense to many traditional workers who did not believe that it could work economically. This was a common refrain from the trade union movement.[47] Furthermore, trade unionists could mobilise a complex and sophisticated statistical case for industry and manufacturing. The strip steel mill at Ravenscraig, for example, was demonstrated to be one of the most efficient in Europe – but to no avail.[48] The statement that there was no such thing as society and the 1988 'Sermon on the Mound' – in which Church of Scotland ministers sat in silence as they were lectured on the importance of wealth creation – confirmed to many that Thatcherism stood for rampant greed and individualism.[49]

The strategies that emerged in both societies to cope with profound socio-economic change did not endear the electorate to government policies. Although there was a shift from manufacturing to the service sector, this often meant movement from well-paid and secure jobs to unskilled, non-unionised and often temporary employment. The impact of the miners' strike, coupled with the Timex dispute in Dundee, the 'Ford Fiasco' and the introduction of legislation that limited trade union rights, added to the perception that the working class was under assault.[50] For many, standards of living could only be maintained by working longer and by a propensity for women to supplement family incomes by part-time work. The take-up for the 'right to buy' council houses was sluggish in both Scotland and Wales, not necessarily as a result of opposition to the policy, but because fears regarding economic stability persisted longer.[51] It was only after 1987, when the worst of the downturn had passed, that the policy picked up; and even then, it was slower than for the rest of the United Kingdom. Furthermore, industrial contraction was long-drawn-out, and good news about new jobs could not generate the same publicity or public interest as high-profile closures. The fate of the Ravenscraig steel mill was a good example, in which repeated reprieves simply prolonged the agony. This surely added to the perception that both societies were net losers from the Thatcherite revolution.[52]

It is also worth pointing out the geographical peculiarities of de-industrialisation in Scotland and Wales, and their electoral impact. Both countries had a higher preponderance of traditional heavy industry that dominated entire communities. The same can be said for Northern Ireland and the north of England, but was distinctly absent in the Tory heartland of the south and less prevalent in the midlands.

The preponderance of traditional or 'old' industry meant that closures provoked widespread fears regarding the knock-on effects. Consequently, the self-employed and independent workers that formed such a crucial backbone of the Conservative electoral hegemony in the midlands and the south were unlikely to turn to Thatcherism on the basis of self-interest. Furthermore, the depressed nature of the economy meant that there was little prospect for growth in self-employment or small business in communities where unemployment was high. As in other parts of the United Kingdom where there was a preponderance of 'old' industry, the Labour vote consolidated and became more geographically specific. In socio-economic terms, Wales and Scotland were part of a wider British divide between areas dependent on the 'old' economy and those which prospered under the 'new' economy. Arguably, it was the coupling of this wider British socio-economic divide with the fact that Scotland and Wales were distinctive 'national' entities that helped promote the growing perception of a distinctive 'territorial' dimension in British politics. The 'national' dimension was part of the mix of British regional anti-Conservatism, but the prime driver was socio-economic.

The difference between Scotland and Wales in the 1980s is that Labour held up better in the latter, where the Liberals failed to make the same level of progress as in Scotland. In the general election of 1983, there was a Falklands factor which maintained Conservative support, but arguably more critical in determining the electoral outcome was a dent in Labour's support. It was in 1987 that the Conservatives appeared to suffer a Celtic backlash, as the Welsh Tories declined from fourteen to eight seats, while the Scots declined from twenty-one to ten. However, the fact that Labour was able to return fifty out of seventy-two Scottish seats somewhat exaggerates the extent of the party's success north of the border. Roughly speaking, the Liberals and Nationalists each secured about a fifth of the popular vote, the Conservatives a quarter and Labour just over 40 per cent. Depending on the perspective adopted it can be claimed that Scotland went anti-Tory, but it can equally be argued that the Tories were simply the main losers in the fragmentation of Scottish politics after 1987. The Liberal Democrats, paradoxically, achieved a proportional representation in 1992, securing three times as many MPs as the SNP on half its share of the vote. The rise of anti-Poll Tax groups and anti-Trident protesters was held up as evidence of the vibrant political culture of a strong civil society, but the cynic might see them as evidence of frustration with conventional politics. Electoral politics in Wales was more stable, with the Labour Party commanding between 45 and 49.5 per cent of the popular vote and the Conservatives around the 29 per cent mark. Whereas in Scotland the Labour and Conservative parties could command over half of the popular vote, in Wales it was nearer three-quarters. Arguably, traditional voting loyalties held their shape better than in Scotland, where the first-past-the-post system masked the extent to which the Labour–Tory bi-polar divide was collapsing.

After 1987, when there was a widespread belief that tactical voting had reduced the Conservatives to a rump in Scotland, problems began to emerge for Labour. Initial expectations that such a decisive electoral rejection of Thatcherism would bring changes in Conservative policy came to nought.[53] If anything, it turned the Conservative spotlight on this bastion of northern resistance. As we have seen, Tory strategy was to play the uncompromising unionist card and deny that there was a constitutional dimension to the lack of Conservative support in Scotland. It was claimed that the right to govern was confirmed by the outcome of the election in the United Kingdom as a whole; if voters in Scotland wanted change, they could turn to nationalism. For Labour particularly, and to a lesser extent the Liberal Democrats, this presaged what was known as the 'doomsday scenario', in which a left-of-centre Scotland would be permanently governed by a right-wing party that held power by virtue of majority United Kingdom support based in the south of England.[54] With the imposition of the Poll Tax one year ahead of England and the SNP victory in the Labour heartland of Govan in 1988, Labour seemed vulnerable to nationalist claims of a choice between independence or perpetual Thatcherism. A critical factor in the creation of the Constitutional Convention in 1988, and the agreement of both Labour and the Liberals to work together for home rule, was the need to find a solution to the problem of British constitutional imbalance and, just as important, a way to head off a potential nationalist challenge. Devolution, it was claimed, would stave off the worst excesses of Tory rule from London, without the need to break the Union.[55] It acknowledged the legitimacy of nationalist aspirations, but within the traditional understanding of the unionist constitutional framework. Thatcher, it was claimed, posed the greatest threat to the Union by her uncompromising and blinkered attitude.

The myth of civil society

Arguably the reason why the Scots used the Thatcherite experience to make a greater case for home rule than the Welsh was their ability to employ the idea of civil society. As a concept, this explained both the need for devolution and the political rejection of Conservatism in the 1980s and 1990s. Yet there is a paradox here. Although the term was only used in the early 1990s, it was retrospectively applied to give a historical coherence to the 1980s. Ironically, civil society was a concept that Thatcher herself could have applauded, and is not that far removed from David Cameron's 'Big Society'. Yet the concepts of 'civic nationalism' and 'civil society' were ideally suited to mobilise the anti-Thatcher/ Conservative lobby, giving it a coherence that might not otherwise have been present. Furthermore, by basing a small-'n' nationalism around civic values, it avoided any association with ethnic or racist ideas, an important issue in the light of the ethnic violence that emerged in the former Yugoslavia. Broadly speaking, the theory went as follows: the Scots were left-of-centre, believed in the mixed economy and expressed these values through their civic institutions. The low vote obtained by the Conservatives was interpreted as an explicit rejection of the values of Thatcherism, facilitated by a belief in anti-Conservative tactical voting.[56] In rejecting the policies of Thatcherism, so the argument went, civil society could be represented through a Constitutional Convention.

This was not necessarily how the rest of the world would have understood 'civil society'. In spite of the spin, the mobilisation of 'civil society' was primarily a defensive manoeuvre by the major losers in the Thatcherite revolution who needed a common denominator. The easiest to hand was discontent with the current constitutional status quo. It is hard to avoid the conclusion that its sponsors were united more by what they did not want than by what they did.

It was argued that, as Thatcher had taken no account of the electoral verdict on her policies in Scotland, a Convention drawing on the support of Labour, the Liberal Democrats, the churches, local government, elements within law and education, and a range of other organisations had sufficient legitimacy to represent the will of the Scottish people. The idea also appealed to Scottish history, invoking the Conventions of 1690 and 1842. Neatly, it bypassed the awkward reality of the splintered nature of Scottish politics; indeed, the Conservative government argued that it did not really have a democratic mandate as none of the elected opposition MPs had stood on that platform.[57] Backed by the Scottish media and press (and what Andrew Neil disparagingly described as Scotland's 'blethering' classes), the Convention was able to articulate the concept of *popular* sovereignty, which was theoretically enshrined in Scottish law, in opposition to British *parliamentary* sovereignty.[58]

However, the movement was also a pragmatic response to the realities of the Thatcherite experience in Scotland. It got round the awkward problem of political impotence for Labour and the Liberal Democrats. It is remarkable just how many concessions Labour made to the Liberal

Democrats, particularly in conceding proportional representation. The trade union movement, the churches and local government had all witnessed a decline in power in the 1980s and this was an opportunity to halt or reverse the tide of growing insignificance. In reality, there is more than a hint of suspicion that 'civil society' in Scotland was simply the remnants of the old corporatist state that Thatcher had so assiduously attacked. Civil society allowed the main losers in the Thatcherite revolution in Scotland to reinvent themselves.

The idea of a strong civil society that rejected Thatcherism in Scotland has many supporters, but has not been tested in any meaningful way. Certainly there is nothing to suggest that the Scots were immune to the growing 'atomisation' of society that existed elsewhere, nor to consumerism, nor to the growing gap that divided the rich from the poor. Voluntary agencies showed a decline in membership. Scots took advantage of the 'right to buy' and bought into privatisation share ownership. A strong civil society may have been an ideal, but it certainly was not a reality. Transmuting civil society into 'civic' nationalism enabled the endorsement of a soft or small-'n' nationalism that could counteract the claims of the SNP. Furthermore, it downgraded the significance of class, and opinion polls showed an increasing conflation of working-class identity with Scottish national identity. In reality, as the sociologist, David McCrone, has pointed out, there was increasing convergence on a wide range of socio-economic indicators between Scotland and England, paradoxically at the time when there was growing political divergence.[59] The concept of civil society could plausibly explain why the leafy middle-class Scottish suburbs, which in England would have voted for the Conservatives, rejected them north of the border. Yet few could deny the significance of class as a mobilising force against Thatcher during the worst of the recession in the 1980s. By presenting anti-Thatcherism or anti-Conservatism as *the* distinctive hallmark of Scottish politics, class ceased to have its dominant role. Instead, civil society and the left-of-centre consensus became a way of drawing together the unionist opposition to Thatcherism.

In part, the poor electoral performance of the Conservatives became a self-fulfilling prophecy. After 1987, when the party did badly, it became expected that it would continue to perform badly. Furthermore, Scottish Tories did not want to hold themselves hostage to constitutional fortune by claiming that they needed a popular electoral endorsement from the Scots for legitimacy. Scottish voters were not necessary for Conservative success, and this realisation did little to discourage an increasing flood of jibes at 'subsidy junkies'. The notion of the 'democratic deficit' was further enforced by the decision to implement the

Poll Tax one year early in Scotland. Furthermore, educational reform and water privatisation were in the political pipeline and seemed to hint that Thatcherism was increasing in intensity.[60] Although the Poll Tax had been implemented at the behest of Scottish Tory activists as part of a long-running campaign against rates, its timing was conditioned by an imminent revaluation that would have pushed them higher. Cuts to the rate support grant from central government ensured that there was no middle-class bonanza from the scrapping of rates and helped create the perception that there were a lot more losers than winners.[61] Worse still, the issue fuelled the argument that Thatcher did not care about the Scots, that their political preferences counted for nothing and that they were being used as guinea pigs. For many, this was enough evidence to show the existence of the democratic deficit and provided the impetus for the formation of the Convention. This made it much easier for the opposition to portray the Conservative Party as alien and anti-Scottish.[62]

Intellectually, the idea of civil society provided a coherence to anti-Thatcherism and arguably imposed a small-'n' nationalist pattern retrospectively on what had been essentially a disparate political response to the Conservative governments of the 1980s. Furthermore, it was a rhetorical device that has been in use up to the present day.[63] By conceding home rule as a matter of urgent political priority, it took the wind out of the sails of any nationalist challenge. The SNP's decision to remain aloof from the Convention was predicated on the belief that should it fail, then they would pick up the political dividend.

The sense of civil society was not as strong in Wales; or rather, the capacity to conjure up a myth of civil society was not as strong. In Wales, class loyalties arguably remained firmer, and there was a greater reluctance to flirt with a nationalist explanation for anti-Thatcherism. The fact that Plaid Cymru was more associated with Welsh-speaking areas made it harder to overcome accusations of ethnic nationalism, even though the party was less committed to independence than the SNP. As mentioned earlier, Wales did not have the same territorial insularity nor the same power of national institutions with which to project anti-Conservatism as a 'national' response to Thatcherism. Labour in Wales did not perceive itself to be under as great a potential threat from a nationalist backlash and had no need to make concessions to the Liberal Democrats. Although Tories were tarred with the anti-Welsh brush, this was less comprehensive and thorough than north of the border, as the Welsh Conservatives' recent revival demonstrates. By contrast, the myth of civil society's response to Thatcher in Scotland still resonates sufficiently to ensure that the prospects of a Conservative revival north of the border seem as far away as ever.

Conclusion

In conclusion, the experience of Thatcherism in Scotland and Wales produced similar socio-economic consequences, but significantly different political outcomes in relation to the demand for devolution. Undoubtedly the Scots' ability to manufacture a more successful 'national' response to Thatcherism was due to the superior resources of their institutions and the existence of a self-contained media that helped project the decline of Conservative fortunes as a result of a 'national' political culture. In this, it is hard to avoid the conclusion that Scottish Conservatives were authors of their own fate. Before Thatcherism, Scottish patriotism had been a mainstay of Toryism north of the border. As Michael Fry has commented, a right-of-centre party that does not have a natural home for patriotism seems doomed to failure.[64] Scottish Conservatives failed to convincingly adapt Thatcherism to a unionism that could accommodate Scottish patriotism. As a consequence, they surrendered constitutional innovation to the Liberals and Labour, who argued that devolution was the best way to preserve and update the Union. Furthermore, they unwittingly came to be associated with the notion that a uniform British nationalism was the only legitimate form of patriotism. For many Scots, Thatcher's Britishness was indistinguishable from Englishness. To some extent this lesson was learned in the Major era, but by then the damage had been done.[65] In Wales, on the other hand, class held its shape better and politics did not fragment. In consequence, there was no need to invoke the idea of civil society to hold it together.

10   'Just another country'? The Irish question in the Thatcher years

Marc Mulholland

In their emblematic song of commercial nihilism, 'Anarchy in the UK' (1977), the Sex Pistols sarcastically reflected on the bathetic fate of that once imperial title, the 'United Kingdom'. The UK was now little more than one acronym among many in a neo-corporate Britain straining under the weight of a proliferation – NEDDY, TUC, CBI, PIB, GLC, etc. Northern Ireland seemed only the most extreme example of a general dissolution, where Parliament and government waned in their effective power of decision and acronym organisations had taken on a life of their own:

> Is this the M.P.L.A. or
> Is this the U.D.A. or
> Is this the I.R.A.
> I thought it was the U.K.
> Or just another country

For Conservatives, of course, punk was part of the disease. Northern Ireland, however, was in their eyes an extreme manifestation of a general malaise: the decline of parliamentary sovereignty, refusal to defend to the hilt irreducible Britishness, and conciliation of subversion and over-mighty interest groups. Indeed, by the later 1970s, it was close to common sense that Britain had made the situation in Northern Ireland worse by trying too hard to resolve it.

The parameters of British policy

The 'Ulster problem' was by no means straightforward. Within Northern Ireland, a hard division existed between Catholics and Protestants: there was no 'floating vote' on the constitutional question. Relations between the unionist establishment in the north and the nationalist establishment in the south were poor. Unionists denied the legitimacy of all-Ireland national allegiance, despite a 'united Ireland' being the bedrock of Irish nationalist ideology for many decades. The

180

constitution of the Irish Republic, in Articles 2 and 3, laid claim to the territory of the six northern counties, a refusal to accept the legitimacy of a neighbour's sovereignty unique within the European Economic Community. Historically, relations between the United Kingdom and Ireland had been rocky. As a historicist creed, Irish nationalism had an obsessively informed memory of British perfidy; as an imperial, culturally Protestant identity, Britishness reacted to Irish nationalism with condescending bafflement and an irritatingly self-assured moral superiority. If the 'totality of relations' comprised a cat's cradle, persistent violence in Northern Ireland, both from the remarkably militaristic and ruthless IRA, and the rougher-hewn sectarian rage of loyalism, ensured that there was rarely time and political space for the British government to steady itself sufficiently to slice the Gordian knot.

It is certainly the case that Britain was fundamentally consistent in its promotion of a framework for settling Northern Ireland, at least from 1972. This was made up of three dimensions. An 'east–west' dimension required cooperation between the sovereign governments in Dublin and London. An 'internal dimension' required the reestablishment of devolved government in Northern Ireland, but now on a cross-community rather than 'majoritarian' basis: any government at Stormont would have to draw in representatives of both the main traditions in Northern Ireland. The 'north–south' dimension would recalibrate relations between the two governments on the island of Ireland, so that they cooperated rather than collided. Finally, the entirety of the 'totality of relations' would have to be sorted out as one coherent interlocking deal if any settlement was to stick.

The east–west, internal 'Catholic–Protestant', and north–south axes were always promoted as the framework for a settlement. Britain, moreover, did not waver from its position that Crown sovereignty over Northern Ireland could not be relinquished without the express consent of the majority within Northern Ireland. However, it is worth emphasising that British parameters for a settlement were inherently ambiguous, being algebraic in form with the values of the various categories up for negotiation. East–west relations, for example, might simply involve neighbourly relations between Dublin and London, and an acknowledgement that the government of Ireland has a particular interest in affairs north of the border. They might, however, go much further than this, with the Irish government being seen as special representatives of Irish nationalists in Northern Ireland, and having an automatic right to be consulted as such. The 'internal' axis might amount to a devolved government in Northern Ireland based upon full power-sharing, with mandatory coalition governments yoking together nationalists and unionists. It might also conceivably mean (and this was the unionists' preferred interpretation), a government based upon a simple majority of deputies in a Stormont parliament, but with powerful parliamentary committees, some chaired by opposition MPs, with the right to see normally confidential governmental paperwork – a kind of extended Privy Council. The 'north–south' axis was perhaps most algebraic in form: would it simply reflect two governments on one island diplomatically cooperating over affairs of common interest, or was it rather an acknowledgement that a single government of Ireland was the logical end-point, and north–south cooperation thus a preparation for such a consummation? Indeed, the original and defunct 'Council of Ireland' in the 1920 Government of Ireland Act, the act which had established partition, had been explicitly designed to serve as a future all-Ireland government in embryo.

During the Troubles, the British government recognised two principles that, logically speaking, were incompatible. By explicitly stating that the Crown would gladly abandon governance in Northern Ireland if a majority in the province concurred, Britain implicitly conceded that Irish sovereignty had a higher moral claim than British sovereignty. No British government, by contrast, declared itself neutral on the intrinsic moral worth of the Union between England, Wales and Scotland, even if in practice majority support for Scottish secession, should it ever come about, could hardly be denied. Britain effectively conceded that all-Ireland sovereignty was a *right*, even if its exercise was blocked by circumstances, while Crown sovereignty in Northern Ireland was a *duty*, to be gracefully abandoned when circumstances allowed. On the other hand, Britain recognised Northern Ireland as the appropriate unit for the exercise of 'democratic consent'. As the six-county province was an entity designedly carved out to save as much of Ireland from Irish nationalism as was compatible with a safe unionist majority, Britain recognised a unionist-crafted *right* of veto on the exercise of all-Ireland (and indeed United Kingdom) self-determination. Britain undertook responsibility for Northern Ireland as a *duty* to unionism so long as it retained majority support within Northern Ireland.

The function of Britain's algebraic framework for a settlement was to square the circle. 'Greening' governance within Northern Ireland, and locating it within a balanced articulation of rights, claims and duties between Britain and Ireland, was a down-payment partly redeeming the *right* of Irish sovereignty. This, hopefully, would reconcile Irish nationalism with Britain's *duty* to uphold Northern Ireland's electorate as the constituency with the right to trigger or withhold all-Ireland sovereignty. Essentially, Britain's strategy was persuasive, attempting to force the contending parties in Northern Ireland to accept *British* realities. As such, the algebraic constancy of Britain's approach was consistent with an exceptionally wide range of approaches to the political actors within Northern Ireland, and indeed Ireland as a whole. I wish to argue here that Britain's approach to the actors of Northern Ireland veered wildly over the course of the Troubles. This had the effect of stoking up fears and promoting hopes within Northern Ireland in such a manner that the conflict was often aggravated. Britain was so obviously negotiating with the parties to the conflict, wilting before their episodic concentrations of strength and exploiting their episodic weaknesses, and so obviously willing to switch tack, that militancy and obduracy were perfectly understandable responses from both nationalism and unionism to Britain's gyrations. In brief, we can divide up British strategies as follows:

- keeping the conflict at arm's length (1921–68, 1976 – *c.* 1984);
- building the political 'centre' in Northern Ireland (1968 – April 1972, August 1972 – 1974, *c.* 1984–9);
- bringing in the political 'extremes' in Northern Ireland (July 1972, 1975, 1990s).

British strategy before Thatcher

After partition, Britain pretty much left Northern Ireland, under the devolved Ulster Unionist-run administration at Stormont, to its own devices. As Catholic grievances about discrimination grew in the 1960s, and the moderate Unionist leadership of Captain Terence O'Neill provoked an ultra and Paisleyite dissidence, this became increasingly untenable. From about 1966, the British government leant upon the devolved Unionist government, encouraging it to introduce civil rights reform. This pressure, however, tended to undermine the position of O'Neill as a liberal Unionist Prime Minister. It was too easy for right-wingers within unionism to accuse him of appeasing a hostile Labour government. When the civil rights movement broke out in Northern Ireland in 1968, Harold Wilson's government insisted upon substantive reform. This contributed to the fall of Terence O'Neill in April 1969, and his replacement by the hapless James Chichester-Clark. Following the commitment of the regular army to keep security control from August 1969, London ministers had a great deal of de facto control over day-to-day policy in Northern Ireland. However, British ministers were well aware that Ulster's Protestants saw Stormont as 'their' government, and a bulwark against treachery. Particularly as the struggle with the IRA ramped up, Britain was loathe to stand down the devolved Unionist government, for fear of provoking a unionist backlash. Britain therefore delivered a robust security policy, particularly evident from the election of Edward's Heath's UK government in June 1970. By vigorously cracking down on Catholic nationalist insurgency, it was hoped that the relatively moderate Unionist government at Stormont, led from March 1971 by Brian Faulkner, could be shored up against the increasingly restive unionist ultras. Hardnosed repression, however – the Falls Road Curfew in July 1970, internment in August 1971, a distinct willingness to use lethal force particularly evident in early 1972 – all served to win Catholic nationalist support for the IRA.

We might describe British strategy from the mid 1960s to the proroguing of Stormont in April 1972 as one of 'shoring up the centre'. The goal was to maintain a moderate Protestant unionist leadership, and to deliver enough civil rights reform to nurture a new and equally moderate Catholic nationalist leadership. This strategy had clearly failed by 1972, as Irish nationalism rejected British pretensions to be a neutral arbiter, and unionist ultras demanded more repression than could be realistically delivered.

When Britain indefinitely suspended Stormont, it seemed temporarily at a loss as to what to do next. For a brief interlude, the Direct Rule administration turned to 'bringing in the extremes'. This involved direct negotiations with the Provisional IRA in July 1972. These quickly broke down, and an embarrassed Secretary of State for Northern Ireland, William Whitelaw, dismissed the episode as nothing more than a means by which Britain had tried to make its determination not to capitulate to violence clear to the IRA. It seems evident, however, that Britain had entertained real hopes that the IRA could be brought into a political process, and there is no reason to believe that Britain would not have offered substantial concessions, not just in terms of the release of prisoners and so on, but also by encouraging open-ended talks, including representatives of militant republicanism, on the status of Northern Ireland.[1]

By the late summer of 1972, however, Britain had reverted to 'shoring up the centre'. This involved dismissing republicanism as a political participant, and encouraging moderate unionists and nationalists to hammer out a deal. This resulted in the power-sharing agreement of 1973, negotiated primarily between the moderate nationalist Social Democratic and Labour Party (SDLP) and the Ulster Unionist Party (UUP), and the ancillary Sunningdale Agreement of 1974 that established an all-Ireland Council of Ireland to undertake executive functions as and when delegated them by the parliaments in Ireland.

Sunningdale collapsed in the face of unionist objections that the institutions agreed were a one-way ratchet towards Irish unity, and a loyalist strike forced the Ulster Unionists to abandon the power-sharing government in May 1974. As the deal was designed to be mutually supportive, the Council of Ireland collapsed as well. The British government (Labour again, since March 1974) reverted to 'bringing in the extremes'. The political wing of the IRA, Sinn Féin, had been legalised in 1974 (as had, briefly, the loyalist Ulster Volunteer Force), and a 'truce' was arranged between British forces and the IRA in 1975. Labour ministers clearly hoped that 'creative' extremists, united if only by a common belief that British sovereignty was incapable of resolving the conflict, would emerge as the political representatives of both nationalist and unionist communities. However, Labour mistook loyalist nostalgia for Stormont as an incipient anti-British 'Ulster nationalism' when in fact Protestant opinion valued the Union far above any particular form of regional governance.[2] By 1976, Britain had decided that its hyperactive attempts at a settlement had only aggravated the conflict in Northern Ireland, by encouraging nationalists and unionists to hope for the best and prepare for the worst. 'The turmoil in Northern Ireland is due in part to inconsistencies in British policy, which is constantly reversing itself', the loyalist leader Andy Tyrie told an interviewer in 1981.[3]

Thatcher and Northern Ireland

Such ideas had significant currency in Conservative circles. Tom Utley, the talented and influential Tory journalist with a particular interest in the Irish question, insisted in 1974: 'what is essential to defeating a revolution … is the will to victory.… [H]ad Britain concentrated single-mindedly on producing that despair in the IRA, the battle for Ulster would now be over.'[4] Enoch Powell, a Unionist MP for South Down since October 1974, argued that the aspirations of the nationalist minority had to be broken because it was not possible for the same territory to belong to two nations: there had to be a total victory for the unionist majority. The British government, he argued, should treat Northern Ireland exactly like the rest of the UK, a policy known as 'integration'. He denounced 'false compromise between incompatible political objectives which has always been the prelude to chaos in Ulster',[5] and urged that the only way the war would come to an end was when one side realised that it could not win.[6] Margaret Thatcher was temperamentally a unionist of the Powell stripe. She shared his desire for military victory, and even for integration. When a Northern Ireland constituency Conservative Association was established in Northern Ireland in 1990, she wrote to it in support, expressing her determination to 'maintain the Union'.[7]

As the new Conservative leader, Thatcher appointed Airey Neave as Shadow spokesman on Northern Ireland. Neave, a former war hero, was close to Thatcher, having been national organiser of Thatcher's successful bid to become party leader. He echoed Utley and Powell in accusing the Labour government of causing deep fear among law-abiding people and democratic politicians in Northern Ireland by studied ambiguity over its constitutional intentions. He pledged his party's commitment to retaining Northern Ireland as part of the United Kingdom, and to maintaining troops there. In 1977, Neave welcomed the visit to the province by the Queen as paving the way to a settlement based on a strengthened Union, and in 1978, he announced that the Conservative Party had formally buried its support for a devolved power-sharing administration in Northern Ireland, where parties from both unionist and nationalist traditions would be required to govern together, as no longer 'practical politics'.[8]

Neave was assassinated by the Irish National Liberation Army (INLA) on 31 March 1979. Thatcher was understandably shocked.[9] She did not, however, cleave to his policies once in office. The new Conservative government abandoned the notion of 'integration'. Most importantly, the Irish government had made clear its unalterable opposition to abandonment of power-sharing devolution with an 'Irish dimension'. As Secretary of State Jim Prior admitted, integration would not destroy Irish nationalist aspirations, and 'it would have scuppered any hope of co-operation with Dublin'.[10] And while Ian Paisley, leader of the Democratic Unionist Party, was impressed by Thatcher's talk of militarily defeating the IRA,[11] it was evident to government ministers that the IRA, following its cellular reorganisation, was more difficult than ever to utterly defeat, even if it could be contained.[12]

James Prior attempted to initiate momentum towards an 'internal settlement' by promoting 'Rolling Devolution'. The idea was that a locally elected assembly would reach agreement on how devolved powers should be exercised, not in one fell swoop but by stages. John Hume of the moderate SDLP attacked the assembly as a 'subterfuge', without power-sharing as of right but as a favour granted by unionists, and entirely ignoring the all-Irish dimension. Unionists, for their part, were quite clear that power-sharing, never mind an 'Irish dimension', was not a price worth paying for devolution.[13]

More important was the development of links between the two sovereign governments. Charles Haughey, who became Taoiseach in late 1979, first met with Thatcher in May 1980. He found her impressive – 'a tough leader' – but was left unsure of her intentions.[14] On 8 December 1980, in the first ever meeting of its kind, the prime ministers, foreign ministers and finance ministers of Britain and Ireland met, largely cutting out the Northern Ireland Office.[15] It was, Paul Arthur notes, 'the most powerful British cabinet presence in Ireland since partition'.[16] Here it was agreed to establish Anglo-Irish 'studies' to examine 'possible new institutional structures, citizenship rights, security matters, economic co-operation and measures to encourage mutual understanding'. Ulster Unionists blamed the malign influence of the Foreign Office and Lord Carrington. Enoch Powell, incidentally, led the way in such conspiracy theorising, believing the Anglo-Irish initiative to be driven by a Foreign Office/American plot to achieve a united Ireland within NATO.[17]

When Argentina invaded the Falkland Islands on 2 April 1982, the unionists felt that their mistrust of the Foreign Office had been vindicated. Ireland at first voted for EEC trade sanctions against Argentina. On 4 May 1982, however, the Dublin government said it was 'appalled' by Britain's sinking of the Argentine warship *Admiral Belgrano* and in May Ireland joined Italy in opposing renewal of EEC trade sanctions against Argentina.[18] In June 1982, breaking with custom, there were no formal talks between Britain and Ireland at the European summit conference in Brussels. When Thatcher met the Republic's new premier, Garrett FitzGerald, during the EEC Heads of Government meeting on 21 March 1983, it was the first such meeting for almost sixteen months.

This diplomatic stand-off came in the aftermath of the hunger strikes in Northern Ireland. Special category status for convicted prisoners – in effect the same regime as allowed unconvicted internees – had been conceded by Secretary of State William Whitelaw in June 1972. When, in November 1975, a later Secretary of State, Merlyn Rees, announced that the special category status of prisoners in Northern Ireland was to cease, he explained that it had engendered illusions in the prisoners that they had political status and were entitled to favoured treatment and future amnesty. 'Criminalisation' was problematic, however, as prisoners suspected of politically motivated ('scheduled') sentences were tried by special 'Diplock' courts, with no jury, and indeed there was ample evidence of confessions being beaten out of suspects. Andy Tyrie, commander of the Ulster Defence Association (UDA), summed it up: 'It's nice to be tough, but it would be better to be tough about issues other than this. There are special courts and special legislation, so why can't there be special prisoners?'[19] A republican hunger strike to the death began on 1 March 1981, when Bobby Sands (26) refused food. The strike resolved into a cruel war of nerves. The British government hinted that substantial concessions would be made after the prisoners ceased their fast, but refused to specify them. In 1991, Sean McKenna, a former prison protester, who had left the IRA after having watched the ten hunger-strikers die in 1981, claimed the IRA leadership in the prison had been 'as intransigent as the Brits'.[20]

For Norman Tebbit, Thatcher's defiance of the hunger-strikers was of a piece with her refusal to heed the Cassandra-like warnings of Tory wets during the aggravated recession of the early 1980s: 'it was becoming clear that she was a Prime Minister unlike any since Churchill'.[21] Thatcher had become a personalised hate figure for the IRA during the hunger strikes.[22] On 12 October 1984, the IRA bombed the Grand Hotel in Brighton, England, in an attempt to murder Margaret Thatcher and senior members of the government staying there during the Conservative Party Conference.

The real significance of the strike was to undermine the pretensions of 'normalisation' (and the concomitant 'criminalisation'), and to thrust 'smash H-Block' candidates, then Sinn Féin itself, into electoral politics. In the 1982 elections to the newly established Northern Ireland Assembly, Sinn Féin candidates got 64,191 first-preference votes. Many observers saw the results as disastrous, giving credibility to Sinn Féin and the provisionals' 'armed struggle'. Speaking privately to Conservative MPs, James Prior expressed his fear that the whole of Ireland could become another Cuba in the event of a Sinn Féin takeover in the north, and he stressed his pessimism about the SDLP's chances of stopping Sinn Féin's electoral advance.[23] Indeed, even the Ulster Unionist Party explicitly decided to go easy on the SDLP in an attempt to shore it up. Should Sinn Féin overhaul the SDLP, said James Molyneaux of the Ulster Unionist Party, it would herald the start of Northern Ireland's 'ultimate nightmare'.[24]

The SDLP's problem was that its moderation appeared to win no favour from the British government, which refused steadfastly to upset the unionist majority. It was vital that it be seen to have a forward strategy if the rise of Sinn Féin was to be stymied. On 11 March 1983, therefore, the Republic's government announced its decision to press ahead with plans for an all-Ireland forum of Irish political parties to discuss the 'national question', along lines suggested by the SDLP. On 2 May 1984, after eleven months of deliberations, the New Ireland Forum came out in favour of unity by consent with guarantees for the protection of both unionist and nationalist identities, but two other options – a federal island and joint sovereignty over Northern Ireland – were also on the table. The real gravamen of the document, however, was on the need to institutionally represent an Irish nationalist identity that, *pace* the integrationists, was not ephemeral:

For nationalists, a central aim has been the survival and development of an Irish identity, an objective that continues in Northern Ireland today as nationalists seek effective recognition of their Irish identity and pursue their rights and aspirations through political means.[25]

Addressing a press conference after an Anglo-Irish summit on 19 November 1984, with FitzGerald sitting horrified at her side, Thatcher with contemptuous off-handedness ruled out the three options proposed by the New Ireland Forum report. The unionist parties reacted with glee. Unionists were optimistic that Thatcher, influenced by her pro-unionist PPS, Ian Gow, would not challenge their core interests.[26] In fact, as early as 1983, Thatcher was aware that an agreement between the British and Irish governments was 'probable rather than possible', as a Northern Ireland minister remembered.[27]

Towards Anglo-Irish rapprochement

Charles Powell, a senior civil service aide to Thatcher, recalled that for the Prime Minister, 'security was paramount ... it was security first, second and third'.[28] This was evident in her enthusiasm for a joint-security zone, allowing Crown forces to pursue IRA suspects across the border. However, it seems clear that it was Garrett FitzGerald and his team who really drove the inter-governmental negotiations. They offered all manner of security cooperation in return for 'Joint Authority' of Northern Ireland by ministers of Britain and Ireland. It is hard to believe that this was really the Irish government's goal. To be sure, 'Joint Authority' had to be the minimum starting point for their negotiators, as otherwise they would have been accused of simply ignoring the agreed nationalist agenda of the New Ireland Forum. However, Joint Authority promised power with a terrifying amount of responsibility. A four-million-strong Irish state simply could not look upon a material engagement in the conflict in Northern Ireland, on their own island, with anything like the *noblesse oblige* of Britain's fifty-five million across the Irish Sea. Should the conflict escalate, loyalism had a proven ability to wreak carnage in southern Irish cities, and the IRA could actually subvert the state. It is prudent to assume that by offering the resources of the Irish state to anti-insurgency efforts north of the border in return for Joint Authority (and massive reform of Northern Ireland's security and judicial system), the Irish were making an offer they knew would be refused, allowing them to fall back on the in fact far more attractive proposition of a right of consultation with minimum strings attached.

Garret FitzGerald's first achievement, according to Geoffrey Howe, was to convince Thatcher that the rise of Sinn Féin was a threat to stability in Ireland, both north and south.[29] Sinn Féin's rise indubitably reflected Catholic 'alienation' from the institutions of state. Thatcher, however, thought that talk of alienation smacked of Marxism, and disliked it proportionately. When Secretary of State for Northern Ireland Douglas Hurd dutifully denied that Catholic alienation existed, John Hume riposted that he would invite Hurd to visit him at his home in the Catholic Bogside of Derry to discuss the matter, only that it would require 'an army of tanks to bring him here'.[30] In November 1984, the strongly anti-republican Catholic Bishop of Down and Conner, Cahal Daly, insisted that he lived in the middle of 'Catholic alienation' and it was not confined to people who voted Sinn Féin.[31]

For the Irish government, the aim was to lessen Catholic alienation by reforming the institutions of governance in Northern Ireland so that the Catholic community there could accept its legitimacy without denying their Irish nationalism. FitzGerald explained his government's thinking to the British thus:

The [Catholic] minority [in Northern Ireland] wanted to live in their own country in peace. Just as [Thatcher] was proud of being English, they took pride in their Irish identity and felt themselves cut off by an arbitrary act from the rest of the nationalist majority in Ireland. They could not express their identity, not being allowed even to fly the flag of their own nation in their own country … A way must be found to enable them to identify with the system of government.[32]

Thatcher clearly found difficult to accept at an emotional level the idea that Irish nationalists could never be brought to accept the democratic legitimacy of British sovereignty. She was obsessed with the idea of solving the problem by somehow creating a purely British enclave state in Ireland. Douglas Hurd said:

I do not know how many times she began a conversation with me by saying that the answer might be to redraw the border so as to be rid of areas which were substantially Nationalist, and retain a loyal and impregnable Unionist province. Repeatedly I had to tell her … [t]here was no tidy dividing line. The intertwining of the communities was hopelessly complex.[33]

Thatcher was unwilling to engage with the unattractive reality that Irish nationalists were inassimilable to British sovereignty. Though quite well-read on Irish history, she found it impossible to synthesise an overall analysis, presumably because to do so would have meant overthrowing cherished assumptions. The head of the Northern Ireland civil service at the time, Sir Kenneth Bloomfield, found Thatcher to be 'inconsistent to the brink of schizophrenia', veering from sentimental unionism to disdain for actually existing Ulster unionism.[34] Robin Ramsay, a former PPS to the Secretary of State for Northern

Ireland, recalled an awkward encounter with her at a formal dinner in 1983:

To my astonishment, she suddenly turned on me and imperiously demanded to know what 'your lot', meaning the Ulster Unionists really wanted ... [S]he thumped the table and said in exasperation, 'I can't get any sense out of the leadership. They just keep mumbling the old slogans. And the others run rings around them.'[35]

Here was the frustration of a political leader exasperated at her inability to intellectually rebut Irish nationalist claims. During the negotiations, Thatcher admired FitzGerald for his intellectual skill and clearly superior knowledge of the issues at stake. By the time she came to write her autobiography out of office, this admiration had curdled into a rather churlish resentment.[36]

Thatcher's lack of a clear line on the Irish question had a positive side. James Molyneaux, who as Ulster Unionist leader had no great cause to speak well of the Prime Minister, contrasted Thatcher favourably with Edward Heath, because she was willing to seek out expert opinion.[37] 'It took a gigantic struggle by many far-sighted-people to persuade her', Geoffrey Howe wrote, but while 'her head was persuaded, her heart was not'.[38]

Thatcher, therefore, was not the real policy-maker on the British side. Sir Robert Armstrong, head of the British civil service, laid the groundwork with Dermot McNally, secretary to the Irish Cabinet. Armstrong was politically supported by Douglas Hurd and Chris Patten, both close to the Foreign Office headed by Geoffrey Howe.[39] A *Times* article from December 1985 said of Armstrong, Howe and Hurd, that they worked easily together and had 'a similar world view and similar personalities. None of them has any enthusiasm for the Union.'[40] The Northern Ireland Office civil service, on the other hand, were almost entirely excluded from negotiations.[41] Indeed, the Conservative elite in general were kept out of the loop. When the draft Anglo-Irish Agreement was finally presented to Cabinet, it was as a fait accompli.[42] All those who still inclined to the view that constitutional initiatives only tended to provoke unionists and tempt nationalists to seek more were ignored.

The Anglo-Irish Agreement

On 15 November 1985, the Anglo-Irish Agreement was signed by Margaret Thatcher and Garret FitzGerald at Hillsborough Castle, County Down. Thatcher cut an impressive figure. FitzGerald was carefully spoken, but nowhere near as 'authoritative and clear spoken' as his counterpart, an Irish minister admitted: 'Thatcher is undoubtedly the sharpest thing out, she looked very well (how can she be 60!), quite feminine, but totally in control and totally on the ball.'[43] This belied the Irish negotiating triumph, however. Substantively, the Agreement obliged Britain to consult Dublin on affairs pertaining to nationalist interests within Northern Ireland.[44] An Inter-Governmental Conference was set up, to be serviced by a full-time secretariat of British and Irish civil servants based in Belfast. The Agreement stated that:

> the Conference shall be a framework within which the Irish Government may, where the interests of the minority community are significantly or especially affected, put forward views on proposals for major legislation and on major policy issues, which are within the purview of the Northern Ireland Departments and which remain the responsibility of the Secretary of State for Northern Ireland.[45]

So long as there was no devolved government in Northern Ireland, *all* legislation and policy issues were the responsibility of the Secretary of State, and so fair game for Irish consultation.

This Agreement was, in many ways, a quite extraordinary British confession of inadequacy. Britain gave up trying to speak for a subset of UK citizens, asking instead the Irish government to act as 'advocates for the Nationalist community'.[46] This was a striking deferral by Britain to a 'foreign government', but, as Tom Wilson, a writer sympathetic to the unionist case, admitted: 'to the Catholic minority in Ulster, the Republic is not a foreign state'.[47]

Thatcher was primarily concerned with winning security cooperation from the Republic of Ireland; at any rate she chose to emphasise this in her memoirs.[48] One might be somewhat sceptical about this. The Agreement was vague on cross-border security cooperation, and purely permissive. It did not of itself materially diminish the IRA's military capacity, and by 1988 Britain had turned to harsher repression on its own behalf. A broadcast ban was introduced on 'direct statements' by representatives or in support of paramilitary organisations.[49] (In September 1990, this led to the bizarre ruling that a historical Ulster Television Schools' series could not include the voices of the former president of the Republic, Eamon de Valera, or of the former Minister for Foreign Affairs, Sean MacBride). On top of this the security forces adopted a demonstrably harder line. By 1992, thirty-seven IRA volunteers had been shot dead by the SAS and undercover units, thirty-one since an intensification of covert operations in 1983, compared to nine by regular army units.[50] All this was very much in defiance of advice proffered by the Irish side of the Inter-Governmental Conference.

The greatest source of angst for the British was extradition. But while the Irish government did amend the 1965 Extradition Act to remove the exemption for 'politically motivated suspects', it also increased the requirements for evidence in warrants issued by the British Attorney General. Thatcher complained that Britain was being treated as a 'least favoured nation', and British–Irish relations nose-dived.[51] In the first year of the legislation, five people were extradited, but thirty-two warrants returned. Despite months of deliberation, officials of the two governments had failed to produce an agreed report on extradition before the end of Thatcher's term.

Thatcher also later evinced surprise at unionist hostility to the Anglo-Irish Agreement: 'it was worse than anyone had predicted to me'.[52] This is hard to credit, as the Agreement was in fact very well trailed. As early as 28 July 1985 the Orange Order had angrily warned of a Protestant backlash that would make the 1974 Ulster Workers' Council strike look like 'a Sunday picnic'.[53] By September 1985, Official Unionist deputy leader Harold McCusker was publicly arguing that unionists had the right to resist British government betrayal, if necessary by force of arms.[54] In November 1985, 'Ulster Clubs' involving unionist politicians and loyalist paramilitaries were established to resist any Anglo-Irish deal.

Ian Gow, a junior minister close to Thatcher, would certainly have predicted unionist fireworks. He resigned from the government in protest at the accord.[55] Unionist protest against the signed Agreement included the petitioning of courts and the Queen, elected representatives boycotting ministers, local councils refusing to conduct normal business, and even default on taxes and rates.[56] A 'day of action' was held on 3 March 1986, during which there was widespread rioting. This, however, exposed the limits of loyalism, for unlike 1974 there was no locally responsible power-sharing administration to bring down, and burning out RUC officers was unlikely to endear the unionist cause to a British audience. On 20 November 1989, Ulster Unionist leader Molyneaux admitted that he had considered resignation when he and Paisley were 'railroaded' into supporting the day of action. Thatcher had effectively broken the British prime-ministerial mould by successfully confronting and facing down the unionists.[57]

The Agreement can be seen as an attempt to bolster the middle ground against the 'extremes'. The rise of Sinn Féin had made bolstering the SDLP as a centre alternative to Sinn Féin a government priority. The government was openly delighted that the Unionists lost the Newry and Armagh seat at Westminster to the SDLP in December 1985, and by a swing of 5 per cent of the nationalist vote away from Sinn Féin to the SDLP. However, the Anglo-Irish Agreement was also calculated to reinforce the unionist centre, by coercively forcing it into serious negotiations for power-sharing with nationalists as the only alternative to direct Irish government involvement.[58] The Agreement had made clear that if unionists could agree devolution with nationalists – which meant paying the price of power-sharing and an Irish dimension – they could roll back the Irish government's right of consultation on Northern Ireland affairs.[59] Unionists, naturally, were outraged at the blackmail implied. 'The paradox of the Anglo-Irish Agreement', Harvey Cox observes, 'was that for several years it appeared to have become in itself the most immediate obstacle to the achievement of its own proclaimed purpose.'[60]

As unionists protested, the Inter-Governmental Conference and its secretariat functioned. A youthful Irish government diplomat later wrote:

The full institutional impact of the Anglo-Irish Agreement has never been highlighted or documented. With good reason. Seeing how mad the Unionists were at its symbolism, they would go crazy altogether if they knew its full practical detail. In one sense, this is a pity, because it would give the lie to those who said that the Agreement was ineffective. How could it be? The Agreement gave the Irish Government a consultative role in all aspects of Northern Irish life … [I]n the absence of a settlement or assembly, the agreement *was* the political system.[61]

It seems certain that the Irish side did succeed in promoting reforms, though for diplomatic reasons this was never admitted. In 1987, the Flags and Emblems Act, which had come close to criminalising the display of the Irish tricolour, was repealed. New public order legislation required seven days' notice for processions, including 'traditional', i.e. loyalist, marches, and the RUC was given wider grounds to impose conditions on such events. An independent Police Complaints Commission for Northern Ireland was established. In March 1990, the Irish minister of foreign affairs, Brian Lenihan, felt able to say that as a result of the Inter-Governmental Conference the RUC was now 'established as a professional police force holding the balance'.[62] The Fair Employment Act, which came into effect in 1990, imposed a new legal duty on firms to monitor the religious composition of their workforces, and this quite rapidly showed a lessening of Catholic disadvantage in the job market.

For all Thatcher's later insistence that she had negotiated for security cooperation, it is clear that she signed a political agreement, as she recognised when addressing an American audience in 1992. She described the Anglo-Irish Agreement as a mechanism to allow the two governments to 'consult together on new items of policy'. Her hope had been that 'the Nationalist community, Republican community, in Northern Ireland might perhaps have more confidence and, on that basis, agree with the Republic of Ireland that Northern Ireland should stay with the United Kingdom as long as that were the wish of her people'.[63] Nonetheless, the Anglo-Irish Agreement was not popularly accepted as a settlement in itself. By January 1990 only 41 per cent of Catholics and 8 per cent of Protestants supported the Agreement. Of Catholics, 62 per cent thought it had made no difference to the political situation.[64] Catholic disaffection owed much to the promotion of the Anglo-Irish Agreement as an instrument designed to marginalise, rather than accommodate, Irish republicanism.

The conflict continues

The marsh breeding political violence had not been drained, however. In March 1988, three unarmed IRA members were shot dead by the SAS in Gibraltar. Back in Northern Ireland, their funeral was attacked by the loyalist, Michael Stone, who killed three men. Then, at the funeral of Stone's victims, two British soldiers in plain clothes were set upon by the crowd, then captured and shot dead by the IRA. Brian Mawhinney, a junior minister in the Direct Rule administration, recalled his fear that 'Northern Ireland was *very* close to the edge of serious and bloody breakdown then'.[65] One outcome was a deliberate channelling of funds to deprived Catholic areas, on the understanding that heavily unionist workplaces such as the shipyards had long been subsidised, and that it was time to even up the balance.[66] For political reasons, therefore, Northern Ireland was 'largely immune' to the hegemony of economic Thatcherism.[67] The 'Making Belfast Work' programme was organised in partnership with the Catholic clergy, hitherto rather sidelined by the government, but now favoured as an alternative to Sinn Féin-influenced community leaders.[68] This was the beginning of 'grantocracy', whereby the British state funded nationalist civil society on the ground. It was a key part of the 1990s peace process that, for the first time, republicans were included in this largesse.

The Anglo-Irish Agreement had played a role in preparing for a new phase, wherein, once again, Britain would concentrate less on 'building the centre' than on 'bringing in the extremes'. The Secretary of State, Peter Brooke, insisted in November 1990 that Britain had no economic or strategic interest in the Union, repeated that it would accept unification by consent, and announced that republicanism could take its place alongside other parties in Northern Ireland if it gave up violence. The government was tentatively moving towards a position of effectively facilitating Sinn Féin's electoral success in return for its moving away from and ultimately abandoning the armed struggle. Thatcher was never convinced by this strategy.[69] Nonetheless, she mostly left politics to those on the ground: Brooke felt that he received more loyal support from Thatcher than he did from her successor, John Major.[70]

On 24 June 1990, in an interview in the *Sunday Tribune*, Gerry Adams said he had 'a major problem' with the IRA causing deaths of 'noncombatants'. Combatants, however, clearly included Thatcher's circle. On 30 July 1990, Ian Gow was murdered by an IRA bomb attached to his car because he was a 'close personal associate' of Thatcher. There was little surprise at Thatcher's determination, when she visited the security forces in Fermanagh shortly before her resignation: 'We must never, never give in to terrorism – never.' Indeed, in February 1990, in an interview with the *Irish News*, Martin McGuinness had admitted that it was the republican movement's military strategy to 'outlast Margaret Thatcher'.[71] On 22 November 1990, Thatcher announced her resignation as Conservative Party leader and Prime Minister. The 'peace process', predicated once more on 'bringing in the extremes', by legitimising Irish republicanism in so far as it abandoned militarism, began its lengthy working out.

Part III

Thatcherism and the wider world

11   Thatcherism and the Cold War

Richard Vinen

On 26 June 1979 Margaret Thatcher's plane made a brief refuelling stop in Moscow on its way to a summit in Japan. A group of Soviet leaders, led by Alexei Kosygin, came out to the airport to have a late supper with the British Prime Minister. The encounter was good-humoured – perhaps because the Russians had already been to a banquet earlier in the evening and were, one assumes, well lubricated by toasts to 'international friendship'. Discussions ranged widely and at one point Thatcher asked whether the Soviet Union would face problems because of Islamic unrest in Afghanistan and Pakistan. Official notes of the meeting record dryly that Kosygin – who must already have been planning the Soviet invasion of Afghanistan that was to take place on Christmas Day 1979 – 'made no comment'.[1]

All this reminds us how much the world has changed in the three decades since 1979 and, in particular, how much of that change is due to the end of the Cold War. Thatcherism coincided with a particular phase of the Cold War, between the fall of Saigon – on the very day that Ronald Reagan wrote his first letter to Margaret Thatcher[2] – and the fall of the Berlin Wall. The subsequent reunification of Germany and its accompanying upheavals helped to bring Margaret Thatcher down. This was a period that began when the West – weakened by Vietnam, Watergate, the oil crisis and the aftermath of internal upheavals in the late 1960s – seemed on the back foot and when the clients of the Soviet Union seemed, in Vietnam and Angola, to be on the march.

In some ways the whole notion of Thatcherism was born out of the communist/anti-communist divide. *Red Star*, the journal of the Soviet armed forces, coined the term 'Iron Lady' in response to Thatcher's speech at Kensington Town Hall in January 1976.[3] Stuart Hall launched the systematic use of the word 'Thatcherism' in an article for *Marxism Today*, published by the Communist Party of Great Britain, in January 1979.[4] References to the Cold War pervaded British politics during the early 1980s – perhaps the time when nuclear annihilation seemed most likely and when debates over the British possession of nuclear weapons were most intense. General Sir John Hackett's novel on *The Third World War* was first published in 1978 and set in 1985.[5] By 1984, it had sold three million copies. Philip Sabin argues that 1980, the first full year of the Thatcher government, was the year in which the 'Third World War Scare' reached its peak: 'The sheer variety of the year's developments in defence and international affairs meant that everyone could see his own particular nightmare coming true.'[6]

In spite of all this, the Cold War does not feature much in discussions of Thatcherism. Hall's seminal article barely mentioned defence policy, foreign affairs or the Soviet Union. At the other end of the political spectrum, Nigel Lawson gave two different definitions of the philosophy that he himself expounded – one, delivered in 1981, emphasised monetarism and one (featured in his memoirs of 1992) ranged more widely over issues such as privatisation, Victorian values and 'nationalism'.[7] At neither point did he mention anti-communism or attitudes to the Soviet Union.[8]

Conservatives in the United States saw the end of the Cold War as a victory, and sometimes presented Thatcher, alongside Reagan and Pope John Paul II, as a heroic crusader against communism. The end of the Cold War also mattered to many in continental Europe. Its importance was greatest in those countries that had actually lived under communist rule, but it was also taken seriously in France precisely because so many French intellectuals, especially historians, had at some point been members of the Communist Party. The fall of the Soviet Union therefore facilitated the tradition of *autocritique* that had begun with Edgar Morin in 1959[9] and that ended with François Furet's *Le passé d'une illusion* in 1995.[10] Historians in continental Europe, however, were generally uninterested in and/or unsympathetic to Thatcherism. Their accounts of the end of communism focused heavily on disillusion among left-wing intellectuals, rather than on the policies pursued by right-wing politicians who had never, in this context at least, had many illusions.

For British writers, by contrast, the end of the Cold War did not have the same resonance: it was neither an occasion for gloating nor one for self-criticism. In addition to this, the way in which Thatcherism is studied has tended to discourage attention to any relations that it might have had with the Cold War. British scholars of Thatcherism focus on economic and social policy rather than on international relations. Even Andrew Gamble's influential analysis, which, in recent years, has made much of 'Anglo-America', views that relationship mainly in terms of attitudes to liberal economics and neo-conservative morality rather than in terms of attitudes to the Soviet world.[11] British writers stress the coherence and unity of Thatcherism, emphasising the qualities that distinguished it from, say, 'the post-war consensus' or 'One-Nation Conservatism'. They are chiefly interested in the place of Thatcherism within a British political tradition – on the ways in which it might be seen as the heir to nineteenth-century liberalism or the Powellism of the 1960s.

Looking at the Cold War gives us a slightly different version of Thatcherism. First, it is a version that lays more emphasis on response to events rather than ideological coherence. Second, it is one that locates Thatcherism more firmly in a particular time and plays down the extent to which it can be understood in terms of similarity with earlier political movements. Third, the Cold War is an area in which Thatcherites are not always easy to distinguish from other Conservatives or, perhaps, from other members of the British establishment generally. Fourth, and related to this point, the study of the Cold War reminds us that it is possible to make too much of the extent to which the right was the only moving part of the British political system during the 1980s. Often the most dramatic transformations occurred on the left. Indeed, there were some areas in which Thatcherites were defenders of a post-war consensus rather than its enemies.

This chapter will be divided into three parts. The first will deal with defence policy; the second with concerns about internal 'subversion'; the third with the way in which the Cold War related to Thatcherite foreign policy, particularly in its dealings with Europe and the United States.

Thatcherism and defence policy

The 1979 election did not bring any sharp change in policy, which continued to revolve around nuclear weapons, NATO membership and the American alliance, and few voters identified defence as an important issue.[12] The Callaghan government of 1976 to 1979 had been particularly hawkish on matters of defence, and it is hard to think of any four ministers in post-war British history who had better relations with the armed forces than Callaghan himself, Denis Healey, David Owen and Roy Mason. The Thatcher government was responsible for the decisions to upgrade Britain's submarine-based nuclear weapons system to Trident and to allow the deployment of American cruise missiles at bases in the UK. These decisions evoked protest and were opposed by the Labour Party, which had turned to the left after the election, but they did not mark a sharp departure from policies pursued by the previous government. After 1979, Denis Healey and James Callaghan continued to support submarine-based strategic missiles while those former Labour ministers who had joined the Social Democratic Party supported cruise missiles but not Trident. The continuity between successive governments was not surprising. Defence had been seen, ever since 1945, as an area in which there should be a high level of consensus between the parties. In any case, because it was an area in which policy depended on specialised and sometimes secret knowledge, politicians were dependent on advice from officers and civil servants.

There was clearly a potential conflict between a commitment to free market economics and a reduction in public spending, on the one hand, and traditional British defence policy, which was both expensive and prone to foster a protected sector of the economy, on the other. Some thinkers who influenced Thatcherism appreciated this conflict. Samuel Brittan, for example, had a low opinion of the whole defence industry.[13] In opposition, Thatcher's Treasury team had been worried by the Labour government's commitment that British defence spending should rise at 3 per cent per annum in line with that of her NATO allies.[14] However, the Conservative Party in opposition had not denounced this commitment and the Conservative government honoured it. The Thatcher government did eventually make some efforts to cut, or contain, defence spending. John Nott, the only hard-core Thatcherite to hold office at defence, instituted a review that was designed to cut naval spending – though its impact, blunted in any case by the aftermath of the Falklands War, was rather smaller than might have been supposed from the vociferous protests of senior naval officers. In any case, the Defence Review was largely about the relative allocation of defence spending rather than its overall size.

There was not, in fact, a particularly distinctive Thatcherite policy with regard to defence. The Thatcherite *domaine réservé* was mainly concerned with economics and it was in the Treasury that Thatcherite ministers exercised most power. Thatcher's first Secretary of State for Defence, Francis Pym, was a conspicuously un-Thatcherite figure, as was Peter Carrington, Thatcher's first Foreign Secretary. Thatcher herself expressed pious admiration for the armed forces, but she had never worn military uniform (a rare position in the almost exclusively male establishment of the late 1970s), never held a defence portfolio and never taken a particular interest in military matters. Some of the abuse directed at Thatcher came from the notion that there was something intrinsically incongruous about a woman taking responsibility for matters of war, and perhaps the idea that absence of military experience disqualified her from any high office. Just as there was not a distinctively Thatcherite position on defence, so there was not a distinctively anti-Thatcherite position. Unlike economic policy, this was not a matter on which the Cabinet could be divided into wets and dries. Those who felt most sceptical about Margaret Thatcher's leadership of the Conservative Party rarely disagreed with her on military questions, and such questions do not seem to have created divisions within the government. The Nott Defence Review of 1981 produced only one resignation – that of a junior minister.[15] As for the flamboyant departure of Michael Heseltine as Secretary of State for Defence in January 1986, this was a dispute about industrial policy, Europe and the future leadership of the Conservative Party. No one imagined that it really had anything to do with defence.

There was, of course, a group of Conservative MPs – which included Alan Clark, Julian Amery, Stephen Hastings and Winston Churchill junior – who took a deep interest in defence during the 1980s. Many of these men admired Margaret Thatcher and believed that she returned their admiration. They were, however, Thatcherians rather than Thatcherites. They were often either uninterested in, or sceptical about, the government's economic policy, while they tended to be right-wing on matters relating to race, South Africa and Rhodesia (matters on which most prominent Thatcherite ministers were either indifferent or liberal). Most importantly, none of these men ever attained significant office under Thatcher – though she seems to have found it convenient to let some of them think that they might do so.

The real innovations of the 1980s on matters of defence came from the left rather than the right. It was the Labour Party that broke most sharply with the post-war consensus, by turning away from the British independent nuclear deterrent. This divided Labour leaders from each other (Callaghan was openly hostile and Healey was evasive), and it helped Labour to lose the 1983 election. Precisely because Labour activists were keen to emphasise that opposition to nuclear weapons was not the same as pacifism, they flirted with an extraordinary range of policy options during this period. Neil Kinnock seems to have been perfectly serious when he talked about 'taking to the hills' in the event of Soviet invasion. It was during the 1980s that the ideas of Tom Wintringham, who had fought in Spain and subsequently tried to turn the Home Guard into a People's Army, were resurrected.[16] Len Scott, an aide to Denis Healey, claims that the reintroduction of conscription was even discussed.[17]

The most important military event of the Thatcher government was, of course, one that seemed at first glance to have little to do with the Cold War. The Falkland Islands lie in the South Atlantic, thousands of miles from the potential Cold War battlefields of Germany and Norway. The

British operation to retake them in the spring of 1982 involved a war with the anti-communist Argentine dictatorship. The Soviet Union did not use its veto in the UN Security Council, and the most influential opponent of the British position was Jeane Kirkpatrick, the American ambassador to the United Nations, a ferocious anti-communist who, in other contexts, attracted admiration from Thatcher.[18] Some senior army officers, unlike their colleagues in the navy, regarded the Falklands as a sideshow.

In spite of all this, the Falklands was clearly related to the Cold War, as any military operation in the early 1980s was bound to be. Support for Britain came partly from the perception that it would not look good if a key member of NATO were to be humiliated – this seems to have had a particular influence on Britain's staunchest supporter, François Mitterrand. The war was also important in changing the whole relationship between Thatcherism and military patriotism. It made Thatcher's personal position in the Conservative Party stronger and it helped the Tories win a large majority in the 1983 election. This electoral influence seems to have sprung from the fact that the 'Falklands factor' intersected with popular thinking about the Cold War. The Falklands War itself was not evoked much in specific terms during the election, but defence more generally was important in the campaign. Victory in the Falklands coincided with an apparent increase in the Soviet threat during the 1980s and with the Labour Party's move to unilateral nuclear disarmament. Over half the electorate believed that Britain would not be adequately defended under a Labour government and about half of voters believed that the Conservatives had the best defence policy. Butler and Kavanagh wrote that 'Not since 1964 had defence loomed so large as an election issue'.[19]

Thatcherism, the Cold War and internal subversion

The Cold War cut across countries as well as dividing them from each other. Some members of the ruling class had always expressed concern about internal 'subversion' by people who were sympathetic to Britain's political enemies abroad; and, during the 1970s, political discussion sometimes acquired a paranoid air. Robert Moss published a spy novel about communist subversion that was marketed with the claim that the truth was so shocking that it could only be told as fiction.[20] Left-wingers worried about the prospect of a military coup. Events in Chile interested both sides – the former worried about Allende and the latter about Pinochet.[21] Peter Jay wrote in *The Times* that Britain's problems might bring an end to democracy.[22]

How much influence did all this have on Thatcher's Conservative Party? A group of men with links to Thatcher were certainly prone to talk about communist subversion: this group included Robert Moss, John Gouriet and Brian Crozier (the first of whom helped to write the 'Iron Lady' speech). Crozier's Institute for the Study of Conflict examined internal subversion. Some of the Conservative MPs who supported Thatcher, notably Airey Neave, belonged to that peculiar world where right-wing politics, Western intelligence agencies, business associations and special forces overlapped. In opposition, Thatcher and some of her frontbench colleagues attended a 'Shield Committee' to study 'security questions'.

It was not, however, obvious that any of this was specifically Thatcherite. Often the men who worried most about the communist threat were old-style Conservatives with military backgrounds – the kind of people who were not particularly interested in radical free-market economics or monetarism. The Shield Committee included Keith Joseph (certainly a Thatcherite, though of a particular kind) but also Whitelaw and Carrington. Most of the Thatcherites associated with the making of economic policy were notably uninterested in subversion. Nigel Lawson alluded to communist infiltration of the Labour Party in a note to Thatcher – but he seems to have assumed that this was a matter of purely electoral concern. As such, it was an opportunity rather than a threat, because it would allow the Conservatives to discredit the Labour Party.[23]

Concern about internal subversion was not limited to the British Conservative Party. It tied British Conservatives into an international network. Part of this was constituted under the aegis of the CIA, but it also involved a variety of right-wingers and Christian Democrats from continental Europe. Antoine Pinay, the former Prime Minister of Fourth Republic France, ran a 'cercle' that took in some of Thatcher's advisors. Concern with communist infiltration also expanded beyond the Conservative Party in Britain itself. A senior civil servant apparently believed that trade union activists were being trained in East Germany during the 1970s.[24] Labour leaders were worried by communist influence in the trade unions and in their own party – Conservatives were sometimes unsure about whether they should be seeking to embarrass Labour leaders or to make common cause with them against extremists in their own ranks.[25]

It is unclear how seriously to take all this. Moss, Gouriet and Crozier were eccentric figures, whose colourful writings sometimes caused amusement even among their own associates.[26] Whitelaw (who had been deeply bruised by the troubles of the Heath government) was worried about subversion, but Carrington sometimes fell asleep in Shield meetings. David Stirling featured in many left-wing fantasies about the prospect of a counter-revolutionary coup – though when he came to see Tory frontbenchers, his concern seems to have been a written constitution rather than martial law.[27] Nicholas Ridley, a backbench Thatcherite MP, prepared a report in late 1977 that is sometimes seen as the blueprint for how the Thatcher government would eventually defeat the National Union of Mineworkers (NUM). Two years earlier, however, he had talked to people who contemplated more radical ways of dealing with union unrest. These people included Walter Walker, a retired general who seems, for a time, to have seen himself as a possible English Pinochet. Walker recalled that Ridley 'talked in riddles' and that 'it seemed to me that what he was trying to convey, but hadn't the guts to say openly, was that the only hope for this country was a military coup'.[28] Senior Conservatives, who knew about Ridley's propensity for extreme statements and tasteless jokes, would probably have paid less attention to such blimpish mutterings.

Thatcherism rose at a time when the nature of the British extreme left was changing. The left-wingers who emerged from the student radicalism of the 1970s rarely supported the Soviet Union. The Heath government still worried about communist influence in the trade unions, but the most direct threats that it had to confront came from new kinds of political movements – from Palestinian terrorism or from the Provisional IRA. Left-wing infiltration of the Labour movement was increasingly likely to come from Trotskyists rather than members of the Communist Party. Changes in trade union leadership during the late 1970s and early 1980s reduced the power of those who were seen as close to communism. Jack Jones, who was believed to have discreet links with the Soviet Union, retired as leader of the Transport and General Workers Union in 1978. Joe Gormley's manoeuvres ensured that the communist Michael McGahey was unable to become leader of the NUM. The post passed instead to Arthur Scargill, classified by MI5 as 'an unaffiliated subversive'.[29] The Heath government had been worried by the extent of communist infiltration of the NUM. The Thatcher government seems to have been less exercised by the matter during the strike of 1984–5. Far from being covert manipulators of union strategy, members of the Communist Party were now often overt critics of that strategy.

Conservatives did not necessarily understand the implications of all this; nor did they draw clear distinctions between different kinds of left-winger. Keith Joseph, a man prone to apocalyptic visions that linked many different elements of decline and crisis, argued that

Labour support for violent picketing at the Grunwick Film Processing Laboratories was linked to the 'fraternal relations' it enjoyed with parties in the Soviet bloc.[30] Some argued that left-wing agitation of any sort was part of a much wider process by which 'Western values' were being undermined in ways that would serve the interests of the Soviet Union.

It is, however, certain that there was a change in Thatcherism's attitude to internal subversion after the 1979 election. Once the Conservative Party was in government, many of the right-wing advisors who had been influential, or at least allowed to imagine that they were influential, in opposition were marginalised. This was particularly noticeable in the case of those men who had been associated with anticommunism. Brian Crozier's project to establish a 'Counter subversion executive' came to nothing and he was discreetly removed from the Institute for the Study of Conflict that he had helped to found.[31] Just after the election, Whitelaw, the Home Secretary, told the head of MI5 that Thatcher had derived much of her information about subversion from 'people who know little or nothing of our work'. Instead, he wanted briefings that would counter 'some of the rather extreme advice' that the Prime Minister had received up to then.[32]

There was also a sense in which the attitude of Thatcherism in power to anti-communism tied in with the longer-term change in the nature of the left. Up until the mid 1970s, it was still possible for some right-wingers to believe that Soviet sympathisers had infiltrated the British establishment. Some even believed that Harold Wilson was a Soviet agent. Walter Walker had told his audience of retired officers, City businessmen and conservative priests in St Lawrence Jewry in February 1975 that there were 'Burgesses and Macleans in every branch of the British state'.[33] (He failed to realise that communists had infiltrated his own movement, which was how these words came to be recorded.) In fact, however, fear of Soviet infiltration diminished during the later 1970s. The exposure of Anthony Blunt in 1979 stimulated a bout of interest in people who might have spied for the Soviet Union, but this affair was in the past. No one seriously imagined that the KGB was still recruiting undergraduates and Blunt himself did not suggest that spying for the Soviet Union had been a good idea. Indeed, for much of the 1980s, Thatcher and her ministers were being advised by senior intelligence officers who knew perfectly well that the KGB station chief in London was not recruiting British citizens, because he had himself been recruited as a spy by them.[34]

The curious symbiotic relation between Thatcherism and *Marxism Today* also contributed to the new view of British communism. Some of the opinions expressed in the journal were to the right of those expressed by the official leaders of the Labour Party. By the late 1980s, a number of influential Conservatives had been interviewed in *Marxism Today*, and Thatcher herself had quoted the magazine in public. It was hard to associate a glossy magazine full of lively and open debate with the notion that the Communist Party of Great Britain was a dark and threatening force.

Thatcherism, the Cold War and the world order

Thatcherism is often identified with particular alliances and enmities. It is seen as being intensely Atlanticist – favourable to alliance with America in general and so close to the politics of Ronald Reagan during the 1980s that some commentators write of British and American politics as though they were parallel tracks towards the same 'revolution'. Thatcherism is also seen as being anti-European. Indeed, after her political demise, Thatcher and her admirers often talked as though all foreign policy roads had led to Bruges. Loyalty to the memory of Margaret Thatcher became associated with Euroscepticism, and Thatcher famously remarked that 'During my lifetime most of the problems the world has faced have come ... from mainland Europe.'[35]

During her time in office, Thatcher did sometimes play up the notion of herself as being close to America and hostile to, or at least exasperated by, Europe. When she met Reagan and American officials at Camp David in December 1984, she praised America and congratulated Reagan on the extent of his recent electoral victory. She then went on to contrast America's mood with that of Europe. According to American records:

She opined that the overall political situation in Europe is not especially encouraging. There is a socialist government in France; neither Holland or Belgium seem to be able to get their act completely together; Germany is a question mark; and the Italians lack guts. There is a socialist government in Spain; Greece is a pain in the neck and certainly no friend of the US.[36]

However, anti-Europeanism was not a consistent feature of Thatcherism. During the 1970s the Conservative Party (or at least the Conservative front bench) was strongly in favour of British membership of the European Community. It may be that Thatcher personally was less sympathetic to European unity than some of her colleagues, but it would have been hard to guess this from statements that she made at the time. It was certainly possible for people like Geoffrey Howe, who regarded themselves as true Thatcherites, to feel a strong emotional attachment to the European project.[37] Conservative pro-Europeanism had many roots: party interest and a desire to embarrass the Labour Party had something to do with it, as did admiration for West European economic performance. Many believed that Britain would benefit from closer association with France and West Germany. However, the Cold War also played a role. Early steps towards European unity had, after all, been taken under the American aegis and as part of a strategy to contain the Soviet Union. During the 1970s, Thatcher often presented support for Europe and support for the West in the Cold War as interrelated. Her speech to the Chelsea Conservative Association in July 1975 (usually considered to be a speech primarily about the Soviet threat) began with a reference to the recent referendum on British membership of the EEC:

This year, we've seen some dramatic changes in world affairs. Here in Britain the question of our membership of the European Community has been clearly and dramatically settled. The policies we have pursued over the past years have been overwhelmingly supported by the British people. Membership is no longer an issue.[38]

Thatcher's relations with other West European leaders owed much to the Cold War. She admired Helmut Schmidt's support for the stationing of American intermediate-range nuclear missiles in Europe and contrasted his 'robustness' with the 'meanderings of US foreign policy under Jimmy Carter'.[39] She also had good relations with François Mitterrand. France was not a member of NATO's combined command structures but it was a power that had built its foreign policy on the independent possession of nuclear weapons. Mitterrand himself was, in many ways, the most articulate opponent of unilateral nuclear disarmament. It was he who gave currency to the phrase: 'the pacifists are in the West but the missiles are in the East'.

The Atlanticist element in Thatcherism can also be overstated. The Thatcherites supported NATO membership and the American alliance but this did not, in fact, take them out of the mainstream of Conservative traditions, or indeed of post-war British politics generally. In the early part of her career as leader, Thatcher was particularly keen to present her American policy in terms of continuity and stressed that her admiration for Macmillan sprang partly from the fact that he had rebuilt the Anglo-American friendship after Suez.[40] It is true that the British government had made rather less of the 'special relationship' under Heath, but this was not an area in which Thatcher's election brought an immediate reversal. Indeed, Thatcherism emerged at a time when the American capacity to exercise leadership in the

West seemed particularly problematic. America had been weakened by Vietnam, Watergate and the oil shock, but also by a sense of internal crisis (especially to do with issues of race, inner cities and education) that evoked particular concern among British Conservatives. Far from being a relationship of mutual support during Thatcher's early years as leader of the Conservative Party, the relationship between America and Britain often seemed to be one of thinly disguised mutual disdain. Henry Kissinger briefed Gerald Ford in these terms on 8 January 1975: 'Britain is a tragedy – it has sunk to begging, borrowing, stealing, until North Sea Oil comes in.'[41]

Relations between Thatcherites and the American leadership improved when Ronald Reagan entered the White House. There was a touch of show business in the way that both Reagan and Thatcher presented this relationship, and it evoked much sneering among Thatcher's British enemies. America and Britain were not, however, completely aligned on Cold War policy during the 1980s. American leaders continued to doubt Britain's value as an ally, especially as the Thatcher government's economic policy (very different from that of Ronald Reagan) appeared to fail in the early 1980s. In July 1981, the American ambassador in London told the President that 'Thatcher has lost her grip on the political rudder … with no British leader seeming to have a clear idea of where or how to go, some political turbulence is likely, with adverse effects on the country's reliability as a US ally.'[42] There were specific disagreements about the American intervention in Grenada in 1983, and about the American attempt to impose sanctions against the Soviet Union after the invasion of Afghanistan. Thatcherite concern with the rule of law and with sovereignty also meant a particular distaste for American 'extra-territoriality'.

There was a more important difference between Reagan and Thatcher. Reagan was a visionary. He had spent the early part of his career in Hollywood and he was good at taking a simple idea and presenting it in dramatic terms. Thatcher had spent the early part of her career holding a succession of unglamorous ministerial posts. She was used to dealing with detail and working her way around complicated realities. In the context of the Cold War, Reagan's two simple ideas were: first, that the Soviet Union was an 'evil empire' and the world would be a better place if it did not exist; and, second, that the prospect of nuclear war was terrible and politicians should work to abolish nuclear weapons. One writer describes Reagan's interventions in Cold War strategy thus:

There were occasions during his presidency when Reagan rose up like some twentieth-century Gulliver and, casting aside the constraints of politics, diplomacy and of his own ignorance, forced upon his administration and indeed the whole world a vision of the future of nuclear weapons that was uniquely his and that was deeply at odds with the policies of his administration.[43]

Thatcher and most of her allies seem to have regarded many of Reagan's ideas with polite scepticism. They were concerned by plans for a Strategic Defence Initiative, because they feared that it would leave Europe unprotected and/or because they simply regarded it as expensive and impractical. As for the collapse of the Soviet Union, this was a prospect that a few of the more intellectually adventurous people in Thatcher's entourage seem to have considered. Keith Joseph certainly made much of Soviet abuses of human rights (he also, for that matter, cared about human rights under right-wing regimes), and he suggested that Conservatives should protest about the visit by Brezhnev to the United Kingdom in 1976.[44] He was interested in the work of dissidents from the Soviet bloc, including Andrei Amalrik, who had published *Will the Soviet Union Survive until 1984?* in 1970.[45]

The most important Thatcherites, however, seem to have approached the Soviet Union with hard-headed realpolitik. In opposition, even Joseph had been careful to distinguish between political parties, which should stay clear of Soviet associations, and states, which had to deal with governments as they stood.[46] Thatcher and her ministers certainly raised the question of human rights when they met Soviet leaders, but Thatcher's main contact with Soviet dissidents seems to have come via Aleksandr Solzhenitsyn, and this contributed to her pessimistic assumption that the Soviet Union was here to stay, and might indeed outlive the Western democracies.[47] Ministers in the Thatcher government generally regarded their Soviet counterparts with cynicism rather than moral outrage. The Thatcherites invested hope in long-term reform of the communist system rather than in its imminent demise, and they had very little faith, at first, that reform was even possible in the Soviet Union. This explains the interest that Thatcher took in Kadar's Hungary, the most economically liberal of the communist states.

A conversation with Mitterrand in 1983 shows how far Thatcher took the continued existence of the USSR for granted as a basis for international relations:

[T]he system is so rigid that one cannot change it. There is no more faith in the system, but there will be no change for a long time, because the survival of the leaders is at stake. If, for example, the Soviet leaders sought to show more flexibility, as the Hungarian leaders do, they would undermine the basis of their own power. For this reason, we have to live with the regime.[48]

In the same conversation, Thatcher did allow for the possibility that some very long-term change might come in the Soviet system from younger leaders – though she added that the Canadian Prime Minister, Pierre Trudeau, had been disappointed by his recent meeting with Mikhail Gorbachev, 'one of the young men that Andropov brought in'. Eventually, of course, Thatcher herself met Gorbachev and began to invest hope in him as a Soviet reformer. This hope, however, always involved change within the Soviet system, not the overthrow of that system.

This emphasis on finding ways to live with the Soviet bloc distinguished Thatcher both from the British left, which, in the early 1980s, spent much time thinking about how NATO and the Warsaw Pact might be disbanded, and from Ronald Reagan. The gulf between Thatcher and Reagan was revealed during a telephone call after Reagan's Berlin speech of 12 June 1987. Reagan recounted his speech and told Thatcher how he had 'called for the wall to come down'. There was a brief embarrassed pause and then Thatcher asked after Nancy.[49]

The end of the Cold War

The Berlin Wall was torn down in November 1989 and Thatcher's own political fall came just over a year later. How were the two events related? Ministers and civil servants were certainly struck by the speed with which events moved in international affairs and the extraordinary change that had come over Europe since Thatcher took power. Some associated the two, linking changes in world politics with developments in Britain. Nicholas Ridley noted that the key moves leading to Thatcher's overthrow occurred 'when the true leader was abroad, signing a treaty bringing the Cold War to an end, an achievement for which she was in large measure responsible'.[50] Thatcher's fall owed much to her increasingly hostile attitude to European unification, and this in turn owed something to the fact that European unity was no longer needed to resist the Soviet threat. The prospect of German reunification, opened up by the fall of the Wall, caused Thatcher particular agitation.[51]

Events between 1988 and 1990 raised particular questions about the personal role of Margaret Thatcher – something rather different from the role of Thatcherism. Thatcher's intervention in matters of foreign policy had been relatively limited during the early years of her government, when she had focused on the economy. Some initiatives (the Rhodesian settlement of 1980, for example) seem to have involved the delegation of power to her ministerial colleagues. Even during the

Falklands War, Thatcher was part of a team – implementing decisions taken by defence chiefs rather than devising policy on her own. The last stages of the Cold War, however, coincided with a period during which Thatcher saw herself increasingly as an international statesperson rather than as a domestic politician. Personal idiosyncrasies played an ever larger part in her attitude to world affairs. She regretted Reagan's departure in 1988 and felt that relations with his successor were less good. She liked Gorbachev, she trusted Mitterrand and she felt an increasing personal antipathy towards Helmut Kohl. She had grown to political maturity during the Cold War and its certainties had provided her with common points of reference with other members of the British establishment. As the Cold War came to an end, Thatcher seems to have reverted to views that had been formed before 1945. In particular, her experience of the Second World War was important. Having experienced the war as a civilian seems to have made her more conscious of the special qualities of Nazism, and especially of the murder of the Jews. She had always been philo-semitic and, in particular, keen that the lessons of the Holocaust should not be forgotten. It is hard not to believe that there was some link in her mind between her opposition to the reunification of Germany and her support at the same time for a British War Crimes Bill.

To some extent, as the Thatcherite ministers who helped to depose her argued, all this merely reflected Thatcher's increasing eccentricity. The end of the Cold War, however, undermined Thatcherism in broader ways. Thatcherism had always been built on the assumption that Britain should be a great power. Thatcher admired Switzerland, but never suggested that Britain itself ought to become a prosperous and independent country that exercised no significant influence beyond its own frontiers.

A belief in great power status was not, of course, unique to the Thatcherites. It was a part of the whole post-war consensus – which was why Enoch Powell denounced it with such fervour. In this context, Thatcher was very much a part of that consensus. Nicholas Henderson's valedictory despatch of 1979 as British ambassador in Paris, on 'British Decline: Its Causes and Consequences',[52] presented the capacity to exercise influence beyond its own frontiers as a necessary attribute of Britain, and saw economic success as a means to secure this influence rather than as an end in itself. The document expounded orthodoxies that had dominated British foreign policy since Bevin, and much of it could have been written by Edward Heath,[53] but it was also picked up with enthusiasm by Thatcher and her ministers.

The Cold War and great power status fitted together in odd ways. On the one hand, it showed that Britain was now overshadowed by America and the Soviet Union. On the other hand, however, the Cold War conferred special status on those European countries, Britain and France, that possessed a level of military power that exceeded their economic power. Jacques Attali was to refer to those countries that had independent nuclear weapons and permanent membership of the United Nations Security Council as the five 'rois thaumaturges' of the modern world. Just as French Gaullism in the 1960s had been built on the capacity to persuade the French that their country was still capable of exercising power around the world, so Thatcherism in the 1980s drew some of its drama, electoral success and self-image from its apparent ability to restore British 'greatness'.

Conclusion

Thatcherism is often presented as a sharp break with the mainstream of post-war British politics, for reasons that owe as much to historiographical tendencies as to the Thatcher governments themselves. In the first instance, studies of Thatcherism have tended to focus on opposition, because the majority of archival sources so far released relate to the pre-1979 period. Some Thatcherites also thought of themselves as returning to opposition after 1990, when they saw themselves as hostile to the direction in which John Major took their party. Second, studies of Thatcherism have tended to emphasise what was *said* rather than what was *done*. This tendency is exacerbated by the fact that the public statements of Margaret Thatcher and her key associates are, courtesy of the Thatcher Foundation website, so easily accessible. Third, historians of Thatcherism have tended to give much attention to extra-parliamentary advisors, such as Alfred Sherman, John Hoskyns or Robert Moss. These men probably enjoyed most access to Thatcher herself before the 1979 election – after this date her advice was more likely to come from civil servants. It is not surprising that advisors have become so important to historians. Their job was to conjure up plausible overall interpretations and to express those interpretations in striking passages – the kind of passages that historians find quotable. Conversely, some ministers are underrepresented in accounts of Thatcherism. Many books, for example, do not contain a single quotation from, say, Willie Whitelaw or Peter Carington.

Nothing epitomises all these tendencies more than the impact of Thatcher's 'Iron Lady' speech of 19 January 1976. This was written by one of her extra-parliamentary advisors without, apparently, much consultation of her frontbench team. It was delivered in opposition and it contained a striking statement of intent against the Soviet Union – made all the more resonant, as was often the case, by the way in which Thatcher's enemies responded to it. It certainly contributed to the tone of Thatcherism, with its 'sense of imminent danger', that so struck some commentators in the late 1970s.[54]

In terms of policy, however, the speech was deceptive. It bore almost no relation to anything that Thatcher did once in government. The 'Iron Lady' speech stressed the threat posed by the Soviet navy; but the Thatcher government's first real intervention in defence policy (the Nott Review of 1981) involved cuts to the British surface fleet. Robert Moss, who had helped write the speech, exercised little influence once Thatcher was in government. On matters of defence and foreign policy, ministers (often from the 'non-Thatcherite' wing of the party) and civil servants exercised a particularly strong influence after 1979. This does not mean that Thatcher renounced all contact with extra-parliamentary advisors or that she abandoned radical rhetoric. On the contrary, Thatcher's political success came partly from her ability to talk the talk of radicalism while walking the walk of pragmatism. The most revealing aspect of George Urban's recollections of having advised Margaret Thatcher is not his insistence on the moral clarity of her vision but the separation conveyed by his book between the speech-writing and Chequers seminars, in which he was involved, and the real business of policy formation.[55]

In their attitudes to the Cold War, the Thatcher governments were notable for the extent to which they fitted into an establishment consensus. Thatcherism went with support for the American alliance, NATO and, at least in the early years, European unity. It also went with a restrained and unsentimental view of the Soviet Union that did not expect, or want, dramatic change. It is true that Thatcher made some dramatic speeches as Leader of the Opposition, but the very fact that she often wrote these speeches without consulting her frontbench colleagues suggests an awareness that the mood they expressed (like some of her speeches on crime or immigration) would not be taken into government.

The absence of radicalism in Thatcherite policy towards the Cold War is highlighted by five comparators. The first is François Mitterrand. It is often suggested that Thatcher had few real affinities with other European leaders, or that her apparently cordial relations with the French President sprang from his capacity to flatter. There were, however, more hard-headed reasons for Thatcher and Mitterrand to feel that they had things in common. Jacques Attali reports the following exchange between the two:

Mitterrand: I too would be against nuclear weapons, if the USSR and the United States were as well.

Thatcher: No, at the moment, I would be against conventional weapons.

Mitterrand: But of course, that is because you are a realist![56]

Second, Enoch Powell, sometimes seen as the intellectual ancestor of Thatcher in terms of economic policy, was at odds with Thatcherism over the Cold War. Powell was dubious about nuclear weapons, against European integration and violently hostile to the United States. His vision of foreign policy was utterly removed from that of Margaret Thatcher. It is, perhaps, indicative of the way in which the end of the Cold War changed Thatcher's personal approach, and also marginalised her in the Conservative Party, that Enoch Powell welcomed the Bruges speech and apparently offered to rejoin the Conservative Party if Thatcher was re-elected as leader in 1990.[57]

Third, it was the British Labour Party that broke with the post-war consensus on defence and foreign policy after 1979. The gulf between the two parties that played such a role in the 1983 election owed much more to change on the left than to change on the right.

Fourth, Ronald Reagan's vision of a world that would be free of nuclear weapons and even of the Soviet Union was alien to the modest ambitions of the Thatcher governments.

Fifth, and most revealingly, Thatcher's position can be compared to that of Tony Blair. Blair is often seen as seen as Thatcher's heir – he accepted much of Thatcher's social and economic legacy and, like Thatcher, was a 'presidential' leader who held power for a long time. On matters of foreign policy, however, the Blair government was conspicuously different from the Thatcher government. Blair came to power with an almost Gladstonian commitment to a 'moral' foreign policy, which was given its most famous expression in his Chicago speech of 1999. Blair's foreign policy involved intervention that was designed to make the world a better place, culminating in the American-led invasion of Iraq in 2003. Some of Thatcher's ministers (notably Kenneth Clarke) openly disapproved of this invasion. Thatcher herself, during the run-up to the first Gulf War of 1991, had apparently insisted that 'regime change' could not be a legitimate aim for such operations.[58] Blair and his front bench were the first generation of politicians to come to power after the Cold War, and their view of the world owed much to the optimism that went with its end. Thatcher, by contrast, had grown up during the Cold War and her politics was overshadowed – until almost the end – by the sense that the Soviet Union was a great and immutable presence in world affairs.

The Cold War played a particularly large part in British internal politics in the early 1980s. This was partly because of the shift in Labour Party policy, partly because of the apparent increase in Soviet aggression and partly because the Falklands War, rather unexpectedly, associated Thatcher with military success. All of these things did a great deal to pave the way for the Tory election victory of 1983 and hence for the high Thatcherism that went with privatisation, the crushing of the NUM and the liberalisation of the City. The end of the Cold War also played a part in British politics. This was partly because it raised questions for all British politicians about the extent to which Britain could claim to be a great power in a multi-polar world: a world in which power, in Europe at least, now had less to do with military force.

12   Europe and America

Andrew Gamble

In 1946 Winston Churchill identified the circles of Europe and America as two of Britain's most important external relationships, empire being the third and, in Churchill's view, still the highest priority.[1] In the decades that followed, empire shrank in significance, and Britain suffered both absolute and relative decline in its political and economic standing. In the post-imperial twilight America and Europe became ever more central to British policy and to the British political imagination. During the Thatcher years there was a significant reconfiguration of these two relationships, which had lasting consequences. These reconfigurations were in part reactive, coming about through responses to particular events as well as changed circumstances in security and political economy, and often reflected institutional and policy shifts. But they also came about through significant political interventions and political choices, the positive re-imagining of territorial space and territorial relationships, and in particular the great transnational spaces of Europe and Anglo-America in which Britain had been so intimately involved for so long.

In this as in many other fields those who identified themselves as adherents of Margaret Thatcher and the new thinking in the Conservative Party did not have a preconceived idea of the changes they wanted to see. The positions that came to be labelled Thatcherite in the 1990s emerged gradually as a result of the political choices that Thatcher and some of her closest colleagues made first in opposition and later in government. At the outset the positions were much less precise than they were subsequently to become, but by the end of the Thatcher government a relatively clear choice had emerged over whether Britain should give greater priority to its relationship with Europe or with America, and the label 'Thatcherite' had become firmly attached to the American option. The choice between Europe and America, despite some protesting that no choice had to be made, had once again become one of the great dividing lines in British politics, both between parties and within parties, and had divided the original Thatcherites themselves into Eurosceptics and

218

Europhiles. Thatcher herself may have been slow at first to articulate this division, but by the end she played a crucial part in defining it, and stamping both Thatcherism and the Conservative Party with a predominantly Eurosceptic identity it was not to lose. She lost several close allies as a result, but she succeeded in changing the stance of her party and the national debate on the relationship of Britain with the European Union over the next twenty years.

Different images of Europe and America played an important part in shaping the ideological evolution of Thatcherism and determining its eventual character. These images were not cast in stone but they were not free-floating either. They were not simply products of political imagination but evolved in relation to particular contexts and events. This was particularly true of attitudes towards Europe. Thatcher inherited a party whose leadership was strongly pro-European. This was the party of Macmillan, Heath, Maudling, Macleod, Whitelaw, Howe, Carrington, Prior, Hurd, Clarke, Walker and Heseltine. The Eurosceptics had some support on the back benches but were not well represented in the leadership. The Conservatives had been a predominantly pro-European party for more than a decade, and had successfully negotiated the entry of Britain into the European Community which was finally accomplished in 1973. Thatcher herself was slow to articulate a more sceptical position. As a member of the Heath government she voted for entry in the 1970s, and as Leader of the Opposition she supported the 'yes' campaign in the 1975 referendum. Only towards the end of her eleven years as Prime Minister did she begin to define the opposition between Europe and America much more sharply, and to treat them as competing rather than complementary priorities.

Her position was still ambiguous, however, partly because of the need in government to deal with the European Union and reach acceptable compromises. She gave full support to the Single European Act in 1986 because this appeared to further Britain's long-standing aim of breaking down barriers to trade and competition in Europe. She also reluctantly eventually agreed to sterling joining the Exchange Rate Mechanism (ERM). She had strongly opposed this when it was advocated by Nigel Lawson, and it was one of the main reasons he resigned in 1989.[2] Having lost one Chancellor over the issue in 1989, she did not want to lose another, and acceded to the arguments of her new Chancellor, John Major, and her Foreign Secretary, Douglas Hurd, supported by the Labour opposition, that it was now time for Britain to join the ERM in 1990. It was not until she left office that her position hardened further and she regretted some of the decisions she had taken in office, and began to argue that Britain should consider leaving the

European Union altogether.[3] But even in government the direction of her thinking about the European Union, and the manner in which she articulated it, helped fuel the conflict in the party which was to consume it for the next fifteen years, and which ended with the exclusion or marginalisation of the pro-European wing of the party. An intransigent Euroscepticism became one of her most important and enduring legacies to her party.

Images of Europe and America have always played a large part in the British political imagination, and in the Conservative political imagination in particular.[4] This chapter seeks to place these images in the spectrum of thought about Europe and America, and will examine a number of contexts which were important for shaping and changing these attitudes, and the various communities – based around security, political economy and ideology – which supported them. In each case the process will be traced by which the Conservative Party moved from being a strongly pro-European party in the 1960s and 1970s to become an increasingly Eurosceptic party in the 1980s and 1990s, while rediscovering and reinvigorating its enthusiasm for Anglo-America.

British decline and the end of empire

Britain's historical involvement with both Europe and the United States is tangled and complex. The expansion of England within the territorial space of the British Isles and then (in the form of Great Britain) throughout the world is the essential context in which British national identity emerged.[5] Britain was part of Europe but increasingly defined itself against Europe.[6] Its European policy was aimed at keeping a balance of power within Europe and preventing any one nation from dominating, but until the world wars of the twentieth century, Britain devoted the greater part of its energies to wars and conquests outside Europe rather than within it. The result was the creation in the nineteenth century of the world's largest territorial empire, as well as a vast informal empire of trade, investment and finance.[7] The dual logic of empire and hegemony[8] made Britain for a time pre-eminent, but it was never a pre-eminence which rested on Britain's dominance of Europe. After the American colonists successfully rebelled against British rule and won independence in 1783, British pre-eminence no longer depended on British dominance of North America.

The decline of British power in the twentieth century was most marked in the disappearance of the territorial empire by the 1970s and the industrial decline which reshaped the British economy radically in the 1970s and 1980s.[9] British government developed two long-term strategies for dealing with these events. It sought for as long as it could to preserve its empire and its world power status through a rapprochement with the United States, which began at the start of the twentieth century and reached its climax in the wartime alliance between 1941 and 1945.[10] Important sections of the British political class came to view Britain's long-term interest, from both geopolitical and political economy considerations, as the assumption by the United States of the leadership and protection of the open and relatively liberal international trading order that Britain had partially created and presided over in the nineteenth century. The second strategy was to manage Britain's relative economic decline through a mixture of protectionist, welfarist and corporatist policies and institutions, which kept the lid on domestic class conflict and allowed Britain to maintain a steady if slow rate of growth.[11]

There were always tensions between these two strategies – preserving Britain's world position for as long as possible and concentrating on promoting domestic economic prosperity. By the 1970s both were in serious trouble. Successive governments had attempted to grapple with the end of empire and the growing mismatch between Britain and the United States by launching a bid, encouraged by the United States, to commit Britain to membership of the European Community.[12] This was seen as complementary to Britain's membership of NATO and to recognising the United States as the leader of the West, rather than as an alternative to it. The French had a very different conception of the European Union: as a means of asserting Europe's independence from the United States, and regaining the capacity to conduct an independent foreign policy. Another reason for British support for membership of the European Community was that by the 1960s it had come to be seen as a way of stimulating growth in the British economy and forcing through modernisation and greater competition. This is why many economic liberals in the Conservative Party, including Enoch Powell and Margaret Thatcher, gave full support to the first application.

As the political ambitions of the European Community developed, however, the more it appeared that the British and French views of the Community were incompatible.[13] The pro-European wing of the Conservatives believed that the British vision of Europe could command sufficient support from other member nations to win the arguments and shape Europe in the way that Britain wanted. But the Eurosceptic wing of the party, which rapidly gained strength in the 1980s, feared that Britain could never control the rest of Europe and that its national sovereignty was increasingly at risk from the deepening process of European integration to which the other member states were committed.

At the same time as concern was growing among Conservatives about the direction of the European Community and Britain's involvement within it, there was also a reassessment of Britain's relationship with the United States. The special relationship identified by Winston Churchill in his 1946 Iron Curtain speech at Fulton, Missouri, had been a reflection on the wartime cooperation between the two powers, but a few years later this had become a permanent post-war alliance through the formation of NATO in 1949. Britain accepted the establishment of military bases of a foreign power on its soil, and participated as a full partner in the prosecution of the Cold War. Although Britain could no longer pretend it was the equal of the United States, it was still a major world player, with a large part of its empire intact, as well as its network of military bases and alliances and commercial interests throughout the world. To demonstrate its continuing importance it had acquired nuclear weapons, was one of the founder members of NATO, and had been installed as one of the permanent members of the UN Security Council.

The special relationship entered a second phase after the Suez debacle in 1956. Britain never again sought to act on its own in a major intervention without the support and agreement of the United States, and in security terms became increasingly dependent on it.[14] The withdrawal from empire accelerated, as Britain reduced its commitments around the world. These new realities led many in the Conservative Party to recognise the attractions of a closer association with the emerging European Community. Europe, however, represented a complex choice. Membership could mean Britain becoming the vehicle for US interests within the Community, as the French feared, or Britain deciding to participate wholeheartedly in the construction of a European union, giving that project greater priority in future than its relationship with the United States. Under Edward Heath's leadership of the Conservatives, for a short while it seemed that the Conservatives were moving in the second direction.[15] With the Labour Party repeatedly shifting its position on Europe, the Conservatives were more and more identified as the pro-European party, and took the initiative in seeking to commit Britain to a European future. For Heath, the European project offered the opportunity of carving out a new post-imperial role in the world for Britain – the answer to Dean Acheson's comment that Britain no longer had a role now that its empire was gone. A European role had the attraction of making Britain less dependent on the United States, and at the same time promoting the modernisation of the British economy and reversing its very visible decline relative to other European economies. Heath was determined to promote it.

The Thatcher years were to interrupt this new trajectory decisively, but it took some time for the new direction and the nature of the choice that was being taken to become clear. But there were some early signs. After becoming leader Thatcher supported the 1975 referendum called by the Labour government to confirm Britain's membership, but she did not play a major role, leaving that to Edward Heath. Her first significant intervention in foreign affairs was the speech she delivered in January 1976,[16] which warned of the dangers of Soviet expansion and led to the bestowing of the title 'Iron Lady' upon her by the Russians, which she gratefully accepted. It signalled an order of priorities in her thinking about the world and Britain's place within it which was to become ever more marked in the course of her premiership.

The security community

Although not confined to security matters, it is significant that this priority first emerged in relation to them. Thatcher was eventually to inaugurate a new phase of the special relationship with the United States through her partnership with Ronald Reagan, which elevated it once more into Britain's most important external relationship. The key to this new articulation of the special relationship was the designation of Britain as the chief ally of the United States, the indispensable friend, the one nation which could always be relied upon to give the United States support. This represented a gradual shift in language and perception by British politicians. Britain no longer made any pretence at being the equal of the United States or as having a foreign policy which was separate from the United States. The new stance that Britain adopted was implicit in the changed realities of international politics after Britain's failure at Suez, but only under Thatcher was the logic fully articulated.

To critics, the British position appeared supine and demeaning. The term 'poodle' to describe Britain's relationship to the United States was first used by Denis Healey about Margaret Thatcher in 1983,[17] long before it was used about Tony Blair at the time of the Iraq War. What the insult was intended to draw attention to in both cases was the apparent subservience of both Margaret Thatcher and Tony Blair to presidents of the United States. This had long been a rule for British prime ministers. They hardly ever broke ranks and criticised American policy in public, preferring to make their arguments in private, using their privileged status as insiders to ally with other members of the inner circle in order to influence policy.[18] There was fierce debate during both the Thatcher and the Blair governments as to whether the trade-off between public subservience and insider influence served British interests. But in the new version of the special relationship articulated by Thatcher and later by Blair there was no trade-off. British interests were at one with the United States because the United States was the leader of the Western world and the guarantor not only of British security through NATO and its other military alliances, but also of economic prosperity through its safeguarding of the international liberal economic order. From this perspective the United States was fulfilling a role which Britain could not undertake on its own, and which was vital to British security and prosperity. Britain was not acting in the interests of the United States but in its own interests when it gave the United States its support.[19]

Thatcher continued with this policy, which had been established since the 1940s, and whose roots went much further back to the beginning of the century.[20] In that sense she did not innovate. What she did was to reinvigorate the special relationship and the security community that upheld it by defining a new purpose for it. Her warnings about the new expansionist threat posed by the Soviet Union in the 1970s helped to make Soviet intentions towards Western Europe once more the focus of security policy after the period dominated by the Vietnam War and détente. If the Soviet Union was once again a threat then the leadership of the United States was vital in confronting it. There was no substitute for American leadership and American power. It was the only plausible leader of the West. Britain acting alone or with its European allies would not be credible. Thatcher's repeated warnings of the Soviet threat identified her and Britain as the staunchest allies of the United States in Europe. Thatcher was to give full support to the US military build-up under President Reagan, which included the siting of cruise and Pershing missiles at bases in Britain in the 1980s.

The battle against the Soviet Union engaged all her energy and enthusiasm, and rekindled her trust in the United States. Thatcher always felt differently towards the rest of Europe. After she left office she wrote in a revealing remark that during her lifetime 'most of the problems the world has faced have come ... from mainland Europe, and the solutions from outside it'.[21] Her antipathy to Germany was revealed after the opening of the Berlin Wall in her strong opposition to the idea of German reunification.[22] She told Gorbachev at the time that Britain did not want a united Germany. The fractious relations with other European leaders, and her dismissive attitudes towards many of them, were also well documented, contrasting strongly with the close relationship she forged with Ronald Reagan. She established no similar rapport with any European leader.

What lay at the root of this attitude was her deep instinct for a form of 'English' exceptionalism, the idea sedulously cultivated for three centuries that Great Britain was set apart from Europe with different interests and different attitudes. Britain had always needed a European policy, but had always avoided becoming too involved in European affairs. The European project as it unfolded represented a fundamental challenge to that idea of 'England' and from the start it attracted resistance from Conservative nationalists and Conservative imperialists. The most intransigent of these nationalists was Enoch Powell, distinctive for his even-handed distaste for Europe and the United States.[23] He wanted Britain to be independent of both. Thatcher was increasingly to share Powell's instincts towards Europe but not his hostility to the United States. She never offered a British Gaullism. She disagreed with Powell over the role the United States played because she fundamentally believed that British and American interests were essentially one. Her emphasis on the continuing security threat from the Soviet Union was the most obvious expression of this, and breathed new life into the muted Atlanticism of her party. After some waning in the previous ten years Anglo-America now acquired a new resonance and strength.

The course of Anglo-American relations was not, however, entirely smooth during the Thatcher years. Two flashpoints between the British and the Americans arose: first, over the occupation of the Falkland Islands in 1982, and, second, over the US intervention in Grenada in 1983. The British response to the seizure of the Falkland Islands by Argentina was to dispatch a task force and seek to regain the islands by force.[24] Without US support the task force could not have succeeded, and its failure would have made the survival of Margaret Thatcher as Prime Minister very difficult, at a time when the government was under huge pressure from the domestic economic situation and the formation of the SDP/Liberal Alliance. The US administration was divided, with some, like Jeane Kirkpatrick, arguing that the US had a greater interest in supporting a friendly South American government like Argentina than in allowing Britain to pursue an old colonial claim. But in this instance the special relationship delivered. Britain's wider importance to US interests was given priority: Galtieri was sacrificed and Margaret Thatcher was preserved. In apparent contravention of the Monroe Doctrine, the United States allowed a European power to intervene in the western hemisphere to repossess one of its colonies. It was a measure of how the relationship between Britain and the United States had changed that this was now a possibility. The United States could afford to make the concession because of its appreciation that the Falklands was symbolic only – British power had long been extinguished in South America, and at that particular juncture it was more important to keep its principal ally happy. Refusal to do so, and forcing Britain to abandon its claim to the Falklands, would have had serious consequences for the special relationship and would have greatly weakened Atlanticist and pro-American sentiment in Britain.

The outcome of the Falklands conflict gave Thatcher a major success which cemented her leadership of the Conservatives and burnished her reputation as a strong leader. She won a landslide majority in the general election in 1983, and her confidence in British national sovereignty and her attachment to the Atlantic Alliance were confirmed. The Grenada episode the following year, however, showed the limits of British influence over the United States. The United States intervened in Grenada, part of the Commonwealth, to depose a regime it did not like, without any reference to either Britain or the United Nations. Britain protested, but to no avail. The United States simply invoked the Monroe Doctrine and defined the issue as one affecting the security of the United States. Britain's impotence to influence this decision was apparent, and its protests were brushed aside. However, the strong personal bond between Thatcher and Reagan survived this friction, as did the new form of the special relationship. An illustration of this came with the US bombing of Libya in 1986 when the Thatcher government gave permission for US airbases in Britain to be used to conduct the raid. Thatcher suffered a great deal of criticism for this in Britain, although it was not a maverick decision, but one fully in line with the role Britain was expected to play in relation to the United States. US leadership had to be respected and US decisions for its own security and the security of the alliance had to be accommodated.

Vindication for the policy of keeping close to the United States came with the collapse of communism in Europe. Britain and the United States acting together had now seen off the challenges mounted to the liberal capitalist order first by the Axis powers and then by the Soviet Union.[25] A certain amount of triumphalism was in order, and there was no shortage of it. A new world order was proclaimed, amidst speculation that the world had never been so united around the same political and economic principles. This victory was a victory for Anglo-America and for its leadership of the free world. The European project was at best a subordinate part of this project, at worst a distraction from it. By the end of the 1980s Thatcher had increasingly come to see it as a distraction, and a dangerous distraction at that.

The political economy community

The European project had widest appeal in Britain when it was presented as an economic project. Many Conservatives became persuaded of the advantages of greater economic cooperation within Europe, especially since more than 50 per cent of British trade came to be conducted with other members of the European Community after the formation of the Common Market in 1956. There was not, however, the same support for initiatives to merge security and defence. Most British politicians preferred to entrust security matters to NATO and the alliance with the United States. Conservatives were also convinced that the kind of cooperation they needed was for Europe to be organised as a single economic space, to allow maximum movement of capital, goods and labour within it. This ideal of a free trade Europe was the one which had initially led Enoch Powell to be a supporter of the first application of membership, and it was the reason that Margaret Thatcher voted for entry in 1971, and why she was such a strong advocate of the Single European Act in the 1980s.

In government Thatcher pursued an ambiguous policy towards Europe.[26] She quickly made herself very unpopular with her fellow leaders by insisting upon a substantial rebate of Britain's contribution to the Community budget on the grounds that Britain was receiving much less from the budget than it was contributing. Other leaders complained that she appeared to have no sense that Europe was a community, with shared tasks and shared burdens. Instead she wanted Britain to get out of the budget exactly the same as it had put in. But on other matters Thatcher and several of her ministers were in the forefront in pushing for the Community to move towards a single market. It quickly became apparent, however, that if the single market was to work, it needed to be supported by institutional and policy innovations in other areas as well. The Single European Act turned out to be one of the most far-reaching measures of European integration; yet it received strong support from Thatcher and her ministers, amidst considerable dismay from the Eurosceptics on the back benches. Many European governments saw the decision to create a single market as inevitably requiring the development at the European level of the kind of state powers that had previously evolved at national level to sustain and regulate markets, including new legal and administrative capacities. Thatcher always rejected this implication. The internal argument as it developed in the Conservative Party came to be between those like Thatcher who recoiled from the prospect of further pooling of national sovereignty, and those who accepted the advantages that would come from further integration. Thatcher believed that the single market did not require supranational regulation, but could remain under the control of the Council of Ministers, and would extend free trade, not bureaucratic powers. Many of her own ministers, including Geoffrey Howe, Leon Brittan, Michael Heseltine and Chris Patten, disagreed with her, seeing the advantages of extending the institutional powers of the European Union to make the single market a reality.[27] A key dividing line between the supporters and opponents of further European integration and cooperation was national sovereignty and whether in the economic sphere at least the major benefits could be secured only by a greater pooling of sovereignty than had already been achieved.[28]

Thatcher's repudiation of the implications of the single market, and in particular the proposals for economic and monetary union, not only split the Conservative Party, it created a new ideological dividing line. It fed into a debate as to what kind of political economy Britain wanted to adhere to. Britain, it was said, had its own distinctive political economy, which had more in common with the United States than with Europe. This idea that there were different models of capitalism, and that Britain was in a different category from many of the other European countries, proved a fertile one during the 1980s and 1990s. Anglo-Saxon capitalism was characterised both by its admirers and its critics as built on free, flexible and competitive markets, with relatively low levels of public spending, taxation and government intervention.[29] As traditional manufacturing industry declined, so new industries in the service sector in general and in financial services in particular developed during the 1980s to fill the gap. The continental model, of which there were several variants, gave much less emphasis to finance and much more to industry, and to safeguarding existing industry and employment. Many of the welfare states in northern Europe were more generous than the British one, inequality was lower, and solidarity more pronounced. On the British side, the third sector of voluntary and philanthropic activity tended to be more developed.

One of Thatcher's lasting legacies was to link the security arguments for American primacy with the political economy arguments. The United States, it was argued, should be Britain's priority not only because it alone could guarantee the security of Europe and the wider free world, but because it also shared with Britain a form of political economy which was superior to anything that Europe possessed. This was a novel argument when it first began to be advanced, because for a time in the 1970s and 1980s at the height of the stagflation and the relative decline and imperial overstretch affecting both Britain and the

United States, it had briefly seemed that other models of capitalism, notably the German and the Japanese, were performing much better than the Anglo-Saxon one, and there was much talk of the Anglo-Saxon countries needing to copy elements of these other models if they were to revive.[30] But by the end of the 1980s the boom engineered by the Reagan administration, and the far-reaching economic reorganisation in the international economy – above all in finance – led to a rapid re-evaluation of the different models, and the realisation that the Anglo-Saxon ones had acquired a new cutting edge which allowed their proponents to position themselves once again as the leading and most innovative part of the capitalist world.[31] This new confidence became encapsulated in a new policy orthodoxy, dubbed 'the Washington Consensus', and reflected the desire of the Thatcher and Reagan administrations to champion the Anglo-American model of capitalism against alternatives such as the European social model. This orthodoxy helped to inaugurate the new financial growth model of the 1980s, with deregulation of the financial markets, and attempts to roll back the state by reducing taxation and cutting spending programmes. By this means, by the end of the 1980s Thatcher and her allies were able to crystallise the strategic choice facing Britain as one between America and Europe not just in security but in political economy terms, and to position Britain firmly as part of Anglo-America rather than as part of Europe.

The ideological community

Arguments about how to interpret the Thatcher years have often centred on whether Thatcherism was an ideological project from the outset, or whether it is better understood as rooted in particular contexts – the product of chance, circumstances and interests rather than grand ideological designs. These two positions are too sharply opposed to be very illuminating, because what is important is how to understand ideas not as some prime mover opposed to interests, but as a necessary part of any context in which political action takes place. The ease with which ideas can be separated from the context in which they are applied, discussed and analysed sometimes makes it appear as though they float above all specific contexts. But in fact no context can be understood apart from the ideas that are constitutive of it.

One of Thatcherism's most distinctive features was its contribution to the reshaping of the images of Europe and the United States. It was certainly not obvious from the outset that this would be so, and particular events and contingencies and particular personalities were crucial for the way the positions crystallised and new narratives were developed.

But there could be no doubt by the time that Thatcher left office as to how indelibly both the Conservative Party and British politics more generally had been shaped by this divide. What gave it such potency as discussed in the last section was that ideas about security came to be united with ideas about political economy, and connected then to ideas about national interest and national identity. It was a heady mixture, and left a lasting legacy.

Thatcher herself was no ideologue, but ideologues were certainly attracted to her, and throughout her period as leader and beyond it there were ideological battles over what she represented and the change that her governments were bringing about. In trying to make sense of these changes, Thatcher and her supporters were able to draw on a number of rich ideological seams in Anglo-America, particularly from liberalism and conservatism. The new formulations of these came to be dubbed neo-liberalism and neo-conservatism, although these are not coherent and unified doctrines. It is better to think of them in the way that Irving Kristol characterised neo-conservatism – as persuasions rather than fixed doctrines, within which a considerable variety of points of view and influences are possible.[32] In the 1970s and 1980s they provided a number of intellectual frameworks and characteristic biases within which policy came to be discussed and evaluated, but they never supplied blueprints, and were not adhered to rigidly.

What was true of both neo-liberalism and neo-conservatism is that they were both part of transatlantic ideological debates, many of whose themes did not resonate in many other countries. The ideological community in Anglo-America is closely knit and has a long history.[33] Since the 1970s new discourses such as neo-liberalism and neo-conservatism have been developed which encouraged interchanges between think-tanks, political parties and public intellectuals across the Atlantic. There are important differences as well as similarities in the ideological discourse of the two nations, but there are many common features, and the emergence of new narratives such as neo-liberalism enriched and deepened the interchange.[34]

Thatcher was determined to reverse British decline. But she came to realise that this was only possible by reinvigorating the ties between Britain and the United States and rekindling the ideal of English-speaking civilisation. Neo-liberalism was an attempt to rethink the contribution of economic liberalism to economic prosperity and political stability, and emerged in its Anglo-American form as a critique of the Keynesianism, welfarism and statism of the post-war period. It laid the intellectual foundations for a practical challenge to the established orthodoxy, and led ultimately to the formulation of a new common sense about economic policy, both national and more importantly international. Monetarism was a part of this, but by no means the whole of neo-liberalism. It was important in a practical sense for offering a set of rules for running monetary policy in the absence of fixed exchange rates and in the inflationary context of the 1970s and 1980s.[35] But the deeper impact of neo-liberalism, associated in particular with Hayek, lay in the rethinking of the role of the state in the economy, and the formulation of a policy that favoured cutting back the state and removing restrictions on the private sector, confirming the market and market relationships as the driving force in the determination of the relationship between civil society and the state. The familiar mantras of neo-liberalism – low taxes, privatisation, deregulation – became the principles of a political economy that sought to reinvigorate the Anglo-Saxon formula that had brought such success in the past.

Thatcher may have struggled with the finer points of monetarism, but she understood very well the conception of the free economy which underlay it and which both Milton Friedman and Friedrich Hayek proclaimed, despite their differences. It fitted her own instincts to draw a parallel between the national budget and the budget of an ordinary housewife. This had long been one of the great simplifying ideas of liberal political economy, but it had been overlain by the ascendancy of Keynesianism, with its explicit separation of the private economy of individual agents from the complexity of the national economy, and its criticism of the attempt to reduce economic aggregates to microeconomic foundations. The move of mainstream economics away from Keynes in the 1970s and the return to favour of orthodox fiscal conservatism also provided a political space for Thatcher and Reagan to articulate the traditional verities of liberal political economy, although in practice Ronald Reagan was a believer in supply-side economics and the need for tax cuts to expand the economy, while Thatcher believed that regaining fiscal balance and defeating inflation must always be the first priority.

Thatcher was also a major contributor to the new international common sense, the Washington Consensus. She was a strong supporter of the free movement of goods and capital, and of encouraging developing countries to become self-sufficient by opening their markets, and accepting the package of neo-liberal reforms, including privatisation and deregulation, which was the condition for gaining access to international loans. Thatcher believed as strongly as Ronald Reagan in creating a world in the image of Anglo-Saxon capitalism. She became a proselytiser for the Anglo-Saxon model, and the virtues it would bring, not just to the developing world but also to parts of the developed world, including other states in Europe. Thatcher drew on several strands of neo-liberal ideas to guide her, both to chart a direction and to justify the evolving pattern of policy. The glimpse of the new international order the neo-liberals were stumbling towards was far from clear to many of them at the height of the stagflation, but they knew quite clearly what they were against, and neo-liberal doctrines gave them the confidence to think that both growth and stability could be returned to the capitalist economy.

The neo-liberal strand of Thatcherism has been well explored,[36] the neo-conservative strand less so. Yet in many ways it is the key to understanding the attraction of Anglo-America over Europe. Many Thatcherites who were economic liberals supported further European integration on the reasonable ground that if the single market was to work it needed a strong state to regulate and police it. That was an argument that never persuaded Thatcher, mainly because she never believed Europe could be an entity that could or would provide security for the UK or leadership for the West. Neo-conservatism was very American in its origins and distinctive characteristics,[37] but the aspect that crossed the Atlantic was the emphasis it placed upon US primacy, and the need for the United States to continue to provide strategic leadership, but only when this was in accordance with its own interests. The new phase of the special relationship over which Reagan and Thatcher presided was based precisely upon this assumption, and it was the willingness of Thatcher to identify British interests with the way in which the United States defined its own interests that was the key to the rehabilitation of Britain in American eyes, and its renewed importance for American strategy. Britain was useful again in the 1980s, 1990s and 2000s in a way it had not been in the 1960s and 1970s.[38] The glue in this new special relationship was partly the renewed strategic threat perceived to be coming from the Soviet Union, and partly the re-creation of the old bond between the English-speaking peoples. Thatcher identified with America in a way many former British imperialists would have found difficult. That was because America was no longer seen as a rival. The days when Britain could think of rivalling America were long gone.

The empathy between Margaret Thatcher and Ronald Reagan drew less from their economic liberalism than from their social and political conservatism. They both instinctively gave the same priority to the nation and its security over other political values, and economic liberalism, while important, gained its particular significance because it distilled the principles on which the nation's economic life should be constructed to best reflect the national character. Although their personalities were quite different, they created a common ideological bond which helped define the era, and in doing so infused new life into the image of Anglo-America.[39]

Thatcher's renewed engagement with America and distancing from Europe were not self-contained phenomena within the political class. They were also deeply affected by popular attitudes, and the way in which American cultural influences had increasingly come to change Britain's image of itself and its place in the world, and shaped popular opinion accordingly. In the nineteenth century and for at least the first half of the twentieth century, British Conservatives tended to be highly resistant to 'Americanisation'. They fought a long rearguard action in defence of hierarchy, authority and order against the mass culture and mass consumerism developed in such powerful ways by the Americans. The British themselves had been responsible for some of the early mass markets, but the Americans took the process much further, and gave mass consumption a centrality it had never had before. This was the other side of America: the vehicle of high modernity and the constant adapting of culture.[40]

The cultural aspects of America still gave British Conservatives some disquiet, but for the Thatcher generation this was generally over-shadowed by the role the United States had come to play as the chief shield and protector of the West and its values and traditions against the threats from internal subversion and external enemies, whether empires or civilisations. Europe was part of this West but it needed to accept American leadership. If Europe would not do so, then Britain's interest was clear. It had to give priority to its relationship with the United States. Security, political economy and ideology all converged as far as Thatcher and her closest supporters were concerned in making this the only possible choice.

13 Decolonisation and imperial aftershocks: the Thatcher years

Stephen Howe

It was long conventional, if inexplicit, wisdom that Britain's era of decolonisation, beginning in the mid to late 1940s, was largely concluded by the mid to late 1960s. Most overviews of the subject end around there, with the remaining African colonies and almost all the larger ones elsewhere having achieved independence, and the 'East of Suez' military commitment abandoned. More recent rethinking, however, has tended to see this as a story which, in so far as it has ever really ended, did so considerably later than once believed. Several important events and, indeed, crises of the Thatcher years can be viewed as involving a politics of decolonisation and/or having a distinctively post-imperial dimension. Most evidently, these include the Falklands War; the transfer of power in Zimbabwe and the complex events leading to the transfer of power in Hong Kong; crises in Commonwealth relations, especially over apartheid South Africa; and, in some eyes, various aspects of domestic politics and policy, such as immigration and European integration.

Yet such varied events and processes have rarely been seen either as a coherent ensemble or as forming parts of some larger narrative, whether of the end of empire as such or of a British 'post-imperialism'. Zimbabwe, the Falklands or Hong Kong are typically viewed as detached 'epilogues' to these narratives, and have quite often literally been thus consigned in overviews of decolonisation. I attempt here both a broad survey of these events and a tentative answer to the question of how far and in what ways such diverse episodes and controversies can be made elements in a coherent single 'end of empire' narrative – one which places the Thatcher era clearly within a more capacious account of decolonisation, both external and internal.

I undertake this task in the face of substantial and widespread doubts about whether it is even possible to construct such a tale for the Thatcher era. Certainly few have tried. Of those major histories of British decolonisation which have titular or otherwise explicit end dates, the great majority close their stories at some point in the 1960s or early 1970s, with 1964 by some margin the most popular concluding

234

date. A very few such surveys, it is true, carry on later; but none among these really treats events after the 1960s/70s as full parts of the empire story. Instead, they are viewed as 'post-' somethings to it: leftovers, afterwords and afterthoughts.[1]

We also, however, face a more substantive historiographical problem than that of chronology: the familiar, long-standing but still vexing one of the centrality or otherwise of empire to domestic British affairs. It is a commonplace – but a largely accurate one – that until very recently imperial and colonial history existed in an almost entirely separate sphere from the writing of 'domestic' British history. In the latter, empire was either excluded altogether (most often without even an explicit recognition of, let alone argument for, its being so) or confined to detached and usually brief sections of the works concerned.

From the 1990s onward, this academic apartheid faced major challenges. A substantial body of writing – and indeed polemic – urged the centrality of empire to every aspect of life in the imperial metropole as well as among the colonised.[2] On this reading, imperial expansion and power were profoundly, even ubiquitously constitutive of metropolitan British culture. The distinction between 'home' and 'empire' was, on this view, blurred or dissolved; there was always what one recent work calls an 'unhappy imbrication' of home/nation and empire, Self and Other.[3] Britishness itself did not exist prior to or independently of empire, but was a product of it. It naturally follows that this long imbrication, this mutually constitutive relationship, should have had powerful enduring effects; and, indeed, that the writing of a separate, national or insular, British history is for any modern period simply an error, both myopic and ideologically charged.

In consequence, a historiographical revolution has been proclaimed, often under the rubric of 'the new imperial history' – or sometimes, especially in North America, a 'new *British* history'.[4] But has that revolution merely been announced, or has it actually taken place? Only, I think we have to say, in relatively restricted academic circles, and mostly among writers coming from the imperial rather than the 'domestic' side of a schism which refuses to disappear. The past few years have seen an outpouring of major works of synthesis on contemporary British history, covering either the whole of the post-war era or significant chunks of it. Yet few of these books bear any marks of the supposed revolution announced by the 'new imperial history'. In such works that treat of the Thatcher years, explicit allusion to imperial or post-imperial themes is ordinarily confined to the Falklands crisis, and even in relation to this often goes little beyond clichés (albeit contested ones) about aggressive atavism, and/or reference to whether there was an electoral 'Falklands

Effect' in 1983 – the dominant view being of course that there was not. Cultural and intellectual histories ordinarily share the same perspective – even if recent essays in the former give decolonisation a slightly larger place than do political ones. In the 1980s the idea of the postcolonial took off in academia – initially and especially in literary and cultural studies. Traditional imperial historians, however, have often reacted to it with disdain or dismay. Writers on 'domestic' British political history have, with very rare and usually hostile exceptions, simply not noticed.

There is, then, some room for doubt whether this chapter has 'a subject' at all, still less one of any importance; and whether 'British empire' and 'the Thatcher era' are linked in any significant way, beyond a heterogeneous list of minor residues. Before returning to these big questions and the potential big story, a few words might usefully be said on Margaret Thatcher herself, and on the key 'imperial' issues of her premiership.

Thatcher and empire

Born in 1925, Margaret Roberts was one of the last generation of politicians to have grown up in an era when empire was a settled fact of British life. Empire, however, seems to have had little direct impact on her upbringing. Neither of her parents, Alfred and Beatrice, appears to have had imperial connections or experiences, and if any more distant relatives did so this has not surfaced either in her memoirs or in any of the major biographies. Alfred's lifetime migrations seem to have been restricted to the area between Northamptonshire and Lincolnshire. Even his strong Methodist commitments do not appear to have involved the kind of empire-wide activities of that church which several recent historians have traced; although, in a 1985 interview, Margaret recalled that 'I knew about overseas missions because we used to have some of the overseas missionaries from Africa coming and talking to us about it. We lived an astonishingly international life for people in a small town.' Kesteven and Grantham Girls' School was certainly not one of those academies that provided a steady stream of servants of empire. Margaret seems never to have travelled outside England in her youth: we are told that her first trip abroad was her honeymoon. Intriguingly, though, she later recalled that: 'I had an ambition as a child. I wanted to be part of the Indian Civil Service, because our Civil Service was the best in the world ... The Indian Civil Service was part of our Civil Service and it was thus the best in the world.'[5]

After leaving Grantham, neither Margaret's Oxford circle and interests nor her brief work as a research chemist in Essex and London involved any apparent imperial – or other international – experiences or interests. At her adoption meeting for the Finchley seat, her speech apparently focused on events in the Middle East, but this was a rather isolated instance in an early political career overwhelmingly concerned with domestic issues – local government, tax affairs and junior office at the Ministry of Pensions.[6] Husband Denis, with a New Zealand-born father, a career in the oil industry and extended stays in several British colonies or semi-colonies, had a background and career far more evidently linked to empire than hers.

All this stands in sharp contrast with so many of her political contemporaries or rivals – from Ted Heath's extensive youthful travels in 1930s Europe, through Tony Benn's wartime service in Africa, to James Callaghan's seafaring background in Portsmouth, an infinitely more cosmopolitan, globalised and indeed 'imperial' town than Grantham. Callaghan's father, incidentally, had been a member of the famous – or notorious – punitive expedition to Benin in Nigeria in 1895, while the family's Baptist faith seems, unlike Thatcher's Methodism, to have had a strong international dimension. Among the major Conservative figures of her era we might note, for example, Enoch Powell's crucially formative Indian experiences, or Geoffrey Howe's National Service in Kenya, followed by strong involvement with African affairs in his student days. Peter Carington's family included a Governor of New South Wales, veterans of Egyptian, Boer and Zulu wars, and much else. Even Thatcher's successor, Brixton boy John Major, had spent several years in Nigeria as a young man. Thatcher may not have been uniquely 'provincial' in her background among British political leaders, as was sometimes sneeringly suggested – all those just mentioned except Benn and Carington came from poorer families than hers – but she was almost uniquely insular and 'a-imperial' in her social and intellectual formation.

What, then – if anything – did shape her view of empire and its legacies? Thatcher apparently first encountered Kipling's work at the age of 11 and became entranced, if not obsessed by it.[7] Such youthful enthusiasms may even be thought to have filled the intellectual gap in someone who, from all indications, simply knew and read less history than any other modern British statesperson (less, even, than Tony Blair). However, it can hardly be argued that the influence profoundly marked either her policies or her public statements. She repeatedly said she was proud of the history of the empire, but reference to that history in speeches and apparently also in conversation was almost invariably generic. Few of her many references to Kipling were specifically 'imperial', and to my knowledge she never explicitly lamented the end of empire, with one ambiguous and anecdotal exception noted below. Thatcher herself famously consulted the opinions of various historians – most notably, of Norman Stone – in relation to her European policies, but so far as I am aware no historian of empire was ever sought out for advice during her years in power.

This apparent mixture of attitudes may, however, have been quite in tune with British public opinion. A Gallup Poll survey for the *Daily Telegraph* which, in August 1997, sought to probe knowledge of and attitudes to empire, discovered ignorance to be at least as profound as the Colonial Office's 1940s surveys had found it to be during the empire's existence. Of those questioned, 53 per cent did not know that the United States had once been a British colony. Only minorities knew that St Helena and Montserrat remained British possessions: 42 per cent and 35 per cent respectively, even though both territories had been in the news in preceding days. Perhaps more remarkably, 47 per cent believed that Australia was still a colonial dependency; while less – often much less – than 30 per cent gave correct answers to any of the survey's other factual historical questions. Perhaps more striking were the general approval ratings: 70 per cent said they took pride in the fact that Britain once had a great empire – of these, 60 per cent regretted that empire no longer existed, although 82 per cent of all respondents thought decolonisation had been 'inevitable'; 58 per cent felt that Britain's rule had done more good than harm to the colonies, with 70 per cent saying that it had been beneficial to Britain itself. Only a minority, however – 44 per cent – believed that Britain still had any duty to help former colonies; while just 19 per cent (perhaps a surprisingly high figure) thought that the Commonwealth was more important to Britain today than were the European Union or the USA.[8] This is a profile of attitudes strikingly like that apparently revealed in Margaret Thatcher's scattered public statements on such questions. Shirley Letwin was surely right to say that unlike any of her predecessors, or the dominant culture of her party before her time, she seemed free (or *relatively* free) of nostalgia for empire or hang-ups about its end.[9]

Her view, though never explicitly formulated in anything like these terms, would appear to have been very like that famously enunciated by the man so often claimed to have been a key intellectual mentor, Enoch Powell. Speaking, significantly, of *England*, not *Britain*, Powell argued that:

the continuity of her existence was unbroken when the looser connections which had linked her with distant continents and strange races fell away. Thus our generation is one which comes home again from years of distant wandering. We discover affinities with earlier generations of English who felt no country but this to be their own. We discover affinities with earlier generations of English who felt there was this deep, this providential difference between our empire and those others, that the nationhood of the mother country remained unaltered through it all, almost unconscious of the strange fantastic structure built around her – in modern parlance 'uninvolved'.[10]

If this was indeed her view – not, I think, one readily reducible to the cliché of 'Little Englandism', but not one suffused either with nostalgia for empire or with some ambient urge to reassert a lost and lamented imperial role – then one would not expect to discern some general overarching 'imperialism' or new or renewed form of global activism and interventionism in the international policies of her governments. Nor do I think we find such a pattern, though by no means all commentators on British foreign policy would agree. Nor, I suspect, do we find the kind of 'unilateralism' that some have identified, and have even seen as a kind of imperial throwback.[11] For instance, unlike Eden over Suez, Thatcher did not simply assume that she would have US backing to retake the Falklands, and made sure that all was firm on the transatlantic diplomatic front before acting there. Although her opposition to sanctions against South Africa famously left her in a minority of one within the Commonwealth, a few recent commentators like James Mayall argue that her role was less negative than usually thought and that she did engage in quiet diplomacy which helped pave the way for the eventual democratic transition.[12] Despite her own opposition to sanctions, and her repeated references to both Rhodesia's and South Africa's black nationalist movements as terrorists, she never gave key posts – let alone in foreign affairs – in her governments to members of the substantial 'kith and kin' or pro-Pretoria lobbies within her party. Figures like Geoffrey Howe, Peter Carington and Douglas Hurd, who *did* have crucial posts, were very much on the other side of those intraparty divisions.

Among her main confidants and ideological soul-mates were few people who expressed an identifiably 'imperialist' orientation in foreign policy. That ardent and emblematic arch-Thatcherite Nicholas Ridley came, not unfairly, to be seen as a thoroughgoing appeaser of Argentina in relation to the Falklands. That crisis was certainly not part of some broad pattern of seeking to maintain political control of overseas possessions. Thatcher's years in power witnessed the 1981 accessions to independence of Belize and of Antigua-Barbuda, then of St Kitts and Nevis in 1983 (Anguilla, in 1980, withdrew from the tiny island federation and opted to remain under British rule) and of Brunei in 1984. There were no significant developments, constitutional changes or British government initiatives in relation to any of Britain's remaining overseas territories during the Thatcher years, except of course for the Falklands. She showed little interest in any of them, and there was certainly no effort to strengthen British control. One finds in the foreign and security policy statements of her years no such sweeping proclamation of the need for global activism as some of those from the later Blair governments.[13] If her supposed scorn for old institutions did not seem to extend to those most associated with the remains of empire, maybe that is just because neither she nor those in her inner circles thought them to be of any great importance.

Incidents and issues

In the absence of clear evidence for a single, overarching Thatcherite programme which might in any obvious way be called 'imperial' – though I shall return to such notions, in a broader perspective, in conclusion – let us briefly survey the key episodes during her years in power which have strong links with the legacies of formal empire. Some candidates for that category must be excluded at the outset. These include Northern Ireland: it is very contestable and contested whether this was or is to be considered in any analytically useful way an imperial or colonial question (a contest in which I have had a certain personal involvement), but it is of undeniable importance that significant actors both within Ireland and internationally conceived of it as such. For present purposes, however, we can merely suggest that, in the earliest stages of the 'Troubles', precedents or connections with then-recent colonial counter-insurgencies were evident on several levels in British policy, personnel and, not least, the military tactics of which Bloody Sunday was the most disastrous though not wholly isolated instance;[14] but that by 1979 and afterwards such connections were far less evident.[15] The economic aspects of 'imperial legacies' in the 1980s also cannot be discussed here. The City was both child and mainstay of empire, in its informal as least as much as its formal manifestations. It did not lose its massive importance for former British colonies or semi-colonies during the tumultuous changes in world financial markets through the 1980s. Yet, as the most influential analysis of the relationship, that by Cain and Hopkins, points out, Thatcherism was not especially friendly to the 'gentlemanly' part of 'gentlemanly capitalism', while the City itself rapidly became a far less 'national', let alone identifiably post-imperial, institution during the decade, with the massive influx of foreign capital and firms.[16]

The fields of security, intelligence and terrorism can also only be gestured towards here. Except for the disputed case of Northern Ireland, none of the significant security threats experienced or indeed feared during the Thatcher years can be directly linked to Britain's formal imperial role – none of the remaining British overseas territories witnessed violent unrest, let alone attacks on Britain's own soil linked to their affairs. Yet Britain's and especially London's role as a magnet for migration and a global financial and media centre, in significant part deriving from its imperial past, clearly contributed to its being the site for attacks or plots from several quarters during those years, from Iraqi, Iranian, Libyan, Palestinian, Sikh and other groups. The homelands of the militants involved had in every case once been de jure or de facto British colonies.

Policies towards the Middle East also deserve, but cannot here receive, a substantial separate analysis. In this region, which had through the first two-thirds of the twentieth century become so central to Britain's empires, both formal and informal, British interests and involvements remained strong throughout the 1980s. Here I can only summarily suggest that the Thatcher era exhibited far more continuities than radical breaks. In relation to the Israeli–Arab conflict Thatcher has sometimes been argued to have been especially pro-Israeli, with a few commentators linking this to her personal 'pro-Jewish' feelings in domestic affairs. Yet it is far from clear that she was more so than, say, Harold Wilson. Certainly 'Arabist' figures within her party found themselves out in the cold, or, like Ian Gilmour, became prominent among her fiercest critics. But this surely owed less to views specifically on the Middle East than to such people's tendency to belong to the party's One Nation, patrician and often ex-Foreign Office circles. If there is a link at all, it might lie in the FCO – seen by Thatcherites as deplorably weak and even unpatriotic in its settled pragmatism, and by pro-Israeli critics as entrenchedly pro-Arab. On the 'other side', none of the important Jewish members of her Cabinets – Leon Brittan, Nigel Lawson, Keith Joseph, David Young – had particularly strong ties to Israel. Conversely, links with Gulf states remained strong, and relations with the Saudis especially became closer than ever in the Thatcher years.

Taking the main relevant episodes in rough chronological order, the first 'imperial' crisis facing the Thatcher government concerned what, in these years, was named in rapid succession Rhodesia, Zimbabwe-Rhodesia, then Zimbabwe.

Margaret Thatcher had been expected by many, including among Rhodesia's whites and her own core supporters, to offer strong support for Ian Smith's regime and the new 'power-sharing' (or puppet) government under Abel Muzorewa which came into office almost simultaneously with her own. So, indeed, her instincts inclined her to do – but to the surprise of many and the dismay of some, she bowed to the views of Carrington, her Foreign Secretary, of the Carter administration and of the Commonwealth to declare herself, at her first Commonwealth Heads of Government meeting in Lusaka, 'wholly committed to genuine black majority rule'.[17] That summit, where she famously danced with and professed herself charmed by Zambia's Kenneth Kaunda, presented an unexpectedly emollient Thatcher to her Commonwealth colleagues, to black Africa and to the world. The image was not to last. She seems to have been almost entirely, and again unexpectedly, 'hands-off' in relation to the ensuing Lancaster House negotiations. If they and the settlement to which they led were a 'triumph', it was not hers but Carrington's – and, as it turned out, Robert Mugabe's – except in so far as she showed wisdom in her virtual abstention.[18]

The world then saw the brief return to Zimbabwe of all the outward show of British colonial rule, but with none of the substance of power. The remarkable recent florescence of work in contemporary history by Zimbabweans – most of them, alas, now operating in exile – has tended to underline both how little real influence Britain had there at any time since the 1960s, and how utterly Thatcher's, or any other British government failed to understand the internal dynamics of its politics.[19] Margaret Thatcher's own deep feelings were perhaps revealed when, watching the independence ceremony on TV, she reportedly exclaimed 'The poor Queen, do you realise the number of colonies that have been handed over ... since she came to the Throne?' – and wept.[20]

At the heart of most contemporary historians' views on an 'imperial' dimension to the Thatcher years lies the Falklands War: indeed as we have noted, for many general accounts it stands alone in being described thus. Bill Nasson, for example, sees the Falklands as 'The last militant episode of an old imperial past ... nothing other than a bizarre imperial episode, [but] unlike Suez, military victory this time seemed to do something to atone for a catalogue of decline and failure at home.'[21] Yet this was evidently an ambiguous case. While the war was very obviously imperial, in being fought over one of Britain's remaining formal colonial possessions, it was also a hybrid: in part, a war of defence against another state's act of aggression, defending the principle of self-determination and the declared wishes of the islanders; in part, anticipating features of the post-colonial wars of intervention that have become so familiar in the more recent past. If the beliefs that drove Thatcher's government into war, and enabled it to command such strong public and opposition support, could be described (as Anthony Barnett did in a pioneering analysis) as a revived 'Churchillism' – an anachronistic vision of national greatness, driven by the inherited ideology of absolute, indivisible sovereignty – then this was far from peculiar to Thatcher. Instead, it reflected, or helped form, a much wider national mood.[22] It was indeed that mood – the apparent renewal during the Falklands War of an aggressive, jingoistic, xenophobic form of popular British patriotism – that was held by many, especially on the left, to be the most significant and unwelcome aspect of the crisis, and perhaps that most clearly and powerfully associated with the popular imperialism of the past.[23] Here can be found, as I have suggested at greater length elsewhere, the starting point for much subsequent debate and investigation about the character of English/British nationalism and national identity, both among historians and other scholars and in a wider public sphere.[24] Thatcher herself appeared, in some public statements during the war's immediate aftermath, to urge that it marked an epochal reassertion of Britain's global greatness – though she refrained from expressing this in too explicitly imperial terms.[25]

Yet it has been much doubted whether the victory had the significant domestic effects often attributed to it.[26] If going to war over the islands indicated a firm resolve to defend both the territorial integrity of Britain's remaining overseas possessions and the rights of their inhabitants, then clearly this did not reflect some general consistent ideological stance on such matters. As is well known, prior to the invasion Thatcher's government had been no less willing than its immediate predecessors to negotiate with Argentina some form of agreement on the transfer of sovereignty. If the war and its aftermath manifested a strident 'Churchillism', preceding policy looked to critics more like Chamberlain's. The 1983 Grenada crisis underlined that upholding sovereignty was certainly not an immovable principle. Despite the figleaves of involvement by various Caribbean micro-states and of retrospective endorsement by the island's Governor-General Sir Paul Scoon; despite, too, the more significant fact that the Grenadian government thus overthrown was the illegitimate product of a coup and of the murder of the previous Prime Minister Maurice Bishop; this was on the face of it quite clearly an act of US aggression against a Commonwealth country still under the British Crown. Britain had not been consulted or even informed before the invasion. On that level Denis Healey was surely correct to describe it as 'an unpardonable humiliation of an ally'.[27] Yet Britain neither publicly condemned the invasion nor supported UN resolutions doing so. It is said that Thatcher was privately very angry, telephoning Reagan to moan that 'You have invaded the Queen's territory and you didn't even say a word to me.'[28] She suggested in her memoirs that she 'felt dismayed and let down by what had happened. At best the British government had been made to look impotent; at worst we looked deceitful.'[29] But the anger was at the lack of consultation rather than at the act itself: at form, rather than substance. Thatcher felt no real regret at the overthrow, by Britain's closest ally and patron, of a rogue Marxist regime. The USA's action had a considerable degree of regional backing and, in retrospect, apparent popularity among most Grenadians. But there was a bitter irony in that the 'excuse' for invasion was the ousting and murder of Maurice Bishop, a leader both Washington and London had hated and sought to undermine when he was in power.[30] British actions – or lack of them – over Grenada were surely strong evidence, if further such were needed, that the Atlantic alliance and the politics of the second Cold War were far more important to Thatcher-era foreign policy than any specifically post-imperial dimension.

Policy towards South Africa presented more permanent, or recurring, dilemmas during the Thatcher years. These too may be viewed as distinctively post-imperial both in that the country was a former colony – albeit one where arguably Britain had been able to exert only influence, not direct power, since about 1910 – and in the crucial role of the Commonwealth. Relations with and within the Commonwealth played as large a role in the multiple crises over South Africa, peaking in 1986–9, as they had done with the Rhodesian settlement.[31] Here too many of Thatcher's apparent personal preferences clashed with the demands of diplomacy and the pressures or pieties of Commonwealth unity. They also appeared increasingly divisive on the 'domestic' British scene, as opposition to apartheid took on an ever higher public profile and mobilised the impassioned sympathies not only of most of the political left, but much of the centre and even of some senior Conservatives.[32] For Thatcher, opposition to sanctions clearly stemmed both from her economic views and from her identification of the African National Congress as a 'terrorist' as well as pro-Communist organisation.[33] Thatcher's relations both with many Commonwealth leaders, and with the organisation's Secretary-General Shridath Ramphal, became, it seems, very poor indeed on a personal as well as a political level. Among the more dramatically public, if symbolic, consequences was the boycott of the 1986 Edinburgh Commonwealth Games by over half the eligible countries. There were straining effects, too, within her own government, such as when at the 1989 Commonwealth Heads of Government meeting in Kuala Lumpur she flatly and imperiously threw out the South African plans negotiated by her then Foreign Secretary, John Major. This issue threatened to bring to a head the notably uncomfortable relationship between premier and monarch. There were several behind-the-scenes clashes between the Queen and Thatcher over Commonwealth relations and Thatcher's stance on South African sanctions. It was a question on which Elizabeth II felt particularly strongly; indeed, it was an at least partial exception to the general avowed political neutrality of the Crown. Ben Pimlott quotes 'a key Whitehall figure' as saying of Elizabeth that 'she is entitled to feel that, whereas she just inherited the title of Queen of England [*sic*], her Headship of the Commonwealth is something she has striven for and earned'.[34] Her Prime Minister, she clearly felt, undermined that role, and this was not forgiven.

Hong Kong was different – from everywhere else. By 1979 it was by far the most important remaining British possession, in terms of population and still more of economic clout. Unlike almost every other colony, its promised future lay not in independence but in (re)absorption by a far larger neighbouring state – itself indeed an imperial state by most definitions. In that it was not, of course, quite unique; but unlike the cases of Gibraltar, Belize or the Falklands, it was generally accepted in London that the neighbour's claims to sovereignty could not be resisted.[35] This had not always been the case. After 1945 Britain briefly considered pursuing a 'nation-building' course in Hong Kong, which might have set the colony on the road to eventual independence as a city-state like Singapore. This course was eventually rejected, in part because of the perceived lack of popular support for a separate identity within the colony, in part because it was thought that China would react to it with the invasion which seemed so possible or probable in 1949.[36] By Thatcher's time the independence option seemed long since foreclosed (it had become so, by a nice historical coincidence, under a Governor named Grantham), even if it is clear that she not only hoped but fought long and hard for a way of maintaining British control. Her subsequent expressions of sorrow, indeed anger, were numerous and seemingly heartfelt.[37] Once again she found herself bitterly and semi-publicly at odds with the 'appeasers' in the Foreign Office. And once again, as with South Africa, the results remained inconclusive, leaving huge dilemmas for her successor. Here, too, the principle of democratic self-determination, so strongly if inconsistently proclaimed in relation to the Falklands, played little apparent part in her or her ministers' calculations. True, there were elections to the Legislative Council for the first time in 1985 – but with an electorate of 70,000 out of a population of six million. Fears that Hong Kong residents might seek to migrate to the UK in unacceptable 'swamping' numbers appeared far more important at No. 10 than hopes or plans that they might exercise any democratic rights. Only under John Major's premiership and Chris Patten's governorship, in what was widely derided as a death-bed conversion before the transfer of power, did Hong Kong achieve anything even vaguely approximating a democracy.

Contrasts and continuities

So far, we have pointed towards a series of 'post-imperial' episodes and issues of the Thatcher years, and have implied that these were indeed essentially discrete episodes, not clearly linked together into some wider pattern of policy or philosophy, of either abidingly imperialist or consistently decolonising kinds. Let us turn now to wider arguments about continuities and/or breaks; to whether or in what ways the Thatcher years might be seen in some bigger end-of-empire story. I look first at debates on domestic British affairs, then at those on Britain's place in the world – while noting, once again, those heated, unresolved disputes as to whether that very distinction should not be dissolved.

Claims that post-war British political debates and developments, not least during and since the 1980s, were distinctively post-imperial, or indeed a form of internal decolonisation, have been advanced in at least four major respects.[38] First and perhaps most generally, numerous economic and political commentators have associated the loss of empire with Britain's comparatively poor economic performance and the widely perceived crisis of confidence in Britain's national purpose and even identity. In one version, the Thatcher era stands in that narrative as the point where this retreat was arrested, the post-imperial perception of inevitable decline thrown off and a new confidence and assertiveness implanted – with the Falklands victory sometimes viewed as the key psychological turning point in that regard.[39] Other stories, of course, are more negative, seeing the 1980s as offering false solutions to 'post-imperial' problems, exhibiting neurotic reactions of denial and an 'inability to mourn' national decline.[40]

The second line of argument focuses on contending and mutating nationalisms. On this reading, the revived, reconfigured English nationalism with which Thatcherism was associated by some critics, and viewed as intimately associated with the legacies of empire or indeed with the reassertion of a distinctively imperialist mindset, helped in its turn to quicken the pace and sharpen the temper of separatist nationalisms in Scotland, Wales and Northern Ireland. In one version at least, all this made the 'Break-Up of Britain' a natural, even inevitable concluding chapter to the end of empire, just as an English imperialism and 'internal colonialism' within these islands had been the necessary prelude and precondition for global expansion.[41]

Third, there was an argument centred on the politics of 'race', suggesting that imperialism and its legacies were decisive in shaping British racial attitudes. Empire had been the incubator of British racism, and an alleged atavistic revival of aggressively imperialist emotions under Thatcher (once again, often seen as crystallised or symbolised by the Falklands campaign) had renewed or intensified this, with the acquiescence or even active encouragement of the Prime Minister herself.[42]

Fourth, it was asserted that the United Kingdom's own governing and constitutional arrangements, involving over-centralism, archaism, secrecy and multiple modes of 'indirect rule', were crucially and damagingly shaped by the legacies of global empire. Structures and attitudes developed in and for the running of a global empire had a powerful effect 'at home', which endured well after empire's external dissolution, and which numerous Thatcher-era measures were seen as actually intensifying. In this sense Britain was, as several 1980s commentators proclaimed, 'the last colony of the empire'.[43] It was a journalistic cliché of both the 1950s and the 1980s to write of British governments sitting atop bubbling pots of discontent, pressure cookers of social protest. In the 1950s these were in Nyasaland and Nigeria, Cyprus and Aden. In Thatcher's years, they were in Liverpool and Glasgow, Brixton and Burnley. Local government leaders from Lambeth to Liverpool frequently protested at being 'treated like a colony' by Whitehall and Westminster. Yet, more importantly, that same rhetorical trope (although it soon proved to be rather more than that) was ever more often heard in Scotland, Wales and Northern Ireland – and in the latter, intriguingly, it was heard now from unionists as well as nationalists.[44]

So a powerful and plausible story – indeed several converging stories – could be told about the Thatcher years as crucial parts of a grand narrative of empire, of the enduring domestic effects of imperialism and its ends. Yet there are also significant grounds for doubt about the explanatory reach of such stories. These cluster around questions as to how significant, indeed how clearly identifiable and distinguishable, may be the specifically 'post-imperial' aspects of each of the developments and debates noted above. How these in turn are answered depends in great part on what view one takes of the sharp, substantially unresolved arguments alluded to at the outset of this chapter, over the salience or otherwise of imperialism to British politics, cultures and identities across the centuries.

It may even be that, from a different and perhaps wider perspective, those debates are misplaced. Ashley Jackson, for example, argues that:

Decolonisation has become too dominant a theme in modern British history ... The focus on decolonisation as the master-narrative of twentieth-century imperial history has blinded us to the continuities in Britain's relations with the world and the many connections between the Britain of 2007 and the Britain of 1967.

If 'decolonisation' is *not* the master key for understanding changes in Britain's modern world role, then it might naturally follow that it is an error to search for signs of 'internal decolonisation' in the 1980s or perhaps any other recent period of British history. For Jackson,

Britain never in fact entirely lost that empire and certainly never lost the appetite and capacity to perform a world role, despite the turn towards Europe that Acheson approvingly discerned, and the relative contraction of British economic, political and military power in the post-war decades. Britain's global interests never vanished, and, even though the Cheshire cat of empire slowly faded, the grin remained.[45]

Jackson's is surely an overstated claim, even if salutary as a corrective to conventional wisdom. Neither the transitions to independence of former colonies, nor the simultaneous decline in Britain's 'informal empire' and capacity to exert global power, was an illusion. Yet it is true that attention to decolonisation has led to neglect of important continuities, including some which contemporary events have brought sharply back into view. As I have suggested, the field has been dominated – not least in considerations of the Thatcher era – by three different basic ways of conceiving the issues involved: as concerning mere residues of empire; as a matter of returns and revivals; and as a tale of continuities. The first has been perhaps the most conventional wisdom among historians. Critics and commentators from the left have often focused most on the second, often focusing especially on the Falklands War. Events since 2001 have given new impetus to the third: an argument that from the 1960s through to the 1990s, Britain did not so much accept a diminished world role as seek new ways of exerting influence outside Europe. The 1998 Strategic Defence Review summarised and updated much of this, linking Britain's national security not only to Europe and the USA but also to Africa, the Mediterranean and the Gulf. It proclaimed continued readiness for global military deployment, which after 2001 was of course increasingly activated and intensified.[46]

The common assumption both of contemporary political commentary on decolonisation, and of earlier historical writing about it, was that this was in some sense an inevitable process, a singular one – in that the post-1945 accessions to independence of dozens of African, Asian and other territories formed in some strong sense a single story – a profoundly transformative one, and one whose central meaning was the triumph of the nation-state model of political organisation over that of the multinational imperial system. Alternative outcomes, including the continuation of a form of imperial relationship, as with Britain's remaining overseas territories or France's *départements* and *territoires d'outre-mer*, were not only aberrant but inherently illegitimate: this remains the operating assumption of the United Nations' Special Committee of the 24 on Decolonisation.

Multiple contemporary developments, both political and historiographical, have recently combined to call much of this into question. Leaving aside the most ambient and contentious of all these, debates over an alleged twenty-first-century renewal of empire and a 'colonial present', four of them appear to me to be of particular pertinence to thinking about the Thatcher years in relation to wider histories of imperial decline, persistence or after-effects.

First has been the recent move towards bringing the Dominions, the former colonies of white settlement, 'back in' to the end-of-empire story. They were mostly excluded from writing and debate over the process of decolonisation after 1945, on the simple basis that they were already politically independent. Recently, though, historians such as Tony Hopkins and James Belich have argued that full decolonisation came to Canada, Australia or New Zealand much later than conventionally thought.[47] It came only, in Belich's terms, after the failure of a project of 'recolonisation' – of increasing economic and cultural integration of the Dominions with Britain – which had dominated the first half of the twentieth century. It involved the erosion or ending of a globalised conception of Britishness, a 'British world' or 'Greater Britain' – both terms which have had an enormous new salience among recent Anglophone historians of empire – and the creation of new national identities. These are processes which, on many levels, are still in train today. Their study still needs, I think, to be more fully integrated with that of the 'subject' (or non-white) empire than is ordinarily done, and indeed with that of Britain itself. The Thatcher years may, as a result, come to seem a crucial moment in this process, as James Curran and Stuart Ward have recently suggested from the 'Australian end' of the story. [48]

Second, a great deal of recent historical work in numerous European countries clusters around the idea of 'internal decolonisations' in Europe, and especially those states which were once major colonial powers. Such debate, once again an intensely politicised one engaging a broad public sphere as well as academic research, and often closely intertwined with questions over the very nature of national identities and national pasts, has emerged in country after country. Recent French exchanges have been perhaps the most dramatic and hotly argued eruption, but Britain, Belgium, Holland, Italy, Germany and more are witnessing vigorous interrogation of colonial histories and their present-day entailments. All have involved a politics of memory (and of forgetting), a strong interest in the relations between ideas about empire and ones about race, and an intense focus on the effects of empire within metropolitan European societies and cultures: this last an emphasis so far strongest, I think, in British history, but with ever-growing analogues almost everywhere else. Fully comparative studies of these phenomena – of the political determinants and implications of new disputation over colonial histories – are only just beginning to emerge.[49] Again, the 1980s in Britain look from this perspective like a crucial moment, not this time in the stories of imperial decline or after-effects themselves so much as in the formation of 'imperial memory' and its relation to changing conceptions of national identity.

Third, closely linked to the foregoing, there is a very recent growth of interest in what we might call the Europeanisation of decolonisation. How did the birth and development of the project of European integration relate to the concurrent declines and decolonisations of Europe's overseas empires? What kind of reality, and what plans and projections, lay behind once popular notions like 'Eurafrica'? A few historians and political scientists like Peo Hansen, Louis Sicking, or more recently Todd Shepard, have in the past discussed such questions and have – sometimes in highly polemical vein – engaged with the 'colonial heritage' of the European Union or possible links between early moves towards European integration and the processes of decolonisation. Some have urged that at least until the early 1960s, many of the visions, movements and institutional plans for European integration envisaged that Africa would be incorporated into the European project – that it would indeed be a *Eurafrican* project.[50] One potential upshot is to call into question the tendency to view European integration and the pursuit of a global, or Atlantic, role as mutually exclusive. Historically, these things were intertwined in far more complex a fashion.

Fourth, and again closely related, historians have been rethinking the relations between decolonisation and the Anglo-American partnership. In sum, the emerging argument from several quarters is that post-1945 American policy was far more, and more importantly, supportive of

Britain's empire than most historians had previously believed. As Roger Louis and Ronald Robinson argued in a pioneering instance of this reappraisal:

It ought to be a commonplace that the post-war British Empire was more than British and less than an *imperium*. As it survived, so it was transformed as part of the Anglo-American coalition. Neglecting the American role, imperial historians often single out British enfeeblement as prime cause of an imperial demise ... To see the transformation of an imperial coalition as if it were the collapse of an imperial state is like mistaking the melting tip for the iceberg.[51]

As the Cold War intensified from 1947, superpower competition came to the rescue of Britain's empire. Despite persisting anti-colonialist rhetoric, in practice America consistently gave priority to anti-communism over anti-colonialism. In multiple regions, the USA's 'most important collaborators' became the British and their empire/Commonwealth. Louis and Robinson carried the story only through the 1950s, though subsequently Louis has sought to extend it as far as the early 1970s.[52] Aspects of their case have been subject to strong criticism. Yet it remains worth exploring how much of the pattern of Britain's international role in the 1980s can aptly be fitted into their picture: how Thatcher-era 'Atlanticism', in its relation to projections of British power in the extra-European world, connects to patterns of British–American cooperation (and dispute) both in the immediate post-war decades and in the period of the Bush–Blair axis.

March 2002 witnessed the death, at the age of 101, of Queen Elizabeth the Queen Mother, the last Queen to have also been an Empress. By then it had already been concluded and proclaimed that Britain's military commitment in Afghanistan would have to be substantial and enduring. Exactly a year later came the invasion of Iraq. On that century-long perspective, the Thatcher years were just an episode in a continuing, in some respects remarkably unchanging, imperial story: but an episode when it was both too late, and too soon, for empire to dare speak its name.

Appendices

Prepared by Peter Sloman

Appendix 1: Timeline

1925–1974 Margaret Thatcher's early career

1925	13 October	Margaret Roberts born in Grantham
1943	October	Margaret Roberts begins chemistry degree at Somerville College, Oxford
1946	October	Margaret Roberts elected president of Oxford University Conservative Association
1950	23 February	Margaret Roberts unsuccessful at Dartford in general election
1951	15 October	Margaret Roberts unsuccessful at Dartford in general election
	13 December	Margaret Roberts marries Denis Thatcher
1953	15 August	Carol and Mark Thatcher born
	1 December	Margaret Thatcher (MT) qualifies as a barrister
1958	31 July	MT adopted as Conservative candidate for Finchley
1959	8 October	MT elected as Conservative MP for Finchley in general election
1961	9 October	MT appointed Parliamentary Under-Secretary at Ministry of Pensions and National Insurance
1964	October	MT appointed Shadow pensions spokesman following Conservatives' general election defeat
1965	18 October	MT becomes Shadow spokesman for housing and land
1966	19 April	MT becomes Shadow Treasury spokesman under Iain Macleod
1967	10 October	MT appointed to Shadow Cabinet, with responsibility for fuel and power
1968	11 October	MT gives Conservative Political Centre Lecture, 'What's Wrong with Politics?'
	14 November	MT becomes Shadow Minister of Transport
1969	21 October	MT becomes Shadow Secretary of State for Education and Science
1970	18 June	General election: Conservatives 330 seats, Labour 287, Liberals 6, Others 7
	19 June	MT appointed Secretary of State for Education and Science
	30 June	MT issues Circular 10/70, withdrawing the compulsion for secondary schools to adopt comprehensive system

1971	14 June	Bill ending free milk for primary school children passes second reading
1972	9 January	Miners begin strike (ends 25 February)
	9 February	Government introduces three-day week
1973	13 November	State of emergency declared as miners prepare overtime ban
1974	28 February	General election: Labour 301 seats, Conservatives 297, Liberals 14, Ulster Unionist parties 11, SNP 7, Plaid Cymru 2, Others 3
	March	MT appointed Shadow Secretary of State for the Environment
	10 October	General election: Labour 319 seats, Conservatives 276, Liberals 13, SNP 11, Ulster Unionist parties 10, Plaid Cymru 3, Others 3
	7 November	MT moves to Shadow Treasury team
	21 November	Sir Keith Joseph tells MT that he will not seek Conservative Party leadership; MT decides to stand

1975–1990 Margaret Thatcher as Conservative Party leader

1975	4 February	First ballot of Conservative leadership election: MT 130, Heath 119. Heath withdraws from contest
	11 February	Second ballot of Conservative leadership election: MT 146, Willie Whitelaw 79. MT elected Conservative Party leader
	5 June	EEC Referendum: 67.2 per cent vote 'yes'
	18 June	First landing of North Sea oil
	11 July	Government and TUC announce voluntary incomes policy
1976	19 January	MT warns against Soviet aggression in speech at Kensington Town Hall
	5 April	James Callaghan becomes Labour leader and Prime Minister in succession to Harold Wilson
	7 April	Labour government loses Commons majority
	21 August	Grunwick dispute on trade union recognition begins
	29 September	UK applies to IMF for $3.9bn
	4 October	Conservative policy document *The Right Approach* published
1977	23 March	Lib–Lab Pact agreed, keeping Callaghan government in office in confidence vote
	13–24 June	Climax of Grunwick mass picket
	9 October	Former Labour minister Reg Prentice defects to Conservatives
1978	30 January	MT refers to 'swamping' by immigrants in television interview
	21 September	Ford workers begin strike against 5 per cent wage offer
	5 December	UK opts out of European Monetary System at Brussels summit
1979	3 January	Lorry drivers' strike begins
	22 January	Public employees' 'day of action', followed by six weeks of strikes

	1 March	Devolution rejected 4–1 in Welsh referendum. In Scotland, 'yes' campaign secures 51.6 per cent, but fails to meet threshold of 40 per cent of total electorate
	28 March	Government loses vote of no confidence, 311 to 310
	30 March	Airey Neave killed by INLA bomb in House of Commons car park
	3 May	General election: Conservatives 339 seats, Labour 268, Liberals 11, Ulster Unionist parties 10, SNP 2, Plaid Cymru 2, Others 3
	7 June	European Parliament elections: Conservatives 60 seats, Labour 14, Others 4
	12 June	Geoffrey Howe's first budget: income tax reduced from 33p to 30p and top rate from 83p to 60p; VAT raised to 15 per cent. Howe also announces a relaxation of exchange controls
	18 July	Government abolishes exchange restrictions on outward direct investment and on portfolio investment in securities in EEC currencies or from international organisations
	1 August	Clegg Commission on Pay Comparability recommends rises of up to 25.8 per cent for public sector workers, half to be paid immediately, half from April 1980
	10 September	Lancaster House conference on Rhodesia begins (agreement reached 21 December)
	23 October	Howe announces abolition of remaining exchange controls
	15 November	Anthony Blunt exposed as 'fourth man' in Soviet spy network
	25 December	Soviet Union invades Afghanistan
1980	2 January	Steel strike begins
	26 March	Howe announces Medium-Term Financial Strategy in budget
	22 September	Iran–Iraq war begins
	10 October	MT tells Conservative Party Conference 'The lady's not for turning'
	15 October	Callaghan retires as Labour Party leader (Michael Foot elected as successor, 10 November)
	27 October	First hunger strike by H-block prisoners in Maze prison, Belfast
	4 November	Ronald Reagan elected President of the United States
1981	5 January	Cabinet reshuffle: Norman St John-Stevas dismissed
	24 January	Labour Party special conference at Wembley introduces electoral college for future leadership elections
	25 January	Council for Social Democracy formed
	10 February	National Coal Board announces plans to close twenty-three pits (withdrawn on 18 February after local strikes)

	February	Government sells off 51.6 per cent of British Aerospace
	1 March	Second IRA hunger strike begun by Bobby Sands
	26 March	Social Democratic Party (SDP) launched by Roy Jenkins, David Owen, Bill Rodgers and Shirley Williams
	30 March	364 economists issue letter condemning the government's economic policies
	11–14 April	Brixton riots
	6 May	Ken Livingstone becomes leader of the Greater London Council
	3 July	Southall riot
	4–8 July	Moss Side riots
	20 July	Michael Heseltine leads task force to Merseyside
	27 July	British Telecommunications Act separates Post Office and telecommunications services
	14–15 September	Cabinet reshuffle: Sir Ian Gilmour, Mark Carlisle and Lord (Christopher) Soames dismissed
	27 September	Denis Healey defeats Tony Benn for deputy leadership of Labour Party
	12 November	Civil Service Department abolished
	25 November	Scarman Report on Brixton riots calls for 'urgent action' against 'racial disadvantage'
	26 November	Shirley Williams (SDP) wins Crosby from Conservatives in by-election
1982	4 January	Young Workers Scheme starts, subsidising employers of under-18s earning less than £40 per week
	26 January	Unemployment passes 3 million
	February	National Freight Corporation bought out by management; Amersham International privatised
	25 March	Roy Jenkins (SDP) wins Glasgow Hillhead in by-election
	2 April	Argentine forces capture Port Stanley in Falkland Islands
	5 April	Francis Pym replaces Lord (Peter) Carrington as Foreign Secretary; task force sails for Falklands
	25 April	South Georgia recaptured
	14 June	Port Stanley recaptured; Argentine garrisons surrender
	2 July	Roy Jenkins becomes SDP leader, defeating David Owen
	20 July	Eight British soldiers killed and fifty-one people injured in two IRA bomb attacks in London
	1 October	Church of England publishes *The Church and the Bomb*
	6 December	Seventeen people, including eleven British soldiers, killed by INLA bomb at Ballykelly
1983	8–12 January	MT visits Falklands
	18 January	Franks Committee clears government of Falklands negligence

	February	Government sells 51.5 per cent of Associated British Ports
	April	Youth Training Scheme introduced
	9 June	General election: Conservatives 397 seats, Labour 209, Alliance 23, Ulster Unionist parties 15, Plaid Cymru 2, SNP 2, Others 2
	10–11 June	Cabinet reshuffle: Howe appointed Foreign Secretary, Nigel Lawson becomes Chancellor
	16 June	Central Policy Review Staff abolished
	13 June	David Owen succeeds Roy Jenkins as SDP leader
	August	Enterprise Allowance Scheme, launched in five pilot areas early in 1982, extended nationwide
	24 September	Thirty-eight IRA inmates escape from Maze prison
	2 October	Neil Kinnock elected Labour Party leader
	14 October	Cecil Parkinson resigns as Trade and Industry Secretary, after pregnant secretary, Sara Keays, says he had promised to marry her
	11 November	First US missiles arrive at Greenham Common
	17 November	Six people killed and eighty injured in IRA bombing of Harrods
1984	8 January	Miners' strike begins in Yorkshire
	25 January	Howe announces ban on trade union membership at GCHQ
	26 February	*Spitting Image* first broadcast
	12 April	Bill to privatise British Telecom enacted
	17 April	Libyans open fire from London embassy on anti-Gaddafi demonstrators, killing WPC Yvonne Fletcher
	29 May	Clash between police and striking miners at Orgreave coke works: 64 injured, 84 arrested
	14 June	European Parliament elections: Conservatives 45 seats, Labour 32, Others 4
	25–26 June	European Council at Fontainebleau: MT obtains UK rebate from EEC budget
	10 July	National dock strike begins
	26 July	Trade Union Bill enacted, removing legal immunity from unions which hold strikes without ballots, and requiring secret ballots for union officers
	18 August	Clive Ponting charged with leaking *Belgrano* documents from Ministry of Defence (acquitted 11 February 1986)
	24 August	Second national dock strike begins
	12 October	IRA bomb attack on Grand Hotel, Brighton, during Conservative Party Conference kills four
	20 November	British Telecom share issue floated
	11 December	Rate-capping of thirteen councils announced
	19 December	Sino-British Joint Declaration, signed by MT, provides for Hong Kong to return to Chinese sovereignty in 1997
1985	29 January	Oxford University votes against conferring an honorary degree on MT

	16 July	Local Government Bill abolishes GLC and metropolitan councils (with effect from 1 April 1986)
	9–10 September	Handsworth riots: 400 youths attack police, two people killed
	28–9 September	Brixton riots: 220 arrests
	1 October	Neil Kinnock attacks Militant Tendency at Labour Party Conference
	6 October	Broadwater Farm (Tottenham) riot: PC Keith Blakelock murdered
	18 October	Nottinghamshire miners form Union of Democratic Mineworkers (UDM)
	15 November	Anglo-Irish Agreement signed at Hillsborough
	1 December	Church of England publishes *Faith in the City* report
	13 December	Westland Helicopters controversy erupts
1986	9 January	Heseltine resigns from Cabinet over Westland
	20 January	MT and François Mitterrand announce plans for Channel Tunnel
	24 January	Leon Brittan resigns from Cabinet over Westland
	28 February	Single European Act signed (for implementation on 1 July 1987)
	18 March	Nigel Lawson budget reduces basic rate of income tax to 29p
	21 May	Kenneth Baker replaces Sir Keith Joseph as Education Secretary
	10 October	Trustee Savings Bank sold
	27 October	'Big Bang' in City of London
	2 December	British Gas privatised
1987	February	British Airways privatised
	17 March	Lawson budget reduces basic rate of income tax to 27p
	28 March	MT visits Moscow during five-day visit to Soviet Union
	May	Rolls Royce privatised
	11 June	General election: Conservatives 375, Labour 229, Alliance 22, Ulster Unionist parties 13, Plaid Cymru 3, SNP 3, Others 5. Cabinet reshuffle follows
	July	British Airports Authority privatised
	16 September	MT's 'Walk in the Wilderness' at Stockton-on-Tees
	19 October	Stock exchange slump ('Black Monday')
	8 November	IRA bomb at Remembrance Day parade in Enniskillen kills eleven, injures sixty-three
	8 December	Reagan and Gorbachev sign Intermediate-Range Nuclear Forces treaty to eliminate ground-based, medium-range missiles stationed in Europe
1988	10 January	Whitelaw resigns from government due to ill health
	2 March	Liberal Party and SDP vote to merge, forming Social and Liberal Democrats (Liberal Democrats from 16 October 1989)

	15 March	Lawson budget cuts standard rate of income tax to 25p in £, top rate to 40p in £
	21 May	MT addresses General Assembly of the Church of Scotland ('The Sermon on the Mound')
	24 May	Section 28 of Local Government Act enacted, forbidding local authorities to promote homosexuality in schools
	13 July	*A Claim of Right for Scotland* published by the Campaign for a Scottish Assembly
	20 September	MT's Bruges speech
	2 November	MT begins three-day visit to Poland
	8 November	George Herbert Walker Bush elected President of the United States
	30 November	*Charter 88* published
	November	British Steel Corporation privatised
	21 December	Bomb explodes on Pan Am flight 103 over Lockerbie, killing 270
1989	5 March	MT addresses Saving the Ozone Conference in London
	30 March	First meeting of the Scottish Constitutional Convention: *Claim of Right* signed by fifty-eight of Scotland's seventy-two MPs
	1 April	Poll Tax introduced in Scotland
	5 April	Mikhail Gorbachev arrives in UK for three-day visit
	15 June	European Parliament elections: Labour 45 seats, Conservatives 32, Others 4. Green Party receives 15 per cent of vote
	12 July	Abbey National Building Society floated on Stock Exchange
	24 July	Cabinet reshuffle: Howe appointed Leader of the House of Commons, John Major becomes Foreign Secretary
	16 October	EEC summit at Madrid: UK agrees to enter Exchange Rate Mechanism when three conditions are met
	26 October	Lawson resigns from government: John Major becomes Chancellor of the Exchequer, Douglas Hurd Foreign Secretary
	9 November	East Germany opens border with West Germany
	5 December	MT defeats Sir Anthony Meyer in leadership ballot, 314 to 33
	December	English and Welsh regional water companies privatised
1990	31 March	Poll Tax riots
	1 April	Poll Tax introduced in England; Strangeways prison riot begins
	3 May	Local elections: Labour gains over 300 council seats

16 May	Closure of Ravenscraig steelworks announced
14 July	Nicholas Ridley resigns from government after *Spectator* interview
30 July	Conservative MP Ian Gow killed by IRA bomb
2 August	Iraq invades Kuwait
3 October	German reunification
8 October	UK joins Exchange Rate Mechanism
1 November	Howe resigns from government over European policy; Environmental Protection Act receives royal assent
20 November	First ballot of Conservative leadership election: MT 204, Heseltine 152
22 November	MT tells Cabinet she will resign
27 November	Second ballot of Conservative leadership election: Major 185, Heseltine 131, Hurd 56. Major's rivals withdraw in his favour
28 November	MT resigns as Prime Minister; John Major succeeds her

1991–2011 Margaret Thatcher since leaving office

1991	7 March	Receives Medal of Freedom from President Bush
	28 May	Addresses Supreme Soviet of the USSR
	July	Thatcher Foundation (established 23 July) applies, unsuccessfully, for charitable status
	20 November	Speaks in Parliament on the Maastricht Treaty, urging a referendum on the single European currency
	22 November	Calls Major 'arrogant' for refusing a referendum on Maastricht
1992	9 April	General election: Conservatives 336, Labour 271, Liberal Democrats 20, Ulster Unionist parties 13, Plaid Cymru 4, SNP 3, SDLP 4. MT proclaims 'the end of Socialism'
	27 April	Article in *Newsweek* ('There isn't such a thing as "Majorism"')
	6 June	Raised to the peerage as Baroness Thatcher of Kesteven
	28 June	Calls Maastricht 'a treaty too far'
	16 September	Britain exits the ERM ('Black Wednesday')
1993	13 April	Condemns British policy towards Bosnia in BBC interview
	24 May	Speech to Europ-Assistance dinner: condemns 'the rise of the new Maastricht Empire'
	18 October	MT publishes first volume of memoirs: *The Downing Street Years*
1995	12 June	MT publishes second volume of memoirs: *The Path to Power*

1996	13 June	MT donates money to Bill Cash's European Foundation, provoking row with Major
1997	1 May	General election: Labour 418, Conservatives 165, Liberal Democrats 46, Ulster Unionist parties 13, SNP 6, Plaid Cymru 4, Others 7
	25 May	MT visits Tony Blair at 10 Downing Street
	18 June	MT endorses William Hague in Conservative leadership election
1997	1 July	MT attends handover ceremony in Hong Kong
1998	22 October	MT writes to *The Times* condemning the arrest of General Augusto Pinochet in London
2001	22 May	MT tells election rally 'The Mummy Returns'
	21 August	MT writes to *Daily Telegraph*, opposing Ken Clarke's bid for the leadership
2002	22 March	MT announces retirement from public speaking
	2 April	MT publishes *Statecraft: Strategies for a Changing World*; calls for renegotiation of Britain's membership of the EU, or withdrawal and membership of NAFTA
2005	September	Margaret Thatcher Centre for Freedom established in Washington DC
2007	13 September	MT visits Gordon Brown in 10 Downing Street

Sources: Brian Harrison, *Finding a Role? The United Kingdom 1970–1990* (Oxford University Press, 2010); Margaret Thatcher Foundation website, brief chronology; various newspapers and BBC archive.

Appendix 2: Statistical tables

(a)   Electoral

(i)   *General election results*

United Kingdom

	Conservative Party		Labour Party		Liberal Party / Alliance / Liberal Democrats		Scottish National Party / Plaid Cymru		Others		Government majority
	Vote share	Seats	Vote share	Seats	Vote share	Seats	Vote share	Seats	Vote share	Seats	
February 1974	37.8	297	37.2	301	19.3	14	2.6	9	3.2	14	None
October 1974	35.7	276	39.3	319	18.3	13	3.4	14	3.3	13	Lab 3
1979	43.9	339	36.9	268	13.8	11	2.0	4	3.4	13	Con 44
1983	42.4	397	27.6	209	25.4	23	1.5	4	3.1	17	Con 144
1987	42.2	375	30.8	229	22.6	22	1.7	6	2.7	18	Con 100
1992	41.9	336	34.4	271	17.8	20	2.3	7	3.5	17	Con 21
1997	30.7	165	43.2	418	16.8	46	2.5	10	6.8	20	Lab 177

England

	Conservative Party		Labour Party		Liberal Party / Alliance / Liberal Democrats		Others	
	Vote share	Seats	Vote share	Seats	Vote share	Seats	Vote share	Seats
February 1974	40.1	268	37.7	237	21.3	9	1.0	2
October 1974	38.8	252	40.1	255	20.2	8	1.0	1
1979	47.2	306	36.7	203	14.9	7	1.2	0
1983	46.0	362	26.9	148	26.4	13	0.7	0
1987	46.1	357	29.5	155	23.8	10	0.5	1
1992	45.5	319	33.9	195	19.2	10	1.4	0
1997	33.7	165	43.5	328	18.0	34	4.8	2

Wales

	Conservative Party		Labour Party		Liberal Party / Alliance / Liberal Democrats		Plaid Cymru		Others	
	Vote share	Seats	Vote share	Seats	Vote share	Seats	Vote share	Seats	Vote share	Seats
February 1974	25.9	8	46.8	24	16.0	2	10.8	2	0.6	0
October 1974	23.9	8	49.5	23	15.5	2	10.8	3	0.2	0
1979	32.2	11	47.0	21	10.6	1	8.1	2	2.2	1
1983	31.0	14	37.5	20	23.2	2	7.8	2	0.4	0
1987	29.5	8	45.1	24	17.9	3	7.3	3	0.2	0
1992	28.6	6	49.5	27	12.4	1	8.9	4	0.6	0
1997	19.6	0	54.7	34	12.3	2	9.9	4	3.4	0

Scotland

	Conservative Party		Labour Party		Liberal Party / Alliance / Liberal Democrats		Scottish National Party		Others	
	Vote share	Seats	Vote share	Seats	Vote share	Seats	Vote share	Seats	Vote share	Seats
February 1974	32.9	21	36.6	40	7.9	3	21.9	7	0.6	0
October 1974	24.7	16	36.3	41	8.3	3	30.4	11	0.3	0
1979	31.4	22	41.5	44	9.0	3	17.3	2	0.8	0
1983	28.4	21	35.1	41	24.5	8	11.8	2	0.3	0
1987	24.0	10	42.4	50	19.2	9	14.0	3	0.3	0
1992	25.6	11	39.0	49	13.1	9	21.5	3	0.8	0
1997	17.5	0	45.6	56	13.0	10	22.1	6	1.9	0

Northern Ireland

	Ulster Unionists		Ulster Democratic Unionists		Ulster Popular Unionists		Alliance Party		SDLP		Sinn Féin		Others	
	Vote share	Seats	Vote share	Seats	Vote share	Seats	Vote share	Seats	Vote share	Seats	Vote share	Seats	Vote share	Seats
February 1974	45.5	7	8.2	1			3.2	0	22.4	1			20.8	3
October 1974	36.5	6	8.5	1			6.4	0	22.0	1			26.7	4
1979	36.6	5	10.2	3			11.9	0	18.2	1			23.2	3
1983	34.0	11	20.0	3	3.0	1	8.0	0	17.9	1	13.4	1	3.7	0
1987	37.8	9	11.7	3	2.5	1	10.0	0	21.1	3	11.4	1	5.4	0
1992	34.5	9	13.1	3	2.5	1	8.7	0	19.7	4	10.0	0	11.5	0
1997	32.7	10	13.6	2			8.0	0	24.1	3	16.1	2	5.6	1

Sources: House of Commons Library Research Paper 04/61, *UK General Election Statistics: 1918–2004* (28 July 2004), accessed at: www.parliament.uk/documents/commons/lib/research/rp2004/rp04–061.pdf; *British Electoral Facts*, 7th edn (2006). Where the Speaker of the House of Commons stood for re-election, he or she is listed as 'Other', rather than under any previous party affiliation.

(ii)   Conservative voting by gender, age and class

Conservative percentage vote share in MORI poll; election aggregates, weighted to final outcome

Great Britain only

		October 1974	1979	1983	1987	1992	1997
	All voters	37		45	44	43	43	31
Sex	Men	32	43	42	43	41	31
	Women	39	47	46	43	44	32
Age group	18–24	24	42	42	37	35	27
	25–34	33	43	40	39	40	28
	35–54	34	46	44	45	43	30
	55+	42	47	47	46	46	36
Social	ABC1	56	59	55	54	54	39
class	C2	26	41	40	40	39	27
	DE	22	34	33	30	31	21

Source: Ipsos MORI Archive, accessed at: www.ipsos-mori.com/researchpublications/researcharchive/101/How-Britain-Voted-Since-October-1974.aspx?view=wide.

(iii)   Opinion poll satisfaction ratings

MORI poll (June)

	Net satisfaction with government	Net satisfaction with Prime Minister
June 1980	−27	−10
June 1981	-43	−27
June 1982	+12	+23
June 1983	Not asked	+20
June 1984	−28	−15
June 1985	−33	−16
June 1986	−41	−32
June 1987	+5	+10
June 1988	−7	+3
June 1989	−36	−26
June 1990	−42	−32

Source: Ipsos MORI Archive, accessed at: www.ipsos-mori.com/researchspecialisms/socialresearch/specareas/politics/trends.aspx.

(b)   Economic

(i)   Macro-economic

	Inflation (annual % change in Retail Price Index)	Unemployment (thousands)		Bank of England base rate (%)		Annual Change in GDP (%)
		Highest monthly figure	Lowest monthly figure	Highest	Lowest	
1974	16.1	628	515	13	11.5	−1.4*
1975	24.2	1,152	738	11.75	9.75	−0.6*
1976	16.5	1,440	1,220	15	9	2.6*
1977	15.8	1,567	1,286	14.25	5	2.4*
1978	8.3	1,608	1,364	12.5	6.5	3.2*
1979	13.4	1,464	1,299	17	12	2.7*
1980	18.0	2,244	1,471	17	14	−2.1
1981	11.9	2,772	2,271	16	12	−1.2
1982	8.6	3,097	2,270	14.5	9	2.2
1983	4.6	3,325	2,984	11	9	3.7
1984	5.0	3,284	3,030	12	8.5	2.7
1985	6.1	3,346	3,179	14	9.5	3.6
1986	3.4	3,408	3,216	12.5	10	4.0
1987	4.2	3,297	2,686	11	8.5	4.6
1988	4.9	2,722	2,047	13	7.5	5.0
1989	7.8	2,074	1,612	15	13	2.3
1990	9.5	1,850	1,556	15	14	0.8
1991	5.9	2,552	1,960	14	10.5	−1.4
1992	3.7	2,983	2,674	12	7	0.1
1993	1.6	3,062	2,679	7	5.5	2.2
1994	2.4	2,887	2,417	6.25	5.25	4.3
1995	3.5	2,503	2,196	6.75	6.25	3.1
1996	2.4	2,311	2,196	6.5	5.75	2.9
1997	3.1	1,908	1,388	7.25	6	3.3

* GDP change calculations for 1974–9 are estimates.

Sources: British Political Facts, 10th edn (2011); *Twentieth Century British Political Facts* (2000); Central Statistical Office, *Social Trends* 12 (1982); OECD Statistics website, GDP growth statistics, at http://stats.oecd.org/index.aspx.

(ii)   *Trade unions*

	Membership of UK-based unions (thousands)	Trade union density (% of employees in employment)	Working days lost to strikes (thousands)
1974	11,764	51.6	14,750
1975	12,193	54.1	6,012
1976	12,386	54.9	3,284
1977	12,846	56.8	9,985
1978	13,112	57.6	9,306
1979	13,289	57.4	29,474
1980	13,289	57.9	11,964
1981	12,106	55.4	4,266
1982	11,593	54.2	5,313
1983	11,236	53.4	3,754
1984	10,994	51.8	27,135
1985	10,821	50.5	6,402
1986	10,539	49.3	1,920
1987	10,475	48.5	3,546
1988	10,376	46.6	3,702
1989	10,158	44.8	4,128
1990	9,947	43.5	1,903
1991	9,585	42.3	761
1992	9,048	40.5	528
1993	8,700	39.5	649
1994	8,278	37.5	278
1995	8,089	36.1	415
1996	7,982	33.8	1,303
1997	7,841	32.4	235

Sources: Andy Charlwood and David Metcalf, 'Trade Union Numbers, Membership and Density', in Susan Fernie and David Metcalf (eds.), *Trade Unions: Resurgence or Demise?* (Abingdon: Routledge, 2005); *British Political Facts*, 10th edn (2011).

(iii)   *Privatisation and housing transfers*

	Net central government proceeds from privatisation (£m)	Sales of local authority housing		Housing stock by tenure at year end (%)	
				Owner-occupied	Rented from local authorities and new towns
1974–5			1974	53.0	30.7
1975–6			1975	53.4	31.1
1976–7			1976	53.7	31.4
1977–8			1977	54.1	31.7
1978–9			1978	54.7	31.7
1979–80	377		1979	55.3	31.5
1980–1	405	2,330	1980	56.2	31.2
1981–2	494	105,200	1981	56.5	30.5
1982–3	455	167,120	1982	58.2	29.2
1983–4	1,132	106,260	1983	59.5	28.3
1984–5	2,060	77,520	1984	59.6	27.4
1985–6	2,706	72,140	1985	60.5	26.6
1986–7	4,458	76,750	1986	61.5	25.9
1987–8	5,140	93,730	1987	62.7	25.1
1988–9	7,069	135,700	1988	64.0	24.0
1989–90	4,219	133,800	1989	65.2	22.8
1990–1	5,346	76,330	1990	65.8	21.9
1991–2	7,923	48,290	1991	66.3	21.2
1992–3	8,114	37,690	1992	66.3	20.5
1993–4	4,632	44,680	1993	66.6	19.9
1994–5	5,648	43,340	1994	66.8	19.1
1995–6	2,426	31,510	1995	66.8	18.4
1996–7	4,500	33,210	1996	67.0	17.9
1997–8		41,330	1997	67.2	17.0

Sources: British Political Facts, 10th edn (2011); Central Statistical Office / Office for National Statistics, *Annual Abstracts of Statistics.*

(iv) Poverty rates

	Before housing costs measure (% living in households with income below 60% of contemporary median income)		After housing costs measure (% living in households with income below 60% of contemporary median income)	
	All	Children	All	Children
1974	14	14	15	16
1975	13	13	14	15
1976	12	14	13	16
1977	11	12	12	14
1978	13	15	13	15
1979	13	13	14	14
1980	15	16	16	17
1981	14	18	14	20
1982	12	15	14	18
1983	13	16	14	19
1984	13	17	15	21
1985	14	19	17	22
1986	16	21	19	25
1987	18	23	21	26
1988	21	24	23	26
1989	22	25	23	27
1990	22	28	24	31
1991	21	26	24	31
1992	22	29	25	34
1993	20	28	24*	34*
1994–5	19	25	25	33
1995–6	18	24	24	33
1996–7	19	27	25	34
1997–8	20	27	24	33

* After housing costs figures are for 1993–4.

Source: Institute for Fiscal Studies website at: www.ifs.org.uk/ fiscalFacts/povertyStats. Figures rounded to nearest percentage point.

(c)   Government revenue, expenditure and borrowing

(i)   *Taxation*

	Taxation (general government receipts) as % of GDP	Income tax revenue as % of total central government revenue*		Standard rate of income tax	Higher rate of income tax	Tax revenues from UK oil and gas production (£million)
1974	40.5	43.4	1974–5	33	38–83	20
1975	40.2	51.2	1975–6	35	40–83	25
1976	41.0	50.4	1976–7	35	40–83	81
1977	39.7	44.9	1977–8	34	40–83	238
1978	38.7	43.5	1978–9	33	40–83	565
1979	38.8	37.9	1979–80	30	40–60	2,313
1980	40.7	36.7	1980–81	30	40–60	3,743
1981	43.7	37.4	1981–2	30	40–60	6,492
1982	43.7	36.6	1982–3	30	40–60	7,822
1983	42.9	35.4	1983–4	30	40–60	8,798
1984	43.4	33.7	1984–5	30	40–60	12,035
1985	42.3	32.6	1985–6	30	40–60	11,348
1986	41.4	35.4	1986–7	29	40–60	4,783
1987	41.1	32.6	1987–8	27	40–60	4,618
1988	40.3	32.4	1988–9	25	40	3,168
1989	40.1	32.1	1989–90	25	40	2,368
1990	39.3	33.1	1990–91	25	40	2,312
1991	38.3	33.5	1991–2	25	40	979
1992	36.7	33.3	1992–3	25	40	1,305
1993	35.9	33.7	1993–4	25	40	1,223
1994	36.9	32.8	1994–5	25	40	1,642
1995	38.0	33.7	1995–6	25	40	2,289
1996	38.1	32.6	1996–7	24	40	3,303
1997	39.3	31.2	1997–8	23	40	3,277

*Income tax figures include capital gains tax revenue from 1993 onwards

Sources: British Political Facts, 10th edn (2011); Central Statistical Office / Office for National Statistics, *Annual Abstracts of Statistics*; HM Revenue and Customs website at: www.hmrc.gov.uk/stats/corporate_tax/table11_11.pdf.

(ii)   Government expenditure

	Government expenditure (total managed expenditure) as per cent of GDP	Total government expenditure (total managed expenditure, £billion)	Social Security	National Health Service	Education	Defence	Public order and safety	Transport
		£billion	£billion					
1974–5		43.7	9.9	5.0	6.8	5.2		
1975–6		55.7	11.9	5.8	7.6	6.1		
1976–7		63.6	14.5	6.5	8.5	6.7		
1977–8		69.4	17.2	7.3	9.4	7.8		
1978–9	45.3	78.5	20.8	8.8	10.9	9.6	2.6	2.9
1979–80	44.8	93.5	25.3	10.8	13.1	11.7	3.2	3.5
1980–81	47.3	112.4	31.0	12.3	14.5	13.1	4.0	4.1
1981–2	48.1	125.5	35.5	13.3	15.5	14.9	4.6	4.6
1982–3	48.5	138.3	38.7	14.3	16.4	16.0	5.2	5.1
1983–4	48.3	149.6	41.7	15.2	16.9	17.6	5.7	5.1
1984–5	48.1	159.9	45.8	16.3	17.7	18.4	6.4	6.4
1985–6	45.5	166.5	48.8	17.7	19.6	18.6	6.6	6.5
1986–7	44.1	172.7	51.1	19.4	21.2	19.1	7.2	6.4
1987–8	42.1	183.2	51.9	21.4	23.1	19.4	8.1	6.4
1988–9	39.4	190.6	55.7	23.4	25.9	21.0	9.0	6.3
1989–90	39.7	210.2	61.8	26.1	28.1	22.0	10.3	7.3
1990–91	40.0	227.5					11.7	8.3
1991–2	42.3	254.2	78.8	29.5	31.3	23.2	13.2	9.2
1992–3	44.2	274.2	87.7	32.7	33.2	23.8	14.4	10.8
1993–4	43.6	286.2	95.3	35.0	34.7	23.5	15.0	10.0
1994–5	43.2	299.2	97.8	36.7	36.2	23.3	15.6	11.5
1995–6	42.6	311.4	100.5	38.4	37.0	22.5	16.0	10.9
1996–7	41.0	315.8	104.1	39.9	37.8	22.1	16.4	9.5
1997–8	39.2	322.0	105.9	41.9	38.6	21.7	17.1	8.7

Sources: British Political Facts, 10th edn (2011); Institute for Fiscal Studies website at: www.ifs.org.uk/ff/lr_spending.xls.

(iii) Government borrowing

	National debt as % of GDP	Public sector net borrowing as % of GDP	Current budget surplus as % of GDP
1974–5	50.0	6.5	−0.9
1975–6	46.0	7	−1.4
1976–7	47.0	5.5	−1.1
1977–8	48.0	4.3	−1.3
1978–9	49.0	5	−2.5
1979–80	46.0	4.1	−1.8
1980–81	43.0	4.8	−2.9
1981–2	46.0	2.3	−1.3
1982–3	44.0	3	−1.4
1983–4	43.0	3.8	−1.9
1984–5	45.0	3.6	−2.1
1985–6	46.0	2.4	−1.2
1986–7	44.0	2	−1.4
1987–8	46.0	1	−0.4
1988–9	44.0	−1.3	1.6
1989–90	39.0	−0.2	1.4
1990–91	35.0	1	0.3
1991–2	35.0	3.7	−1.9
1992–3	36.0	7.4	−5.6
1993–4	40.0	7.7	−6.3
1994–5	46.0	6.2	−4.8
1995–6	49.0	4.7	−3.3
1996–7	52.0	3.4	−2.7
1997–8	53.0	0.7	−0.1

Source: Institute for Fiscal Studies website at:
www.ifs.org.uk/ff/debt_borrowing.xls.

Notes

INTRODUCTION: VARIETIES OF THATCHERISM

1 C. Moore, 'The Mellowing of Margaret Thatcher', *Daily Telegraph*, 12 October 2005; MTFW 110596.
2 For an extended bibliography, see 'Further reading' at the end of this volume.
3 E. H. H. Green, *Thatcher* (London: Hodder Arnold, 2006); R. Vinen, *Thatcher's Britain: The Politics and Social Upheaval of the 1980s* (London: Simon & Schuster, 2009); B. Harrison, *Finding a Role? The United Kingdom, 1970–1990* (Oxford University Press, 2010).
4 Interview for *Sunday Telegraph*, 23 October 1969, Thatcher CD-ROM.
5 M. Thatcher, *The Path to Power* (London: HarperCollins, 1995), p. 38.
6 *The Sun*, 25 November 1971.
7 J. Campbell, *Margaret Thatcher: The Grocer's Daughter* (London: Random House, 2001). For 'ordinariness' as a Conservative language of class, see Jon Lawrence and Florence Sutcliffe-Braithwaite, Chapter 7 in this volume.
8 Declaring that 'our human stock is threatened', Joseph warned that a 'rising proportion of children are being born to mothers least fitted to bring children into the world'. As a solution, he suggested greater use of birth control by 'these classes of people'. Keith Joseph, speech at Edgbaston, 19 October 1974, MTFW 101830.
9 Unless otherwise stated, all figures are taken from the statistical information in Appendix 2.
10 Reproduced in P. Booth (ed.), *Were 364 Economists All Wrong?* (London: IEA, 2006), pp. 122–3.
11 For a good introduction to the debate, see *ibid.*
12 K. O. Morgan, *Michael Foot: A Life* (London: HarperCollins, 2007), pp. 411–12.
13 David Sanders *et al.*, 'Government Popularity and the Falklands War: A Reassessment', *British Journal of Political Science*, 17 (1987), 281–313.
14 See www.hmrc.gov.uk/stats/corporate_tax/rates-of-tax.pdf (accessed 6 April 2011).
15 Vinen, *Thatcher's Britain*, p. 155.
16 D. Butler and G. Butler, *Twentieth Century British Political Facts, 1900–2000*, 8th edn (Basingstoke: Palgrave Macmillan, 2000), p. 275.
17 Thirty-three voted for Meyer, while a further twenty-seven abstained.

18 Speech to the College of Europe, 20 September 1988, MTFW 107332; House of Commons statement, 30 October 1990, MTFW 108234.

19 Hansard, HC Deb., 5th series, vol. 180, cols. 463–5 (13 November 1990).

20 'Where Were You When You Heard She Was Going?', *New Statesman*, 26 February 2009.

21 'The Thatcher Years: Winners and Losers in an Age of Ideology', *The Guardian*, 23 November 1990. Explaining her attachment to the Thatcher era, she stressed its inspirational effect on women and noted that 'It's made me fucking rich.'

22 'Where Were You When You Heard She Was Going?'

23 For example, 'I'm in Love with Mrs Thatcher', The Notsensibles (1979); 'Stand Down Margaret', The Beat (1980); 'Margaret on the Guillotine', Morrissey (1988); 'Tramp the Dirt Down', Elvis Costello (1989); 'The Day that Thatcher Dies', Hefner (2000); 'Merry Christmas Maggie Thatcher', Elton John (*Billy Elliot the Musical*, 2005).

24 'The Thatcher Years'; 'Where Were You When You Heard She Was Going?'

25 One early visitor was apparently 'moved to tears by the sight of a small, slight, fair and rather vulnerable woman getting down to her first day of work'. Patrick Cosgrave told readers that 'Her skin is, of course, very pale, and her hair very fine ... She is fortunate, too, in that her skin is remarkably unlined: even around the neck': P. Cosgrave, *Margaret Thatcher: Prime Minister* (London: Arrow, 1979), pp. 13, 17.

26 P. Riddell, 'Ideology in Practice', in A. Adonis and T. Hames (eds.), *A Conservative Revolution? The Thatcher–Reagan Decade in Perspective* (Manchester University Press, 1994), pp. 22–5.

27 Quoted in Green, *Thatcher*, p. 7.

28 As Ewen Green has noted, terms like 'Gladstonism' and 'Beaconsfieldism' had some currency in the nineteenth century. However, their usage was limited and was not endowed with the ideological significance attributed to 'Thatcherism'. *Ibid.*, p. 22.

29 See Robert Saunders, Chapter 1 in this book.

30 S. Hall, 'The Great Moving Right Show', *Marxism Today* (January 1979), pp. 14–20; S. Hall and M. Jacques (eds.), *The Politics of Thatcherism* (London: Lawrence & Wishart, 1983); A. Gamble, *The Free Economy and the Strong State: The Politics of Thatcherism* (Basingstoke: Macmillan, 1988; 2nd edn 1994).

31 M. Jacques, 'Breaking out of the Impasse', *Marxism Today* (October 1979), pp. 6–15.

32 For a critique of *Marxism Today*, see R. McKibbin, 'The Way We Live Now', *London Review of Books*, 11 January 1990. For further discussion of Thatcherism and neo-liberalism, see Ben Jackson, Chapter 2 in this volume.

33 J. Bulpitt, 'The Discipline of the New Democracy: Mrs Thatcher's Domestic Statecraft', *Political Studies*, 34 (1986), 19–39. For further discussion of Bulpitt, see Jim Tomlinson, Chapter 3 in this book.

34 Green, *Thatcher*, p. 130. See also R. McKibbin, 'Why Did It End So Badly?', *London Review of Books*, 18 March 2004.

35 S. R. Letwin, *The Anatomy of Thatcherism* (London: Fontana, 1992).

36 See Matthew Grimley, Chapter 4 in this volume.

37 Interview for *Sunday Times*, 1 May 1981, MTFW 104475.

38 Vinen, *Thatcher's Britain*, p. 11.

39 D. Marsh and R. Rhodes (eds.), *Implementing Thatcherite Policies* (Buckingham: Open University Press, 1992); B. Jessop, K. Bonnett, S. Bromley and T. Ling, *Thatcherism: A Tale of Two Nations* (Cambridge: Polity, 1988).

40 For example, PMQ, 10 July 1986; Letter to Neil Kinnock, 15 May 1986; phone-in for Radio London, 6 January 1987 (all on Thatcher CD-ROM).

41 Inequality statistics from D. Coates, *Prolonged Labour* (Basingstoke: Palgrave, 2005), p. 19.

42 I. Crewe, 'Has the Electorate Become Thatcherite?', in R. Skidelsky (ed.), *Thatcherism* (London: Chatto & Windus, 1988). See also R. Jowell, S. Witherspoon and L. Brook (eds.), *British Social Attitudes: The Fifth Report* (London: Gower, 1988).

43 E. Evans, *Thatcher and Thatcherism*, 2nd edn (London: Routledge, 2004), p. 76.

44 Vinen, *Thatcher's Britain*, p. 205.

45 For Thatcherism as an alien growth, see M. Garnett and I. Gilmour, 'Thatcherism and the Conservative Tradition', in M. Francis and I. Zweiniger-Bargielowska (eds.), *The Conservatives and British Society, 1880–1990* (Cardiff: University of Wales Press, 1996).

46 D. Willetts, *Modern Conservatism* (Harmondsworth: Penguin, 1992); E. H. H. Green, 'Thatcherism: A Historical Perspective', in his *Ideologies of Conservatism* (Oxford University Press, 2002); Green, *Thatcher*; S. Evans, 'Thatcher and the Victorians: A Suitable Case for Comparison?', *History*, 82 (1997), 601–20; R. Blake, *The Conservative Party from Peel to Major*, rev. edn (London: Heinemann, 1997). For an insistence on the pragmatic nature of Thatcher's Conservatism, see P. Riddell, *The Thatcher Era and its Legacy* (Oxford: Blackwell, 1991).

47 A. Roberts, *Eminent Churchillians* (London: Weidenfeld & Nicolson, 1994), p. 253. See also N. Lawson, *The New Conservatism* (London: CPS, 1980).

48 A. Adonis, 'The Transformation of the Conservative Party in the 1980s', in Adonis and Hames, *A Conservative Revolution?*, pp. 148–52.

49 I. Gilmour, *Dancing with Dogma: Britain under Thatcherism* (London: Simon & Schuster, 1992). See also S. Evans, '"A Tiny Little Footnote in History": Conservative Centre Forward', *Parliamentary History*, 29 (2010), 208–28.

50 Lawson, *The New Conservatism*, pp. 3, 11.

51 For example, R. Walsha, 'The One Nation Group and One Nation Conservatism, 1950–2002', *Contemporary British History*, 17 (2003), 69–120; S. Evans, 'The Not So Odd Couple: Margaret Thatcher and One Nation Conservatism', *Contemporary British History*, 23 (2009), 101–21.

52 For a useful survey, see C. Hay, 'Whatever Happened to Thatcherism?', *Political Studies Review*, 5 (2007), 183–201.

53 J. Tomlinson, *The Politics of Decline: Understanding Post-War Britain* (Harlow: Pearson, 2000); C. Hay, 'Chronicles of a Death Foretold: The Winter of Discontent and Construction of the Crisis of British Keynesianism', *Parliamentary Affairs*, 63 (2010), 446–70.

54 We are grateful to David Howell for drawing our attention to this point.

1 'CRISIS? WHAT CRISIS?' THATCHERISM AND THE SEVENTIES

1 Foreword to Conservative Party manifesto, 1979, MTFW 103999; M. Thatcher, *The Downing Street Years* (London: HarperCollins, 1993), p. 10.

2 G. Howe, endorsement of R. McIntosh, *Challenge to Democracy: Politics, Trade Union Power and Economic Failure in the 1970s* (London: Politico's, 2006).

3 C. Hay, 'Chronicles of a Death Foretold: The Winter of Discontent and Construction of the Crisis of British Keynesianism', *Parliamentary Affairs*, 63 (2010), 464–6.

4 The etymology of Thatcherism is a subject in its own right; but for early usages of this kind, see *The Guardian*, 25 April 1975, p. 16, and 29 December 1975, p. 10; *The Observer*, 23 May 1976, p. 12.

5 P. Williamson, *Stanley Baldwin: Conservative Leadership and National Values* (Cambridge University Press, 1999), pp. 14–17; my emphasis. For a similar approach, see A. Hindmoor, *New Labour at the Centre: Constructing Political Space* (Oxford University Press, 2004), especially pp. 9–10.

6 K. Joseph, *Reversing the Trend: A Critical Re-appraisal of Conservative Economic and Social Policies* (Chichester: Rose, 1975), p. 4.

7 Notably the Selsdon Group (1973), the Centre for Policy Studies (1974), the Conservative Philosophy Group (1975) and the Salisbury Group (1978). For Tory literature, see R. Blake and J. Patten (eds.), *The Conservative Opportunity* (London: Macmillan, 1976); R. Boyson, *Centre Forward: A Radical Conservative Programme* (London: Temple Smith, 1978); M. Cowling (ed.), *Conservative Essays* (London: Cassell, 1978); I. Gilmour, *Inside Right: Conservatism, Policies and the People* (London: Hutchinson, 1977); Joseph, *Reversing the Trend*; R. Scruton, *The Meaning of Conservatism* (London: Macmillan, 1980).

8 D. Butler and D. Kavanagh, *The British General Election of 1979* (London: Macmillan, 1980), pp. 2, 10, 350.

9 R. Blake, 'A Changed Climate', in Blake and Patten, *The Conservative Opportunity*, pp. 2–3.

10 Speech on accepting the Conservative Party leadership, 20 February 1975, MTFW 102629.

11 That claim first appeared in H. Young, *One of Us: A Biography of Margaret Thatcher* (London: Macmillan, 1989), p. 406. His source was Jonathan Aitken, roughly thirteen years after the event. At such a distance, it is unlikely to have been a verbatim quotation, and it sits uneasily with Thatcher's characteristic disdain for 'ideology'. As the overuse of this remark suggests, there is no other known instance of Thatcher making such a demand. See I. Trewin (ed.), *The Hugo Young Papers: Thirty Years of British Politics – Off the Record* (London: Allen Lane, 2008), p. 271.

12 Interview, *The Observer*, 12 January 1979; BBC Radio 2, Jimmy Young interview, 31 January 1979; *Daily Express*, Gale interview, 10 April 1979 (all on Thatcher CD-ROM). Press conference at Melbourne, 7 October 1981, MTFW 104713.

13 Conference, 10 October 1975, MTFW 102777.

14 A. Sherman, *Paradoxes of Power: Reflections on the Thatcher Interlude* (Exeter: Imprint, 2005), pp. 82–5. Like other writers, Sherman noted how much personal attention Thatcher gave to her speeches, insisting that

'every phrase, every word had to earn her approval' (pp. 84–5). For similar testimonies, see P. Cosgrave, *Margaret Thatcher: Prime Minister* (London: Arrow, 1979), pp. 25–6; F. Mount, *Cold Cream: My Early Life and Other Mistakes* (London: Bloomsbury, 2008), pp. 328–30.

15 Foreword to R. Blake, *Conservatism in an Age of Revolution* (London: Churchill Press, 1976); Conference, 12 October 1979, MTFW 104147.

16 'What's Wrong with Politics?', 11 October 1968, MTFW 101632; McIntosh, *Challenge to Democracy*, p. 205.

17 Speech at Cardiff, 16 April 1979, MTFW 104011; speech to Scottish Young Conservatives, 2 September 1978, MTFW 103494.

18 A. Burnet, 'Is Britain Governable?' (London: CPC, 1975), p. 21; D. Hurd, *An End to Promises: A Sketch of Government, 1970–74* (London: Collins, 1979), pp. 140–1.

19 Blake, *Conservatism in an Age of Revolution*, p. 11.

20 Joseph, *Reversing the Trend*, pp. 7, 71.

21 'Themes', 16 February 1978 (by A. Maude, R. Boyson, D. Howell, N. Lawson and N. Tebbit), MTFW 109853; emphasis in original.

22 Speech at Hofstra University, New York, 27 March 2000, MTFW 108387; speech at Leningrad State University, 29 May 1991, MTFW 108273.

23 Sherman called her 'a woman of beliefs, and not of ideas'; Sherman, *Paradoxes of Power*, p. 25.

24 'Dimensions of Conservatism', 4 July 1977, MTFW 103411.

25 Speech to Canadian Parliament, 26 September 1983, MTFW 105440.

26 BBC *Today* programme, 2 September 1977 (Thatcher CD-ROM).

27 Speech to Conservative Central Council, 15 March 1975, MTFW 102655; my emphasis.

28 Lecture at Roosevelt University, Chicago, 22 September 1975, MTFW 102465; interview for PBS *Firing Line*, 25 July 1977 (Thatcher CD-ROM).

29 PMQ, 28 February 1980, MTFW 104315. But for the close association between some of her supporters and these intellectuals, see Ben Jackson, Chapter 2 in this volume.

30 Peter Jay claims to have found Thatcher almost entirely ignorant of monetarism in 1985, and joked that 'explaining monetarism to Thatcher was "like showing Genghis Khan a map of the world"': W. Keegan, 'Mrs Thatcher, Myth Snatcher', *The Observer*, 9 May 2004.

31 Speech to Chambers of Commerce, 10 January 1979, MTFW 103922.

32 House of Commons, 28 February 1980, MTFW 104316.

33 Speech to the Press Association, 11 June 1980, MTFW 104377.

34 Interview with George Gale for the London Broadcasting Corporation, 17 May 1974, MTFW 102366.

35 In 1981, Thatcher promised to turn back the forces of socialism 'democratically, and I use the word in the dictionary sense, not the Bennite sense'. Regrettably, she did not elaborate on either definition. Conference, 16 October 1981, MTFW 104717.

36 'Themes'.

37 Lord Hailsham, *The Dilemma of Democracy: Diagnosis and Prescription* (London: Collins, 1978), pp. 15, 22.

38 A. King, 'The Problem of Overload', in A. King (ed.), *Why Is Britain Becoming Harder to Govern?* (London: BBC, 1976), p. 26; S. Brittan, 'The Economic Contradictions of Democracy', *British Journal of Political Science*, 5 (1975), 129, 132 (quoting NOP poll, September 1974); P. Jay, 'How Inflation Threatens British Democracy with its Last Chance Before Extinction', *The Times*, 1 July 1974. See also S. Brittan, *The Economic Consequences of Democracy* (New York: Doubleday, 1977).

39 Conference, 8 October 1976, MTFW 103105.

40 LWT *Weekend World*, 18 September 1977, MTFW 103191.

41 McIntosh, *Challenge to Democracy*, p. 5.

42 Labour Party manifesto, October 1974, quoted in D. Butler and D. Kavanagh, *The British General Election of October 1974* (London: Macmillan, 1975), p. 60.

43 For example, *Another Bill of Rights? A Report by a Committee of the Society of Conservative Lawyers* (London: CPC, 1976); Hailsham, *Dilemma of Democracy*; W. Waldegrave, *The Binding of Leviathan: Conservatism and the Future* (London: Hamish Hamilton, 1978); P. Johnson, *A Tory Philosophy of Law* (London: CPC, 1979).

44 K. Joseph, *Freedom Under the Law* (London: CPS, 1975). For Hayek's proposals for second chamber reform, see F. A. Hayek, *Economic Freedom and Representative Government* (London: IEA, 1973).

45 Speech to the American Enterprise Institute, 25 June 1998, MTFW 108377.

46 Joseph at Upminster, 22 June 1974, in Joseph, *Reversing the Trend*, pp. 6, 9.

47 Thatcher, 'It's Your Freedom They Hate', *Sunday Express*, 23 November 1975, MTFW 102808.

48 Speech at Grosvenor Square, 20 February 1975, MTFW 102629; Party Political Broadcast, 5 March 1975, MTFW 102644.

49 Press conference, 18 September 1975, MTFW 102464.

50 Speech to Grantham Conservatives, 4 March 1977, MTFW 103329.

51 Interview for *Hornsey Journal*, 21 April 1978, MTFW 103662.

52 'Dimensions of Conservatism', 4 July 1977, MTFW 103411.

53 Speech at Cardiff, 16 April 1979; speech at Finchley, 2 May 1979, MTFW 104072.

54 Interview for *Woman* magazine, 13 April 1988 (Thatcher CD-ROM).

55 Speech at St Lawrence Jewry, 30 March 1978, MTFW 103522.

56 Conference, 8 October 1976, MTFW 103105.

57 Speech at St Lawrence Jewry, 30 March 1978.

58 Conference, 13 October 1978, MTFW 103764.

59 House of Commons, 22 May 1975, MTFW 102697, quoting Thomas Mann.

60 *Why Britain Needs a Social Market Economy; With a Foreword by Sir Keith Joseph* (London: CPS, 1975), p. 14. This argument was given a more academic cast in S. Beer, *Britain Against Itself: The Political Contradictions of Collectivism* (London: Faber & Faber, 1982).

61 Speech in Wellington, New Zealand, 10 September 1976, MTFW 103095.

62 N. Lawson, *The New Conservatism* (London: CPS, 1980), p. 2; my emphasis.

63 John Parker, House of Commons, 25 July 1978, MTFW 103736.

64 J. Hoskyns and N. Strauss, 'Stepping Stones', 14 November 1977, MTFW 111771, p. 35; emphasis in original.

65 D. Butler and D. Kavanagh, *The British General Election of February 1974* (London: Macmillan, 1975), p. 42.

66 Conference, 16 October 1981, MTFW 104717.

67 See P. Cormack (ed.), *Right Turn: Eight Men who Changed their Minds* (London: Leo Cooper, 1978).

68 Reg Prentice, Lord Chalfont and Edward Pearce, *ibid.*, pp. 3, 13, 49, 68.

69 Conference, 8 October 1976; conference, 14 October 1977, MTFW 103443.

70 N. Beloff, *Freedom Under Foot: The Battle over the Closed Shop in British Journalism* (London: Temple Smith, 1976).

71 R. Cockett, *Thinking the Unthinkable: Think-Tanks and the Economic Counter-Revolution, 1931–1983* (London: HarperCollins, 1995), p. 222.

72 House of Commons, 15 July 1976, MTFW 103077.

73 *The Campaign Guide, 1977* (London: CCO, 1977), pp. 471–4, MTFW 110799.

74 S. Heffer and C. Moore (eds.), *A Tory Seer: The Selected Journalism of T. E. Utley; With an Introduction by Margaret Thatcher* (London: Hamish Hamilton, 1989), p. 113; *The Right Approach to the Economy* (London: CPC, 1977), MTFW 112551.

75 Speech to Conservative Trade Unionist Conference, 28 February 1976, MTFW 102970.

76 Speech in Wellington, New Zealand, 10 September 1976, MTFW 103095.

77 Speech in Glasgow, 21 February 1975, MTFW 102454. Labour councillors at Clay Cross had refused to implement the 1972 Housing Finance Act, holding down council house rents and running a deficit of £1,000 a week on the housing fund. For a near-contemporary account, see A. Mitchell, 'Clay Cross', *Political Quarterly*, 45 (1974), 165–78.

78 *Campaign Guide, 1977*, p. 461.

79 Joseph, *Freedom under Law*, p. 6.

80 K. Joseph, *The Economics of Freedom* (London: CPS, 1975), p. 10.

81 Thatcher, 'It's Your Freedom They Hate'.

82 Conference, 10 October 1975.

83 Joseph, 'Freedom Under Law', p. 7.

84 N. Lawson, 'Thoughts on the Coming Battle', 15 October 1973, MTFW 110312; conference, 10 October 1975.

85 Conference for Management in Industry, 9 January 1978, MTFW 103502.

86 D. Howell, *Time to Move On: An Opening to the Future for British Politics* (London: CPC, 1976), p. 21.

87 'Themes'. See also Sherman to Thatcher, 11 December 1978, MTFW 112002; and Thatcher, *The Path to Power* (London: HarperCollins, 1995), p. 313.

88 For the improving economic reputation of the Callaghan government, see J. Tomlinson, *The Politics of Decline: Understanding Post-War Britain* (Harlow: Pearson, 2001), p. 86, and B. Ingham, *Kill the Messenger* (London: Fontana, 1991), p. 153. The Lib–Lab Pact was agreed on 23 March 1977.

89 'Themes'.

90 *The Campaign Guide: Supplement* (London: CCO, 1978), p. 8. See also *Briefing Note: Labour's False Prospectus, 28 September 1978* (London: CPC, 1978), p. 2.

91 Conference, 13 October 1978.

92 Cormack, *Right Turn*, p. 13.

93 Speech to Paddington Conservatives, 18 December 1978, MTFW 103804.

94 Conference, 8 October 1976.

95 *Ibid.*

96 Speech to Conservative Trade Unionist Conference, 5 March 1977 (Thatcher CD-ROM).

97 Conference, 14 October 1977, MTFW 103443.

98 K. O. Morgan, *Callaghan: A Life* (Oxford University Press, 1997), p. 645.

99 Sherman to Thatcher, 11 December 1978.

100 Thatcher, *Path to Power*, p. 417.

101 Hay, 'Chronicles of a Death Foretold', p. 460.

102 D. Marsh, *The New Politics of British Trade Unionism: Union Power and the Thatcher Legacy* (Basingstoke: Macmillan, 1992), pp. 49–52.

103 'Stepping Stones', S-1.

104 For press coverage, see C. Hay, 'Narrating Crisis: The Discursive Construction of the "Winter of Discontent"', *Sociology*, 30 (1996), 262–72.

105 For Callaghan's ill-judged remarks at Heathrow Airport, 10 January 1979, see Morgan, *Callaghan*, pp. 661–2.

106 Thatcher, *Path to Power*, p. 414. For the disorientation of the union leadership, see G. A. Dorfman, *British Trade Unionism Against the Trades Union Congress* (London: Macmillan, 1983), p. 120.

107 Conference, 10 October 1980, MTFW 104431.

108 Joseph, *Reversing the Trend*, p. 7.

109 Speech to Conservative Central Council, 15 March 1975.

110 Howe, too, dedicates less space in his memoirs to oil than to the 'amusing theft of his trousers from a train': A. Marr, *A History of Modern Britain* (Basingstoke: Macmillan, 2008), p. 435.

111 See, for example, interview for CBS *60 Minutes*, 15 February 1985, MTFW 105964.

112 For example, speech to Irano-British Chamber of Commerce, 29 April 1987, MTFW 103667.

113 E.g. interview for IRN, 28 November 1980, MTFW 104452; interview for UPI/ITN, 31 December 1980, MTFW 104471.

114 Speech to Conservative Central Council, 20 March 1976, MTFW 102990.

115 Speech to Scottish Conservative Conference, 12 May 1990, MTFW 108087.

2 THE THINK-TANK ARCHIPELAGO: THATCHERISM AND NEO-LIBERALISM

1 A. Seldon to K. Joseph, 19 August 1970, Institute of Economic Affairs papers, Hoover Institution Archives, Stanford University (hereafter IEA), 333/5.

2 The IEA was formally created in 1955, but only began operating seriously in 1957, after Harris and Seldon began to work there.

3 'Programme of Speakers for the MPS Conference, Oxford – September 1959', MPS papers, Hoover Institution Archives, Stanford University (hereafter MPS), 13/3; R. Harris and A. Seldon, 'The Tactics and Strategy of the Advance to a Free Economy', paper to 1959 MPS Conference, Oxford, MPS 13/9, pp. 7, 8; emphasis in original.

4 A. Gamble, *The Free Economy and the Strong State: The Politics of Thatcherism*, 2nd edn (Basingstoke: Palgrave, 1994), pp. 34–68; R. Desai, 'Second-Hand Dealers in Ideas: Think-Tanks and Thatcherite Hegemony', *New Left Review*, no. 203 (1994), 27–64; B. Harrison, 'Mrs Thatcher and the Intellectuals', *Twentieth Century British History*, 5 (1994), 206–45; R. Cockett, *Thinking the Unthinkable: Think Tanks and the Economic Counter-Revolution, 1931–1983* (London: HarperCollins, 1995); E. H. H. Green, *Thatcher* (London: Hodder Arnold, 2006).

5 A. Denham and M. Garnett, 'The Nature and Impact of Think-Tanks in Contemporary Britain', *Contemporary British History*, 10 (1996), 50–6; R. Vinen, *Thatcher's Britain* (London: Simon & Schuster, 2009), pp. 7, 108.

6 F. A. Hayek, 'The Intellectuals and Socialism', *University of Chicago Law Review*, 16 (1949), 417–33.

7 D. Plehwe, B. Walpen and G. Neunhöffer (eds.), *Neo-Liberal Hegemony: A Global Critique* (London: Routledge, 2005); P. Mirowski and D. Plehwe (eds.), *The Road from Mont Pèlerin: The Making of the Neo-Liberal Thought Collective* (Cambridge, MA: Harvard University Press, 2009); K. Phillips-Fein, *Invisible Hands: The Making of the Conservative Movement from the New Deal to Reagan* (New York: W. W. Norton, 2009); 'Learning From the Rise of the Free-Market Right', special issue of *Renewal: A Journal of Social Democracy*, 17/4 (2009).

8 For criticism of Cockett's account, see K. Tribe, 'Liberalism and Neo-Liberalism in Britain, 1930–80', in Mirowski and Plehwe, *Road*, pp. 93–4, 96–7.

9 M. Friedman, *Capitalism and Freedom* [1962] (Chicago University Press, 2002), p. 17.

10 See, inter alia, R. Backhouse, 'The Rise of Free Market Economics: Economists and the Role of the State Since 1970', *History of Political Economy*, 37 (2005), 378–81; Phillips-Fein, *Invisible Hands*; P. Mirowski and R. Van Horn, 'The Rise of the Chicago School of Economics and the Birth of Neo-Liberalism', in Mirowski and Plehwe, *Road*.

11 C. Muller, 'The Institute of Economic Affairs: Undermining the Post-War Consensus', *Contemporary British History*, 10 (1996), 93; R. Heffernan, '"Blue-Print for a Revolution?" The Politics of the Adam Smith Institute', *Contemporary British History*, 10 (1996), 76. Beyond the initial financial support given to the IEA by its founder, Antony Fisher, Cockett does not discuss the funding of the free market think-tanks in any detail in *Thinking the Unthinkable*.

12 P. Mirowski, 'Review of Harvey, *A Brief History of Neo-Liberalism*', *Economics and Philosophy*, 24 (2008), 117.

13 Harris and Seldon, 'Tactics and Strategy', p. 6.

14 A. Fisher, *Must History Repeat Itself?* (London: Churchill Press, 1974), p. 104. On the origins of the IEA, see Desai, 'Second-Hand Dealers', 45; Cockett, *Thinking*, pp. 122–33.

15 'Corporate Subscribers and Subscriptions', undated [*c*. 1968], IEA 87/6.

16 See e.g. *The Institute of Economic Affairs Progress Report 1970* (London: IEA, 1970), pp. 10–12, copy in IEA 87/3a.

17 R. Harris to M. Friedman, 13 May 1977, Milton Friedman papers, Hoover Institution Archives, Stanford University (hereafter MF), 154.

18 'Annual Report 1968: Year to 30 June 1968', IEA 64/3; 'Annual Report 1981: Year to 30 June 1981', IEA 65/7.

19 'Annual Report 1974: Year to 30 June 1974', IEA 64/9; 'Annual Report 1975: Year to 30 June 1975', IEA 65/1; 'Annual Report 1977: Year to 30 June 1977', IEA 65/3; 'Annual Report 1979: Year to 30 June 1979', IEA 65/5.

20 B. Harrison, *Finding a Role? The United Kingdom 1970–90* (Oxford University Press, 2010), p. 337.

21 N. Cayzer to R. Harris, 10 November 1972, IEA 72/11; record of donations to IEA from Cayzer Irvine Ltd, IEA 72/11.

22 G. Blundell to H. Smith, 3 March 1964, IEA 72/10; G. Blundell to H. Smith, 3 October 1968, IEA 72/10.

23 R. Harris to H. Smith, 11 October 1974, IEA 72/10; R. Harris to H. Smith, 11 October 1974, IEA 72/10; R. Harris to P. Fenwick-Smith, 4 October 1978, IEA 72/10 (first quote); R. Harris to A. E. Wieler, 16 February 1981, IEA 72/6 (second quote).

24 R. Harris, 'Memorandum to John Wood and Arthur Seldon', 14 March 1975, IEA 295/12; R. Harris to K. Joseph, 1 April 1974, IEA 295/12; R. Harris to K. Joseph, 30 May 1974, IEA 295/12. On the origins of the CPS, see Harrison, 'Mrs Thatcher and the Intellectuals', 211–20.

25 K. Joseph to E. Woodroofe, 18 April 1974, Keith Joseph papers, Conservative Party Archive, Bodleian Library, Oxford (hereafter KJ), 10/8.

26 See, for example, L. Robbins, 'Hayek on Liberty', *Economica*, 28 (1961), 66–81.

27 S. Brittan to M. Friedman, 22 December 1958, MF 21/33; M. Friedman to S. Brittan, 6 January 1959, MF 21/33.

28 D. Plehwe, 'Introduction', in Mirowski and Plehwe, *Road*, pp. 17–20.

29 A. Seldon to M. Friedman, 16 March 1961, MF 33/2; R. Harris to M. Friedman, 15 September 1960, MF 154.

30 M. Friedman to the editor of *The Times*, 1 October 1991, MF 154, p. 2.

31 J. Buchanan to G. Tullock, 13 June 1965, 26 June 1965, 12 July 1965, 8 July 1965 and 19 July 1965, all in Gordon Tullock papers, Hoover Institution Archives, Stanford University (hereafter GT), 109.

32 G. Tullock to A. Seldon, 21 July 1977; A. Seldon to G. Tullock, 26 August 1977; A. Seldon to G. Tullock, 4 August 1977, all in IEA 26/2. Tullock later recollected that he first came into contact with the IEA in the early 1960s: see his 'The Intellectual Situation in the United States in the Post-War Years and its Connection with the IEA', in *A Conversation with Harris and Seldon* (London: IEA, 2001), p. 89.

33 For helpful accounts of these ideas, see N. Bosanquet, *After The New Right* (London: Heinemann, 1983), pp. 1–88; Gamble, *Free Economy*, pp. 34–68.

34 E.g. A. Walters, *Money in Boom and Slump* (London: IEA, 1969); M. Friedman, *The Counter-Revolution in Monetary Policy* (London: IEA, 1970); J. Wood, *How Much Unemployment?* (London: IEA, 1972); S. Brittan, *Second Thoughts on Full Employment* (London: CPS, 1976); P. Jay, *Employment, Inflation and Politics* (London: IEA, 1976); M. Friedman, *Inflation and Unemployment* (London: IEA, 1976).

35 E.g. E. G. West, *Education and the State* (London: IEA, 1965); J. Buchanan, *The Inconsistencies of the National Health Service* (London: IEA, 1965); A. Seldon, *Universal or Selective Social Benefits* (London: IEA, 1967); A. Seldon, *After the NHS* (London: IEA, 1969); A. Seldon, *Whither the Welfare State?* (London: IEA, 1981).

36 F. A. Hayek, *A Tiger by the Tail* (London: IEA, 1972); F. A. Hayek, *Economic Freedom and Representative Government* (London: IEA, 1973); W. Niskanen, *Bureaucracy: Servant or Master?* (London: IEA, 1973); S. Brittan, *Participation Without Politics* (London: IEA, 1975); J. Buchanan and R. Wagner, *The Consequences of Mr Keynes* (London: IEA, 1978); J. Buchanan, *The Economics of Politics* (London: IEA, 1978); R. Harris, *The End of Government?* (London: IEA, 1980); N. Thompson, 'Hollowing out the State: Public Choice Theory and the Critique of Keynesian Social Democracy', *Contemporary British History*, 22 (2008), 355–82. For further discussion of the critique of trade unions, see B. Jackson, 'An Ideology of Class: Neo-Liberalism and the Trade Unions, c. 1930–79', in C. Griffiths, J. Nott and W. Whyte (eds.), *Classes, Cultures and Politics: Essays for Ross McKibbin* (Oxford University Press, 2011), pp. 263–81.

37 R. Harris, 'Strategy and Tactics in Presenting the Case for the Free Market', paper to 1964 MPS Meeting, Semmering, F. A. Hayek papers, Hoover Institution Archives, Stanford University (hereafter Hayek), 84/15; Cockett, *Thinking*, pp. 130–1, 188–91.

38 Harrison, 'Mrs Thatcher and the Intellectuals', 223; see too Desai, 'Second-Hand Dealers', 61–2.

39 P. A. Hall, 'The Movement from Keynesianism to Monetarism: Institutional Analysis and British Economic Policy in the 1970s', in S. Steinmo, K. Thelen and F. Longstreth (eds.), *Structuring Politics* (Cambridge University Press, 1992), pp. 90–113; P. A. Hall, 'Policy Paradigms, Social Learning

and the State: The Case of Economic Policy Making in Britain', *Comparative Politics*, 25 (1993), 284–92.

40 C. Hay, 'Chronicles of a Death Foretold: The Winter of Discontent and Construction of the Crisis of British Keynesianism', *Parliamentary Affairs*, 63 (2010), 446–70.

41 J. Bulpitt, 'The Discipline of the New Democracy: Mrs Thatcher's Domestic Statecraft', *Political Studies*, 34 (1986), 19–39. For further discussion of Bulpitt's work, and of Conservative Party political strategy in this period, see Jim Tomlinson, Chapter 3 in this volume.

42 D. Kynaston, *The Financial Times: A Centenary History* (London: Viking, 1988), pp. 406–19, 427–9; J. Grigg, *The History of The Times*, vol. VI: *The Thomson Years, 1966–81* (London: HarperCollins, 1993), pp. 340–4, 396–402.

43 I am grateful to Robert Saunders for this point.

44 A. Shrimsley to A. Seldon, 30 September 1977, IEA 329/1.

45 R. Harris to M. Friedman, 3 November 1978, MF 154, and M. Friedman to R. Harris, 4 December 1978, IEA 296/11. According to Harris, this dinner had been intended to bring Friedman and Keith Joseph together, but Joseph was forced to cancel and proposed Thatcher as his substitute: *Conversation with Harris and Seldon*, p. 56.

46 The lecture was published as Friedman, *Counter-Revolution in Monetary Policy*.

47 Transcript of *Controversy*, broadcast 23 September 1974, MF 55/13; R. Harris to M. Friedman, 24 September 1974, MF 85/7.

48 This paragraph draws on the analysis of W. Parsons, *The Power of the Financial Press: Journalism and the Formation of Economic Opinion in Britain and the USA* (London: Edward Elgar, 1996), pp. 98–106.

49 Kynaston, *Financial Times*, pp. 329–30, 368–9; Grigg, *History*, pp. 37–8, 222–4, 287–93; Brittan, *Second Thoughts*, pp. 11–13; Cockett, *Thinking*, pp. 184–8; Parsons, *Power*, pp. 107–9, 175–84; M. Friedman, 'The Role of Monetary Policy', *American Economic Review*, 58 (1968), 1–17.

50 S. Brittan, 'How to End the Strike-Threat System', *Financial Times*, 5 September 1974; S. Brittan, 'The Political Economy of British Union Monopoly', *Three Banks Review*, 111 (1976), 3–32; P. Jay, 'The Good Old Days of Stop-Go Economics', *The Times*, 5 December 1973; P. Jay, 'How Inflation Threatens British Democracy with its Last Chance Before Extinction', *The Times*, 1 July 1974.

51 Parsons, *Power*, p. 182; Grigg, *History*, pp. 287–93, 386–9.

52 Kynaston, *Financial Times*, pp. 399–406, 429–30, 433–9, 456–9.

53 A. Seldon to L. Chickering, 18 May 1981, IEA 332/4; G. Wheatcroft, 'Welch, (James) Colin Ross (1924–1997)', *Oxford Dictionary of National Biography* (Oxford University Press, 2004); W. Deedes, 'Green, (James) Maurice Spurgeon (1906–1987)', *ibid.*; Cockett, *Thinking*, pp. 183–4.

54 R. Dudley Edwards, *The Pursuit of Reason: The Economist 1843–1993* (London: Hamish Hamilton, 1993), pp. 590–1, 831, 839–40; Parsons, *Power*, p. 191.

55 R. Harris, 'Aide Memoire: Dinner with Alastair Burnet on 12 October 1970', IEA 294/5. See also the correspondence with Burnet in IEA 295/10, spanning *c.* 1966–73.

56 Parsons, *Power*, pp. 189–92.

57 M. Swann to R. Harris, 3 October 1974; R. Harris to M. Swann, 27 January 1978, both in IEA 295/2; A. Seldon to M. Swann, 18 February 1980, IEA 333/6.

58 K. Joseph to W. Whitelaw, 10 September 1976; G. Howe to K. Joseph, 16 September 1976, KJ 18/9; Note of IEA/CPS Dinner, 19 October 1976, IEA 333/6.

59 A. Seldon, 'IEA on the Air', memo, 2 July 1980, IEA 333/6, p. 1.

60 Harrison, *Finding*, p. 329.

61 R. Harris and A. Seldon to Prince Philip, 3 February 1977, IEA 330/8; 'Minutes of the 63rd Meeting of IEA Managing Trustees', 27 July 1977, IEA 90/3, p. 1; R. Harris, 'IEA Dinner: 22nd February', 3 February 1978, IEA 330/8; Prince Philip to R. Harris, 3 March 1977, IEA 298/2; 'Dinner for the Duke of Edinburgh: Thursday, 26th November 1981', memo, IEA 298/2; R. Davies to Lord Harris, 24 November 1980, IEA 298/2.

62 A. Seldon to E. Heffer, 27 June 1978, and E. Heffer to A. Seldon, 3 July 1978, both IEA 23/4.

63 MPS Membership List, 1970, GT 58; 'Guests Attending MPS Cambridge Meeting', 1980, MPS 25/8; 'Guests Attending MPS St Andrews Meeting', 1976, MPS papers, Liberaal Archief, Ghent. I am grateful to Gilles Christoph for sending me a copy of the latter reference.

64 M. Friedman to W. Buckley, 2 December 1970, MF 22/13.

65 R. Harris to J. Jewkes, 30 September 1960, IEA 297/4.

66 See the correspondence between Howe and Seldon collected in IEA 332/3, spanning *c.* 1969–82.

67 A. Seldon to G. Watson, 14 February 1977, IEA 327/3; R. Harris to M. Friedman, 1 March 1974, IEA 85/7. For a flavour of Harris's unhappiness with the Heath government, see his 'Who are the Guilty Men?', *Spectator*, 23 February 1974.

68 Cockett, *Thinking*, pp. 232–3; A. Denham and M. Garnett, *Keith Joseph* (Chesham: Acumen, 2001), p. 238.

69 R. Harris, memo to John Wood and Arthur Seldon, 14 March 1974, IEA 295/12.

70 K. Joseph to R. Harris, 8 August 1974, IEA 295/12.

71 Denham and Garnett, *Keith Joseph*, pp. 255–7.

72 K. Joseph, *Reversing the Trend: Seven Speeches by Sir Keith Joseph* (London: Barry Allen, 1975), pp. 7, 70.

73 John Ranelagh's anecdote about Thatcher slamming a copy of *The Constitution of Liberty* on the table during a meeting in the late 1970s has been recounted ad nauseam, but it is certainly not representative of Thatcher's outlook in this period. In any case, the evidence on which this story is grounded (recollections some years after the event) does not look very secure. J. Ranelagh, *Thatcher's People* (London: Fontana, 1992), p. ix.

74 See A. Seldon to K. Joseph, 14 September 1981, IEA 333/6; A. Seldon, *The Riddle of the Voucher* (London: IEA, 1986); Harris and Seldon, *Conversation*, p. 57.

75 Correspondence between Seldon and Howe, IEA 332/3; K. Joseph to R. Boyson, 20 November 1975, KJ 19/1; Denham and Garnett, *Keith Joseph*, pp. 207–11, 369–73.

76 M. Wickham-Jones, 'Monetarism and its Critics: The University Economists' Protest of 1981', *Political Quarterly*, 63 (1992), 171–85.

3 THATCHER, MONETARISM AND THE POLITICS OF INFLATION

1 M. Thatcher, *The Path to Power* (London: HarperCollins, 1995), p. 298.
2 D. Cannadine, 'Apocalypse When? British Politicians and British "Decline" in the Twentieth Century', in P. Clarke and C. Trebilcock (eds.), *Understanding Decline* (Cambridge University Press, 1997), pp. 261–84; E. H. H. Green, *Thatcher* (London: Hodder, 2006), pp. 55–6; J. Tomlinson, 'Mrs Thatcher's Macro-economic Adventurism, 1979–1981, and its Political Consequences', *British Politics*, 2 (2007), 3–19.
3 On declinism, see J. Tomlinson, 'Thrice Denied: "Declinism" as a Recurrent Theme in British History in the Long Twentieth Century', *Twentieth Century British History*, 20 (2009), 227–51.
4 R. McKibbin, 'Class and Conventional Wisdom: The Conservative Party and the "Public" in Inter-war Britain', in R. McKibbin, *The Ideologies of Class* (Oxford University Press, 1990), pp. 259–93; D. Jarvis, 'Mrs Maggs and Betty: The Conservative Appeal to Women Voters in the 1920s', *Twentieth Century British History*, 5 (1994), 129–52.
5 A. Booth, 'Inflation, Expectations and the Political Economy of Conservative Britain 1951–64', *Historical Journal*, 43 (2001), 827–47.
6 E. H. H. Green, 'The Treasury Resignations of 1958: A Reconsideration', *Twentieth Century British History*, 11 (2000), 409–30.
7 R. Jones, *Wages and Employment Policy 1936–1985* (London: Allen & Unwin, 1987), pp. 54–8.
8 Conservative Party manifesto, 1970, in I. Dale (ed.), *Conservative Party General Election Manifestos 1900–1997* (London: Routledge, 2000), p. 183.
9 Jones, *Wages*, pp. 84–92; Selsdon Group, 'The Selsdon Manifesto', 19 September 1973: 'Inflation is at present a serious long-term threat to our economic wealth and to the survival of our free society, but the Government's attempt to overcome it by prices and incomes policies presents an even greater threat', MTFW 110860.
10 J. Bulpitt, 'The Discipline of the New Democracy: Mrs Thatcher's Domestic Statecraft', *Political Studies*, 34 (1986), 19–39; R. Middleton, *Charlatans or Saviours? Economists and the British Economy from Marshall to Meade* (Cheltenham: Elgar, 1998), pp. 334–42.
11 J. Keynes, *The Economic Consequences of the Peace* [1919] (London: Macmillan, 1971), p. 143; F. Fetter, 'Lenin, Keynes and Inflation', *Economica*, 44 (1977), 77–80; R. White and K. Schaler, 'Who said "Debase the Currency": Keynes or Lenin?', *Journal of Economic Perspectives*, 23 (2009), 213–22.
12 L. Robbins, 'Chairman's Introduction' to L. Robbins *et al.*, *Inflation: Economy and Society* (London: IEA, 1972), p. 7; L. Robbins, *Against Inflation: Speeches in the Second Chamber 1965–1977* (London: Macmillan, 1979).
13 F. A. Hayek, *A Tiger by the Tail: The Keynesian Legacy of Inflation*, 2nd edn (London: IEA, 1978); J. Tomlinson, *Hayek and the Market* (London: Pluto, 1990), pp. 68–80.

14 F. A. Hayek, *New Studies in Philosophy, Politics, Economics and the History of Ideas* (London: Routledge & Kegan Paul, 1978), p. 216.

15 R. Johnson, *The Politics of Recession* (London: Macmillan, 1985), p. 131.

16 *The Banker*, March 1974, p. 205.

17 *The Economist*, 17 May 1975, p. 9. There was much more in the same vein: J. Tomlinson, *The Politics of Decline: Understanding Post-War Britain* (Harlow: Pearson, 2001), pp. 85–90.

18 A. Beckett, *Pinochet in Piccadilly: Britain and Chile's Secret History* (London: Faber & Faber, 2002), pp. 192–202; for Thatcher's defence, see speech to the Conservative Party Conference, 6 October 1999, MTFW 108383.

19 The discussions drawn on here are mainly from the Economic Reconstruction Group (ERG) and the Shadow Cabinet, usually called the Leader's Consultative Committee (LCC).

20 'If the Public Sector Borrowing Requirement continues to grow, we will be moving further and further towards the Weimar mechanism of hyper-inflation': 'Note on Discussion at Fentiman Road', 18 May 1975, MTFW 109968. Fentiman Road was the home of Geoffrey Howe.

21 A. Ridley, 'Inflation, Pay Determination and the Labour Market', 16 March 1978, MTFW 109759.

22 K. Joseph, speech at Preston, 5 September 1975, MTFW 110607.

23 J. Prior, 'Counter-Inflation Policy', 13 May 1975, MTFW 110103.

24 *Glasgow Herald*, 21 February 1975.

25 Hansard, HC Deb., 5th series, vol. 892, col. 1638 (22 May 1975).

26 Speech at Beechwood, 21 June 1975, MTFW 102721.

27 Green, *Thatcher*, pp. 65–6.

28 J. Wood, *How Much Unemployment? The Methods and Measures Dissected* (London: IEA, 1972); Middleton, *Charlatans or Saviours?*, p. 275; later references on this include LCC, 15 July 1974, MTFW 111901; for Joseph regretting not supporting Heath on this issue, see 'Notes Towards the Definition of Policy', 4 April 1975, MTFW 110908.

29 Speech at Roosevelt University, Chicago, 22 September 1975, MTFW 102465. In this speech Thatcher cites Weimar Germany as a case study of the damage done by inflation.

30 Speech, 1 May 1974, cited in Green, *Thatcher*, p. 67.

31 Joseph to Thatcher, 27 January 1979, enclosing draft speech on unions, MTFW 111880.

32 Speech at Roosevelt University, 22 September 1975; speech to Zurich Economic Society, 14 March 1977, MTFW 10336.

33 N. Lawson, *The View from Number 11: Memoirs of a Tory Radical* (London: Bantam, 1992), pp. 27, 29.

34 Correlli Barnett's *Collapse of British Power* (London: Eyre Methuen, 1972), did not receive much notice. His *Audit of War: The Illusion and Reality of Britain as a Great Nation* (London: Macmillan, 1986) was widely noted; see also Martin Wiener's *English Culture and the Decline of the Industrial Spirit, 1850–1980* (Cambridge University Press, 1981).

35 Speech at Kensington Town Hall, 19 January 1976, MTFW 102939.

36 Notes of Shadow Cabinet meeting by Lord Hailsham, 11 April 1975, Churchill Archives Centre, Papers of Lord Hailsham, HLSM 1/1/10, reproduced at MTFW 111134. Speaking to his own paper, Joseph asserted:

'The 100 years of relative decline (since the Great Exhibition) is objectively demonstrable.'

37 J. Hoskyns and N. Strauss, 'Stepping Stones', 14 November 1977, MTFW 111771; J. Hoskyns, 'Stepping Stones Programme', 19 January 1978, MTFW 109848; discussion at Shadow Cabinet, 30 January 1978, MTFW 109832.

38 Ridley, 'Inflation, Pay Determination and the Labour Market', 16 March 1978.

39 Joseph to Thatcher, 27 January 1979, enclosing draft speech on unions.

40 Thatcher, *Path to Power*, pp. 296–304, 403–5.

41 Bulpitt, 'Discipline', 21–2.

42 A. Ridley, 'The Monetary Approach to Forecasting Inflation', 26 May 1976, MTFW 110141, makes clear his view that the 1975–6 inflation stemmed from monetary expansion two years earlier; Thatcher, *Path to Power*, p. 299. In a memo to Thatcher in 1976 Joseph said explicitly that 'more recently Labour inherited the lagged results of the Tory expansion of demand in the early 1970s', but I have found no case of this being said so explicitly in public: K. Joseph, 'Case Against Incomes Policy', 4 May 1976, MTFW 103191; G. Howe, speech to Finchley Conservatives, 13 June 1975, MTFW 102676.

43 M. Friedman, *Counter-Revolution in Monetary Theory* (London: IEA, 1970), p. 24.

44 Green, *Thatcher*, pp. 102–6.

45 In Conservative policy-making circles anti-unionism was expressed most vehemently in the 'Stepping Stones' analysis, which asserted that in pursuing Conservative policies 'there is one major obstacle – the negative role of unions. Unless a satisfying and creative role can be developed, national recovery will be virtually impossible': 'Stepping Stones'. To some Conservatives this degree of hostility was inappropriate, but not for Thatcher: discussion at Shadow Cabinet, 30 January 1978; G. Howe, *Conflict of Loyalty* (London: Macmillan, 1994), pp. 104–7.

46 Thatcher partly recognises this in her memoirs when she notes that 'time and again inflation registered in the opinion polls as the public's top priority for action, though often in tandem with strong support for pay policy as supposedly the only means of fighting it': Thatcher, *Path to Power*, p. 299.

47 Joseph to Thatcher, 27 January 1979, enclosing draft speech on unions.

48 Bulpitt, 'Discipline', 29–31.

49 Joseph to Thatcher, 27 January 1979, enclosing draft speech on unions.

50 Ridley, 'Inflation, Pay Determination and the Labour Market', 16 March 1978.

51 Thatcher, *Path to Power*; ERG, 27 June 1975, MTFW 110214.

52 G. Pepper and M. Oliver, *Monetarism Under Thatcher: Lessons for the Future* (London: IEA, 2001) give one typology, including 'genuine monetarism', against which standard Howe and Lawson are found wanting: only Thatcher and Joseph escape censure for lack of genuine attachment to the creed (pp. 21–9).

53 ERG, 'Interim Report', 24 July 1975, MTFW 110116.

54 Howe, though increasingly committed to a monetary view of inflation, was also a strong supporter of some form of West German style 'Concerted

Action' council, as a way of educating the population on economic realities (i.e. the need to reduce wage demands). This was an argument with surprising life in Conservative policy-making circles in these years, though one which Thatcher opposed more stridently at the time than her memoirs suggest: Thatcher, *Path to Power*, p. 301; 'The Economic Education of the Public: Proposals for "Concerted Action" and Fighting Inflation', 16 May 1977, MTFW 109761. Thatcher scribbled on it that she 'disagrees most strongly with this paper'.

55 ERG, 20 November 1975, MTFW 110226.

56 Joseph, 'Case Against Incomes Policy', 4 May 1976.

57 A. Ridley, 'Countering Inflation', 15 December 1976, MTFW 110239.

58 ERG, 'Interim Report', 24 July 1975.

59 Minutes of Shadow Cabinet meeting, 11 April 1975, MTFW 109958.

60 ERG, 30 October 1975, MTFW 110222.

61 Bulpitt, 'Discipline', 37; Tomlinson, 'Mrs Thatcher's Macroeconomic Adventurism'.

62 Bulpitt, 'Discipline', 33.

63 *Ibid.*, 26.

64 For Thatcher on Adam Smith, see her lecture at Roosevelt University. This, of course, is only one version of Smith; for an alternative, see I. McLean, *Adam Smith: Radical and Egalitarian* (Edinburgh University Press, 2006). On the rise of this economic liberalism in British politics, see Ben Jackson, Chapter 2 in this volume.

65 Lawson, *View from Number 11*, pp. 299–301.

66 The debate was characterised by great exaggerations about the scale of spending: M. Friedman, 'The Line We Dare Not Cross: The Fragility of Freedom at 60%', *Encounter*, 47 (1976), 8–14; for a corrective to such exaggerations, see R. Middleton, *Government versus the Market* (Cheltenham: Elgar, 1996), pp. 526–9.

67 As noted above in reference to the 1970 election manifesto, the link between higher taxation and inflation could be posed in a non-monetarist way as driven by those resentful of higher taxes pushing harder to raise their pre-tax incomes.

68 G. Howe, 'The Economic Prospect and the Party's Political Position', 16 December 1975, MTFW 110128.

69 J. Fforde, 'Setting Monetary Objectives', *Bank of England Quarterly Bulletin*, 23 (1983), 200–8.

70 Lawson, *View from Number 11*, pp. 17–18.

71 G. Pepper, *Inside Thatcher's Monetarist Revolution* (Basingstoke: Macmillan, 1998), p. 31.

72 The non-housing aspect of this was, of course, to be pursued by the privatisation of nationalised industries in the mid 1980s, but though privatisation was talked about before 1979, there seems to have been little discussion of its role in creating 'popular capitalism'.

73 For example, speech to Conservative Party Conference, 10 October 1975, MTFW 102777; speech to Conservative Women's Conference, 19 May 1976, MTFW 103029.

74 Lawson, *View from Number 11*, p. 11; see also 'Houses: The Tory Christmas Box', *Sunday Times*, 29 September 1974.

75 Lawson, *View from Number 11*, p. 11.
76 Owner occupation rose from 51 per cent to 68 per cent of households between 1979 and 1992: H. Young, *Thatcherism: Did Society Survive?* (London: Catholic Housing Aid Society, 1992), p. 10.
77 Lawson, *View from Number 11*, pp. 629–30; C. Hay, 'Good Inflation, Bad Inflation? The Housing Boom, Economic Growth and the Disaggregation of Inflationary Preferences in the UK and Ireland', *British Journal of Politics and International Relations*, 11 (2009), 461–78.
78 The Conservatives were very successful in reducing the PSBR, but not initially by cutting spending, rather by increasing taxes.
79 Though Samuel Brittan had stressed the importance of the exchange rate in 1978: Joseph to Thatcher, 9 October 1978, MTFW 111869.
80 D. Cobham, *The Making of Monetary Policy in the UK 1975–2000* (Chichester: Wiley, 2002), p. 142.
81 Tomlinson, 'Mrs Thatcher's Macroeconomic Adventurism'.
82 I. Crewe, 'How to Win a Landslide Without Really Trying', in A. Ranney (ed.), *Britain at the Polls 1983: A Study of the General Election* (Durham, NC: American Enterprise Institute, 1985), pp. 178–9.
83 Thatcher, *Path to Power*, pp. 420–30; C. Hay, 'Narrating Crisis: The Discursive Construction of the "Winter of Discontent"', *Sociology*, 30 (1996), 253–77.

4 THATCHERISM, MORALITY AND RELIGION

1 K. Joseph, speech at Edgbaston, 19 October 1974, MTFW 101830.
2 A. M. Smith, *New Right Discourse on Race and Sexuality 1968–1990* (Cambridge University Press, 1994), p. 2.
3 P. Williamson, 'The Doctrinal Politics of Stanley Baldwin', in M. Bentley (ed.), *Public and Private Doctrine: Essays in British History Presented to Maurice Cowling* (Cambridge University Press, 1994), pp. 181–208.
4 S. Hall, *The Hard Road to Renewal* (London: Verso, 1988), p. 91.
5 *Ibid.*, p. 137.
6 S. R. Letwin, *The Anatomy of Thatcherism* (London: Fontana, 1992), p. 337.
7 D. Marquand, 'The Paradoxes of Thatcherism', in R. Skidelsky (ed.), *Thatcherism* (Oxford: Blackwell, 1988), p. 165.
8 See D. Sandbrook, 'Against the Permissive Society: The Backlash of the Late 1960s', in W. R. Louis (ed.), *More Adventures with Britannia* (London: I.B. Tauris, 2009), pp. 55–71.
9 F. Mount, *Cold Cream: My Early Life and Other Mistakes* (London: Bloomsbury, 2008), p. 288.
10 For Thatcher's voting record on permissive legislation in the 1960s, see G. K. Fry, 'Parliament and "Morality": Thatcher, Powell and Populism', *Contemporary British History*, 12 (1998), 139–47.
11 H. L. A. Hart, *Law, Liberty and Morality* (London: Oxford University Press, 1963).
12 M. Thatcher, *The Path to Power* (London: HarperCollins, 1995), pp. 152–3.
13 P. Devlin, *The Enforcement of Morals* (London: Oxford University Press for the British Academy, 1959).

14 'What Lies Ahead in the Seventies?', *Finchley Press*, 2 January 1970, MTFW 101709.

15 BBC *Woman's Hour* interview, 9 April 1970, MTFW 101845.

16 Draft letter from Whitehouse to the *Birmingham Post* and other papers, 7 May 1970, NVALA papers, Box 54, Albert Sloman Library, University of Essex. For Whitehouse's work with NVALA, see L. Black, 'There was Something about Mary: The National Viewers' and Listeners' Association (NVALA) and Social Movement History', in N. J. Crowson, M. Hilton and J. McKay (eds.), *NGOs in Contemporary Britain: Non-State Actors in Society and Politics since 1945* (Basingstoke: Palgrave Macmillan, 2009), pp. 182–200.

17 A. Maude, *The Common Problem* (London: Constable, 1969), pp. 197, 51.

18 *Ibid.*, p. 273.

19 For a detailed account of the circumstances of this speech, and the reaction to it, see A. Denham and M. Garnett, *Keith Joseph* (Chesham: Acumen, 2001), pp. 265–75.

20 Joseph, speech at Edgbaston, 19 October 1974.

21 Thatcher, *Path to Power*, p. 262.

22 Speech to Conservative Central Council, 15 March 1975, MTFW 102655.

23 Speech to the English-Speaking Union, Houston, Texas, 9 September 1977, MTFW 103268.

24 Speech to the Scottish Conservative Conference, Perth, 13 May 1978, MTFW 103684.

25 Sherman to Thatcher, 22 March 1979, Alfred Sherman papers, Box 8, AR MT/M/2115, Royal Holloway, University of London.

26 Lord Hailsham, undated article, 'Moral Behaviour, Not Economic Failure', circulated by Keith Joseph as part of his 'Notes Towards the Definition of Policy', 7 April 1975, MTFW 110098.

27 Speech at St Lawrence Jewry, 30 March 1978, MTFW 103522.

28 Maude, *Common Problem*, p. 41.

29 Interview with *Woman's Own*, 23 September 1987 (Thatcher CD-ROM).

30 C. Hay, 'Narrating Crisis: The Discursive Construction of the "Winter of Discontent"', *Sociology*, 30 (1996), 253–77. See also Robert Saunders, Chapter 1 in this volume.

31 Speech at Finchley, 11 April 1979, MTFW 104002.

32 Election address, 11 April 1979, MTFW 104003; speech to Young Conservatives, Bournemouth, 10 February 1979, MTFW 103942; speech at Cardiff, 16 April 1979, MTFW 104011.

33 K. O. Morgan, *Callaghan: A Life* (Oxford University Press, 1997), p. 320; Bernard Donoughue, *The Heat of the Kitchen*, rev. and updated edn (London: Politico's, 2004), p. 271.

34 Conference speech, Blackpool, 14 October 1977, MTFW 103443. Thatcher apparently did not get her speechwriters' joke, trying to change the punch-line to 'keep taking the pills': A. Watkins, *A Conservative Coup: The Fall of Margaret Thatcher* (London: Duckworth, 1991), p. 27; S. Hoggart, *A Long Lunch: My Stories and I'm Sticking to Them* (London: John Murray, 2010), p. 191.

35 Speech at Cardiff, 16 April 1979.

36 Speech to Finchley Inter-Church Luncheon Club, 17 November 1969, reported in *Finchley Press*, 21 November 1969, MTFW 101704; speech presenting Templeton Prize, 13 April 1976, MTFW 103008; speech to Conservative Women's Conference, 24 May 1978, MTFW 103696; interview with *Catholic Herald*, 22 December 1978, MTFW 103793.

37 Speech to the Bow Group, 16 May 1978, MTFW 103674.

38 Sherman, 'Memo to MT proposing a talk on "A Christian View of Society"', 1 May 1980, Sherman papers, Box 8, ARMT/M/3/10.

39 A. Sherman, *Paradoxes of Power: Reflections on the Thatcher Interlude* (Exeter: Imprint Academic, 2005), p. 56.

40 Speech at St Lawrence Jewry, 30 March 1978.

41 For the NFOL, see A. Whipple, 'Speaking for Whom? The 1971 Festival of Light and the Search for the "Silent Majority"', *Contemporary British History*, 24 (2010), 319–39.

42 Whitehouse to E. Heath, 17 April 1973, NVALA papers, Box 111.

43 J. Poulton, *Dear Archbishop* (London: Hodder & Stoughton, 1976), p. 18.

44 D. Coggan, foreword to Poulton, *Dear Archbishop*, p. 7.

45 R. Wood to Archbishop D. Coggan, 26 March 1975, Coggan papers, vol. 190, fol. 8, Lambeth Palace Library.

46 Speech to Greater London Young Conservatives (Iain Macleod Memorial Lecture), 4 July 1977, MTFW 103411.

47 Press release, 25 October 1979, NVALA papers, Box 59; Thatcher to Whitehouse, 19 April 1979, NVALA papers, Box 4 (2002 accession).

48 Sherman, *Paradoxes of Power*, p. 41.

49 Memorandum, 31 January 1979, KJ 18/6, Keith Joseph papers, Conservative Party Archive, Bodleian Library, Oxford. The quotation from Temple was omitted from the final version.

50 M. Cowling (ed.), *Conservative Essays* (London: Cassell, 1978), p. 5.

51 Shadow Cabinet, 17 April 1978, Thatcher papers, THCR 2/6/1/162, quoted in E. H. H. Green, *Thatcher* (London: Hodder Arnold, 2006), p. 128. See also Jon Lawrence and Florence Sutcliffe-Braithwaite, Chapter 7 in this volume.

52 'Themes', 16 February 1978 (by A. Maude, R. Boyson, D. Howell, N. Lawson and N. Tebbit), MTFW 109853.

53 See Camilla Schofield, Chapter 5 in this volume.

54 'The Moral Basis of a Free Society', *Daily Telegraph*, 16 May 1978, MTFW 103687.

55 Speech to Greater London Young Conservatives, 4 July 1977.

56 Speech at Conservative Political Centre Summer School, 6 July 1979, MTFW 104107.

57 Speech at St Lawrence Jewry, 4 March 1981, MTFW 104587.

58 R. Butt, 'Mrs Thatcher: The First Two Years', *Sunday Times*, 1 May 1981.

59 R. Samuel, 'Mrs Thatcher and Victorian Values', in R. Samuel, *Island Stories: Unravelling Britain* (London: Verso, 1998), p. 337.

60 D. Willetts, 'The Family', in D. Kavanagh and A. Seldon (eds.), *The Thatcher Effect: A Decade of Change* (Oxford University Press, 1989),

pp. 266–7. Mount calls the Family Policy Group 'pretty much my own idea': email correspondence with the author, 9 November 2010.

61 G. Douglas, 'Family Law under the Thatcher Government', *Journal of Law and Society*, 17 (1990), 411–26. See also M. Durham, *Sex and Politics: The Family and Morality in the Thatcher Years* (Basingstoke: Macmillan, 1991). The term limit for abortions was, however, reduced from 28 to 24 weeks in 1990.

62 Speech to Finchley Inter-Church Luncheon Club, 17 November 1969.

63 See e.g. Thatcher to Whitehouse, 20 October 1975, NVALA papers, Box 54.

64 Notes for conference speech, 'Thoughts on the Moral Case I' (undated, but before 6 October 1979), MTFW 112195.

65 F. Sutcliffe-Braithwaite, 'The Origins and Development of Thatcherite Social Policy, 1975–1979', unpublished MPhil dissertation, University of Cambridge, 2010, p. 27. I am grateful to the author for allowing me to consult her dissertation.

66 Letwin, *Anatomy of Thatcherism*, p. 39.

67 'The Moral Basis of a Free Society', *Daily Telegraph*, 16 May 1978.

68 Interview with *Catholic Herald*, 22 December 1978, MTFW 103793; see also speech to Scottish Conservative Conference, 13 May 1978; speech to Conservative Women's Conference, 24 May 1978.

69 Thatcher, *Path to Power*, p. 556.

70 See also her second speech at St Lawrence Jewry, 4 March 1981.

71 M. Alison and D. Edwards (eds.), *Christianity and Conservatism* (London: Hodder & Stoughton, 1990), p. 10.

72 Thatcher reputedly asked her staff to tell her the name of the only book in the Bible that did not mention God, and was delighted when no one correctly identified the Book of Esther, adding, 'it is a very *gory* book': H. Young, *One of Us*, rev. edn (London: Pan, 1990), p. 426.

73 For a critical exegesis of the 'Sermon on the Mound', see J. Raban, *God, Man and Mrs Thatcher* (London: Chatto & Windus, 1989), especially pp. 32–3.

74 'Speech Module for Thatcher: A Nation Under God', 17 November 1978, Sherman papers, Box 6, AR/MT/5/2/2.

75 'Draft Questions for Mrs Thatcher, to be first considered by Mr Whitelaw', undated, KJ 8/22, Conservative Party Archive.

76 *Church Times*, 17 February 1978, p. 20. Leonard's remarks were criticised by other bishops, including the Bishop of Lichfield: see *Church Times*, 3 March 1978, p. 1.

77 For a discussion of the actual, rather than imputed, political beliefs of 1980s Anglican clergy, see C. Field, 'Rendering unto Caesar? The Politics of Church of England Clergy Since 1980', *Journal of Anglican Studies*, 5 (2007), 89–108.

78 Young, *One of Us*, p. 418.

79 Interview with *Woman's Own*, 23 September 1987.

80 E. H. H. Green, *Ideologies of Conservatism: Conservative Political Ideas in the Twentieth Century* (Oxford University Press, 2002), pp. 278–9.

81 I. Gilmour, *Dancing with Dogma: Britain under Thatcherism* (London: Simon & Schuster, 1992), p. 201.

82 Speech to Conservative Women's Conference, 25 May 1988, MTFW 107248; speech at National Children's Home, 17 January 1990, MTFW 107922.

83 Sherman to R. Ryder, 23 March 1978, TCHR 2/6/1/225, Margaret Thatcher papers, Churchill Archives Centre, Cambridge; Sherman to A. Howarth, 7 February 1977, TCHR 2/6/1/226.

84 See e.g. Thatcher, Sir Robert Menzies Lecture, Monash University, 6 October 1981; speech to Board of Deputies of British Jews, 15 December 1981; interview with *Sunday Telegraph*, 19 July 1986; interview with *Paris Match*, 2 March 1990; Pankhurst Lecture to 300 Group, 18 July 1990 (all on Thatcher CD-ROM).

85 A. Friedlander, 'Immanuel Jakobovits', *Oxford Dictionary of National Biography* (Oxford University Press, 2004); Young, *One of Us*, pp. 422–4.

86 See M. Grimley, 'The Religion of Englishness: Puritanism, Providentialism and "National Character", 1918–45', *Journal of British Studies*, 46 (2007), 884–906.

87 For the best account of twentieth-century decline, see S. J. D. Green, *The Passing of Protestant England: Secularisation and Social Change, c. 1920–1960* (Cambridge University Press, 2011).

88 Whitehouse to Thatcher, 27 May 1988, NVALA papers (2002 accession), Box 4.

89 For 'discursive Christianity' and 'Christian Britain', see C. Brown, *The Death of Christian Britain: Understanding Secularisation 1800–2000* (London: Routledge, 2001); also J. Garnett *et al.*, *Redefining Christian Britain: Post-1945 Perspectives* (London: SCM Press, 2007); for sabbatarianism, see G. I. T. Machin, *Churches and Social Issues in Twentieth-Century Britain* (Oxford University Press, 1998), pp. 214–15.

90 J. Campbell, *Margaret Thatcher: The Iron Lady* (London: Jonathan Cape, 2003), pp. 250–2.

91 See e.g. N. Boyle, 'Understanding Thatcherism', *New Blackfriars*, 69 (1988), reprinted as chapter 1 in N. Boyle, *Who Are We Now? Christian Humanism and the Global Market from Hegel to Heaney* (Edinburgh: T. & T. Clark, 1998); Marquand, 'Paradoxes of Thatcherism'.

92 Remarks on becoming Prime Minister, 4 May 1979, MTFW 104078. For a speechwriter's account of this episode, see R. Millar, *A View from the Wings: West End, West Coast, Westminster* (London: Weidenfeld & Nicolson, 1993), p. 266. Mary Whitehouse wrote to the new premier that 'it was a wonderful thing to hear a Prime Minister utter the marvellous words of St Francis before the whole world – already one senses a lifting of the spirit!' Whitehouse to Thatcher, 9 May 1979, NVALA papers, Box 59.

5 'A NATION OR NO NATION?' ENOCH POWELL AND THATCHERISM

1 Bill Schwarz interview with Enoch Powell, 26 April 1988 (private recording). See also J. E. Powell, *A Nation or No Nation? Six Years in British Politics*, ed. R. Ritchie (London: Elliot Right Way Books, 1978), pp. 121–74. In this collection of speeches, Powell posed four questions to 'the nation': 'A free

economy?', 'A sovereign Parliament?', 'What place for Ulster?' and 'An end to immigration?'

2 S. Heffer, *Like the Roman: The Life of Enoch Powell* (London: Weidenfeld & Nicolson, 1998), p. 153.

3 See, for instance, Powell speech at the South-West Norfolk Conservative Fete, 15 June 1963, POLL 4/1/1, Enoch Powell papers, Churchill Archives Centre, Cambridge: '[We must] seek to re-establish our self-confidence and faith in ourselves upon a new basis and to find, as it were, a new patriotism befitting this changed world, to replace the old, imperial patriotism of the past. To help the nation in this work to express its purpose is uniquely the mission of the Tory Party: to proclaim to ourselves and to our fellow countrymen that the reserves of energy, of resource, of enterprise, from which our past achievements sprang, are not exhausted.'

4 Speech at Kensington Town Hall, 19 January 1976, MTFW 102939.

5 *The Right Approach*, Conservative policy document, 4 October 1976, MTFW 109439.

6 P. B. Rich, 'Conservative Ideology and Race in Modern British Politics', in P. Rich and Z. Layton-Henry (eds.), *Race, Government and Politics in Britain* (London: Macmillan, 1986), p. 54.

7 A. Gamble, *The Conservative Nation* (London: Routledge & Kegan Paul, 1974), p. 218.

8 Powell in *Odd Man Out*, BBC TV profile by Michael Cockerell, transmitted 11 November 1995, POLL 5/69.

9 J. E. Powell to E. and A. Powell, 9 March 1943, POLL 1/1/5.

10 For a discussion of Thatcher as Cold Warrior, see Richard Vinen, Chapter 11 in this volume.

11 D. Marquand, 'The Paradoxes of Thatcherism', in R. Skidelsky (ed.), *Thatcherism* (London: Chatto & Windus, 1988), p. 171.

12 Powell, Bill Schwarz interview, 26 April 1988.

13 Marquand, 'Paradoxes', p. 172.

14 J. Hoskyns and N. Strauss, 'Stepping Stones', 14 November 1977, MTFW 111771.

15 See N. Lawson, 'The New Conservatism' (lecture to the Bow Group), 4 August 1980, MTFW 109505.

16 R. Vinen, *Thatcher's Britain: The Politics and Social Upheaval of the Thatcher Era* (London: Simon & Schuster, 2009), p. 16.

17 E. H. H. Green, *Ideologies of Conservatism: Conservative Political Ideas in the Twentieth Century* (Oxford University Press, 2002), pp. 216, 236–7.

18 T. Nairn, *The Break-up of Britain* (London: Verso, 1981), p. 384.

19 Speech at Kensington Town Hall, 19 January 1976.

20 D. Schoen, *Enoch Powell and the Powellites* (London: Macmillan, 1977), p. 240.

21 Powell speech 'To the Annual General Meeting of the West Midlands Area Conservative Political Centre', 20 April 1968, in *Reflections: Selected Writings and Speeches of Enoch Powell* (London: Bellew Publishing, 1992), p. 168.

22 S. Hall, C. Critcher, T. Jefferson, J. Clarke and B. Robert, *Policing the Crisis: Mugging, the State and Law and Order* (London: Palgrave Macmillan, 1978).

23 S. Hall, 'Racism and Reaction', in *Five Views of Multi-Racial Britain* (London: Commission for Racial Equality, 1978), p. 30, cited in J. Procter, *Stuart Hall* (London: Routledge, 2004), p. 83.

24 C. Schofield, *Enoch Powell and the Making of Postcolonial Britain* (Cambridge University Press, forthcoming).

25 *Sunday Times*, 3 September 1968.

26 Powell, *Reflections*, p. 168.

27 Labour Research Department, *Powell and His Allies* (London, 1969), p. 10.

28 Enoch Powell held the 'realist' position that state sovereignty was an absolute. With such thinking, civil society is 'state-contained', and 'relations between societies [are] subordinate to, and dependent on, political relations between states'. Powell's 'civil society' was synonymous with a peaceful community at war – with a community able to wage war outside of itself. J. Anderson, 'Rethinking National Problems in a Transnational Context', in D. Miller (ed.), *Rethinking Northern Ireland: Culture, Ideology and Colonialism* (London: Longman, 1998), p. 129.

29 For the Powellite analysis of Northern Ireland and its relationship to Margaret Thatcher's, see Marc Mulholland, Chapter 10 in this volume.

30 Powell, *A Nation or No Nation?*, p. 19.

31 For a discussion of black and anti-racist cultural forms as a critique of capitalism, see P. Gilroy, 'Diaspora, Utopia and the Critique of Capitalism', in P. Gilroy, *There Ain't No Black in the Union Jack* (London: Routledge, 2002), pp. 200–302.

32 Report of Sir Kenneth Newman (Commissioner of Metropolitan Police), October 1984, cited *ibid.*, p. 137.

33 B. Särlvik and I. Crewe, *Decade of Dealignment: The Conservative Victory of 1979 and Electoral Trends in the 1970s* (Cambridge University Press, 1983).

34 'Selection of Letters From Public Following 20 April 1968', POLL 8/1/8.

35 Rich, 'Conservative Ideology', pp. 55–7.

36 For Powellight, see Heffer, *Like the Roman*, pp. 569–70.

37 Z. Layton-Henry, *The Politics of Race in Britain* (London: Allen & Unwin, 1984), pp. 145–6.

38 Report to Lord Thorneycroft, June 1976, THCR 2/6/1/140, Margaret Thatcher papers, Churchill Archives Centre.

39 K. Joseph, speech at Edgbaston, 19 October 1974, MTFW 101830.

40 T. Nairn, *Pariah: Misfortunes of the British Kingdom* (London: Verso, 2002), p. 22; J. Casey, 'Tradition and Authority', in M. Cowling (ed.), *Conservative Essays* (London: Cassell, 1978), p. 87.

41 K Joseph, 'Our Tone of Voice and our Tasks', 12 July 1976, MTFW 110178.

42 R. Butt, 'The Link Between Public Money and Public Morality', *The Times*, 24 October 1974.

43 Joseph to Thatcher, 27 January 1979, enclosing draft speech on unions, MTFW 111880.

44 Casey, 'Tradition and Authority', p. 87.

45 'Stepping Stones', pp. 9, 27, 36, A-9.

46 Powell, speech to Wessex Area Young Conservative Weekend School, Weymouth, 1 October 1966, POLL 4/1/2.
47 Powell, speech to Manchester Convention Dinner, 6 November 1965, POLL 4/1/2.
48 J. E. Powell, 'Truth, Politics and Persuasion', *Advertising Quarterly* (Spring 1965), 12.
49 S. Beer, *Modern British Politics: A Study of Parties and Pressure Groups* (London: Faber & Faber, 1965).
50 Heffer, *Like the Roman*, p. 825.
51 Hansard, HC Deb., 5th series, vol. 968, cols. 955–7 (18 June 1979).
52 Powell, 'International Charity', draft copy, *New Society*, 5 June 1965, POLL 6/1/1. According to Powell, the market is an evolutionary entity and the the-atre of innumerable human interactions. In this schema, the market is not a set of abstractions but is fundamentally contingent – it cannot be planned, controlled or universalised. The market is the expression of the community through which the moral individual can exist. The habits and expectations of a market order are, then, culturally and historically specific.
53 Interview for the *Sunday Times*, 1 May 1981, MTFW 104475.
54 M. Cowling, 'The Present Position', in Cowling (ed.), *Conservative Essays*, p. 4.
55 Speech to Greater London Young Conservatives (Iain Macleod Memorial Lecture), 4 July 1977, MTFW 103411. For further discussion of Thatcherism and Christianity, see Matthew Grimley, Chapter 4 in this volume.
56 Rich, 'Conservative Ideology', p. 61.
57 Letters Report, July 1976, Immigration File, THCR 2/6/1/140. I would like to thank Andrew Riley, archivist for the Margaret Thatcher papers at the Churchill Archives Centre, for kindly opening previously closed files for this research, including letters from the public to Margaret Thatcher on immigra-tion. Those who wrote to her, like Powell's letter-writers, were predominantly working-class. Many noted concern that 'Britain is over-populated, under housed and under employed' (Thatcher's underline). Thatcher's assistant believed that the main motivation of writing the letters seemed to be 'undoubt-edly much more fear of the unknown and of being swamped in the future, than dislike of those immigrants already here' (Thatcher's underline).
58 A. Neave, report on Race Relations Bill HAC(76)1, 16 July 1976, THCR 2/6/1/140.
59 Layton-Henry, *The Politics of Race*, pp. 104, 148.
60 *Ibid.*, p. 149 and C/10, papers of the Indian Workers Association, MS2141, Birmingham City Archives.
61 Thatcher recognised the impact of Powellism on the 1970 general election. Her files on immigration from early 1978 include an excerpt from J. Wood (ed.), *Enoch Powell and the 1970 Election* (London: Elliot Right Way Books, 1970), with a note attached. Wood's book itself quotes letters from Powell's supporters across the country asserting that they voted Conservative thanks to his work in the election campaign. It includes speeches by Powell and

Heath and a discussion of the electoral significance of anti-immigration, all of which are used to assert that it was Enoch Powell who won the 1970 general election for the Conservative Party. The excerpt included in Thatcher's personal file on immigration is a speech by Heath in 1970, which called for strict control of immigration and subsidised voluntary repatriation. The book describes this speech as a virtual copy of Powell's arguments. Powell's 'enemies within' speech of June 1970 is also copied for Thatcher, which begins: 'Britain at this moment is under attack'. The note attached to the excerpt reads that Norman Tebbit had 'come across some interesting pronouncements by Ted Heath and Enoch Powell'. Thatcher noted and underlined the text and had it copied for Willie Whitelaw.

62 Speech to Young Conservative Conference, 12 February 1978, MTFW 103487.
63 B. Evans, 'Thatcherism and the British People', in S. Ball and I. Holliday (eds.), *Mass Conservatism: The Conservatives and the Public since the 1880s* (London: Frank Cass, 2002), p. 224.
64 *Daily Telegraph*, 25 April 1981.
65 Powell, quoted in 'Sure Signs that Britain has Returned to Normal', *The Economist*, 26 July 1982.
66 'At the End of the Day', *The Economist*, 19 June 1982.
67 A. Barnett, *Iron Britannia* (London: Allison and Busby, 1982).
68 Speech to Conservative rally at Cheltenham, 3 July 1982, MTFW 104989.
69 Heffer, *Like the Roman*, pp. 844, 879.
70 Powell, in *Enoch Powell on 1992*, ed. R. Ritchie (London: Anaya, 1989), p. 50.
71 Vinen, *Thatcher's Britain*, pp. 225–6.
72 Speech to the College of Europe, Bruges, 20 September 1988, MTFW 107332.
73 Gilroy, *There Ain't No Black in the Union Jack*, p. 133.
74 A. Sivanandan, 'Why Muslims Reject British Values', *The Observer*, 16 October 2005.
75 D. Feldman, 'Why the English like Turbans: Multicultural Politics in British History', in D. Feldman and J. Lawrence (eds.), *Structures and Transformations in Modern British History* (Cambridge University Press, 2011).
76 Cowling, 'The Present Position', p. 1.
77 D. Dixon, 'Thatcher's People: The British Nationality Act 1981', *Journal of Law and Society*, 10 (1983), 161–80, at 171–2.
78 The poster is reproduced in Gilroy, *There Ain't No Black in the Union Jack*, p. 64.
79 Dixon, 'Thatcher's People', 165.
80 Gilroy, *There Ain't No Black in the Union Jack*, p. 65.
81 J. Casey, 'The Revival of Tory Philosophy', *The Spectator*, 17 March 2007.
82 D. Hayes and A. Hudson, *Basildon: The Mood of a Nation* (London: Demos, 2001), p. 19, cited in B. Evans, 'Thatcherism and the British People', in Ball and Holliday, *Mass Conservatism*, p. 237.

6 THATCHER AND THE WOMEN'S VOTE

1 I. Zweiniger-Bargielowska, 'Explaining the Gender Gap: The Conservative Party and the Women's Vote, 1945–1964', in M. Francis and I. Zweiniger-Bargielowska (eds.), *The Conservatives and British Society, 1880–1990* (Cardiff: University of Wales Press, 1996), pp. 194–223, at p. 202.

2 I. Zweiniger-Bargielowska, *Austerity in Britain: Rationing, Controls, and Consumption, 1939–1955* (Oxford University Press, 2000); D. Jarvis, 'Mrs Maggs and Betty: The Conservative Appeal to Women Voters in the 1920s', *Twentieth Century British History*, 5 (1994), 129–52.

3 R. Campbell, *Gender and the Vote in Britain: Beyond the Gender Gap?* (Colchester: ECPR Press, 2006).

4 P. Norris and J. Lovenduski, 'Gender and Party Politics in Britain', in P. Norris and J. Lovenduski (eds.), *Gender and Party Politics* (London: SAGE, 1993), p. 39.

5 D. Butler and D. Kavanagh, *The British General Election of 1983* (New York: Oxford University Press, 1984), p. 296.

6 MORI, 'How Britain Voted since October 1974', available at http://ipsos-rsl.com/researchpublications/researcharchive/poll. aspx?oItemId=101&view=wide (accessed 14 August 2010).

7 Labour Party, *Report of the National Executive Committee Women's Committee, 1992–93*, p. 11. The ITN/Harris polls give a 5 per cent gap in 1983 and a 10 per cent gap in 1992.

8 R. Rose and I. McAllister, *The Loyalties of Voters: A Lifetime Learning Model* (London: SAGE, 1990).

9 The early academic writing on the gender gap in the US includes, 'Men and Women: Is Realignment Under Way?', *Public Opinion* (April/May 1982), 21–32; K. Frankovic, 'Sex and Politics – New Alignments, Old Issues', *Political Studies*, 15 (1982), 438–48; E. Klein, *Gender Politics: From Consciousness to Mass Politics* (Cambridge, MA: Harvard University Press, 1984). Bob Worcester began a 1984 memorandum to the Labour Party polls committee on the subject of the 'gender gap' by noting that 'there has been a great deal of attention drawn recently in the United States to the gender gap': 'The Gender Gap: Women in Britain', confidential memorandum, 16 July 1984. Unless otherwise noted, this and all other MORI material is located in the uncatalogued files of the Labour Party, held at the People's History Museum, Manchester.

10 For a summary of the Thatcher governments' policies affecting women, see J. Lovenduski and V. Randall, *Contemporary Feminist Politics: Women and Power in Britain* (Oxford University Press, 1993), pp. 40–54.

11 The *Red Book 1983* (the collated collection of privately commissioned polls and memoranda prepared by MORI for the Labour Party in the aftermath of the 1983 election) contains a lengthy memorandum entitled 'Women', dated 17 May 1983, addressed to Joyce Gould and apparently prepared at her request.

12 P. Norris, 'Gender: A Gender-Generation Gap?', in G. Evans and P. Norris (eds.), *Critical Elections: British Parties and Voters in Long-Term Perspective* (London: SAGE, 1999), pp. 148–63.

13 Campbell, *Gender and the Vote*, p. 1.

14 B. Campbell, *Iron Ladies: Why Do Women Vote Tory?* (London: Virago, 1987).

15 *Ibid.*, p. 3.

16 'No, I am Not a Feminist': interview with *Hornsey Journal*, 21 April 1978, MTFW 103662.

17 Poster 197/9–33, Digitized Poster Collection, Conservative Party Archive, Bodleian Library, Oxford (hereafter CPA).

18 Interview for *Shropshire Star*, 7 September 1978, MTFW 103750.

19 Speech to Conservative Women's Conference, 24 May 1989, MTFW 107675. For her characterisation of feminists as strident, see interview for *Hornsey Journal*, 21 April 1978, and Scottish press conference, 26 April 1979, MTFW 104045.

20 Speech to British Society of Magazine Editors, 29 July 1988, MTFW 107300. At the same time, Thatcher did increase the budget of the EOC annually throughout her time in office: J. Lovenduski, *Feminising Politics* (London: Polity, 2005), p. 40.

21 B. Campbell and J. Lovenduski, 'What's in it for Women?', *The Guardian*, 2 June 1987.

22 On society, or the lack of it, see interview in *Woman's Own*, 31 October 1987, MTFW 106689. On Thatcher's use of women's media, see W. Webster, 'First Among Unequals', *The Guardian*, 2 May 1989; H. Nunn, *Thatcher, Politics and Fantasy: The Political Culture of Gender and Nation* (London: Lawrence & Wishart, 2002), pp. 126–8.

23 Speech to British Society of Magazine Editors, 29 July 1988.

24 Poster 1978/9–31, CPA.

25 Radio interview for London Broadcasting, 28 April 1979, MTFW 104051.

26 Scottish press conference, 26 April 1979; emphasis in original.

27 Interview for Channel 4 News, 13 June 1986, MTFW 106422; interview for Scottish TV, 4 September 1986, MTFW 106467.

28 Eleanor Rathbone, the inter-war independent MP and leader of the National Union of Societies for Equal Citizenship, was continually frustrated by such suggestions in the 1920s and 1930s. See E. Rathbone, 'Changes in Public Life', in R. Strachey (ed.), *Our Freedom and its Results* (London: Hogarth Press, 1936), pp. 256, 258.

29 Interview with ITN, 11 February 1975, MTFW 102618.

30 E. H. H. Green, *Thatcher* (London: Hodder Arnold, 2006), p. 16.

31 One of the first discussions of this issue occurred in 1950. See H. J. Parry and H. M. Crossley, 'Validity of Responses to Survey Questions', *Public Opinion Quarterly*, 14 (1950), 61–80.

32 Lovenduski and Randall, *Contemporary Feminist Politics*, p. 53.

33 J. Lovenduski, P. Norris and C. Burness, 'The Party and Women', in A. Seldon and S. Ball (eds.), *Conservative Century* (Oxford University Press, 1994), p. 634.

34 Campbell, *Iron Ladies*, p. 233.

35 Nunn, *Thatcher*, p. 17.

36 Notes for MORI polling presentation to Labour Party campaign committee, 25 April 1979. The results were recorded as the 'men lead' in response to the question 'Would you prefer a man as X?' Results were given first for the full panel, then for only the women members. The largest gap was for 'as a trade union official' (full panel +27, women only +10). The response to 'as a magistrate' was full panel +28, women only +31.

37 *Ibid.* As in the above poll, the results were broken down by full panel and women only. The figures for those who believed Thatcher to be each of the following were (full panel, women only): devious (20 per cent, 16 per cent); snobbish (32 per cent, 26 per cent); emotional (16 per cent, 12 per cent); compassionate (16 per cent, 18 per cent); intelligent (52 per cent, 54 per cent). While 52 per cent of the full panel believed Callaghan to be intelligent, only 35 per cent of women did.

38 Lovenduski and Randall, *Contemporary Feminist Politics*, p. 27.

39 MORI poll of 'Women's Attitudes', 1985.

40 D. Smith Wilson, 'A New Look at the Affluent Worker: The Good Working Mother in Post-War Britain', *Twentieth Century British History*, 17 (2006), 206–29.

41 On Thatcher's rhetorical distinctions between 'ordinary' Britons and socialists, see Lawrence and Sutcliffe-Braithwaite, Chapter 7 in this volume.

42 MORI poll of 'Women's Attitudes', 1985.

43 P. Cosgrave, *Thatcher: The First Term* (London: Bodley Head, 1985), p. 5.

44 R. Worcester, memorandum, 26 May 1983, in *Red Book 1983*.

45 The enduring appeal of Thatcher to even self-professed feminists is addressed in J. Burchill, 'Slimeballs Always Hate a Strong Woman', *The Times*, 14 November 2004.

46 Since female enfranchisement, attempts to encourage women to vote for women qua women as candidates have all failed spectacularly. This was most evident in the Women for Westminster campaign, which was launched in 1942, but which foundered in the face of the partisanship surrounding the 1945 election campaign. See L. Beers, 'Women for Westminster: Feminism and the Limits of Non-Partisan Associational Culture', paper presented at the Pacific Coast Conference on British Studies, Seattle, WA, March 2011.

47 26 May 1987 national poll; 2 June 1987 poll in marginals, both in *Red Book 1987*.

48 Campbell, *Iron Ladies*, p. 200.

49 Cosgrave, *The First Term*, p. 6.

50 Radio interview for IRN, 28 November 1980, MTFW 104452.

51 MORI poll of 'Women's Attitudes' 1985. The question on shopping formed part of a broader survey of the division of labour in married households, from which it emerged that 'one job in the house which has traditionally been seen as the husband's role is removing spiders from the bath, but this is one area where major steps have been made towards equality – 65 per cent of wives said that if they found a spider in the bath they would get rid of it themselves', although interestingly only 51 per cent of 18–24-year-olds would do so.

52 Worcester, memorandum, 26 May 1983.

53 Jarvis, 'Mrs. Maggs and Betty', 143.

54 Worcester, memorandum, 26 May 1983; P. Hewitt and D. Mattinson, *Women's Votes: The Key to Winning*, Fabian Research pamphlet no. 353 (London: Fabian Society, 1989), pp. 6–9.

55 Hewitt and Mattinson, *Women's Votes*, pp. 6–9.

56 Rosie Campbell's recent research on gender ideology and issue preference finds women's greater interest in education to be the most substantial difference between the sexes: Campbell, *Gender and the Vote*, pp. 57–8.

57 R. Worcester and N. Grant, confidential memorandum, 1 February 1983, in *Red Book 1983*.

58 Handwritten results of MORI poll, January 1985.

59 L. Elder and S. Greene, 'Parenthood and the Gender Gap', in L. D. Whitaker (ed.), *Voting the Gender Gap* (Urbana, IL: University of Illinois Press, 2008), p. 128.

60 MORI memorandum, 1 June 1987, in *Red Book 1987*.

61 E. Evans, *Thatcher and Thatcherism*, 2nd edn (London: Routledge, 2004), p. 71.

62 I. Dale (ed.), *Conservative Party General Election Manifestos, 1900–1997* (London: Routledge, 2000), p. 320.

63 Hewitt and Mattinson, *Women's Votes*, p. 6.

64 MORI memorandum, 1 June 1987.

65 *Ibid.*

66 National Labour Women's Advisory Committee, *Report to the National Conference of Labour Women* (London, 1988).

67 B. Harrison, *Finding a Role? The United Kingdom 1970–1990* (Oxford University Press, 2010), p. 386.

68 MORI memorandum, 12 May 1987, in *Red Book 1987*.

69 MORI memorandum, 2 June 1987, in *Red Book 1987*.

70 *Ibid.*

71 MORI memorandum, 7 June 1987, in *Red Book 1987*.

72 D. Butler and D. Kavanagh, *The British General Election of 1987* (New York: St Martin's Press, 1988), p. 183.

73 Hewitt and Mattinson, *Women's Votes*, pp. 4–5.

74 R. Worcester and P. Hutton, memorandum to Labour Party Campaign Committee, re. pensioners, 2 June 1987, in *1987 Red Book*; *The Labour Party Advertising Campaign 1987* (commemorative booklet presented by Peter Mandelson to members of the NEC).

7 MARGARET THATCHER AND THE DECLINE OF CLASS POLITICS

1 S. Fielding, 'Rethinking Labour's 1964 Campaign', *Contemporary British History*, 21 (2007), 309–24, and S. Fielding, *The Labour Governments, 1964–70*, vol. I: *Labour and Cultural Change* (Manchester University Press, 2003), chapters 3 and 4.

2 *The New Britain* (Labour Party manifesto, 1964) eschewed class language altogether – appealing instead to 'the people' in various guises, including

'ordinary people' and 'go-ahead people'; see also D. Edgerton, *Warfare State: Britain, 1930–1970* (Cambridge University Press, 2006), esp. chapters 5 and 6, and M. Savage, *Identities and Social Change in Britain Since 1940: The Politics of Method* (Oxford University Press, 2010), esp. chapters 3 and 9.

3 M. Meacher, 'The Coming Class Struggle', *New Statesman*, 4 January 1974.

4 R. Kilroy-Silk, 'Why There Must be no Truce in the Class War', *The Times*, 15 December 1976.

5 *Let us Work Together – Labour's Way out of the Crisis* (Labour Party manifesto, February 1974); *Britain will Win with Labour* (Labour Party manifesto, October 1974); *The Times*, 19 February 1974, p. 4, 25 March 1974, p. 13, and 15 April 1974, p. 7; D. Howell, 'First Draft of Edinburgh Speech', p. 8, HWLL, 2/4/2/1, David Howell papers, Churchill Archive Centre, Cambridge; Thatcher speech to Conservative rally in Edinburgh, 25 April 1979, MTFW 104043: 'There was Denis Healey promising to squeeze the rich until the pips squeaked. He did – only it wasn't just the rich he squeezed, it was all of us *[applause]*'.

6 P. Hutber, *The Decline and Fall of the Middle Class and How it Can Fight Back* (London: Associated Business Programmes, 1976); R. King and N. Nugent (eds.), *Respectable Rebels: Middle-Class Campaigns in Britain in the 1970s* (London: Hodder & Stoughton, 1979).

7 G. H. Gallup, *The Gallup International Public Opinion Polls: Great Britain, 1937–1975*, vol. II: *1965–1975* (New York: Random House, 1976), pp. 1288 [November 1973], 1293 [January 1974], 1295 [February 1974], 1318 [April 1974], and 1404 [May 1975]. Asked 'Do you think there is class struggle in this country or not?', the proportion of respondents agreeing peaked at 62 per cent in the heated context of the February 1974 election; it was at its lowest, 57 per cent, in November 1973. See also D. Butler and D. Stokes, *Political Change in Modern Britain: The Evolution of Electoral Choice*, 2nd edn (London: Macmillan, 1974), p. 477. Butler and Stokes asked: 'On the whole, do you think there is bound to be some conflict between different social classes or do you think they can get along together without any conflict?' The proportion agreeing that there is 'bound to be some conflict' peaked in 1964, when 42 per cent of the sample agreed with this statement, and was at its lowest in 1970, when only 32 per cent agreed.

8 *The Times*, 25 October 1974, p. 17; *Sunday Times*, 9 February 1975, p. 14 (editorial); Thatcher article, 'How Tories Will Face the Unions', *Daily Telegraph*, 15 May 1977, MTFW 103384.

9 J. Campbell, *Margaret Thatcher: The Grocer's Daughter* (London: Pimlico edn, 2001), p. 287; *Sunday Times*, 9 February 1975, p. 14 (editorial: 'The Case for William Whitelaw'); David Kemp interviewing Thatcher for Granada TV's *World in Action* on the eve of the first ballot for the Conservative Party leadership, 31 January 1975, MTFW 102450.

10 R. King, 'The Middle Class Revolt and the Established Parties', in King and Nugent, *Respectable Rebels*; R. King, 'Petit-Bourgeois Conservatism', *Parliamentary Affairs*, 34 (1981), 308–21; E. H. H. Green, *Thatcher* (London: Hodder Arnold, 2006), p. 21.

11 M. Cockerell, *Live From Number 10: The Inside Story of Prime Ministers and Television* (London: Faber, 1988), pp. 215–20, 234–5; Campbell, *Grocer's Daughter*; D. Kavanagh, *Thatcherism and British Politics: The End of Consensus?* 2nd edn (Oxford University Press, 1990), pp. 268–76; P. Cosgrave, *Margaret Thatcher: A Tory and her Party* (London: Hutchinson, 1978).

12 S. Hall and M. Jacques (eds.), *The Politics of Thatcherism* (London: Lawrence & Wishart in association with *Marxism Today*, 1983); A. O'Shea, 'Trusting the People: How Does Thatcherism Work?', in Formations Collective, *Formations of Nation and People* (London: Routledge & Kegan Paul, 1984), pp. 19–41, for whom discourse is as important as ideology; B. Jessop, K. Bonnett, S. Bromley and T. Ling, *Thatcherism: A Tale of Two Nations* (Cambridge: Polity, 1988); A. Gamble, *The Free Economy and the Strong State: The Politics of Thatcherism*, 2nd edn (Basingstoke: Macmillan, 1994).

13 Green, *Thatcher*, pp. 17–21, though Green acknowledges that Thatcher 'felt [middle class] values were widely held' especially within 'the aspirational sector of the skilled working class' (p. 19).

14 D. Cannadine, *Class in Britain* (New Haven and London: Yale University Press, 1998), pp. 171–80, at pp. 173, 177.

15 *Ibid.*, pp. 178, 179.

16 'Thatcherite' here refers to the personal advisors and trusted speech-writers who did most to shape Thatcherite public discourse in opposition: figures such as John Hoskyns, David Howell, Paul Johnson, Ronnie Millar, Alfred Sherman, Norman Strauss and T. E. Utley, as well as Thatcher's key political allies such as Keith Joseph and Geoffrey Howe.

17 A. Sherman, 'The Will-o-the-wisp of the Classless Society', THCR 2/6/1/173 ['Speech Notes on the Classless Society'], Margaret Thatcher papers, Churchill Archives Centre; Sherman, 'Class and Nation (Possible Talk for Blenheim)', 11 July 1977, CPS 6/1 ['MT (Margaret Thatcher) Various Drafts and Speeches (in date order)'], Centre for Policy Studies papers, London School of Economics Archive, London; Thatcher speech to Greater London Young Conservatives (Iain Macleod Memorial Lecture), 4 July 1977, MTFW 103411.

18 See especially S. Evans, 'The Not so Odd Couple: Margaret Thatcher and One Nation Conservatism', *Contemporary British History*, 23 (2009), 101–21; also O'Shea, 'Trusting the People', p. 26. Below we argue that Thatcher recast the 'One Nation' trope in terms of the struggle of the disempowered 'masses' against a bureaucratic, socialist 'elite'.

19 J. Pakulski and M. Waters, *The Death of Class* (London: SAGE, 1996); also A. Gorz, *Farewell to the Working Class* (London: Pluto, 1982).

20 E.g. G. Radice and S. Pollard, *Any Southern Comfort?* Fabian Society pamphlet no. 568 (London: Fabian Society, 1994), pp. 1, 4; P. Gould, *The Unfinished Revolution: How the Modernisers Saved the Labour Party* (London: Little, Brown, 1998), esp. pp. 1–17 – 'Not disadvantaged, not privileged, not quite working-class, not really middle-class – they don't even have a name. I will call them the new middle class' (p. 17).

21 Speech to the Conservative Women's Conference, 21 May 1975, MTFW 102694; speech to the Welsh Conservative Conference, 14 June 1975, MTFW 102713; and speech to the Federation of Conservative Students, 12 July 1975, MTFW 102741. On the ambiguities inherent in talk of 'Middle Britain', see M. Wakefield, 'Is Middle Britain Middle-Income Britain?', Briefing Note 38 (London: Institute for Fiscal Studies, 2003).

22 V. Bogdanor, '1974: The Crisis of Old Labour', in A. Seldon and K. Hickson (eds.), *New Labour, Old Labour: The Wilson and Callaghan Governments, 1974–79* (London: Routledge, 2004); also J. H. Goldthorpe, 'The Current Inflation: Towards a Sociological Account', in F. Hirsch and J. H. Goldthorpe (eds.), *The Political Economy of Inflation* (London: M. Robertson, 1978), esp. pp. 196–201.

23 S. R. Letwin, *The Anatomy of Thatcherism* (London: Fontana, 1992), esp. chapter 2. Matthew Grimley, Chapter 4 in this volume, also traces back a proto-Thatcherite distaste for growing materialism and acquisitiveness to Angus Maude's *The Common Problem* (London: Constable, 1969).

24 S. Brooke, 'Gender and Working-Class Identity in Britain During the 1950s', *Journal of Social History*, 34 (2001), 773–95; also L. Segal, 'Look Back in Anger: Men in the 50s', in R. Chapman and J. Rutherford (eds.), *Male Order: Unwrapping Masculinity* (London: Lawrence & Wishart, 1988), esp. pp. 80–93.

25 N. Dennis, F. Henriques and C. Slaughter, *Coal Is our Life: An Analysis of a Yorkshire Mining Community* (London: Eyre & Spottiswoode, 1956); R. Hoggart, *The Uses of Literacy: Aspects of Working-Class Life with Special Reference to Publications and Entertainments* [1957] (London: Penguin, 1981); M. Young and P. Willmott, *Family and Kinship in East London* [1957] (London: Penguin, 1986).

26 *Seven plus Seven* (1970) and *21* (1977), *Up Series* DVD, discs 2 and 3 (Granada Ventures, 2009); S. Bruzzi, *Seven Up* (London: Palgrave Macmillan, 1999), pp. 16, 77–9.

27 K. Coates and R. Silburn, *Poverty: The Forgotten Englishmen* (London: Penguin, 1970).

28 R. M. Titmuss, *Income Distribution and Social Change: A Study in Criticism* (London: G. Allen & Unwin, 1962); B. Abel-Smith and P. Townsend, *The Poor and the Poorest: A New Analysis of the Ministry of Labour's Family Expenditure Surveys of 1953–54 and 1960* (London: Bell, 1965); P. Townsend, *Poverty in the United Kingdom: A Survey of Household Resources and Standards of Living* (London: Allen Lane, 1979).

29 B. Jackson, *Working Class Community* [1968] (London: Pelican, 1972), esp. chapter 10; J. Seabrook, *The Unprivileged: A Hundred Years of Family Life and Tradition in a Working-Class Street* [1967] (London: Penguin, 1973), p. 147; cf. his later *Working-Class Childhood: An Oral History* (London: Gollancz, 1982); Hoggart, *Uses of Literacy*.

30 J. H. Westergaard, 'Sociology: The Myth of Classlessness', in R. Blackburn (ed.), *Ideology in Social Science: Readings in Critical Social Theory* (London: Fontana, 1972). The essay was written in 1964; a postscript in 1971 suggested that right-wingers might now be graduating towards a

different argument, that society should 'recognize ... the tenacious hold of inequalities as welcome evidence of their inevitability and moral necessity' (p. 153).

31 The debate is summarised in J. H. Goldthorpe *et al.*, *The Affluent Worker in the Class Structure*, 3 vols. (Cambridge University Press, 1968–9), I, p. 1, and III, pp. 21–9, 104–5; also M. Abrams, 'Why Labour Has Lost Elections', *Socialist Commentary* (August 1960), 5–6; M. Abrams and R. Rose, *Must Labour Lose?* (London: Penguin, 1960); F. Zweig, *The Worker in an Affluent Society: Family, Life and Industry* (London: Heinemann, 1961).

32 J. H. Goldthorpe, 'Intellectuals and the Working Class in Modern Britain', in D. Rose (ed.), *Social Stratification and Economic Change* (London: Hutchinson, 1988), p. 54.

33 Goldthorpe *et al.*, *Affluent Worker*, III, pp. 26–7, 107–8.

34 See Meacher, 'Coming Class Struggle', p. 10; R. W. Johnson, 'Must Labour Lose?', in R. W. Johnson, *The Politics of Recession* (London: Macmillan, 1985), p. 263.

35 J. E. Cronin, *New Labour's Pasts: The Labour Party and its Discontents* (Harlow: Pearson/Longman, 2004), chapter 4.

36 'The Shape of Things to Come', *Whatever Happened to the Likely Lads?* series 2, episode 13; P. Wickham, *The Likely Lads* (London: BFI, 2008), pp. 48–9.

37 Savage, *Identities and Social Change*, p. 221; see also M. Savage, 'Working-Class Identities in the 1960s: Revisiting the Affluent Worker Study', *Sociology*, 39 (2005), 929–46.

38 Savage, *Identities and Social Change*, pp. 216–25.

39 M. Savage, 'Sociology, Class and Male Manual Work Cultures', in J. McIlroy *et al.* (eds.), *British Trade Unions and Industrial Politics*, vol. II: *The High Tide of Trade Unionism, 1964–79* (Aldershot: Ashgate, 1999).

40 R. E. Pahl, *Divisions of Labour* (Oxford: Blackwell, 1984), pp. 323–7.

41 *Ibid.*, pp. 322, 324, 326–7; see also R. E. Pahl and C. D. Wallace, 'Neither Angels in Marble nor Rebels in Red: Privatization and Working-Class Consciousness', in Rose, *Social Stratification and Economic Change*.

42 Pahl and Wallace, 'Neither Angels nor Rebels', p. 145.

43 Savage, *Identities and Social Change*, p. 166.

44 Goldthorpe *et al.*, *Affluent Worker*, III, pp. 9, 22–8, 46, 116, 164.

45 F. Zweig, *The New Acquisitive Society* (Chichester: Rose for the Centre for Policy Studies, 1976), pp. 16–17; here he might have been on to something: Goldthorpe and Lockwood downplayed 'normative convergence', apparently unwilling to admit that it might be a highly significant sociological phenomenon in itself.

46 *Ibid.*, p. 26.

47 *Ibid.*, p. 7. For Vaizey's account of his conversion to Conservatism across the 1970s see *The Times*, 3 December 1980.

48 Zweig, *New Acquisitive Society*, pp. 7, 27.

49 *Ibid.*, p. 8.

50 L. Black, *The Political Culture of the Left in Affluent Britain, 1951–64* (Basingstoke: Palgrave, 2003), esp. chapter 6; L. Black and H. Pemberton

(eds.), *An Affluent Society?: Britain's Post-War 'Golden Age'* (Aldershot: Ashgate, 2004); J. Lawrence, 'Class, "Affluence" and the Study of Everyday Life in Britain, c. 1930–1964', *Journal of Cultural and Social History* (forthcoming, 2013).

51 J. Tomlinson, *The Politics of Decline: Understanding Post-War Britain* (Harlow: Longman, 2000); Green, *Thatcher*, pp. 55–6, 71–2; CRD paper, 'Election Strategy: Some Thoughts on a Strategy for an Election Held this Spring', 31 January 1979, THCR, 2/7/1/57; the emphasis is Thatcher's. See also Jim Tomlinson, Chapter 3 in this volume.

52 K. Joseph, *Reversing the Trend: A Critical Re-appraisal of Conservative Economic and Social Policies. Seven Speeches by Sir Keith Joseph* (Chichester: Rose, 1975); A. Denham and M. Garnett, *Keith Joseph* (Chesham: Acumen, 2001), pp. 239–76.

53 K. Joseph, speech on 5 January 1975, in *Reversing the Trend*, pp. 55–6.

54 E. Hobsbawm, 'The Forward March of Labour Halted?', *Marxism Today* (September 1978), 279–86; Joseph, *Reversing the Trend*, p. 57.

55 'The Middle-Class Struggle', 24 August 1976, THCR 2/6/1/173; Hutber, *Decline and Fall*. Keith Joseph and Jonathan Sumption co-authored a book about why equality of outcome was, in fact, absurd: *Equality* (London: J. Murray, 1979). Alfred Sherman made the point bluntly in 'Will-o-the wisp, Notes on Speech (2)', 18 January 1977, THCR 2/6/1/173, arguing that differentiation – i.e. inequality of outcomes – is necessary in order that there are 'prizes for the aspiring'; as for the failures, or 'the deprived' as they were often called, Sherman was damning: 'no one has deprived them of anything, they are inadequate'.

56 Interview, Granada TV *World in Action*, 3 February 1975, MTFW 102450.

57 Speech to Parliamentary Press Gallery, 26 January 1977 (Thatcher CD-ROM). See also Thatcher article, 'My Kind of Tory Party', *Daily Telegraph*, 30 January 1975, MTFW 102600.

58 'How Tories Will Face the Unions', *Sunday Telegraph*, 15 May 1977, MTFW 103384.

59 'The Moral Basis of a Free Society', *Daily Telegraph*, 16 May 1978, MTFW 103687; speech at Finchley, 11 April 1979, MTFW 104002.

60 Speech to the Conservative Trade Unionist Conference, Bradford, 11 March 1978, MTFW 103640.

61 Interview, Granada TV *World in Action*, 3 February 1975; speech to Grantham Conservatives, 4 March 1977, MTFW 103329.

62 Interview, Granada TV *World in Action*, 3 February 1975; interview for *Hornsey Journal*, 21 April 1978, MTFW 103662.

63 For an important argument about the right-wing populist claim to 'ordinariness' in 1960s and 1970s Britain, see A. Whipple, '"Ordinary People": The Cultural Origins of Popular Thatcherism in Britain, 1964–79', unpublished PhD thesis, Northwestern University, 2004 – though as Wilson's populism demonstrated in the 1960s, the discourse of 'ordinariness' remained a contested field shaped largely by the fall-out from imperial (and with it patrician) decline.

64 Conservative Party Election Broadcast (PEB), 'Crisis, What Crisis?', 23 April 1979, available at: www.screenonline.org.uk/tv/id/1389915/index. html (accessed 2 July 2010); 'How Tories Will Face the Unions', *Sunday Telegraph*, 15 May 1977.

65 Speech at Cardiff, 16 April 1979, MTFW 104011; see also Thatcher's talk of 'ordinary working men and women' at Grantham, 4 March 1977.

66 Speech to Conservative Trade Unionists, 29 April 1979, MTFW 104053; emphasis added.

67 Zweig, *New Acquisitive Society*, p. 7.

68 D. Jarvis, '"Behind Every Great Party": Women and Conservatism in Twentieth-Century Britain', in A. Vickery (ed.), *Women, Privilege and Power: British Politics, 1750 to the Present* (Stanford University Press, 2001), pp. 309–14; T. Fitzgerald, 'The New Right and the Family', in M. Loney, D. Boswell and J. Clarke (eds.), *Social Policy and Social Welfare: A Reader* (Milton Keynes: Open University Press, 1983).

69 On the Conservatives' remarkable faith in the health of the nuclear family in the 1970s, see F. Sutcliffe-Braithwaite, 'The Origins and Development of Thatcherite Social Policy, 1975–1979', unpublished MPhil dissertation, University of Cambridge, 2010, and Matthew Grimley, Chapter 4 in this volume.

70 Speech to Grantham Conservatives, 4 March 1977.

71 Speech to Greater London Young Conservatives, 4 July 1977.

72 E. Biagini, *Liberty, Retrenchment and Reform: Popular Liberalism in the Age of Gladstone, 1860–1880* (Cambridge University Press, 1992); A. Howe, *Free Trade and Liberal England, 1846–1946* (Oxford: Clarendon Press, 1997); F. Trentmann, *Free Trade Nation: Commerce, Consumption and Civil Society in Modern Britain* (Oxford University Press, 2008).

73 On Thatcherism's links to 1960s radical populism, see R. Cockett, 'The New Right and the 1960s: The Dialectics of Liberation', in G. Andrews *et al.* (eds.), *New Left, New Right and Beyond: Taking the Sixties Seriously* (Basingstoke: Palgrave, 1999).

74 P. Rock, CRD paper on 'Housing Finance', 20 November 1975, THCR 2/6/1/42; original emphasis.

75 Green, *Thatcher*, p. 20; G. K. Fry, *The Politics of the Thatcher Revolution: An Interpretation of British Politics, 1979–1990* (Basingstoke: Palgrave Macmillan, 2008), p. 11. Green is adamant that this was party code for 'the middle classes' but we argue that it should rather be seen as code for all those, of whatever class, who had already embraced the vigorous 'bourgeois' virtues of self-help and independence.

76 Speech to the Bow Group, 16 May 1978, MTFW 103674. At about this time Patrick Dunleavy was developing his influential thesis about the politics of housing and the new 'consumption classes': see P. Dunleavy, 'The Urban Bases of Political Alignment', *British Journal of Political Science*, 9 (1979), 409–43.

77 Interview for Tyne-Tees TV, 1 July 1977, MTFW 103410.

78 Interview with Gordon Burns, Granada TV *World in Action*, 27 January 1978, MTFW 103485.

79 Conservative PEB, 'The International Prosperity Race', 19 April 1979, MTFW 104028.
80 Sutcliffe-Braithwaite, 'The Origins and Development of Thatcherite Social Policy'.
81 R. Thaler and C. Sunstein, *Nudge: Improving Decisions About Health, Wealth and Happiness* (New Haven, CT, and London: Yale University Press, 2008); M. Thatcher, 'Reflections on Liberty', in S. Pugliese (ed.), *The Political Legacy of Margaret Thatcher* (London: Politico's, 2003), p. 3.
82 Letwin, *Anatomy of Thatcherism*.
83 Hoskyns, 'Election "Game-Plan"', 4 April 1979, HOSK 1/241, Sir John Hoskyns papers, Churchill Archives Centre.
84 Conservative PEB, 'The International Prosperity Race', 19 April 1979, and similarly in Conservative PEB, 25 April 1979, available at Keele University: www.politicsresources.net/area/uk/pebs/con79.htm (accessed 2 July 2010).
85 Conservative PEB, 27 April 1979, MTFW 104050.
86 J. Hoskyns and N. Strauss, 'The Stepping Stones Programme', 19 January 1978, THCR 2/6/1/245; emphasis in original. This was indeed about selling a moralised vision of 'the healthy society' to the electorate, a point drawn out by Matthew Grimley, Chapter 4 in this volume.
87 Conservative PEBs, 19 and 23 April 1979. Some ascribe undue significance to these broadcasts: see D. Haigron, 'Targeting "Essex Man" and "C2 Wives": The Representation of the Working Class Electorate in the Conservative Party Political Broadcasts (1970s and 1980s)', in A. Capet (ed.), *The Representation of Working People in Britain and France* (Newcastle-upon-Tyne: Cambridge Scholars, 2009). More generally see B. Evans, 'Thatcherism and the People', in S. Ball and I. Holliday (eds.), *Mass Conservatism: The Conservatives and the Public since the 1880s* (London: Frank Cass, 2002).
88 'Speechwriters Conference, 19 April 1979', Conservative Central Office, p. 3, HWLL, 2/4/2/3; 'Game-Plan No. 2', 21 April 1979, p. 3, HOSK 1/248; D. Butler and D. Kavanagh, *The British General Election of 1979* (London: Macmillan, 1980), pp. 138–41, 222–3.
89 Conservative PEB, 7 June 1983, MTFW 105382.
90 Quoted in A. H. Halsey, *A History of Sociology in Britain: Science, Literature, and Society* (Oxford University Press, 2004), pp. 131 ff.
91 Evidence of correspondence with sociologists and social scientists is found in KJ 18/1, 18/2, and 29/5, Keith Joseph papers, Conservative Party Archive, Bodleian Library, Oxford. On Joseph's experience with the SSRC-funded research programme on 'Transmitted Deprivation' in the early 1970s, see Denham and Garnett, *Keith Joseph*, pp. 197, 379 (n. 31); J. Welshman, 'Where Lesser Angels Might Have Feared to Tread: The Social Science Research Council and Transmitted Deprivation', *Contemporary British History*, 23 (2009), 199–219.
92 'If You See Sid, Tell Him' (1986).
93 Speech to Scottish Conservative Conference, Perth, 15 May 1987, MTFW 106814.
94 *Ibid.*

8 DEFIANT DOMINOES: WORKING MINERS AND
THE 1984–5 STRIKE

1 D. H. Lawrence, 'The Miner at Home', originally published in *The Nation*, 16 March 1912.

2 *The Times*, 7 March 1984.

3 For example, PMQ, 26 July 1984, MTFW 105730; interview for the *Financial Times*, 31 August 1984, MTFW 105508.

4 H. Francis, 'Learning From Bitter Experience: The Making of the NUM', in A. Campbell, N. Fishman and D. Howell (eds.), *Miners, Unions and Politics 1910–47* (Aldershot: Ashgate, 1996), pp. 253–72.

5 For the origins and politics of the Power Group, see R. Ottey, *The Strike: An Insider's Story* (London: Sidgwick and Jackson, 1985).

6 For Areas identified with the NUM right, see C. Griffin, *The Leicestershire Miners*, vol. III: *1945–1988* (Coalville: NUM Leicester Area, 1988); D. Howell, *The Politics of the NUM: A Lancashire View* (Manchester University Press, 1989); K. Gildart, *North Wales Miners: A Fragile Unity, 1945–1996* (Cardiff: University of Wales Press, 2001).

7 The politics of the NUM is covered in two volumes by A. Taylor, *The NUM and British Politics* (Aldershot: Ashgate, 2003).

8 The rise of the left in Yorkshire is analysed in A. Taylor, *The Politics of the Yorkshire Miners* (Beckenham: Croom Helm, 1984).

9 Scargill's opponents were Trevor Bell (COSA), Ray Chadburn (Nottinghamshire) – who failed to secure the formal support of his own Area – and Bernard Donaghy (Lancashire), a nomination designed to prevent Gormley's Area from being tempted by Scargill.

10 Monopolies and Mergers Commission, *National Coal Board: A Report on the Efficiency and Costs in the Development, Production and Supply of Coal by the NCB*, 2 vols. (London: HMSO, 1983). For an analysis of one Area in this context, see J. Phillips, 'Workplace Conflict and the Origins of the 1984–85 Miners' Strike in Scotland', *Twentieth Century British History*, 20 (2009), 152–72.

11 The Derbyshire case was Langwith, where the NUM fragmented over a proposal for a national overtime ban. See Howell, *Politics of the NUM*, pp. 62–5. The Nottinghamshire ballot on Teversal is in NUM Nottinghamshire Area Minutes, March 1979; these and other records of the NUM Nottingham Area are held at the Area office in Mansfield.

12 Taylor, *NUM and British Politics*, II, pp. 122–33; also Howell, *Politics of the NUM* pp. 48–58.

13 See Taylor, *NUM and British Politics*, II, pp. 153–66.

14 NUM Special Delegate Conference, October 1983, pp. 849–50. Papers relating to the NUM's National Executive Committee (NEC) and national conferences are held at the NUM national office in Barnsley.

15 For Scotland, see Phillips, 'Workplace Conflict'.

16 NUM NEC, 8 March 1984.

17 For the text, see National Union of Mineworkers Rules.

18 Ottey, *The Strike*, pp. 60–9. The three were Ottey, Trevor Bell and Ted Mackay of North Wales.

19 J. Winterton and R. Winterton, *Coal Crisis and Conflict: The 1984–85 Miners' Strike in Yorkshire* (Manchester University Press, 1989), pp. 66–8, and more generally Taylor, *NUM and British Politics*, II, pp. 174–93.

20 For an attempt to construct a pro-ballot NEC majority, see Ottey, *The Strike*, pp. 79–84; Howell, *Politics of the NUM*, pp. 118–20.

21 NUM Special Delegate Conference, 19 April 1984.

22 For the background to Nottinghamshire mining politics, see R. Waller, *The Dukeries Transformed: The Social and Political Development of a Twentieth Century Coalfield* (Oxford: Clarendon Press, 1983); W. J. Morgan and K. Coates, 'The Nottinghamshire Coalfield and the British Miners' Strike 1984–85', *University of Nottingham Occasional Papers in Local History*, 5 (1991); D. Gilbert, *Class, Community and Collective Action: Social Change in Two British Coalfields, 1850–1926* (Oxford: Clarendon Press, 1992); C. Griffin, '"Notts Have Some Very Peculiar History": Understanding the Reaction of the Nottinghamshire Miners to the 1984–85 Strike', *Historical Studies in Industrial Relations*, 19 (2005), 63–99. Nottinghamshire colliery studies emphasising attitudes to work and cooperation are presented in J. Krieger, *Undermining Capitalism: State Ownership and the Dialectic of Control in the British Coal Industry* (London: Pluto, 1984).

23 The analyses of Gilbert and Waller focus on contrasting parts of the coalfield. In 1984 their behaviour was similar. The Yorkshire NUM branches close to Nottinghamshire included pits in the Doncaster area with political traditions well to the left.

24 Richardson had defeated David Prendergast by 4,147 to 3,973 on the sixth count with 8,716 votes non-transferable: NUM Nottinghamshire Area Minutes, 1982.

25 NUM Nottinghamshire Area Minutes, Executive Council, 10 March 1984.

26 For an account from within the Nottinghamshire Constabulary, including material on the death of David Jones, see C. Sheppard and G. Marsden, 'The Policing of the NUM Dispute 1984/5: Part A, The Nottinghamshire Experience; Part B, In the National Context' (unpublished typescript in possession of the author). I am grateful to the late Ken Coates for this material.

27 The details of the ballot are in NUM Nottinghamshire Area Minutes. See Conference of Branch Officials and Committee Men, 18 March 1984, Executive and Council Minutes 1984.

28 The pickets' experience is presented in *Thurcroft: A Village and the Miners' Strike, by the People of Thurcroft* (Nottingham: Spokesman, 1986), pp. 63–99.

29 NUM Nottinghamshire Area Minutes, Executive Council, 20 April 1984; Executive, 26 April 1984; also Meeting of Branch Officials and Committee Men, 25 April, with Scargill and Heathfield present.

30 For a description by a member of the anti-strike lobby, see C. Butcher and M. Seymour, *The Link-Up of Friendship: The Story of 'Silver Birch' and the Working Miners During the 1984–85 Strike* (privately printed, 1991), pp. 6–10.

31 NUM National Executive Committee minutes, 10 May 1984.

32 The changeover can be charted in the membership and subsequent decisions of the Area's institutions. See Morgan and Coates, 'The Nottinghamshire Coalfield', for the thoroughness of this change. Details of some branch ballots are in the *Mansfield Chronicle and Advertiser*, 5 July 1984.

33 For Leicestershire, see Griffin, *The Leicestershire Miners*, pp. 230–68; D. Bell, *The Dirty Thirty: Heroes of the Miners' Strike* (Nottingham: Five Leaves, 2009); and for Nottinghamshire, K. Stanley, *Notts Miners Do Strike!* (Mansfield: NUM, 2010). See Morgan and Coates, 'The Nottinghamshire Coalfield', for an estimate of the long-term number of Nottinghamshire strikers.

34 Butcher and Seymour, *The Link-Up of Friendship*, pp. 12–18.

35 *New Statesman*, 14 December 1984. See also the appeal tabled by Bottomore's Bentinck branch, NUM Nottinghamshire Area Minutes, 26 November 1984, calling for public disassociation from the Working Miners' Committees.

36 Author's discussions with Jim Lord, 1987.

37 *New Statesman*, 14, 21 December 1984.

38 For an analysis see K. D. Ewing, 'The Strike, the Courts and the Rule-Books', *Industrial Law Journal*, 14 (1985), 160–75.

39 The only case where the union won in court on the question of the strike's official status was in Scotland: see *ibid.*, 162–3.

40 *New Statesman*, 21 December 1984.

41 See *Taylor and Foulstone v. National Union of Mineworkers (Yorkshire Area) and National Union of Mineworkers*, 28 September 1984, in *Industrial Relations Law Reports* (1985).

42 NUM Nottinghamshire Area Minutes, Council, 20 December 1984.

43 *Clarke and others v. Chadburn and others*, 18 July 1984, in *Industrial Relations Law Reports* (1985).

44 NUM Nottinghamshire Area Minutes, Council, 20 December 1984.

45 These developments can be traced in the Nottinghamshire Area Records, January–July 1985. Opinions of Nottinghamshire miners about the split can be found in A. J. Richards, *Miners on Strike: Class Solidarity and Division in Britain* (Oxford: Berg, 1996), chapter 7.

46 National Union of Mineworkers, Report of Special Rules Revision Conference, 1985.

47 F. Beckett and D. Hencke, *Marching to the Fault Line: The 1984 Miners' Strike and the Death of Industrial Britain* (London: Constable, 2009), pp. 219–28 (based on NCB Records 31/443, 444, 465 in the National Archives).

48 NUM Nottinghamshire Area Minutes, Council, 25 March 1985, receiving report of meeting held on 14 March.

49 NUM Nottinghamshire Area Minutes, Special Executive, 23 August 1985.

50 For Leicestershire, see Griffin, *The Leicestershire Miners*, pp. 269–307; for North Wales, Gildart, *North Wales Miners*, pp. 189–201; for Lancashire, Howell, *Politics of the NUM*, pp. 179–92.

51 In addition, Newark had a significant mining vote between 1950 and 1979. In the north of the county, many of Bassetlaw's miners were members of

the NUM's Yorkshire Area. Its political trajectory in the 1980s showed no post-strike shift against Labour.

52 The socially mixed Newark seat was gained by the Conservatives.

53 The rejected NUM nominee, Jimmy Hood, an Ollerton branch official, was also a Scot. Having taken a leading role in the strike, he was elected for Clydesdale in 1987. I am grateful to Jimmy Hood and Andy Stewart for their insights.

54 For a pre-strike portrait of his mining constituents, see Stewart's maiden speech in the Commons: Hansard, HC Deb., 5th series, vol. 48, cols. 746–8 (11 November 1983).

55 The note was dated 15 September 1984. The meeting included three officials, Stewart, Thatcher and her PPS, Michael Alison. When Stewart disagreed with the official position on two issues, Thatcher turned to her officials and said: 'I told you we were wrong, Andy has confirmed my view.' Copy of letter and supporting material provided by Andy Stewart. It may be significant that this meeting took place immediately after the collapse of apparently fruitful talks between the NUM and the Coal Board.

56 Hansard, HL Deb., 5th series, vol. 457, col. 240 (13 November 1984).

57 See, for example, *Mansfield Chronicle and Advertiser*, 1 November 1984.

58 For example: 'A Vote for the Left-Wing Labour Candidate is a Vote Against the Majority of the Nottinghamshire Miners and their Families', *Mansfield Chronicle and Advertiser*, 4 June 1987.

59 Charles Hendy, in Hansard, HC Deb., 5th series, vol. 235, col. 764 (18 January 1994).

60 Hansard, HC Deb., 5th series, vol. 72, col. 641 (4 February 1985).

61 Hansard, HC Deb., 5th series, vol. 155, col. 770 (26 June 1989).

62 The Conservative vote fell heavily in Mansfield but only slightly in Ashfield. Stewart's vote in Sherwood showed a very small increase. The swing to Labour in the coalfield seats was based significantly on a sharp decline in the Liberal Democrat vote.

9 THATCHERISM, UNIONISM AND NATIONALISM: A
COMPARATIVE STUDY OF SCOTLAND AND WALES

1 The study of devolution is dominated by political scientists, and recent contributions include: J. Mitchell, *Devolution in the United Kingdom* (Manchester University Press, 2009); V. Bogdanor, *Devolution in the United Kingdom* (Oxford University Press, 2001); H. Bochel, D. Denver, J. Mitchell and J. Pattie, *Scotland Decides: The Devolution Issue and the 1997 Referendum* (London: Frank Cass, 2000); J. B. Jones and D. Balsom (eds.), *The Road to the National Assembly for Wales* (Cardiff: University of Wales Press, 2000); and B. Taylor and K. Thomson (eds.), *Scotland and Wales: Nations Again?* (Cardiff: University of Wales Press, 1999).

2 The phrase was coined by John Smith.

3 The classic account of Scottish unionism is J. Mitchell, *Conservatives and the Union: A Study of Conservative Party Attitudes to Scotland* (Edinburgh University Press, 1990), but see also C. Kidd, *Union and Unionisms: Political Thought in Scotland, 1500–2000* (Cambridge University Press, 2008) for the

longer perspective. For Wales, see J. Osmond, *The National Question Again: Welsh Political Identity in the 1980s* (Dyfed: Gomer Press, 1985); M. Cragoe, *Culture, Politics and National Identity in Wales, 1832–1886* (Oxford University Press, 2004), demonstrates the limited historical impact of unionism on Welsh politics, as does F. Abdul, 'The Conservatives in Wales, 1880–1935', in M. Francis and I. Zweiniger-Bargielowska (eds.), *The Conservatives and British Society, 1880–1990* (Cardiff: University of Wales Press, 1996).

4 See, for example, *Scottish Control, Scottish Affairs: Unionist Policy* (Glasgow: Scottish Unionist Association, 1949), and Churchill's speech in Edinburgh, 14 February 1950, denouncing London control: *The Times*, 15 February 1950, p. 4. Labour's Secretary of State for Scotland in the 1960s, William Ross, made great play of the threat of nationalism in order to secure greater state investment north of the border: see S. Wilkes, *Industrial Policy and the Motor Industry* (Manchester University Press, 1984), p. 286.

5 I. G. C. Hutchison, *Scottish Politics in the Twentieth Century* (Basingstoke: Palgrave, 2000), pp. 104–17.

6 Cragoe, *Culture, Politics and National Identity,* demonstrates that the party did try to project an image of itself as patriotically Welsh and British but was handicapped by its association with the aristocracy, pp. 99–111.

7 The difference between a unitary and a union state in a British context was first theorised by S. Rokkan and D. Urwin, *Economy, Territory, Identity: Politics of West European Peripheries* (London: SAGE, 1983), p. 218.

8 Thatcher's frustration with the Scots is clearly apparent in M. Thatcher, *The Downing Street Years* (London, HarperCollins, 1993), pp. 618–24.

9 See D. Stewart, *The Path to Devolution and Change: A Political History of Scotland Under Margaret Thatcher* (London: I.B. Tauris, 2009), which highlights the impact of socio-economic change; K. D. George and Lynn Mainwaring, *The Welsh Economy* (Cardiff: University of Wales Press, 1988); and, more generally, J. Davies, *A History of Wales* (London: Penguin, 2007), pp. 650–70.

10 Bochel *et al.*, *Scotland Decides.*

11 This is particularly prominent in Scotland, due to the comparative ease of accessing memoirs such as Canon Kenyon Wright, *The People Say Yes: The Making of Scotland's Parliament* (Glendaruell: Argyll Press, 2003); or the Scottish Constitutional Convention's *Claim of Right*, ed. Owen Dudley Edwards (Edinburgh: Polygon, 1989), and *Towards Scotland's Parliament: A Report to the Scottish People* (Edinburgh: Convention, 1990); and the populist work of journalists such as the former *Herald* editor Arnold Kemp, *The Hollow Drum: Scotland Since the War* (Edinburgh: Mainstream, 1993); Chris Harvie and Peter Jones, *The Road to Home Rule: Images of Scotland's Cause* (Edinburgh: Polygon, 2000); and the BBC's political commentator, Brian Taylor, *The Road to the Scottish Parliament* (Edinburgh University Press, 2002). All these rely more on personal anecdote than on statistical evidence.

12 For the significance of civil society as an explanatory force for home rule, particularly among political and social scientists, see P. Lynch, *Scottish Government and Politics: An Introduction* (Edinburgh University Press, 2001), p. 184; D. McCrone, *Understanding Scotland: The Sociology of a*

Nation (New York: Routledge, 2001), p. 122; A. Brown, D. McCrone and L. Paterson, *Politics and Society in Scotland*, 2nd edn (Basingstoke: Macmillan, 1998), p. 122; and L. Paterson, *The Autonomy of Modern Scotland* (Edinburgh University Press, 1994), p. 12.

13 See R. J. Finlay, 'Thatcherism, Civil Society and the Road to Home Rule: Scotland 1980–1997', in A. J. Murdoch (ed.), *The Scottish Nation: Identity and History, Essays in Honour of William Ferguson* (Edinburgh: John Donald, 2007), pp. 136–56.

14 Mitchell, *Conservatives and the Union*, pp. 17–38.

15 *Ibid.*, and Hutchison, *Scottish Politics*.

16 T. Devine, 'The Break-Up of Britain? Scotland and the End of Empire', *Transactions of the Royal Historical Society*, 16 (2006), 163–80, for the role of the state in revitalising the Union.

17 The differential in the share of the vote between the Conservatives and Labour between 1955 and 1979 was 7.9 per cent and actually declined to 6.5 per cent in 1983. The real gap appeared in 1987 with Labour at an unprecedented 18 per cent margin.

18 R. Johnston *et al.*, 'Labour Electoral Landslides and the Changing Efficiency of Voting Distributions', *Transactions of the Institute of British Geographers*, 27 (2002), 336–61.

19 McCrone, *Understanding Scotland*, pp. 84, 103–7.

20 Scottish Tories still constantly referred to themselves as unionists, unlike Welsh colleagues. There may be a chicken-and-egg scenario here: Scots felt the Union to be more under threat than their Welsh colleagues, so were more likely to use the unionist label as a badge of identity.

21 For the tradition of an 'Orange' vote for Conservatism in Scotland, see I. G. C. Hutchison, 'Working Class Politics', in R. A. Cage (ed.), *The Working Class in Glasgow, 1750–1914* (London: Croom Helm, 1987), pp. 128–30; T. Gallagher, *Glasgow, the Uneasy Peace: Religious Tension in Modern Scotland, 1819–1914* (Manchester University Press, 1987), pp. 134–82; E. McFarland, *Protestants First: Orangeism in Nineteenth Century Scotland* (Edinburgh University Press, 1990); and for its influence into the 1950s see D. Seawright and J. Curtice, 'The Decline of the Scottish Conservative and Unionist Party, 1950–92', *Contemporary Record*, 9 (1995), 319–42.

22 P. R. Roberts 'The Act of Union in Welsh History', *Transactions of the Honourable Society of Cymmodorion* (1974), 49–72.

23 Contemporaries paid little attention to the impact of the electoral system in Scotland and Wales. See, for example, A. H. Wood, *The Times Guide to the House of Commons* (London: Times Newspapers, 1987); *Newsweek*, 22 June 1987, p. 10; *Contemporary Review*, 251 (1987), p. 251; and an academic endorsement from D. Denver, 'The British General Election of 1987: Some Preliminary Reflections', *British Journal of Political Science*, 19 (1989), 448–57.

24 Publicly it was asserted that 'Northern Ireland was as British as Finchley', although recently released documents suggest that Thatcher was not prepared to stand in the way of Irish unity. See W. V. Shannon (former US

ambassador to Ireland), 'The Anglo-Irish Agreement', *Foreign Affairs* (Spring 1986), 849–70.

25 See Marc Mulholland, Chapter 10 in this volume, for the Northern Irish dimension of the Thatcher years.

26 D. Torrance, *We In Scotland: Thatcherism in a Cold Climate* (Edinburgh: Birlinn, 2010), pp. 138–9.

27 For the 'Scotland is British' group and the attitude of Scottish Young Conservatives, see *ibid.*, pp. 20, 184.

28 *The Economist*, 29 April 1989, p. 32; P. Walker, *Staying Power: An Autobiography* (London: Bloomsbury, 1991), chapter 15.

29 Speech to Glasgow Conservatives, 19 January 1979, MTFW 103929.

30 See Devine, 'Break-Up of Britain', and R. J. Finlay, *Modern Scotland, 1914–2000* (London: Profile, 2004), pp. 235–316.

31 Speech to Scottish Conservative Conference, 13 May 1988, MTFW 107240; but see also I. McLean, 'Adam Smith and the Modern Left', available at: www.nuff.ox.ac.uk/politics/papers/2005/mclean %20smith.pdf.

32 Quoted in *Scottish Field*, 8 March 1989, and repeated in the press at the time.

33 For example, the 1984–5 miners' strike was associated with the destruction of a British industry and the communities that depended on it, but did not have a separate Scottish or Welsh dimension: see the near-contemporary M. Adeney and J. Lloyd, *The Miners' Strike, 1984–85: Loss Without Limit* (London: Routledge, 1986). A British outlook was also maintained by workers in the steel industry, although as the closure of Ravenscraig became more likely, the Scottish novelist James Kelman published *Fighting for Survival: The Steel Industry in Scotland* (Glasgow: Clydeside Press, 1990).

34 This was reinforced at the Conservative Party Conference on 10 October 1986 when Thatcher reacted to the fact that the Labour Party had adopted the red rose as its new symbol by proclaiming that 'The rose I am wearing is the rose of England', MTFW 106498.

35 The issue was highlighted in the Scottish Television broadcast by George Rosie, *Scotching the Myth* (September 1990).

36 For example, Malcolm Rifkind in Hansard, HC Deb., 5th series, vol. 143, col. 779 (15 December 1988).

37 As 'old' employment gave way to 'new' employment by 1986 a gap had emerged between average wages in Scotland and England: 'Average Earnings of Employees: Scotland and Great Britain', in Scottish Executive, *Scottish Economic Statistics* (Edinburgh: HMSO, 2001), p. 99.

38 According to John Home Robertson, for Labour, 'The hard right of the Conservative Party would be happy for Scotland to be out of the Union': Hansard, HC Deb., 5th series, vol. 152, col. 727 (3 May 1989). Jim Wallace for the Liberals claimed that 'The most serious threat to the Union comes from this Tory government': Hansard, HC Deb., 5th series, vol. 126, col. 350 (27 January 1988).

39 *Radical Scotland*, 29 (October/November 1987), p. 6, concluded that there was a 'national' dimension in determining the outcome of the election in

Scotland and this analysis quickly became the orthodoxy in the Scottish media.

40 *Ibid.* The initial analysis was that the Scots and the Welsh were more egalitarian and supportive of the public sector and rejected the selfish individualism of Thatcherism, but this was not related, as yet, to a demand or a need for political devolution.

41 A good example of this backward projection of the significance of nationalism that emerged in the late 1980s is L. Paterson (ed.), *A Diverse Assembly: The Debate on a Scottish Parliament* (Edinburgh University Press, 1998).

42 *Radical Scotland* was foremost in championing tactical voting and though the debate was carried into the Scottish broadsheets, with a probable readership of not more than 300,000, it is questionable whether it substantively influenced the outcome of the 1987 general election.

43 See Finlay, 'Thatcherism, Civil Society and the Road to Home Rule', for social and economic change.

44 A. Midwinter, M. Keating and J. Mitchell, *Politics and Public Policy in Scotland* (Basingstoke: Macmillan, 1991), p. 113, charts the increase in public spending and employment.

45 '[M]oney that could have been invested in new industries, new opportunities, went instead trying to keep yesterday's jobs alive': speech to Scottish Conservative Conference, 13 May 1988, MTFW 107240.

46 The Scottish novelist William McIlvanney claimed that Scottish identity was rooted in industrial history: *Radical Scotland* (December/January 1988), p. 20.

47 See Kelman, *Fighting for Survival.*

48 *The Economist*, 22 December 1990, pp. 28–9.

49 As David Torrance points out, the 'sermon' was received rather neutrally by ministers: Torrance, *We in Scotland*, pp. 169–74. Nonetheless, like the Scottish Cup Final in 1988, when fans showed the Iron Lady the red card, this was soon incorporated into a demonology of Thatcherism.

50 'Scotland's Industrial Armies', *Radical Scotland* (December/January 1985), p. 20; 'Scottish Low Pay Unit', *STUC Review*, 42 (1989); many more examples are cited in Stewart, *The Path to Devolution.*

51 'Changes in Housing Tenure, Scotland 1949–99', in Scottish Executive, *Scottish Economic Statistics*, p. 129, shows that the rate of right-to-buy only increased after 1987 when the worst of the downturn was over. The same trend is apparent in Wales where the number of sales reached a peak in 1989 which was more than double the 1985 level.

52 This is demonstrated in average earnings and rates of employment relative to the United Kingdom as a whole throughout the 1980s: see http://new.wales. gov.uk/topics/statistics/headlines/pop-2007/hdw200704181/?lang=en and Scottish Executive, *Scottish Economic Statistics.*

53 This was very apparent in Thatcher's speech to the Scottish Conservative Conference, 13 May 1988: 'I won't be discouraged by temporary setbacks. I did not come into politics to take short cuts, or court easy popularity. My principles are not at the mercy of the opinion polls.'

54 J. Ross, 'Grasping the Doomsday Nettle – Methodically', *Radical Scotland*, 30 (December/January 1988), p. 7.

55 As is explicitly stated in the 1988 *Claim of Right*.
56 This was something that Scottish Tories came to believe themselves, particularly the perception that they were anti-Scottish: see *The Scotsman*, 10 September 1987.
57 Government reaction to the Convention's claims is covered in A. Brown and J. Parry (eds.), *The Scottish Government Yearbook 1990* (Edinburgh: Paul Harris, 1991), pp. 24–40.
58 See Wright, *The People Say Yes*: the notion of popular sovereignty harked back to a ruling in the 1950s by Lord Cooper that parliamentary sovereignty was not a constitutional idea recognised in Scots law.
59 McCrone, *Understanding Scotland*, pp. 104–27, 149–75.
60 As was indicated in the Scottish Conservative Conferences in 1989 and 1990. The appointment of John Redwood in 1993 and Michael Forsyth in 1995, both dedicated Thatcherites, as Welsh and Scottish Secretaries respectively, increased the perception of a continuing Thatcherite revolution, despite John Major's succession.
61 *The Scotsman*, 2 February 1989, covering the delivery of a 300,000-strong petition against the Poll Tax to Downing Street.
62 See the evidence of annual opinion poll surveys in the *Scottish Government Yearbook* (Edinburgh: Paul Harris, 1988–94).
63 For a more positive interpretation of the role of civil society, see L. Paterson and R. Wyn Jones, 'Does Civil Society Drive Constitutional Change?', in Taylor and Thomson, *Scotland and Wales*, pp. 169–99, and 'Why Didn't Scots Vote Tory', *BBC Scotland Investigates*, broadcast 9 May 2010.
64 M. Fry, 'Scotland Alone', *Prospect*, 16 December 2006.
65 See, for example, Michael Forsyth's gesture of returning the Stone of Destiny taken by Edward I, and John Major's decision to hold the 1992 European summit in Edinburgh.

10 'JUST ANOTHER COUNTRY'? THE IRISH QUESTION
IN THE THATCHER YEARS

1 See M. Mulholland, 'Irish Republican Politics and Violence before the Peace Process', *European Review of History: Revue européenne d'histoire*, 14 (2007), 403–4.
2 'The historical significance of devolution was to hold Ulster for the Union': A. Aughey, *Under Siege: Ulster Unionism and the Anglo-Irish Agreement* (London: C. Hurst & Co., 1989), p. 103.
3 P. O'Malley, *The Uncivil Wars: Ireland Today* (Belfast: Blackstaff Press, 1983), p. 331.
4 T. E. Utley, *Lessons of Ulster* (London: Dent, 1975), p. 147.
5 S. Heffer, *Like the Roman: The Life of Enoch Powell* (London: Weidenfeld & Nicolson, 1998), p. 762.
6 *Belfast Telegraph*, 11 September 1974.
7 *Belfast Telegraph*, 11 May 1990.
8 *Belfast Telegraph*, 13 August 1977, 8 April 1978.
9 M. Dillon, *The Dirty War* (London: Hutchinson, 1988), p. 287.

10 J. Prior, *A Balance of Power* (London: Hamish Hamilton, 1986), p. 194.

11 E. Moloney and A. Pollak, *Paisley* (Dublin: Poolbeg, 1986), p. 339.

12 Humphrey Atkins, quoted in E. Moloney, *The Secret History of the IRA* (London: Allen Lane, 2002), p. 171.

13 E. P. Kaufmann, *The Orange Order: A Contemporary Northern Irish History* (New York: Oxford University Press, 2007), p. 121.

14 B. Arnold, *What Kind of Country?: Modern Irish Politics, 1968–1983* (London: Jonathan Cape, 1984), pp. 147–8.

15 C. O'Leary, S. Elliott and R. A. Wilford, *The Northern Ireland Assembly, 1982–1986: A Constitutional Experiment* (London: C. Hurst & Co., 1988), p. 47.

16 P. Arthur, 'Anglo-Irish Relations and Constitutional Policy', in P. Mitchell and R. Wilford (eds.), *Politics in Northern Ireland* (Boulder, CO: Westview Press, 1999), p. 248.

17 See, for example, Heffer, *Like the Roman*, p. 831. Oddly, an Irish minister involved in the Anglo-Irish Agreement of 1985 was later to claim that the US government had tried to link support for the Agreement to banning Aeroflot from Shannon airport! *Irish Times*, 25–29 August, 1989; P. Keatinge, 'Ireland's Foreign Relations in 1989', *Irish Studies in International Affairs*, 3 (1990), 155.

18 P. Arthur, *Special Relationships: Britain, Ireland and the Northern Ireland Problem* (Belfast: Blackstaff Press, 2000), pp. 209–11.

19 T. Collins, *The Centre Cannot Hold: Britain's Failure in Northern Ireland* (Dublin: Bookworks Ireland, 1983), p. 144.

20 *Irish News*, 12 August 1991.

21 N. Tebbit, *Upwardly Mobile* [1988] (London: Futura edn, 1989), p. 228.

22 G. McGladdery, *The Provisional IRA in England: The Bombing Campaign, 1973–1997* (Dublin: Irish Academic Press, 2007), pp. 128–9.

23 *Belfast Telegraph*, 11 November 1984.

24 *Belfast Telegraph*, 21 April 1984.

25 *The New Ireland Forum* (Dublin: Stationary Office, 1984), paragraph 4.6.

26 G. Walker, *A History of the Ulster Unionist Party: Protest, Pragmatism and Pessimism* (Manchester University Press, 2004), pp. 233–4.

27 R. Needham, *Battling for Peace: Northern Ireland's Longest-Serving British Minister* (Belfast: Blackstaff Press, 1998), p. 80.

28 E. Mallie and D. McKittrick, *Endgame in Ireland* (London: Hodder & Stoughton, 2001), p. 45.

29 G. Howe, *Conflict of Loyalty* (London: Macmillan, 1994), p. 415.

30 R. Smith, *Garret: The Enigma* (Dublin: Aherlow, 1985), p. 422.

31 *Irish News*, 26 November 1984.

32 G. FitzGerald, *All in a Life: An Autobiography* (Dublin: Gill and Macmillan, 1991), p. 516.

33 D. Hurd, *Memoirs* (London: Abacus, 2003), p. 335. All major memoirs of the period record Thatcher's attraction to the option of re-partition.

34 K. Bloomfield, *A Tragedy of Errors: The Government and Misgovernment of Northern Ireland* (University of Liverpool Press, 2007), p. 58.

35 R. Ramsay, *Ringside Seats: An Insider's View of the Crisis in Northern Ireland* (Dublin: Irish Academic Press, 2009), p. 215.

36 Hurd, *Memoirs*, p. 339; Howe, *Conflict of Loyalty*, p. 427.
37 A. Purdy, *Molyneaux: The Long View* (Antrim: Greystone Books, 1989), p. 127.
38 Howe, *Conflict of Loyalty*, p. 422.
39 Hurd, *Memoirs*, p. 336; M. Stuart, 'Douglas Hurd: Foreign Secretary, 1989–95', in K. Theakston (ed.), *British Foreign Secretaries Since 1974* (London: Routledge, 2004), p. 198.
40 Quoted in F. Cochrane, *Unionist Politics and the Politics of Ulster Unionism Since the Anglo-Irish Agreement* (Cork University Press, 1997), p. 16.
41 K. Bloomfield, *Stormont in Crisis: A Memoir* (Belfast: Blackstaff Press, 1994), p. 253.
42 N. Lawson, *The View From No. 11: Memoirs of a Tory Radical* [1992] (London: Corgi edn, 1993), pp. 669–70.
43 G. Hussey, *At the Cutting Edge: Cabinet Diaries, 1982–1987* (Dublin: Gill & Macmillan, 1990), pp. 179–80.
44 This was certainly new. In 1982 the Foreign Office had explicitly declared that no such obligation then existed: P. O'Malley, 'The Anglo-Irish Agreement: Placebo or Paradigm', in H. Giliomee and J. Gagiano (eds.), *The Elusive Search for Peace: South Africa, Israel, Northern Ireland* (Cape Town: Oxford University Press, 1990), p. 186.
45 Anglo-Irish Agreement (available at CAIN Web Service, http://cain.ulst. ac.uk/events/aia/aiadoc.htm), Article 5 (c).
46 M. Cunningham, *British Government Policy in Northern Ireland, 1969–2000* (Manchester University Press, 2001), p. 50.
47 T. Wilson, *Ulster: Conflict and Consent* (Oxford: Basil Blackwell, 1989), p. 197.
48 *Ibid.*, p. 403.
49 See extracts from 'BBC Guidelines for Factual Programmes, 1989', in B. Rolston and D. Miller (eds.), *War and Words: The Northern Ireland Media Reader* (Belfast: Beyond the Pale, 1996), pp. 146–7.
50 Ed Moloney, interview with Mark Urban, *Fortnight* (July/August 1992). See also M. Urban, *Big Boys Rules: The Secret Struggle Against the IRA* (London: Faber & Faber, 1992), pp. 238–9.
51 PMQ, 1 December 1987, MTFW 106975; A. E. Owen, *The Anglo-Irish Agreement: The First Three Years* (Cardiff: University of Wales Press, 1994), p. 251.
52 M. Thatcher, *The Downing Street Years* (London: HarperCollins, 1993), p. 403.
53 *Belfast Telegraph*, 29 July 1985.
54 *Belfast Telegraph*, 11 September 1985.
55 For a summary of the debate on the Agreement at Westminster and in Dáil Éireann, see A. Kenny, *The Road to Hillsborough: The Shaping of the Anglo-Irish Agreement* (Oxford: Pergamon Press, 1986), pp. 105–17.
56 D. Hume, *The Ulster Unionist Party, 1972–92: A Political Movement in an Era of Conflict and Change* (Lurgan: Ulster Society, 1996), pp. 109–21.
57 D. McKittrick and D. McVea, *Making Sense of the Troubles* (Belfast: Blackstaff Press, 2000), p. 237.
58 B. O'Leary and J. McGarry, *The Politics of Antagonism: Understanding Northern Ireland* (London: Athlone Press, 1993), p. 238.

59 Anglo-Irish Agreement, Article 2 (b).
60 W. H. Cox, 'From Hillsborough to Downing Street – and After', in P. Catterall and S. McDougall (eds.), *The Northern Ireland Question in British Politics* (London: Macmillan, 1996), p. 186.
61 E. Delaney, *An Accidental Diplomat: My Years in the Irish Foreign Service, 1987–1995* (Dublin: New Island, 2001), p. 289.
62 *Fortnight* (April 1990), p. 18.
63 Thatcher, answering questions from cadets at the Virginia Military Institute, Lexington, Virginia, 24 January 1992: in J. S. Thompson and W. C. Thompson (eds.), *Margaret Thatcher: Prime Minister Indomitable* (Boulder, CO: Westview Press, 1994), p. 321.
64 *Belfast Telegraph*, 29 January 1990.
65 B. Mawhinney, *In the Firing Line: Politics, Faith, Power and Forgiveness* (London: HarperCollins, 2000), p. 109; emphasis in original.
66 Unemployment had neared 20 per cent for males by 1986, and 40 per cent in some Catholic areas. Though it later declined, republican areas remained blighted. B. Rowthorne and N. Wayne, *Northern Ireland: The Political Economy of Conflict* (Cambridge: Polity Press, 1988), pp. 85–6.
67 F. Gaffiken and M. Morrissey, *Northern Ireland: The Thatcher Years* (London: Zed Books, 1990), p. 205.
68 Mawhinney, *In the Firing Line*, pp. 108–11.
69 P. Taylor, *Brits: The War Against the IRA* (London: Bloomsbury, 2001), pp. 238, 310–11.
70 D. Bloomfield, *Political Dialogue in Northern Ireland: The Brooke Initiative, 1989–92* (Basingstoke: Macmillan, 1998), p. 181.
71 *Irish News*, 23 February 1990.

11 THATCHERISM AND THE COLD WAR

1 'The Prime Minister's Stop-Over in Moscow 26 June', MTFW 112149.
2 Reagan to Thatcher, 30 April 1975, MTFW 110357.
3 Speech at Kensington Town Hall, 19 January 1976, MTFW 102939.
4 S. Hall, 'The Great Moving Right Show', *Marxism Today* (January 1979), 14–20.
5 Sir J. Hackett, *The Third World War: A Future History* (London: Sidgwick & Jackson, 1978).
6 P. Sabin, *The Third World War Scare in Britain: A Critical Analysis* (Basingstoke: Macmillan, 1986), p. 45.
7 N. Lawson, *The View from No. 11: Memoirs of a Tory Radical* [1992] (London: Corgi, 1993), p. 64.
8 N. Lawson, speech to Zurich Society of Economics, 14 January 1981, MTFW 109506.
9 E. Morin, *Autocritique* (Paris: René Julliard, 1959).
10 F. Furet, *Le passé d'une illusion: essai sur l'idée communiste au XXe siècle* (Paris: Laffont, 1995).
11 See Andrew Gamble, Chapter 12 in this volume.
12 D. Butler and D. Kavanagh, *The British General Election of 1979* (Basingstoke: Macmillan, 1980).

13 For Brittan's views, see S. Brittan, *Against the Flow: Reflections of an Individualist* (London: Atlantic, 2005).

14 G. Howe, *Conflict of Loyalty* (Basingstoke: Macmillan, 1994), p. 144.

15 K. Speed, *Sea Change: The Battle for the Falklands and the Future of Britain's Navy* (Bath: Ashgrove, 1982).

16 Peter Tatchell, the Labour candidate in the 1983 Bermondsey by-election, praised Wintringham in his pamphlet, *Democratic Defence, A Non-Nuclear Alternative* (London: GMP, 1985). Wintringham acquired a certain cult status in the 1980s and the term 'People's War', originally coined by him, became an important part of the anti-Thatcher vocabulary.

17 Interview with Len Scott, Imperial War Museum, Sound Archive, 2000, catalogue number 22260.

18 Thatcher later read and admired an article by George Urban and Jeane Kirkpatrick for *Encounter*. G. Urban, *Diplomacy and Disillusion at the Court of Margaret Thatcher: An Insider's View* (London: I.B. Tauris, 1996), p. 35.

19 D. Butler and D. Kavanagh, *The British General Election of 1983* (Basingstoke: Macmillan, 1984), p. 282.

20 R. Moss, *The Collapse of Democracy* (London: Temple Smith, 1975).

21 A. Beckett, *Pinochet in Piccadilly: Britain and Chile's Secret History* (London: Faber & Faber, 2002).

22 P. Jay, 'How Inflation Threatens British Democracy with its Last Chance Before Extinction', *The Times*, 1 July 1974.

23 'I believe that the problem with this card is not whether to play it, but how': N. Lawson, 'Thoughts on the Coming Battle', MTFW 110312. This document seems to have been drafted on 15 October 1973 but sent to Thatcher on 15 January 1978. Lawson was a rare example of a mainstream Thatcherite who cited work by the Institute for the Study of Conflict.

24 Centre for Contemporary British History witness seminar, 'The Civil Service Reforms of the 1980s', 17 November 2006.

25 K. Joseph, 'Notes Towards the Definition of Policy', 4 April 1975, MTFW 110098: 'The fact that the Labour Party and the trades union movement are less concerned than ever to prevent pro-communists taking leading positions at all levels is something which we can legitimately point out – with tacit approval from the patriotic and democratic members of the Labour movement.'

26 S. Hastings, *The Drums of Memory: An Autobiography* (London: Leo Cooper, 1994), p. 236.

27 Hailsham diary entry, 8 November 1974, Churchill Archives Centre, Papers of Lord Hailsham, HLSM 1/1/9, reproduced at MTFW 111124.

28 Beckett, *Pinochet in Piccadilly*, p. 198.

29 Quoted in C. Andrew, *The Defence of the Realm: The Authorized History of MI5* (London: Allen Lane, 2009), p. 677.

30 K. Joseph, speech at Doncaster Racecourse, 24 June 1977, MTFW 111944.

31 B. Crozier, *Free Agent: The Unseen War, 1941–1991* (London: HarperCollins, 1993), pp. 128–48.

32 Quoted in Andrew, *Defence of the Realm*, p. 670.

33 Beckett, *Pinochet in Piccadilly*, pp. 199–200.

34 For the career of the KGB station chief in London, Oleg Gordievsky, see Andrew, *Defence of the Realm*.

35 M. Thatcher, *Statecraft: Strategies for a Changing World* (London: HarperCollins, 2002), p. 320.

36 Record of Thatcher/Reagan meeting, 22 December 1984, dated 28 December 1984, MTFW 109185.

37 Howe sent his own children to the French *lycée* in London: Howe, *Conflict of Loyalty*, p. 134.

38 Speech to Chelsea Conservative Association, 26 July 1975, MTFW 102750.

39 M. Thatcher, *The Path to Power* (London: HarperCollins, 1995), p. 342.

40 *Ibid.*, p. 91: 'Harold Macmillan's great and lasting achievement was to repair the relationship with the United States.'

41 H. Kissinger, briefing for Ford, 8 January 1975, MTFW 110510.

42 R. Allen, memorandum for Reagan, 31 July 1981, MTFW 110522.

43 S. Head, 'Reagan, Nuclear Weapons and the End of the Cold War', in C. Hudson and G. Davies (eds.), *Ronald Reagan and the 1980s: Perceptions, Policies, Legacies* (New York: Palgrave, 2008), pp. 81–101, at p. 82.

44 Hailsham diary, 17 March 1976, HLSM 1/1/10, reproduced at MTFW 111156.

45 On Joseph's relations with Amalrik, see Thatcher to Max Gammon, 21 January 1977, MTFW 111251.

46 Joseph, speech at Doncaster Racecourse, 24 June 1977.

47 Thatcher, *Path to Power*, p. 364.

48 J. Attali, *Verbatim*, vol. I: *Deuxième partie, 1983–1986* (Paris: Fayard, 1993), p. 790; author's translation.

49 Recounted in R. Aldous, *Reagan and Thatcher* (London: Random House, 2012).

50 N. Ridley, *My Style of Government: The Thatcher Years* (London: Fontana, 1991), p. 241.

51 Thatcher, *Statecraft*, pp. 2–3.

52 The dispatch was leaked to *The Economist*, which published it in June 1979.

53 Heath had, in fact, been staying at the Paris embassy shortly before Henderson sent his dispatch.

54 Brian Walden on *Weekend World*, 18 September 1977, MTFW 103191.

55 For Thatcher's supposed moral clarity, see Urban, *In the Court of Margaret Thatcher*, p. 3.

56 Attali, *Deuxième partie*, p. 787.

57 S. Heffer, *Like the Roman: The Life of Enoch Powell* (London: Weidenfeld & Nicolson, 1998), p. 934. See also Camilla Schofield, Chapter 5 in this volume.

58 See D. Hurd, 'Several Careers Open to Talent' (review of Ferdinand Mount, *Cold Cream: My Early Life and Other Mistakes* (London: Bloomsbury, 2008)), *The Spectator*, 12 April 2008.

12 EUROPE AND AMERICA

1 R. Churchill (ed.), *The Sinews of Peace: Post-War Speeches of Sir Winston Churchill* (London: Cassell, 1948).

2 S. George, *An Awkward Partner: Britain in the European Community* (Oxford University Press, 1994), p. 191.

3 M. Thatcher, *Statecraft: Strategies for a Changing World* (London: HarperCollins, 2002). She described the EU as perhaps the greatest folly of the modern era, and recommended that a future Conservative government should reassess its European strategy and apply to join NAFTA, withdrawing from the EU common agricultural and common fisheries policies. In order to secure its objectives Britain should be prepared, if necessary, unilaterally to withdraw from EU membership (p. 402).

4 C. Hitchens, *Blood, Class and Nostalgia: Anglo-American Ironies* (London: Vintage, 1991); A. Gamble, *Between Europe and America: The Future of British Politics* (London: Palgrave Macmillan, 2003).

5 N. Davies, *The Isles: A History* (London: Macmillan, 1999).

6 L. Colley, *Britons: Forging the Nation* (New Haven, CT: Yale University Press, 1992).

7 E. Hobsbawm, *Industry and Empire* (London: Weidenfeld & Nicolson, 1968).

8 J. Ikenberry, 'Liberalism and Empire: Logics of Order in the American Unipolar Age', *Review of International Studies*, 30 (2004), 609–30.

9 D. Coates, *The Question of UK Decline* (London: Harvester Wheatsheaf, 1994); A. Gamble, *Britain in Decline* (London: Macmillan, 1994). For the legacy of imperial decline during the Thatcher years, see Stephen Howe, Chapter 13 in this volume.

10 D. C. Watt, *Succeeding John Bull: America in Britain's Place 1900–1975* (Cambridge University Press, 1984); I. Adams, *Brothers Across the Ocean: British Foreign Policy and the Origins of the Anglo-American 'Special Relationship' 1900–1905* (London: I.B. Tauris, 2005).

11 K. Middlemas, *Politics in Industrial Society* (London: Deutsch, 1979).

12 George, *An Awkward Partner*.

13 L. Siedentop, *Democracy in Europe* (London: Allen Lane, 2000).

14 J. Dumbrell, *A Special Relationship: Anglo-American Relations in the Cold War and After* (London: Macmillan, 2001).

15 D. Dimbleby and D. Reynolds, *An Ocean Apart* (London: Guild Publishing, 1988).

16 Speech at Kensington Town Hall, 19 January 1976, MTFW 102939.

17 Hansard, HC Deb., 5th series, vol. 47, col. 294 (26 October 1983).

18 P. Riddell, *Hug Them Close: Blair, Bush, Clinton and the 'Special Relationship'* (London: Politico's, 2003).

19 Thatcher sets out this argument particularly strongly in *Statecraft*: 'Britain as a European power is in a league of her own. Our language, our links through trade and political influence, our outlook, our closeness with America, our nuclear deterrent – all make us a global power' (p. 399).

20 Adams, *Brothers Across the Ocean*.

21 Thatcher, *Statecraft*, p. 320.
22 M. Thatcher, *The Downing Street Years* (London: HarperCollins, 1993), pp. 692–6.
23 S. Heffer, *Like the Roman: The Life and Times of Enoch Powell* (London: Weidenfeld & Nicolson, 1998). See also Camilla Schofield, Chapter 5 in this volume.
24 M. Hastings and S. Jenkins, *The Falklands War* (London: Michael Joseph, 1983); Dumbrell, *A Special Relationship*, pp. 159–68.
25 K. van der Pijl, *Global Rivalries from the Cold War to Iraq* (London: Pluto, 2006).
26 J. Buller, *National Statecraft and European Integration: The Conservative Government and the European Union, 1979–1997* (London: Pinter, 2000).
27 M. Heseltine, *The Challenge of Europe: Can Britain Win?* (London: Pan, 1991).
28 G. Howe, *Conflict of Loyalty* (London: Macmillan, 1994).
29 M. Albert, *Capitalism Against Capitalism* (London: Whurr, 1993).
30 D. Coates, *Models of Capitalism* (Cambridge: Polity, 2000); P. Kennedy, *The Rise and Fall of the Great Powers* (London: Unwin Hyman, 1986).
31 G. Maynard, *The Economy Under Mrs Thatcher* (Oxford: Blackwell, 1988); J. Bennett, *The Anglosphere Challenge: Why the English-Speaking Nations will Lead the Way in the Twenty-First Century* (Lanham, MD: Rowman & Littlefield, 2004).
32 I. Kristol, *Neoconservatism: The Autobiography of an Idea* (New York: Free Press, 1995).
33 D. Bell, *The Idea of Greater Britain: Empire and the Future of World Order, 1860–1900* (Princeton University Press, 2007).
34 R. Cockett, *Thinking the Unthinkable: Think-Tanks and the Economic Counter-Revolution, 1931–1983* (London: HarperCollins, 1993); P. Mirowski and D. Plehwe (eds.), *The Road from Mont Pèlerin: The Making of the Neo-Liberal Thought Collective* (Cambridge, MA: Harvard University Press, 2009). See also Ben Jackson, Chapter 2 in this volume.
35 For further discussion of monetarism's significance, see Jim Tomlinson, Chapter 3 in this volume.
36 N. Barry, *The New Right* (London: Croom Helm, 1986); Cockett, *Thinking the Unthinkable*; R. Turner, *Neo-Liberal Ideology: History, Concepts, and Policies* (Edinburgh University Press, 2008).
37 I. Stelzer (ed.), *The Neocon Reader* (New York: Grove Press, 2004).
38 Riddell, *Hug them Close*.
39 For an argument that there were also significant contrasts between Reagan and Thatcher, see Richard Vinen, Chapter 11 in this volume.
40 C. Offe, *Reflections on America* (Cambridge: Polity, 2005).

13 DECOLONISATION AND IMPERIAL AFTERSHOCKS: THE THATCHER YEARS

1 John Darwin's *The Empire Project* (Cambridge University Press, 2009), perhaps the most impressive of such overviews, ends in 1970. The biggest publishing effort of all in the field, *British Documents on the End of Empire*

(London: The Stationery Office, 1992 onwards), carries its 'domestic' volumes to 1964 – or 1971 if one counts the differently focused *East of Suez and the British Commonwealth* volumes.

2 Of many works arguing on these lines, among the most powerful was C. Hall, *Civilising Subjects: Metropole and Colony in the English Imagination, 1830–1867* (Cambridge: Polity, 2002). The strongest sceptical counterblast was B. Porter, *The Absent-Minded Imperialists: Empire, Society, and Culture in Britain* (Oxford University Press, 2005).

3 T. W. Nechtman, *Nabobs: Empire and Identity in Eighteenth-Century Britain* (Cambridge University Press, 2010), p. 9.

4 For an attempted overview, see S. Howe (ed.), *The New Imperial Histories Reader* (Abingdon: Routledge, 2009).

5 Interview for Yorkshire Television *Woman to Woman*, 2 October 1985, MTFW 105830. The ICS was not, in fact, 'part of our Civil Service' but an entirely separate establishment – one, moreover, which recruited very few women indeed, and few people from Ms Roberts's non-patrician background.

6 Speech at Finchley adoption meeting, 31 July 1958, MTFW 100941.

7 See, among many such allusions, remarks at Bungay High School prize-giving, 7 November 1975, MTFW 102799; speech at Royal Academy banquet, 27 May 1980, MTFW 104370; speech to the Conservative Party Conference, 9 October 1987, MTFW 106941.

8 *Daily Telegraph*, 26 August 1997. Compare the surveys conducted in 1948 and 1951, and summarised in D. Goldsworthy, *Colonial Issues in British Politics, 1945–1961* (Oxford University Press, 1971), Appendix III, pp. 398–400.

9 S. R. Letwin, *The Anatomy of Thatcherism* (London: Flamingo, 1992), p. 37.

10 J. E. Powell, speech to Royal Society of St George, London, 23 April 1961. This speech has been widely reproduced, including at: www.churchill-society-london.org.uk/StGeorge.html.

11 See, for instance, P. Sharp, *Thatcher's Diplomacy: The Revival of British Foreign Policy* (London: Palgrave Macmillan, 1997).

12 J. Mayall, 'Introduction', in J. Mayall (ed.), *The Contemporary Commonwealth: An Assessment 1965–2009* (Abingdon: Routledge, 2010), pp. 16–18.

13 For instance, Cm. 3999, *The Strategic Defence Review* (London: The Stationery Office, 1998); *Building on Progress: Britain in the World* (HM Government Policy Review: Cabinet Office/Prime Minister's Strategy Unit, April 2007). Richard Vinen makes a similar point in Chapter 11 of this volume.

14 See, for example, A. Edwards, 'Misapplying Lessons Learned? Analysing the Utility of British Counter-Insurgency Strategy in Northern Ireland, 1971–76', *Small Wars and Insurgencies*, 21 (2010), 303–30.

15 See Marc Mulholland, Chapter 10 in this volume, for a fuller discussion of Northern Ireland during the Thatcher years.

16 P. J. Cain and A. G. Hopkins, *British Imperialism*, vol. II: *Crisis and Deconstruction 1914–1990* (London: Longman, 1993).

17 Speech at the opening of the Lusaka Commonwealth Meeting, 1 August 1979, MTFW 104126.

18 There is still no fully documented account of the negotiations, but see S. J. Stedman, *Peacemaking in Civil War: International Mediation in Zimbabwe, 1974–1980* (Boulder, CO: Lynne Rienner, 1991); also Lord Carrington, *Reflect on Things Past: The Memoirs of Lord Carrington* (London: Collins, 1988), pp. 287–307.

19 For a fine synthesis of this recent work, see B. Raftopoulos and A. Mlambo (eds.), *Becoming Zimbabwe: A History from the Pre-Colonial Period to 2008* (Harare: Weaver Press, 2009).

20 As recounted in J. Campbell, *Margaret Thatcher: The Iron Lady* (London: Jonathan Cape, 2003), pp. 74–5.

21 B. Nasson, *Britannia's Empire: Making a British World* (Stroud: Tempus, 2006), p. 176.

22 A. Barnett, 'Iron Britannia', *New Left Review*, no. 134 (1982), 5–96.

23 See, for example, E. Hobsbawm, 'Falklands Fallout', *Marxism Today* (January 1983), 13–19.

24 S. Howe: 'Internal Decolonisation? British Politics since Thatcher as Postcolonial Trauma', *Twentieth Century British History*, 14 (2003), 286–304; S. Howe, 'Empire in the Twenty-first Century British Imagination', in W. Roger Louis (ed.), *Penultimate Adventures with Britannia* (London: I.B. Tauris, 2007); S. Howe, 'Some Intellectual Origins of Charter 88', *Parliamentary Affairs*, 62 (2009), 552–67.

25 The often-quoted exception was her speech to a Conservative rally at Cheltenham, 3 July 1982, MTFW 104989.

26 The classic 'sceptical' argument here is D. Sanders *et al.*, 'Government Popularity and the Falklands War: A Reassessment', *British Journal of Political Science*, 17 (1987), 281–313.

27 Hansard, HC Deb., 5th series, vol. 47, col. 144 (25 October 1983).

28 Campbell, *Iron Lady*, p. 274.

29 M. Thatcher, *The Downing Street Years* (London: HarperCollins, 1993), p. 331.

30 See G. Williams, '"Keeping a Line Open": Britain and the 1979 Coup in Grenada', *Journal of Imperial and Commonwealth History*, 39 (2011), 479–508; G. Williams, *US–Grenada Relations: Revolution and Intervention in the Backyard* (New York: Palgrave Macmillan, 2007).

31 For an overview, see R. Hyam and P. Henshaw, *The Lion and the Springbok: Britain and South Africa Since the Boer War* (Cambridge University Press, 2003).

32 In his memoirs, Geoffrey Howe contrasted his abhorrence of apartheid, stemming from extensive experience of Africa, with Thatcher's approach which was, he sneered, 'derived mainly, I suspect, via Twickenham and Gleneagles (the golf-course not the Agreement)'. He also distanced himself from her anti-immigrant – indeed, Howe very clearly implies, racist – feelings: G. Howe, *Conflict of Loyalty* (London: Macmillan, 1994), p. 477.

33 See, among many instances, her description of the ANC as 'a typical terrorist organisation': press conference at Vancouver Commonwealth summit, 17 October 1987, MTFW 106948.

34 B. Pimlott, *The Queen: A Biography of Queen Elizabeth II* (London: HarperCollins, 1996), p. 464.

35 See J. Dimbleby, *The Last Governor: Chris Patten and the Handover of Hong Kong* (London: Little, Brown, 1997); and for a broader survey, F. Welsh, *A History of Hong Kong* (London: HarperCollins, 1994).

36 S. Yui-Sang Tsang, *Democracy Shelved: Great Britain, China, and Attempts at Constitutional Reform in Hong Kong, 1945–1952* (Hong Kong: Oxford University Press China, 1988); J. M. Brown and R. Foot (eds.), *Hong Kong's Transitions, 1842–1997* (Basingstoke: Macmillan, 1997).

37 For example, interview for CNN, 29 June 1997, MTFW 109211.

38 My own views on these debates are more fully suggested in the writings listed at note 24 above.

39 Among many such claims, see especially Thatcher's speech at Cheltenham, 3 July 1982.

40 P. Gilroy, *After Empire: Melancholia or Convivial Culture?* (London: Routledge, 2004).

41 The key formulation of this argument was in T. Nairn, *The Break-Up of Britain: Crisis and Neo-Nationalism* (London: Verso, 1977; 2nd edn, 1981). See also Chapters 9 and 10 in this volume by Richard Finlay and Marc Mulholland, respectively.

42 An influential early version of this view was in Centre for Contemporary Cultural Studies, *The Empire Strikes Back: Race and Racism in Seventies Britain* (London: Hutchinson, 1982).

43 The phrase may originally have been Tony Benn's in his *Arguments for Democracy* (Harmondsworth: Penguin, 1982), chapter 1 ('Britain as a Colony').

44 See, for instance, G. Adams *et al.*, *Ulster – The Internal Colony* (Belfast: Queen's University Unionist Association pamphlet, 1989).

45 A. Jackson, 'Empire and Beyond: The Pursuit of Overseas National Interests in the Late Twentieth Century', *English Historical Review*, 123 (2007), 1351, 1366.

46 Cm. 3999, *The Strategic Defence Review*.

47 A. G. Hopkins, 'Rethinking Decolonization', *Past and Present*, 200 (2008), 211–47; J. Belich, *Replenishing the Earth: The Settler Revolution and Rise of the Anglo-World, 1780–1930* (Oxford University Press, 2009).

48 J. Curran and S. Ward, *The Unknown Nation: Australia After Empire* (Melbourne University Press, 2010).

49 See, for example, D. Lefeuvre *et al.* (eds.), *L'Europe face à son passé colonial* (Paris: Broche, 2008); K. A. Nicolaides and B. Sebe (eds.), *Echoes of Imperialism: The Present of Europe's Colonial Pasts* (forthcoming); R. Tombs and A. Versaille (eds.), *L'histoire coloniale en debat en France et en Grande-Bretagne* (Brussels: Éditions Versaille, 2010). My own preliminary view may be consulted in my contribution to the last of these volumes, and in S. Howe, 'Colonising and Exterminating? Memories of Imperial Violence in Britain and France', *Histoire@Politique. Politique, Culture, Société*, 11 (2010), 1–18.

50 L. Sicking, 'A Colonial Echo: France and the Colonial Dimension of the European Economic Community', *French Colonial History*, 5 (2004), 207–28; A. Deighton, 'Entente Neo-Coloniale? Ernest Bevin and the Proposals for Anglo-French Third World Power, 1945–1949', *Diplomacy*

and Statecraft, 17 (2006), 835–52; R. W. Heywood, 'West European Community and the Eurafrica Concept in the 1950s', *Journal of European Integration*, 4 (1981), 199–210; J. Kent, *The Internationalization of Colonialism: Britain, France, and Black Africa, 1939–1956* (Oxford: Clarendon Press, 1992); P. Hansen, 'European Integration, European Identity and the Colonial Connection', *European Journal of Social Theory*, 5 (2002), 483–98; T. Shepard, *The Invention of Decolonization: The Algerian War and the Remaking of France* (Ithaca, NY: Cornell University Press, 2006).

51 W. R. Louis and R. Robinson, 'The Imperialism of Decolonization', *Journal of Imperial and Commonwealth History*, 22 (1994), 462.

52 W. R. Louis, 'The Dissolution of the British Empire in the Era of Vietnam' (presidential address to the American Historical Association), *American Historical Review*, 107 (2002), 1–25.

Further reading

WEB RESOURCES

Margaret Thatcher: Complete Public Statements, 1945–1990 (Thatcher CD-ROM) (Oxford University Press, 1999)
Searchable database including all known public statements by Margaret Thatcher before 1990.

Thatcher Foundation website (www.margaretthatcher.org)
A treasure trove of documents on the Thatcher era, including speeches, articles and official papers.

GENERAL STUDIES

Evans, Eric, *Thatcher and Thatcherism*, 2nd edn (London: Routledge, 2004).
A useful textbook, surveying the major themes and events in the Thatcher era.

Fry, Geoffrey K., *The Politics of the Thatcher Revolution: An Interpretation of British Politics, 1979–1990* (Basingstoke: Palgrave Macmillan, 2008).
A broadly sympathetic account, full of waspish judgements, by a self-styled 'untrue believer'.

Gamble, Andrew, *The Free Economy and the Strong State: The Politics of Thatcherism*, 2nd edn (Basingstoke: Macmillan, 1994).
A hugely influential work with a Marxist inflection, locating Thatcherism within the Anglo-American 'New Right'.

Green, E. H. H., *Thatcher* (London: Hodder Arnold, 2006).
A historically informed study of Thatcher's public reputation, by a leading scholar of the Conservative Party.

Harrison, Brian, *Finding a Role? The United Kingdom, 1970–1990* (Oxford University Press, 2010).
The latest volume in the *New Oxford History of England*, paying substantial attention to Thatcher and Thatcherism.

Kavanagh, Dennis, *Thatcherism and British Politics: The End of Consensus?*, 2nd edn (Oxford University Press, 1990).
An important early study locating Thatcherism within the breakdown of consensus politics.

Letwin, Shirley Robin, *The Anatomy of Thatcherism* (London: Flamingo, 1992).
An analysis of Thatcherism by a Conservative philosopher, associating it with 'the vigorous virtues'.

Riddell, Peter, *The Thatcher Era and its Legacy* (London: Blackwell, 1991).
An insightful study by a political journalist, covering a range of different policy areas.

Vinen, Richard, *Thatcher's Britain: The Politics and Social Upheaval of the Thatcher Era* (London: Simon & Schuster, 2009).
A revisionist and historically informed study, stressing Thatcher's orthodoxy in many areas of policy.

COLLECTIONS OF ESSAYS

Adonis, Andrew, and Tim Hames (eds.), *A Conservative Revolution? The Thatcher–Reagan Decade in Perspective* (Manchester University Press, 1994).
Hall, Stuart, and Martin Jacques (eds.), *The Politics of Thatcherism* (London: Lawrence & Wishart in association with *Marxism Today*, 1983).
Kavanagh, Dennis, and Anthony Seldon (eds.), *The Thatcher Effect: A Decade of Change* (Oxford University Press, 1989).
Marsh, David, and R. A. W. Rhodes (eds.), *Implementing Thatcherite Policies* (Buckingham: Open University Press, 1992).
Skidelsky, Robert (ed.), *Thatcherism* (London: Chatto & Windus, 1988).

BIOGRAPHIES, MEMOIRS AND DIARIES

THATCHER

Campbell, John, *Margaret Thatcher: The Grocer's Daughter* (London: Random House, 2001).
Margaret Thatcher: The Iron Lady (London: Jonathan Cape, 2003).
Thatcher, Margaret, *The Downing Street Years* (London: HarperCollins, 1993).
The Path to Power (London: HarperCollins, 1995).
Statecraft: Strategies for a Changing World (London: HarperCollins, 2002).
Young, Hugo, *One of Us: A Biography of Margaret Thatcher* (London: Macmillan, 1989).

MINISTERS

Carrington, Lord Peter, *Reflect On Things Past: The Memoirs of Lord Carrington* (London: Collins, 1988).
Denham, Andrew, and Mark Garnett, *Keith Joseph* (Chesham: Acumen, 2001).
Heseltine, Michael, *Life in the Jungle* (London: Methuen, 2009).
Howe, Geoffrey, *Conflict of Loyalty* (London: Macmillan, 1994).
Hurd, Douglas, *An End to Promises: A Sketch of Government, 1970–74* (London: Collins, 1979).

Memoirs (London: Abacus, 2003).

Lawson, Nigel, *The View From No. 11: Memoirs of a Tory Radical* (London: Corgi, 1992).

Prior, Jim, *A Balance of Power* (London: Hamish Hamilton, 1986).

Ridley, Nicholas, *My Style of Government: The Thatcher Years* (London: Fontana, 1991).

Tebbit, Norman, *Upwardly Mobile* (London: Futura, 1988, 1989).

Walker, Peter, *Staying Power: An Autobiography* (London: Bloomsbury, 1991).

ADVISORS

Hoskyns, John, *Just in Time: Inside the Thatcher Revolution* (London: Aurum, 2000).

Ingham, Bernard, *Kill the Messenger* (London: Fontana, 1991).

Millar, Ronald, *A View From the Wings: West End, West Coast, Westminster* (London: Weidenfeld & Nicolson, 1993).

Mount, Ferdinand, *Cold Cream: My Early Life and Other Mistakes* (London: Bloomsbury, 2008).

Ranelagh, John, *Thatcher's People* (London: HarperCollins, 1991).

Sherman, Alfred, *Paradoxes of Power: Reflections on the Thatcher Interlude* (Exeter: Imprint, 2005).

Urban, George, *Diplomacy and Disillusion at the Court of Margaret Thatcher: An Insider's View* (London: I.B. Tauris, 1996).

DIARIES

Benn, Tony, *Conflicts of Interest: Diaries, 1977–1980*, ed. R. Winstone (London: Hutchinson, 1990).

The End of an Era: Diaries, 1980–1990, ed. R. Winstone (London: Hutchinson, 1990).

Clark, Alan, *Diaries* (London: Weidenfeld & Nicolson, 1993).

McIntosh, Ronald, *Challenge to Democracy: Politics, Trade Union Power and Economic Failure in the 1970s* (London: Politico's, 2006).

The Journals of Woodrow Wyatt, ed. S. Curtis, 3 vols. (London: Pan, 1999–2001).

POLITICAL STUDIES

POLITICS IN THE 1970S

Ball, Stuart, and Anthony Seldon (eds.), *The Heath Government* (London: Longman, 1996).

Beckett, Andy, *When the Lights Went Out: Britain in the 1970s* (London: Faber, 2009).

Black, Lawrence, and Hugh Pemberton, 'The Winter of Discontent in British Politics', *Political Quarterly*, 80 (2009).

Campbell, John, *Edward Heath: A Biography* (London: Jonathan Cape, 1993).

Hay, Colin, 'Chronicles of a Death Foretold: The Winter of Discontent and Construction of the Crisis of British Keynesianism', *Parliamentary Affairs*, 63 (2010).

'Narrating Crisis: The Discursive Construction of the "Winter of Discontent"', *Sociology*, 30 (1996).

Morgan, Kenneth, *Callaghan: A Life* (Oxford University Press, 1997).

Särlvik, Bo, and Ivor Crewe, *Decade of Dealignment: The Conservative Victory of 1979 and Electoral Trends in the 1970s* (Cambridge University Press, 1983; repr. 2010).

THATCHERISM AND THE CONSERVATIVE PARTY

Bale, Tim, *The Conservative Party: From Thatcher to Cameron* (Cambridge: Polity, 2010).

Ball, Stuart, and Ian Holliday (eds.), *Mass Conservatism: The Conservatives and the Public Since the 1880s* (London: Frank Cass, 2002).

Bulpitt, Jim, 'The Discipline of the New Democracy: Mrs Thatcher's Domestic Statecraft', *Political Studies*, 34 (1986).

Clarke, Peter, 'The Rise and Fall of Thatcherism', *Historical Research*, 72 (1999).

Cowley, Philip, and Matthew Bailey, 'Peasants' Uprising or Religious War? Re-examining the 1975 Conservative Leadership Contest', *British Journal of Political Science*, 30 (2000).

Evans, Stephen, 'The Not so Odd Couple: Margaret Thatcher and One Nation Conservatism', *Contemporary British History*, 23 (2009).

Francis, Martin, and Ina Zweiniger-Bargielowska (eds.), *The Conservatives and British Society, 1880–1990* (Cardiff: University of Wales Press, 1996).

Gilmour, Ian, *Dancing with Dogma: Britain under Thatcherism* (London: Simon & Schuster, 1992).

Gilmour, Ian, and Mark Garnett, *Whatever Happened to the Tories? The Conservative Party since 1945* (London: Fourth Estate, 1997).

Green, E. H. H., 'Thatcherism: A Historical Perspective', in E. H. H. Green, *Ideologies of Conservatism: Conservative Political Ideas in the Twentieth Century* (Oxford University Press, 2002).

Watkins, Alan, *A Conservative Coup: The Fall of Margaret Thatcher* (London: Duckworth, 1991).

Wickham-Jones, Mark, 'Right Turn: A Revisionist Account of the 1975 Conservative Leadership Election', *Twentieth Century British History*, 8 (1997).

THE LABOUR PARTY

Cronin, James E., *New Labour's Pasts: The Labour Party and its Discontents* (Harlow: Pearson/Longman, 2004).

Morgan, Kenneth, *Michael Foot: A Life* (London: HarperCollins, 2007).

Seldon, Anthony, and Kevin Hickson (eds.), *New Labour, Old Labour: The Wilson and Callaghan Governments, 1974–79* (London: Routledge, 2004).

Westlake, Martin, *Kinnock* (London: Little, Brown, 2001).

THE SDP

Crewe, Ivor, and Anthony King, *SDP: The Birth, Life and Death of the Social Democratic Party* (Oxford University Press, 1995).

THATCHERISM AND NEW LABOUR

Hay, Colin, 'Whatever Happened to Thatcherism?', *Political Studies Review*, 5 (2007).
Heath, Anthony, Roger Jowell and John Curtice, *The Rise of New Labour* (Oxford University Press, 2001).
Heffernan, Richard, *New Labour and Thatcherism: Political Change in Britain* (Basingstoke: Palgrave Macmillan, 2000).
Jenkins, Simon, *Thatcher and Sons: A Revolution in Three Acts* (London: Allen Lane, 2006).

THE CONSTITUTION

Bogdanor, Vernon, *Politics and the Constitution: Essays on British Government* (Ashgate: Farnham, 1996), chapter 2.
Howe, Stephen, 'Some Intellectual Origins of Charter 88', *Parliamentary Affairs*, 62 (2009).
Marquand, David, *The Unprincipled Society* (London: Jonathan Cape, 1988).

IDENTITIES

GENDER AND SEXUALITY

Campbell, Beatrix, *Iron Ladies: Why Do Women Vote Tory?* (London: Virago, 1987).
Campbell, Rosie, *Gender and the Vote in Britain: Beyond the Gender Gap?* (Colchester: ECPR Press, 2006).
Lovenduski, Joni, and Vicky Randall, *Contemporary Feminist Politics: Women and Power in Britain* (Oxford University Press, 1993).
Nunn, Heather, *Thatcher, Politics and Fantasy: The Political Culture of Gender and Nation* (London: Lawrence & Wishart, 2002).
Smith, Anna Marie, *New Right Discourse on Race and Sexuality 1968–1990* (Cambridge University Press, 1994).

RACE AND IMMIGRATION

Dixon, David, 'Thatcher's People: The British Nationality Act 1981', *Journal of Law and Society*, 10 (1983).
Gilroy, Paul, *There Ain't No Black in the Union Jack* (London: Routledge, 2002).

Hall, Stuart, Charles Critcher, Tony Jefferson, John Clarke and Brian Robert, *Policing the Crisis: Mugging, the State and Law and Order* (London: Palgrave Macmillan, 1978).

Hansen, Randall, *Citizenship and Immigration in Post-War Britain* (Oxford University Press, 2000).

Rich, Paul, and Zig Layton-Henry (eds.), *Race, Government and Politics in Britain* (London: Macmillan, 1986).

Saggar, Shamit, 'A Late, Though Not Lost, Opportunity: Ethnic Minority Electors, Party Strategy and the Conservative Party', *Political Quarterly*, 69 (1998).

ECONOMY AND SOCIETY

THE ECONOMY AND ECONOMIC POLICY

Glyn, Andrew, *Capitalism Unleashed* (Oxford University Press, 2006).

Hall, Peter, 'Policy Paradigms, Social Learning and the State: The Case of Economic Policy Making in Britain', *Comparative Politics*, 25 (1993).

Johnson, Christopher, *The Economy Under Mrs Thatcher* (Harmondsworth: Penguin, 1991).

Maynard, Geoffrey, *The Economy Under Mrs Thatcher* (Oxford: Blackwell, 1988).

Oliver, Michael, *Whatever Happened to Monetarism? Economic Policy-Making and Social Learning in Britain Since 1979* (Aldershot: Ashgate, 1997).

Pepper, Gordon, and Michael Oliver, *Monetarism Under Thatcher: Lessons for the Future* (London: Institute of Economic Affairs, 2001).

Stephens, Philip, *Politics and the Pound: The Conservatives' Struggle with Sterling* (Basingstoke: Macmillan, 1996).

Stevens, Richard, 'The Evolution of Privatisation as an Electoral Policy, c.1970–90', *Contemporary British History*, 18 (2004).

Tomlinson, Jim, 'Mrs Thatcher's Macroeconomic Adventurism, 1979–1981, and its Political Consequences', *British Politics*, 2 (2007).

DECLINE AND DECLINISM

Clarke, Peter, and Clive Trebilcock (eds.), *Understanding Decline* (Cambridge University Press, 1997).

English, Richard, and Michael Kenny (eds.), *Rethinking British Decline* (Basingstoke: Macmillan, 2000).

Gamble, Andrew, *Britain in Decline* (London: Macmillan, 1994).

Tomlinson, Jim, *The Politics of Decline: Understanding Post-War Britain* (Harlow: Pearson, 2001).

'Thrice Denied: "Declinism" as a Recurrent Theme in British History in the Long Twentieth Century', *Twentieth Century British History*, 20 (2009).

TRADE UNIONS

Marsh, David, *The New Politics of British Trade Unionism: Union Power and the Thatcher Legacy* (Basingstoke: Macmillan, 1992).

Taylor, Robert, *The Trade Union Question in British Politics* (Oxford: Blackwell, 1993), chapters 6–8.
Towers, Brian, 'Running the Gauntlet: British Trade Unions under Thatcher, 1979–88', *Industrial and Labor Relations Review*, 42 (1989).

THE MINERS' STRIKE (1984–5)

Adeney, Martin, and John Lloyd, *The Miners' Strike, 1984–85: Loss Without Limit* (London: Routledge, 1986).
Beckett, Francis, and David Hencke, *Marching to the Fault Line: The 1984 Miners' Strike and the Death of Industrial Britain* (London: Constable, 2009).
Howell, David, *The Politics of the NUM: A Lancashire View* (Manchester University Press, 1989).
Phillips, Jim, 'Workplace Conflict and the Origins of the 1984–85 Miners' Strike in Scotland', *Twentieth Century British History*, 20 (2009).
Taylor, Andrew, *The NUM and British Politics*, vol. I: *1944–1968*; vol. II: *1968–1995* (Aldershot: Ashgate, 1995).
Winterton, Jonathan, and Ruth Winterton, *Coal Crisis and Conflict: The 1984–85 Miners' Strike in Yorkshire* (Manchester University Press, 1989).
Thurcroft: A Village and the Miners' Strike, By the People of Thurcroft (Nottingham: Spokesman, 1986).

CLASS AND SOCIAL WELFARE

Cannadine, David, *Class in Britain* (New Haven, CT: Yale University Press, 1998).
Davis, John, 'The London Cabbie and the Rise of Essex Man', in Clare Griffiths, James Nott and William Whyte (eds.), *Classes, Cultures, and Politics: Essays on British History for Ross McKibbin* (Oxford University Press, 2011).
Hobsbawm, Eric, *et al.*, *The Forward March of Labour Halted?* (London: NLB, 1981).
Lowe, Rodney, *The Welfare State in Britain Since 1945*, 3rd edn (Basingstoke: Palgrave Macmillan, 2004), part 3.
Mold, Alex, 'Making the Patient-Consumer in Margaret Thatcher's Britain', *Historical Journal*, 54 (2011).
Offer, Avner, 'British Manual Workers: From Producers to Consumers, c. 1950–2000', *Contemporary British History*, 22 (2008).
Pierson, Paul, *Dismantling the Welfare State? Reagan, Thatcher and the Politics of Retrenchment* (Cambridge University Press, 1994).
Welshman, John, 'Where Lesser Angels Might Have Feared to Tread: The Social Science Research Council and Transmitted Deprivation', *Contemporary British History*, 23 (2009).

THE ENVIRONMENT

McCormick, John, *British Politics and the Environment* (London: Earthscan, 1991), chapter 3.

THATCHERISM AND THE NEW RIGHT

THINK-TANKS AND INTELLECTUALS

Cockett, Richard, *Thinking the Unthinkable: Think-Tanks and the Economic Counterrevolution 1931–1983* (London: HarperCollins, 1993).
Denham, Andrew, and Mark Garnett, 'The Nature and Impact of Think Tanks in Contemporary Britain', *Contemporary British History*, 10 (1996).
Desai, Radhika, 'Second-Hand Dealers in Ideas: Think-Tanks and Thatcherite Hegemony', *New Left Review*, no. 203 (1994).
Hall, Stuart, 'The Great Moving Right Show', *Marxism Today* (January 1979).
Harrison, Brian, 'Mrs Thatcher and the Intellectuals', *Twentieth Century British History*, 5 (1994).
Jessop, Bob, Kevin Bonnett, Simon Bromley and Tom Ling, *Thatcherism: A Tale of Two Nations* (Cambridge: Polity, 1988).
Mirowski, Philip, and Dieter Plehwe (eds.), *The Road from Mont Pèlerin: The Making of the Neo-Liberal Thought Collective* (Cambridge, MA: Harvard University Press, 2009).
Thompson, Noel, 'Hollowing Out the State: Public Choice Theory and the Critique of Keynesian Social Democracy', *Contemporary British History*, 22 (2008).

MORALITY AND THE 'PERMISSIVE SOCIETY'

Black, Lawrence, 'There was Something about Mary: The National Viewers' and Listeners' Association (NVALA) and Social Movement History', in N. J. Crowson, Matthew Hilton and James McKay (eds.), *NGOs in Contemporary Britain: Non-State Actors in Society and Politics Since 1945* (Basingstoke: Palgrave Macmillan, 2009).
Durham, Martin, *Sex and Politics: The Family and Morality in the Thatcher Years* (Basingstoke: Macmillan, 1991).
Fry, Geoffrey K., 'Parliament and "Morality": Thatcher, Powell and Populism', *Contemporary British History*, 12 (1998).
Samuel, Raphael, 'Mrs Thatcher and Victorian Values' (1992), reprinted in Raphael Samuel, *Island Stories: Unravelling Britain, Theatres of Memory*, vol. II (London: Verso, 1998).

POWELLISM

Brooke, Peter, 'India, Post-Imperialism and the Origins of Enoch Powell's "Rivers of Blood" Speech', *Historical Journal*, 50 (2007).
Heffer, Simon, *Like the Roman: The Life of Enoch Powell* (London: Weidenfeld & Nicolson, 1998).
Powell, J. Enoch, *A Nation or No Nation? Six Years in British Politics*, ed. Richard Ritchie (London: Elliot Right Way Books, 1978).
   Reflections: Selected Writings and Speeches of Enoch Powell (London: Bellew Publishing, 1992).
Schofield, Camilla, *Enoch Powell and the Making of Postcolonial Britain* (Cambridge University Press, forthcoming).

DEVOLUTION AND THE UNION

DEVOLUTION

Bogdanor, Vernon, *Devolution in the United Kingdom* (Oxford University Press, 2001).

McLean, Iain, and Alistair McMillan, *The State of the Union* (Oxford University Press, 2005).

Mitchell, James, *Devolution in the United Kingdom* (Manchester University Press, 2009).

Nairn, Tom, *The Break-Up of Britain* (London: Verso, 1981).

SCOTLAND

Finlay, Richard J., 'Thatcherism, Civil Society and the Road to Home Rule: Scotland 1980–1997', in A. J. Murdoch (ed.), *The Scottish Nation: Identity and History, Essays in Honour of William Ferguson* (Edinburgh: John Donald, 2007).

Kidd, Colin, *Union and Unionisms: Political Thought in Scotland, 1500–2000* (Cambridge University Press, 2008)

Mitchell, James, *Conservatives and the Union: A Study of Conservative Party Attitudes to Scotland* (Edinburgh University Press, 1990).

Phillips, Jim, *The Industrial Politics of Devolution: Scotland in the 1960s and 1970s* (Manchester University Press, 2008).

Stewart, David, *The Path to Devolution and Change: A Political History of Scotland Under Margaret Thatcher* (London: I.B. Tauris, 2009).

Torrance, David, *We in Scotland: Thatcherism in a Cold Climate* (Edinburgh: Birlinn, 2010).

WALES

Barry Jones, J., and Denis Balsom (eds.), *The Road to the National Assembly of Wales* (Cardiff: University of Wales Press, 2000).

Davies, John, *A History of Wales* (London: Penguin, 2007).

Osmond, John, *The National Question Again: Welsh Political Identity in the 1980s* (Dyfed: Gomer Press, 1985).

The Welsh Economy (Cardiff: University of Wales Press, 1988).

NORTHERN IRELAND

Aughey, Arthur, *Under Siege: Ulster Unionism and the Anglo-Irish Agreement* (London: C. Hurst & Co., 1989).

Cochrane, Feargal, *Unionist Politics and the Politics of Ulster Unionism Since the Anglo-Irish Agreement* (Cork University Press, 1997).

Cunningham, Michael, *British Government Policy in Northern Ireland, 1969–2000* (Manchester University Press, 2001).

Gaffiken, Frank, and Mike Morrissey, *Northern Ireland: The Thatcher Years* (London: Zed Books, 1990).

Kenny, Anthony, *The Road to Hillsborough: The Shaping of the Anglo-Irish Agreement* (Oxford: Pergamon Press, 1986).

McGladdery, Gary, *The Provisional IRA in England: The Bombing Campaign, 1973–1997* (Dublin: Irish Academic Press, 2007).

BRITAIN AND THE WIDER WORLD

GENERAL

Beckett, Andy, *Pinochet in Piccadilly: Britain and Chile's Secret History* (London: Faber & Faber, 2002).

Gamble, Andrew, *Between Europe and America: The Future of British Politics* (London: Palgrave Macmillan, 2003).

Sharp, Paul, *Thatcher's Diplomacy: The Revival of British Foreign Policy* (London: Palgrave Macmillan, 1997).

BRITAIN AND EUROPE

Buller, Jim, *National Statecraft and European Integration: The Conservative Government and the European Union, 1979–1997* (London: Pinter, 2000).

Crowson, N. J., *The Conservative Party and European Integration Since 1945: At the Heart of Europe?* (Abingdon: Routledge, 2007).

Forster, Anthony, *Euroscepticism in Contemporary British Politics: Opposition to Europe in the British Conservative and Labour Parties Since 1945* (Abingdon: Routledge, 2002).

George, Stephen, *An Awkward Partner: Britain in the European Community*, 3rd edn (Oxford University Press, 1998).

Young, Hugo, *This Blessed Plot: Britain and Europe from Churchill to Blair* (London: Macmillan, 1998).

Young, John, 'Conservative Governments and the Challenge of European Integration, 1984–97', in Adolf M. Birke, Magnus Brechtken and Alaric Searle (eds.), *An Anglo-German Dialogue* (Munich: Saur, 2000).

BRITAIN AND AMERICA

Aldous, Richard, *Reagan and Thatcher* (London: Random House, 2012).

Dumbrell, John, *A Special Relationship: Anglo-American Relations in the Cold War and After* (London: Macmillan, 2001).

Williams, Gary, '"Keeping a Line Open": Britain and the 1979 Coup in Grenada', *Journal of Imperial and Commonwealth History*, 39 (2011).

EMPIRE AND COMMONWEALTH

Howe, Stephen, 'Internal Decolonisation? British Politics since Thatcher as Postcolonial Trauma', *Twentieth Century British History*, 14 (2003).

Jackson, Ashley, 'Empire and Beyond: The Pursuit of Overseas National Interests in the Late Twentieth Century', *English Historical Review*, 123 (2007).

Mayall, James, *The Contemporary Commonwealth: An Assessment 1965–2009* (Routledge: Abingdon, 2010).

THE FALKLANDS WAR

Barnett, Anthony, 'Iron Britannia', *New Left Review*, no. 134 (1982); reprinted as a book (London: Allison and Busby, 1982).
Freedman, Lawrence, *The Official History of the Falklands Campaign*, 2 vols. (Abingdon: Routledge, 2005).
Hastings, Max, and Simon Jenkins, *The Falklands War* (London: Michael Joseph, 1983).
Hobsbawm, Eric, 'Falklands Fallout', *Marxism Today* (January, 1983).
Sanders, David, *et al.*, 'Government Popularity and the Falklands War: A Reassessment', *British Journal of Political Science*, 17 (1987).

Index

Made in the USA
Middletown, DE
28 February 2021